LOW-WAGE WORK IN THE WEALTHY WORLD

LOW-WAGE WORK IN THE WEALTHY WORLD

Jérôme Gautié and John Schmitt
Editors

Russell Sage Foundation • New York

The Russell Sage Foundation

The Russell Sage Foundation, one of the oldest of America's general purpose foundations, was established in 1907 by Mrs. Margaret Olivia Sage for "the improvement of social and living conditions in the United States." The Foundation seeks to fulfill this mandate by fostering the development and dissemination of knowledge about the country's political, social, and economic problems. While the Foundation endeavors to assure the accuracy and objectivity of each book it publishes, the conclusions and interpretations in Russell Sage Foundation publications are those of the authors and not of the Foundation, its Trustees, or its staff. Publication by Russell Sage, therefore, does not imply Foundation endorsement.

Library of Congress Cataloging-in-Publication Data
Low-wage work in the wealthy world / Jérôme Gautié and John Schmitt, editors.
    p. cm. — (The Russell Sage Foundation case studies of job quality in
    advanced economies)
Includes bibliographical references and index.
ISBN 978-0-87154-061-4 (alk. paper)
 1. Wages.   2. Minimum wage.   3. Manpower policy.   4. Labor market.
 I. Gautié, Jérôme.   II. Schmitt, John.
HD4917.L69 2010
331.2'1—dc22

2009018701

The paper used in this publication meets the minimum requirements of American National Standard for Information Sciences—Permanence of Paper for Printed Library Materials. ANSI Z39.48-1992.

Text design by Suzanne Nichols.

RUSSELL SAGE FOUNDATION
112 East 64th Street, New York, New York 10065
10 9 8 7 6 5 4 3 2 1

The Russell Sage Foundation's Project on Low-Wage Work in Europe and the United States

Denmark
Niels Westergaard-Nielsen, National Research Team Coordinator

Ann-Mette Sonne Andersen
Lars Esbjerg
Jingkun Li
Ole Henning Sorensen

Nuka Buck
Jacob Eskildsen
Niels Moller

Tor Eriksson
Klaus G. Grunert
Anna-Kristina Lokke Nielsen

France
Ève Caroli and Jérôme Gautié, National Research
Team Coordinators

Anne Marie Arborio
Jean-Baptiste Berry
Thierry Colin
Christine Guégnard
Sylvie-Anne Meriot

Philippe Askenazy
Jacques Bouteiller
Emilie Fériel
Annie Lamanthe
Philippe Mossé

Mathieu Beraud
Lise Causse
Benoit Grasser
Philippe Méhaut
Sophie Prunier-Poulmaire

Germany
Gerhard Bosch and Claudia Weinkopf, National Research
Team Coordinators

Larz Czommer
Achim Vanselow

Karen Jaehrling
Dorothea Voss-Dahm

Thorsten Kalina

Netherlands
Wiemer Salverda and Maarten van Klaveren, National Research
Team Coordinators

Ria Hermanussen
Marc van der Meer

Wim Sprenger
Arjen van Halem

Kea Tijdens

United Kingdom
Geoff Mason and Ken Mayhew, National Research
Team Coordinators

Marilyn Carroll
Damian Grimshaw
Dennis Nickson
Philip Stevens

Johanna Commander
Susan James
Matthew Osborne
Chris Warhurst

Eli Dutton
Caroline Lloyd
Jonathan Payne

Other Volumes in the Low-Wage Work Project

Low-Wage America: How Employers Are Reshaping Opportunity in the Workplace, edited by Eileen Appelbaum, Annette Bernhardt, and Richard J. Murnane

Low-Wage Work in Denmark, edited by Niels Westergaard-Nielsen

Low-Wage Work in France, edited by Ève Caroli and Jérôme Gautié

Low-Wage Work in Germany, edited by Gerhard Bosch and Claudia Weinkopf

Low-Wage Work in the Netherlands, edited by Wiemer Salverda, Maarten van Klaveren, and Marc van der Meer

Low-Wage Work in the United Kingdom, edited by Caroline Lloyd, Geoff Mason, and Ken Mayhew

PROJECT ADVISORS

Eileen Appelbaum
Rosemary Batt
Annette Bernhardt
Robert M. Solow

Francine D. Blau
Anne Pitts Carter
Sheldon Danziger
Chris Tilly

Françoise Carré
Thomas D. Cook
Richard J. Murnane

Contents

Contributors

JÉRÔME GAUTIÉ is professor of economics at the University of Paris 1 Panthéon-Sorbonne.

JOHN SCHMITT is senior economist with the Center for Economic and Policy Research in Washington, D.C.

EILEEN APPELBAUM is professor and director of the Center for Women and Work in the School of Management and Labor Relations at Rutgers University.

ROSEMARY BATT is Alice H. Cook Professor of Women and Work at the ILR School at Cornell University.

PETER BERG is associate professor in the School of Labor and Industrial Relations at Michigan State University.

ANNETTE BERNHARDT is policy co-director of the National Employment Law Project.

GERHARD BOSCH is professor of sociology and executive director of the Institute for Work, Skills and Training (IAQ) at the University of Duisburg-Essen.

FRANÇOISE CARRÉ is research director at the Center for Social Policy at the J. W. McCormack Graduate School of Policy Studies at the University of Massachusetts–Boston. She also is affiliated fellow at the Center for Women and Work at Rutgers University and research affiliate at the Institute for Research on Labor and Employment at the University of California–Los Angeles.

LAURA DRESSER is associate director of the Center on Wisconsin Strategy.

JACOB ESKILDSEN is professor in the department of marketing and statistics at the Aarhus School of Business, University of Aarhus.

DAMIAN GRIMSHAW is professor of employment studies and director of the European Work and Employment Research Centre (EWERC) at the University of Manchester.

KLAUS G. GRUNERT is professor in the department of marketing and statistics and director of MAPP at the Aarhus School of Business, University of Aarhus.

KAREN JAEHRLING is senior researcher at the Institute for Work, Skills and Training (IAQ) at the University of Duisburg-Essen.

SUSAN JAMES is a research fellow at the ESRC Centre on Skills, Knowledge and Organisational Performance (SKOPE), Department of Education, University of Oxford.

CAROLINE LLOYD is reader in the School of Social Sciences and senior research fellow at the ESRC Centre on Skills, Knowledge and Organisational Performance (SKOPE) at Cardiff University.

GEOFF MASON is senior research fellow at the National Institute of Economic and Social Research, London and visiting professor at the Institute of Education, University of London.

KEN MAYHEW is professor of education and economic performance at Oxford University, fellow in economics at Pembroke College, Oxford, and director of the ESRC Centre on Skills, Knowledge and Organisational Performance (SKOPE).

PHILIPPE MÉHAUT is senior researcher at the Institute of Labour Economics and Industrial Sociology (LEST) at the University of Aix-Marseille.

PHILIP MOSS is professor and chair in the Department of Regional Economic and Social Development at the University of Massachusetts–Lowell.

WIEMER SALVERDA is director of the Amsterdam Institute for Advanced Labour Studies (AIAS) at the University of Amsterdam, and coordinator of the European Low-Wage Employment Research Network (LoWER).

CHRIS TILLY is professor of urban planning and director of the Institute for Research on Labor and Employment at University of California–Los Angeles.

MARC VAN DER MEER is director at ecbo-CINOP (Expertise Center Vocational Training), Den Bosch, the Netherlands.

MAARTEN VAN KLAVEREN is researcher at the Amsterdam Institute for Advanced Labour Studies (AIAS) at the University of Amsterdam and senior consultant at STZ Consultancy and Research, Eindhoven, the Netherlands.

ACHIM VANSELOW is senior researcher at the Institute for Work, Skills and Training (IAQ) at the University of Duisburg-Essen.

DOROTHEA VOSS-DAHM is senior researcher at the Institute for Work, Skills and Training (IAQ) at the University of Duisburg-Essen.

CHRIS WARHURST is professor of labour studies at the University of Strathclyde Business School, director of the Scottish Centre for Employment Research (SCER), and coeditor of the journal *Work, Employment and Society*.

CLAUDIA WEINKOPF is deputy director of the Institute for Work, Skills and Training (IAQ) at the University of Duisburg-Essen.

NIELS WESTERGAARD-NIELSEN is professor of economics at the Aarhus School of Business, University of Aarhus, and is director of the Center for Corporate Performance (CCP).

Foreword

The seal of the Russell Sage Foundation features the ambitious slogan: "For the Improvement of Social and Living Conditions." For over a century, the research projects undertaken by the Foundation, whatever their specific aims, have also sought to serve this broader purpose. The Russell Sage–sponsored study of low-wage work, of which this volume is the culmination, is no exception. Indeed, this study returns to some of the Foundation's earliest concerns.

In 1907 the Russell Sage Foundation's very first large grant financed an extensive survey of the harsh working and living conditions faced by steel workers and coal miners and their families in Pittsburgh, Pennsylvania. The Pittsburgh survey became a model for subsequent social surveys and helped energize Progressive Era reform initiatives that led eventually to occupational health and safety laws, workman's compensation, and the regulation of hours, wages, and the workweek. Modern American workers are the beneficiaries of these reforms, which have vastly improved working conditions over the last hundred years. But recent decades have witnessed a troubling retrenchment, especially for workers in the lower tiers of the U.S. labor market.

Joint Russell Sage/Rockefeller Foundation studies of some twenty-five American industries between 1999 and 2001, summarized in the RSF volume *Low-Wage America*, reveal a disturbingly common pattern: firms, facing intensifying economic pressures due to globalization, technological change, and other economic forces, have sought to hold the line on labor costs by freezing wages, cutting benefits, and reorganizing production, often in ways that intensify work and erode job quality. In the United States, where unions are weak, minimum wages are low, and workers with limited education are plentiful, the deterioration of low-wage work has been widespread. Exceptions have been few and far between and are found mainly where local labor market institutions make it difficult for firms to compete by reducing wages and job quality. Interestingly, in such cases firms have found other ways to compete successfully—often by making investments in training or capital equipment to increase worker productivity and thereby bear the costs of maintaining higher wages and better working conditions.

The coordinated international project reported in this volume compares these recent American developments with labor market trends in five European countries. The comparison builds on intensive study of frontline jobs in five industries, which are predominantly low-paying jobs in the United States. At issue is whether U.S. trends are the inexorable result of worldwide intensification of economic competition, or whether European institutions have been more successful in resisting economic forces and maintaining a higher level of pay and job quality for workers on the lower rungs of the labor market.

The standard measures of a country's economic performance—real income or consumption per person, output per hour worked, and the like—are important but incomplete. When Keynes remarked modestly that "economists are not the guardians of civilization, but they are the guardians of the possibility of civilization," he had this incompleteness in mind. So did we in the planning of this project, even though it is focused on the characteristics of workers, jobs, and labor markets. There is more to a job than the money income that it brings in, though adequate wage income is clearly part of the "possibility of civilization." Likewise, there is more to an economy than the surplus it generates for consumers. An economy affects the well-being of those who take part in it in many other ways as well; the quality of the environment is one, but so too is the quality of the jobs on offer. And job quality is no less real because it is invisible in national economic statistics. That is why this study of low-wage work in Europe and America was planned to augment the standard range of statistical information about low-wage workers and low-wage jobs with intensive case studies of low-wage work that involved site visits to multiple establishments in each industry and interviews with managers and workers.

We speak of "job quality"—just as, in a still broader context, we speak of "the quality of life"—to refer to the nonpecuniary aspects of a job. It is impossible and unnecessary to give an exhaustive list of the components of job quality. The most important items would certainly include: safety and freedom from harmful physical dangers; a degree of job security; some certainty, continuity, and advance notice about hours of work; regular rest periods and paid vacations; a reasonable possibility of upward mobility in pay and status; and a degree of personal autonomy and opportunity for sociability during the workday. In the American context, one would want to add access to health care and provision for retirement. Of course, there are limits and trade-offs imposed by finite productivity. These limits and trade-offs are relevant all up and down the occupational distribution, but they become most acute at the bottom of the labor market, where efforts to hold down labor costs may severely erode the quality of jobs and the quality of workers' lives.

A double objective motivated the decision to extend to Europe the research plan first embodied in *Low-Wage America*. The first was simply to gain some systematic knowledge about the variety of outcomes in some national economies that are basically similar, but obviously not identical, to the American economy. That is why we chose only high-income, successful capitalist economies. If all low-wage labor markets looked exactly the same in wages and job quality, the implication would have been that there was probably little scope for feasible public policy to affect outcomes. That proved not to be the case: there is plenty of variety across these six countries—both in the overall incidence of low-wage work and in the quality of specific jobs in specific industries. It is that variety, if we can understand its origins, that offers scope for policy-induced change.

The second goal, then, was to explore and test the hypothesis that the nature of labor market institutions plays a decisive role in shaping the earnings and other qualities of low-wage jobs as compared with those higher up in the occupational hierarchy. One pretty definite conclusion is that routine economic factors, like technology and market competition, while they play a very important role in governing outcomes, are far from the whole story. They leave a considerable area of slack in which historical, attitudinal, and institutional factors can operate and in which, therefore, public policy can have influence.

We can illustrate with examples from both sides of the street. Looking at the narrowly economic factors at work, it is clear that the intensification of competition leads business firms to urgent cost reduction. This has come about in the hotel industry through consolidation into large, often publicly owned chains intent on streamlining operations and raising profit margins; it has come about in the food processing industry through increased price pressure from large food retailers with significant market clout and from competition from producers in low-wage countries. These pressures on costs then translate easily into pressure on the wages and working conditions of the low-paid, because workers in frontline jobs generally have little firm-specific human capital, are easily replaced if they quit their jobs, and often lack union representation.

On the institutional side, it is generally observed that collective bargaining tends to compress wage distributions and to do perhaps even more to equalize nonwage benefits. Low-wage workers tend to do better in countries with strong union movements. Union strength is not necessarily measured by union density, especially in countries where governments have the capacity and the willingness to extend collective bargaining agreements beyond the actual participants. In these countries, the coverage of collective bargaining agreements may extend to workers who might otherwise have low-wage, low-quality jobs. Another important example is the role of a statutory or informal minimum wage: in France, for instance, the high legal minimum wage is very close to the low-wage threshold and seems to support it, whereas the Netherlands allows a long tail of subminimum wages for young workers. The effects are seen in the distribution of wages and in the composition of the population of low-wage workers.

Still another instructive example of the scope for institutional factors to affect the organization of unskilled work comes from big-box food retailing. In the United States and the United Kingdom, individual workers engaged in stocking shelves work in isolation on simple, repetitive, fully specified tasks. They require little skill and are easily monitored, easily shifted, and easily replaced. In similar stores in Germany, even many frontline workers have had some vocational training. As a result, they can take responsibility for several stages of a supermarket department, from ordering goods to stocking shelves, merchandising products, and advising customers. They have substantial discretion in arranging the necessary work. Vocational education makes this possible.

A different influence, one that crosses the boundary between the narrowly economic and the institutional, comes from the level of the "social wage." The availability of nationally provided health care, pension arrangements, long-lasting unemployment insurance, and social assistance for the poor makes the lives of low-wage workers much more secure in some countries than others. These benefits may also set a floor under the conditions of low-wage work from the supply side. Really bad jobs will attract few takers. And on the demand side, employers may be loath to offer low-wage jobs if they entail costly fringe benefits. In some countries, these supply-and-demand effects have been cited as a cause of high unemployment. In this connection, it is interesting that across the six countries studied here, there is no simple trade-off between job quantity and job quality.

Countries with generous social benefits are not necessarily doomed to high unemployment—at least across our sample of countries—nor are those countries with the thinnest social safety net guaranteed the lowest unemployment rates. Evidently, much depends upon how the social safety net is designed and financed, and perhaps also on the social context in which it is implemented.

The notion of "inclusiveness" emerges from the national comparisons as an important underlying determinant of both wages and job quality. It is partly a matter of informal, often historically embedded, social institutions and partly a matter of explicit public policy, as summed up in the "social wage" and also in the character of the educational system. In our sample of countries, Denmark offers the clearest (and most self-conscious) example of an inclusive, but still market-oriented, system. There has been an explicit national commitment that "no Dane should suffer economic hardship." It has led to a well-developed social safety net and a compressed distribution of earnings with much the smallest incidence of low-wage work. France also scores high on the inclusiveness scale, but in a pattern that involves more direct state involvement in the economy.

The United States exemplifies the non-inclusive end of the scale, not only in practice but in explicit individualistic intent. The United Kingdom and Germany offer contrasting histories. In the United Kingdom, the Thatcher era marked a sharp turn away from earlier inclusiveness, and that move left clear traces in the low-wage labor market. The Blair government made some moves in the reverse direction, notably in the institution of a (rather low) national minimum wage and tax benefits for working families. The results, however, have not been dramatic. Germany has moved in the opposite direction, toward a more individualistic system. German labor laws now permit "mini-jobs"—low-paying part-time jobs exempt from social security taxes—and there have been other attempts to make labor markets more competitive and less "corporatist." Here the consequences have been more noticeable, especially an increase in the incidence of low-wage work and a deterioration of some indicators of job quality. We read this history as containing two general lessons. First, inclusiveness, however it is described in the local policy language, is indeed open to debate and choice. Second, actually having a measurable effect on the quality of low-wage jobs is not easy; changes in policy and in informal behavior have to be fairly deep and have to be pursued persistently.

Another of the lessons of this study is, as the reader will discover, that there is not a simple, one-dimensional U.S.-versus-Europe story. There is variation within Europe too, and the variation occurs along several dimensions. One of the forces that drives change in Europe is that most job-related amenities—job security, regular hours, and so on—are costly. That does not mean that they are simply expendable; there are benefits that may offset the costs. But it does mean that the "high road" to achieving job quality, wherever it exists, is under pressure from intense competition. Firms that have to compete with lower costs elsewhere would like to pass their costs to governments, and governments have to find revenue at a time when raising taxes is unpopular. It is a little ironic that just when the Danish system of "flexicurity" has become a buzzword in Europe and elsewhere, questions have arisen in Denmark as to whether the necessary high tax rates are sustainable.

This is just one aspect of a much broader issue of social policy. No one doubts that, at any instant, the aggregate of goods, services, and quality of life that a society can provide is limited by its capacity to produce. Anything a society does to change the allocation and distribution of goods, services, and amenities is likely also to affect its capacity to produce those things. Wage compression diminishes inequality but weakens incentives; job protection improves security for those employed but adds to the risk assumed by a firm when it creates a job. The deep question for social policy is whether there are acceptable ways for formal legislation and informal negotiation to maneuver along these trade-offs to improve the distribution of incomes and nonpecuniary amenities and the allocation of risks in ways that the consensus will regard as an "improvement of social and living conditions."

Robert M. Solow
Foundation Scholar
Russell Sage Foundation
Institute Professor, Emeritus
Massachusetts Institute of Technology

Eric Wanner
President
Russell Sage Foundation

CHAPTER 1

Introduction and Overview

Eileen Appelbaum, Gerhard Bosch, Jérôme Gautié, Geoff Mason, Ken Mayhew, Wiemer Salverda, John Schmitt, and Niels Westergaard-Nielsen

This volume grows out of the research on the United States summarized in *Low-Wage America: How Employers Are Reshaping Opportunity in the Workplace* (Appelbaum, Bernhardt, and Murnane 2003), which sought to understand how U.S. firms were responding to economic globalization, deregulation, and technological progress and the impact of these responses on typical low-wage frontline workers.

Two broad conclusions emerged from the array of qualitative and quantitative data presented in *Low-Wage America*. First, while most U.S. firms responded to the economic pressures of the last three decades by engaging in cost-cutting efforts that resulted in deteriorating pay and working conditions for their frontline workers, some firms chose different competitive strategies that yielded better outcomes for workers. These alternative "high-road" labor market strategies included focusing on reorganizing the work process, increasing capital intensity, introducing new technology, implementing innovations in products and services, and providing more and better training. These measures generally sought to raise the productivity or lower the turnover of low-wage workers in ways that would offset the higher initial investments or ongoing costs of taking the "high road."[1]

The second broad conclusion of *Low-Wage America* was that labor market institutions have an important impact on firms' choices about how to respond to competitive pressures. From the end of the 1970s to the present, the decline in unionization rates and the erosion of the real value of the minimum wage, for example, have made it substantially easier for U.S. firms to respond to market challenges by taking the "low road." But still, some firms did choose high-road workplace practices in organizing and rewarding the work of less-skilled employees. And these decisions appear to have been shaped by labor market institutions—an employers' association in North Carolina that facilitated training and modernization, fostered new product development, sought new markets, and improved outcomes for both workers and companies; a training facility, jointly managed by hospitals and the health care union in New York City, that improved skills and pay for less-skilled hospital workers; high union density in a vacation destination city with upmarket hotels that led to substantially higher wages and better working conditions for hotel housekeepers. Nevertheless, only a small minority of the firms studied followed such high-road practices.

In research focused solely on the United States, it is difficult to draw conclusions about the role of institutions in determining outcomes for workers in low-paid jobs. There is little institutional variation across the United States—the examples just given of strong labor market institutions in particular locales are widely recognized as exceptions to the general pattern of weak employers' associations, a low level of union density, and the failure of employers to train frontline workers. Our idea was that there might be much to be learned about the nature of jobs that are low-wage in the United States by studying these same jobs in other advanced industrial nations with very different institutional settings. More precisely, our key assumption was that the effects on national economies of changing technology, increasing globalization, and intensifying competition are filtered through institutional structures and, further, that these effects can be observed in the strategic decisions made by firms and in the quality of jobs held by workers.

Indeed, this thinking was the genesis of the Russell Sage Foundation's decision to undertake industry-based case studies of job quality in foreign economies in 2005–2006. Selecting the comparison countries required balancing a set of factors. To be most useful, the comparison economies had to be different from the United States (and from each other), but not so radically different with respect to economic, political, and institutional (including cultural) institutions that they would bring little to a U.S.-focused discussion. Ultimately, three large economies—France, Germany, and the United Kingdom—and two smaller northern European economies—Denmark and the Netherlands—were selected.

Researchers in all five countries followed a common methodology built around firm-level case studies in five industries—call centers, food processing, hospitals, hotels, and retail trade.[2] Within each firm and industry, country teams focused on specific tasks typically performed in the United States by low-wage frontline workers: call center operators; operators in food processing; nursing assistants and cleaners in hospitals; hotel housekeepers; and cashiers and stock or sales clerks in retail. To complement these case studies, national researchers also used available data to draw the broader contours of low-wage and less-skilled work in each country.[3] To measure the extent of low-wage work, national teams defined low-wage workers as those workers earning a gross hourly wage of less than two-thirds of each country's median gross hourly wage. The relative definition of low-wage work has several advantages over an absolute definition. The relative definition abstracts from differences in wages that simply reflect differences in average incomes across the six countries.[4] More importantly, the relative definition reflects the view that relative pay matters both economically and socially. Firms are continuously making hiring and investment decisions based on the relative costs of different kinds of workers and different technologies. And workers are intrinsically concerned about the implied social valuation of their work that is included in the relative wage. This social aspect of pay suggests that relative pay is also a key dimension of job quality.

Indeed, beyond pay, job quality is at the center of the analytical focus of this research. European countries have seen a renewed interest in this issue since the 1990s, and job quality has acquired an important place in the social and employment agenda of the European Union (see Gallie 2007). In this volume, we use the concept of job quality in its broadest sense, covering all the terms of employment and working conditions that may have an impact on the well-being of workers, both at work and in their private lives. Measuring job quality inevitably involves striking a balance between objective job characteristics and workers' subjective perceptions, including those related to job satisfaction. Most analyses of the key determinants of job quality focus on: compensation, including benefits or social entitlements (such as health insurance, pension, paid vacation, parental leave, paid sick days, and other nonwage compensation); contractual status, in particular whether the job is permanent or temporary (one of the fundamental determinants of job security); training and career opportunities; task discretion and other aspects of job design, such as work pace; health and safety conditions; and work schedules, including the scope for finding a balance between work and family life.

The project's firm-level case studies, which focused on specific oc-cupations in the same industries in all six countries, were particularly well suited to comparing these many dimensions of job quality across a variety of national institutional structures. As far as possible, na-tional teams attempted to study eight firms in each industry in each country.[5] In each firm, employers, executives, employees' representa-tives, and a sample of workers were interviewed following shared guidelines. The case studies also included workplace visits and, where possible, quantitative data provided by the firms.

The results of each national research effort were first published in five national monographs.[6] This volume seeks to extract some of the comparative lessons, reintroducing the American case. The main sources of the evidence and analysis here are the national mono-graphs for the five European countries; this volume also draws less directly on earlier research presented in *Low-Wage America*, which has been updated and supplemented by U.S.-based researchers work-ing with the European teams.

The remainder of this chapter summarizes the main findings of the project.

EXPLAINING DIFFERENCES IN SHARES OF LOW-WAGE WORK

One of the main challenges of the research presented here is to ex-plain the international differences in the prevalence of low-wage work. In the mid-2000s, according to our coordinated analysis of separate national household surveys in each of the six countries, the United States had the highest share of low-wage employment, with about 25 percent of workers earning less than two-thirds of the na-tional median wage (see table 2.1).[7] Germany, contrary to widespread expectations, was the European country in the mid-2000s with the next-highest share of low-wage work (22.7 percent), followed closely by the United Kingdom (21.7 percent). The Netherlands (17.6 per-cent) fell about midway between these three low-wage-intensive economies, on the one hand, and France (11.1 percent) and Den-mark (8.5 percent), on the other hand, both of which had substan-tially smaller low-wage shares.[8]

A closely related task facing this volume is to explain the divergent trends over time in the shares of low-wage work in each country (see figure 2.1). Since the 1970s, the low-wage employment share has been falling steadily in France. Over the same period, low-wage shares were relatively constant in Denmark (at a low level) and the United States (at a high level, with some cyclical variation). In the remaining three countries, however, low-wage employment was much higher in the mid-2000s than it had been at the end of the 1970s. The Netherlands and the United Kingdom both saw large increases in the low-wage share over the 1980s and 1990s, with no further increases in the 2000s. In Germany, before reunification, the low-wage share was flat or falling, but from the mid-1990s, the German low-wage share also increased steadily.

Taken together, the evidence on the national prevalence of low-wage work in the mid-2000s, the longer-term trends in the national incidence of low-wage work, and the differences in low-wage work across industries in the same country all suggest that there is no simple story of the United States versus Europe. Low-wage work is more common in the United States than it is in the five European countries examined here—twice as likely as in France and three times as likely as in Denmark. Nevertheless, two European economies—the United Kingdom and Germany—have low-wage employment rates that are much closer to the rate in the United States than they are to those in Denmark and France.[9] Moreover, the United Kingdom, the Netherlands, and, surprisingly, Germany saw sizable increases in low-wage work in the 1990s and 2000s. Even in countries with relatively few low-wage workers, some industries still have important shares of low-wage work, such as hotels in Denmark and France.

These differences in the share of low-wage work are all the more remarkable given that our six countries have all been exposed over the last several decades to the same increases in globalization, technology, and competition within national product markets. The rising share of global trade in domestic GDP, heightened capital mobility, the growing pervasiveness of information and communication technologies, and developments in financial and product markets have increased competitive pressures on companies, strengthened the bargaining power of employers, and undermined the ability of unions and individual workers to defend their wages and other interests. Almost all of the countries studied also have faced large increases in immigration or in the number of migrant workers in recent years (France is the exception).[10] Employer strategies in each country are affected by rising exposure to increasingly globalized markets for goods and services, by intensified competition in product and service markets, and by growing supplies of workers who are less able to defend themselves in the workplace—less-skilled immigrant and migrant workers and, in some countries, women.[11] All five European countries studied here are members of the European Union. During the past twenty-five years, the European integration process has brought some movement toward harmonization of social rights and labor market regulations (for instance, in the domains of working time and equal treatment of part-time and temporary workers; see chapters 2 and 3), which had some impact on the least regulated countries, notably the United Kingdom. Nevertheless, because the integration process was aimed at building a "single market," it was mainly based on the liberalization and deregulation of capital and product markets, and that focus induced increased competitive pressures for many European firms. From the beginning of the 2000s, the entry of new members from eastern Europe, where labor costs are notably lower than in western Europe, also contributed to an increase in these pressures.[12]

Country-specific, long-run, economic structural factors seem to have played little role in explaining international differences in low-wage work. National shares of low-wage work do not appear to be correlated with a country's GDP per capita, GDP growth rate, hourly labor productivity, productivity growth rate, or a range of long-term demographic factors, including female employment rates. Nor do between-country differences in the labor share of total value-added appear to play a decisive role in explaining the incidence of low-wage work. The incidence of low pay, however, is strongly related to the distribution of income *within* the labor share of value-added in each country, a phenomenon on which we hope our findings here shed some light (Mason and Salverda 2008).

Macroeconomic policy and events do, however, appear to influence the evolution of low-wage work over time in some countries. The unification of Germany, for example, produced an unemployment shock that set in motion a deterioration in the collective bargaining regime that led to a significant rise in the low-wage share there. In the United States, the share of low-wage work, while showing no clear long-term trend, falls when the economy is booming and rises when the economy is in a slump.

Nevertheless, the impact of macroeconomic factors on the labor market is clearly mediated by national institutional systems. The national overviews and the case studies suggest that the most important influence on the observed differences in low-wage work is the "inclusiveness" of a country's labor market institutions (chapter 3). For example, the two countries examined here with the smallest low-wage shares, Denmark and France, have labor relations systems that are highly inclusive. By "inclusive" we mean that the systems have formal—and sometimes informal—mechanisms to extend the wages, benefits, and working conditions negotiated by workers in industries and occupations with strong bargaining power to workers in industries and occupations with less bargaining power. In Denmark, about 70 percent of workers are union members and collective bargaining agreements cover about 90 percent of all workers. Moreover, solidaristic wage-bargaining practices there act to raise pay, benefits, and working conditions the most for workers at the bottom, further reducing the share of low-wage workers. In France, despite relatively low levels of union membership (union membership rates in France are even lower than in the United States), more than 90 percent of the workforce is covered by collective agreement rates because agreements are extended by law to non-union workers and firms. These high rates of union coverage, alongside a high minimum wage, appear to have had a substantial impact on reducing the share of low-wage workers in France.

The Netherlands traditionally has also had a fairly inclusive industrial relations system. In important respects, the degree of inclusiveness in the Netherlands is close to that of France. A key feature of the Dutch industrial relations system, however, is that the government and the social partners have agreed to a lower minimum wage for young workers. As a result, the share of low-wage work in the Netherlands lies somewhere between Denmark and France, on the inclusive end of the spectrum, and the United Kingdom and the United States, at the less inclusive end. The negotiated deterioration in the real value of the minimum wage in the Netherlands, as well as agreements among the social partners to allow extensive use of temporary contracts (especially for younger workers) and low-paid part-time employment (especially for women and younger workers), contributed to the rise from the mid-1980s through the mid-1990s in the share of low-wage work.

Historically, the German industrial relations system has also had a high degree of inclusiveness. Since the mid-1990s, however, the inclusiveness of the German system has declined substantially because many employers, especially in small and medium-sized enterprises, have decided not to participate in nationally negotiated wage agreements. The deterioration in the inclusiveness of the system derives from the creation (encouraged through legislative changes) of largely unregulated "mini-jobs," the use of temporary agency and "posted" workers,[13] and the outsourcing of some work to small and medium-sized enterprises that are not covered by national collective bargaining agreements; all of these factors have contributed to a sharp increase over the last decade in the share of low-wage workers in Germany.

The two countries with the least inclusive labor market institutions and industrial relations system are the United States and the United Kingdom. These countries also have among the highest shares of low-wage workers in our study. Only about 13 percent of U.S. workers are members of a union or covered by a union contract. The U.S. system also provides only weak legal regulation of wages, benefits, and working conditions, and its minimum wage is low relative to the average production-worker wage. The United Kingdom has a higher unionization rate than the United States (about 29 percent of British workers were in a union in 2007, and the same share were covered by a union contract), but the British system is far less inclusive than the industrial relations systems in place in the rest of the European countries in our study. The national minimum wage, introduced in 1999 at a level that was substantially more generous than that of the United States (measured either in absolute terms or relative to the median wage), nevertheless remains below the national low-wage threshold and therefore has not had the same effect on the incidence of low pay in the United Kingdom as the minimum wage has had in France.[14]

Inclusiveness is not simply a question of collective bargaining coverage. As suggested in several examples already mentioned, minimum wages are often an important mechanism of inclusiveness. The high French minimum wage (about $7.75 per hour in purchasing power parity [PPP] terms in 2006, compared to $5.15 in the United States in the same year), for example, is one of the principal reasons for the country's low incidence of low-wage work. Denmark does not have a legislated minimum wage but does have a widely recognized, collectively bargained, national-level minimum wage set above the value of what is available from state-provided income support. The low value of the minimum wage relative to the median in the United States, even in the many states that have decided in recent years to set minimum wages above the federal standard, has been too low to have an effect on the prevalence of low-wage work. In Germany, where there is no national minimum wage, a national debate is considering the introduction of a minimum wage in order to shore up the traditionally inclusive but deteriorating German industrial relations system. Beyond the degree of inclusiveness of institutional arrangements, the degree of commitment (from both governments and social partners) to wage compression and equality also plays a crucial role, as the differences across countries in the relative level of statutory minimum wages illustrate. For example, institutional differences in the legal mechanism that sets the minimum wage in France and the United States—Congress must vote for increases in the United States, while the French minimum wage is indexed to inflation as well as to the average blue-collar wage—explain only part of the gap between the U.S. and French minimum wages. Successive French governments also appear to be more committed to wage compression and have enacted discretionary increases in the minimum wage that have had an important impact on the evolution of its value relative to the national median wage.

Employment protection legislation (EPL) plays an ambiguous role in the inclusiveness of national systems and the national incidence of low-wage work. On the one hand, EPL increases the bargaining power of incumbent workers by making it harder for employers to fire them. This greater bargaining power can help to reduce the number of workers earning low pay. On the other hand, EPL that covers only regular workers may create incentives for employers to hire workers under legal arrangements designed to provide little or no employment protection. These less-protected jobs can become havens for low-wage work. In the Netherlands, for example, many low-wage workers are on temporary contracts or are employees of temporary agencies. In Germany, mini-jobbers, posted workers, and temporary agency workers make up an important portion of low-wage workers.

Beyond EPL narrowly defined, much depends on how countries choose to apply labor market regulations and broader worker social rights to nonstandard work arrangements. In Denmark, for example, agency workers receive the same pay as their counterparts employed on standard contracts, and posted workers are generally covered by collective bargaining agreements; in France, agency workers also benefit (at least officially) from equal treatment and receive an additional 10 percent "insecurity premium" relative to their permanent counterparts. In France, the Netherlands, and the United Kingdom, minimum wages apply to posted workers. Generally, the European Union's 1997 Directive on Equal Treatment for Part-Time Workers requires that part-time workers receive pay equal to, and nonwage benefits proportional to, those of full-time workers.[15]

The effective inclusiveness of national industrial relations systems also depends on product market regulations (chapter 3).[16] The changes in product market regulation in the six countries over the last quarter-century—privatization of state-owned enterprises and state-run activities, deregulation of sectors such as finance and telecommunications, and the opening up of national service sectors to intra-European competition—may have had the effect of reducing workers' bargaining power by reducing industry rents and thereby contributing to an increase in the share of low-wage workers. The impact of deregulation, however, appears to depend in an important way on both the specifics of deregulation—in Denmark and the Netherlands, for example, important product market deregulations included protections for existing workforces—and the broader inclusiveness of the national labor relations system.

National institutional systems also play a crucial role on the supply side of the low-wage labor market (chapter 4). In recent years, immigration policy and regulations concerning migrant work have been much more restrictive in France and somewhat more restrictive in Denmark than in the United Kingdom and the United States (with Germany and the Netherlands somewhere in between the two poles).[17] But, as suggested earlier, the impact of immigration and migrant work is "filtered" through national institutions. Strongly inclusive industrial relations systems appear able to absorb current levels of immigration and migrant work without significant increases in the national share of low-wage work. For example, in 2004 in Denmark, France, the Netherlands, and the United Kingdom, immigrants accounted for between 4 and 6 percent of the national labor force, yet the low-wage shares in the national labor force ranged from less than 10 percent in the more inclusive Denmark and France to more than 20 percent in the less inclusive United Kingdom.[18]

Immigrant or migrant workers are not the only source of potential low-wage workers. Also playing a role in determining the inclusiveness of national wage-setting institutions are the availability and generosity of government benefits for nonworking adults. Set high enough, income support can create an effective floor for wages in the low-wage labor market.[19] Workers will be unlikely to accept work at low wages if they are also eligible for income supports that provide a roughly comparable standard of living without the need to work. For example, the country with the most accessible and generous benefits for nonworking adults—Denmark—is also the country with the lowest incidence of low-wage work. High income supports in Denmark effectively constitute an independent wage floor, reinforcing the collectively bargained minimum wage. The country where benefits for nonworking adults are hardest to access and least generous relative to a typical worker's wages—the United States—is the country where low-wage work is most common.

Changes over time in the generosity of benefits appear to have had relatively little role to play in explaining the rise in low-wage work in Germany after the mid-1990s and in the Netherlands between the mid-1980s and the mid-1990s.[20] Benefit generosity and access to benefits have been either stable or increasing in both countries, even as the share of low-wage work has been on the rise. The case of the United Kingdom, the other country that saw a long, steady increase in low-wage work between the early 1980s and mid-1990s, is more complicated. Over the last three decades, out-of-work benefits have generally become less generous, while in-work benefits, such as the Working Tax Credit, have become more generous, especially since the late 1990s.

Overall, our analysis suggests that the inclusiveness of national institutions is the principal determinant of the national share of low-wage work. As the preceding discussion has illustrated, however, national systems, even the most inclusive, offer employers at least some "exit options" from the institutional arrangements that provide inclusiveness, and this facilitates the emergence of a low-wage sector. These exit options take many forms, including: the ability of employers to withdraw from national collective bargaining agreements (as many small and medium-sized enterprises have chosen to do in Germany); the opportunity for firms to outsource at least part of their activities to sectors and firms with lower (even no) collective bargaining standards, including the use of posted employees, who are officially employed by foreign firms and therefore work under the labor laws of their country of origin rather than the law of the country where they are employed; the existence of youth subminimum wages (in the Netherlands, in the United Kingdom, and in the retail sector in Denmark); and the existence of nonstandard work arrangements, such as temporary contracts, temporary agency employment, part-time work, and German mini-jobs. In some cases, exit options are legal and formal; in others, the lack of enforcement of existing laws is a form of exit option. (For example, legal and collectively bargained labor standards are widely violated in the hotel sector, probably owing in part to the extensive use of immigrants in the sector.)

The increase in the use of various exit options in Germany—the decline in employer participation in collective labor agreements, the rise in outsourcing, and the dramatic expansion in mini-jobs—has probably been the principal factor behind the rise in low-wage work there since the mid-1990s. Similarly, the negotiated youth subminimum wage and the intentional expansion of short-hour part-time work for women explain much of the rise of low-wage work in the Netherlands in the 1990s.

ASSESSING DIFFERENCES IN THE OTHER DIMENSIONS OF JOB QUALITY

An important aspect of job quality lies in career opportunities—and in particular the extent to which low-wage jobs lead to higher-paying positions. Unfortunately, internationally comparable data on wage mobility are scarce. The available evidence, however, generally indicates that movement out of low-wage work is at least as high in European economies as it is in the United States. The two countries with the lowest share of low-wage work, Denmark and France, for example, appear to offer low-wage workers the best opportunities for exiting low-wage employment; the United States does not appear to make up for its high share of low-wage work by offering a higher degree of upward mobility (for some evidence on wage mobility, see chapter 2). These findings are consistent with a large body of research that finds higher income mobility in Europe over individuals' working lives and across generations.[21] The array of social supports available for less-skilled workers in Europe, from child care to training, may play a role in the relatively high mobility there.

Nonwage benefits are another key dimension of job quality. Indeed, even between "high-wage" Denmark and "low-wage" America, the differences in statutory and negotiated nonwage benefits—what could be labeled the "social wage" (see chapters 2 and 3)—are substantially more important for the standard of living of low-wage workers (as well as the employment costs facing employers) than the observed wage differences. Low-wage workers in all five European countries, for example, have access either to health insurance or to state-financed health care (as a right of citizenship and often of residency); paid vacation and holidays (at least twenty days per year are mandated by the European Union); paid sick leave; paid parental leave; a much greater likelihood of free or low-cost child care; and, in most countries, legal rights to request or demand scheduling flexibility. As a result, the "social meaning" of low-wage work is different in Europe, even in the United Kingdom, than it is in the United States. In the United States, over one-fourth of low-wage workers have no health insurance (private or public); more than one-fourth have no paid vacation or paid holidays; and more than one-half have no paid sick days (see chapter 2).[22]

At the industry and occupational levels, the case studies in the second half of this volume also examine other aspects of employment and working conditions (see chapter 5 for an extensive overview of the findings). For some occupations—such as hotel room attendants (chapter 7)—differences in job quality across countries are slight. Even in highly regulated and (formally) highly inclusive national labor markets—such as Denmark and France—the lack of both individual and collective bargaining power in the hotel sector, along with a workforce drawn from groups with the lowest individual bargaining power (less-skilled immigrants, women, and young people), appears to have led to the emergence of legal and illegal exit options. Legal exemptions to national laws and regulations, for example, are widespread in France, and existing regulations are often difficult to enforce in all six countries, even in Denmark. In these circumstances, despite some exceptions, the differences in job quality for room attendants between hotels with high and low standards do not appear to be very significant.

Nevertheless, even in frontline occupations for which wages and working conditions appear to be similar to those in the United States, one must remember that, as mentioned earlier, almost all low-wage workers in Europe have nonwage benefits by law or by a collective bargaining agreement that are far less common in the U.S. versions of the same jobs.

The most substantial differences across countries with respect to both the nature of work and the quality of jobs were found in hospitals. What are relatively low-skilled and poorly paid jobs as cleaners and nursing assistants in the United States have been transformed into more-skilled, better-paid jobs, with broader tasks and in less

Taylorized work organizations, in Denmark, the Netherlands, and, to a lesser extent, France (see chapter 8).[23] The United Kingdom has tended to move in the same direction since the beginning of the 2000s, even if the impact on work organization has been modest and the share of low-wage work remained high at the time of the study. In the United Kingdom, sector-specific institutions—strong unions and public-sector employment—appear to override partly the weaknesses in broader British national-level institutions. In contrast, the deterioration in wage levels and job quality for cleaners in German hospitals reflects intensive outsourcing, falling collective bargaining coverage, and the lack of a minimum wage, encapsulating the declining degree of inclusiveness in the German national institutional system. France offers a mixed picture in public hospitals, with clear differences between a core of civil servants and an important periphery of workers on short-term contracts. With respect to international differences in job design, terms of employment, and working conditions, the other three industries examined here—retail trade, food processing, and call centers—lie somewhere in between hotels, where differences in the quality of frontline jobs are relatively small, and hospitals, where the differences are striking.

At first glance, cashiers and sales clerks in retail chains across the six countries appear to work in broadly similar conditions (chapter 6). However, some important differences exist. In Germany and, to a lesser extent, Denmark, many frontline retail workers participate in an apprenticeship system that provides a level of vocational training generally not found in the other countries, where employees are largely less skilled. (France is an exception; there the average retail worker tends to have a higher level of general education than in the other countries.) This translates into a broader range of tasks for retail workers, in contrast with the more Taylorized organizations of work found particularly in the United States and the United Kingdom. In Denmark, upward mobility in the retail sector is also higher than it is elsewhere.

National as well as sectoral institutions have an impact on other dimensions of job quality. In France, for instance, a collective agreement has limited the opportunity for employers to offer part-time contracts of less than twenty-six hours a week (unless explicitly desired by the worker)—involuntary (short) part-time work having disproportionately affected women workers. In Germany, conversely, employers have exercised exit options especially with respect to mini-jobs, which take advantage of women's secondary-earner status.

In the United States, because of lower fringe benefit costs, part-time work is also intensively used as an exit option. In the Netherlands, retailers responded to increased competitive pressures at the beginning of the 2000s by replacing adults (often women) with young workers paid the youth minimum wage (see chapter 3). The retail sector also illustrates how the exclusiveness of an institutional system, here at the industry level, may also derive from the behavior—more or less voluntary—of unions in the sector. In the United States, unions have in some cases acceded to two-tier compensation agreements that offer lower wages and benefits to new workers; in Germany, in some big retail companies, hard-pressed unions have accepted the intensive use of mini-jobs in order to protect core worker employment conditions.

In food processing (chapter 9), the share of low-wage work and other dimensions of job quality differ across countries. High levels of R&D and capital investment in automation in the Danish meat sector have helped to support higher frontline worker wages there in ways not found in the other five countries, where competitive pressures have put substantial strain on wages. National institutions have played an important role in shaping the sector in Denmark, including a well-funded institute dedicated to research, development, and related training in the sector and mandatory job rotation to improve working conditions. The French meat sector and large employers in the Netherlands and Germany (mainly in the confectionery sector) also make use of functional flexibility and multi-skilling.[24] By contrast, in the United Kingdom and the United States, low wages, numerical flexibility, and Taylorized work organization remain widespread. Migrant workers make up an important part of the meat-processing workforce in Germany and in the food-processing sector as a whole in the United Kingdom and the United States. Migrant workers are often on special contracts (as temps or posted workers) that are less protective and that may facilitate or merely reflect employers' decisions to follow low-road employment strategies.

Job design and employment conditions for call center operators also differ across countries (chapter 10). In the Netherlands, the United Kingdom, and the United States, the share of low-wage workers in this industry is high, and the workplaces have taken a more Taylorized approach to work organization, with an extensive use of electronic performance monitoring. Wages are higher and high-discretion jobs are more common in Denmark and, to a lesser extent, France than they are in the Netherlands, the United Kingdom, and the United States. German call centers lie somewhere in between these two models. Worker discretion is relatively high and job tasks are more varied in Germany, but the share of low-wage workers is relatively high, especially at subcontractors. These call center examples also demonstrate that the same contextual factor (high unemployment and reduced employment opportunities, both of which are found in Germany and France) may lead to different outcomes in different institutional frameworks. In Germany, the pressure has been on wages, while institutions such as unions and work councils seem to have succeeded in maintaining rather good working conditions relative to other countries; in France, however, the minimum wage and other inclusive institutions have protected wages but may have directed competitive pressures toward work intensification. The British case is also interesting since firms have responded to tightening labor markets by offering a mix of improvement in wages and working conditions, but firms generally have not changed job design or work organization.

These vignettes are not intended to give an overview of the industry case studies (for that, see chapter 5) but only to give some examples of how differences in labor market institutions can shape differences in job quality for frontline workers. Some more general lessons can also be drawn.

The outcomes in several industries (the hotel industry is the obvious case) confirm that high-road product market strategies (for example, based on high-quality goods or services) do not necessarily entail high-road human resources practices. The case studies demonstrate that high-road human resource practices generally emerge only when the appropriate institutional arrangements at the national or industry level are already in place.

Functional flexibility (broadly defined jobs with a high degree of worker discretion) appears to be neither a necessary nor sufficient condition for high pay, good working conditions, and high job satisfaction. In French retail, for example, wages are high in the traditional big supermarket chains, but so is work intensity (which is much higher than it is for cashiers in the United States), and the working conditions are particularly bad. In German retail, meanwhile, relatively high-skilled workers engage in a range of tasks, including a high level of customer service, but wages are low, primarily because of the high incidence of mini-jobs. Developing job rotation and multi-skilling in the Danish and French food-processing firms did not always lead to increased job satisfaction. The same was true in U.S. hospitals, where attempts by some firms to redesign jobs had only limited impact on job satisfaction. These examples may illustrate the ambiguity of partial solutions: task enrichment may have limited impact on satisfaction if it is not supported by training and compensated by a wage increase or if multi-skilling is used to cut the number of jobs and to increase workloads. All these examples suggest the usefulness of a multidimensional assessment of job quality rather than a simple distinction between a high road and a low road.

Another general remark relates to the relationship between job quality and workforce characteristics. In all the countries, even in more egalitarian Denmark, gender plays a key role in the low-wage labor market. Several occupations studied here—housekeepers in hotels and hospitals, nursing assistants, cashiers in retail, packers in food processing—are often, if not mainly, done by women. Because of the complex interaction between job segregation and wage discrimination, it is not easy to disentangle the forces at play at the industry level. Frontline workers in retail food (who are disproportionately women) consistently earn less than sales clerks in retail electronics (who are disproportionately men) even though available data suggest that productivity levels are roughly the same across the two sectors within each country. Moreover, recruitment of managers from rank-and-file workers is largely limited to men. In food processing, operators in packing (more often women) are usually paid less than operators in production. Women's individual bargaining power is usually more limited owing to difficulties in reconciling work and family constraints. Women are more often employed in less protective employment statuses—such as the German mini-jobs, seasonal contracts, and other forms of temporary or part-time jobs. The same goes for immigrants and, to a lesser extent, youths. The opportunity for all these "secondary" labor force groups to avoid taking low-wage and low-quality jobs depends partly on the national institutions that have an impact on their labor supply, including the income tax system, child care benefits, student grants, and wider access to out-of-work benefits (see chapter 4).

THE TRADE-OFF BETWEEN JOB QUANTITY AND JOB QUALITY

A widely shared view—at least among economists—is that Europe may have better but, as a consequence, fewer jobs than the United

States does. Higher wage and nonwage costs—including any costs to employers of higher job quality—might create a trade-off between wages (as well as benefits and job quality) and the quantity of jobs. Do the countries in our sample with a low share of low-wage workers suffer higher unemployment or fewer employment opportunities than they would if they had more low-wage workers? (see, for example, Krugman 1994). The case study approach that lies at the heart of this project is ideal for studying both the firm-level determinants of the prevalence of low-wage work and the differences across firms and countries in the nature and quality of frontline jobs. Case studies, however, are not well suited for an analysis of aggregate employment issues—especially the issue of whether there is a national trade-off between the level of low-wage employment and employment opportunities for less-skilled workers.[25] Nevertheless, the detailed information contained in the case studies may provide clues for researchers using national-level data to analyze the potential for the wage-employment trade-off that has been a key feature in labor market policy debates in Europe since at least the early 1990s (see, for example, OECD 1994).

The data on the shares of low-wage work provide only weak support for the view that European labor market institutions lead inevitably to fewer employment opportunities for entry-level workers. The country in our study with what is arguably the most generous social welfare state, Denmark, also has the highest employment rate and the lowest unemployment rate, not just overall but also for younger workers and less-educated workers (see table 2.6). The Netherlands, which has a far more generous social welfare system than the United States or the United Kingdom, also does at least as well as both those countries on most employment measures and actually surpasses the United States and the United Kingdom when it comes to the employment of the young and the less-educated. At first glance at least, the experience of Germany over the last decade also runs somewhat counter to the standard inequality-unemployment trade-off. The share of low-wage workers in Germany has increased sharply since the mid-1990s, but through 2004, the overall employment rate changed little. Between 2004 and 2007, German employment rates did jump, however, and the earlier German employment performance might well have been worse in the absence of the rising low-wage share. In the United Kingdom, the introduction of a national minimum wage in 1999 and the increase in this wage since then do not seem to have had a negative impact on employment (for a detailed survey, see Metcalf 2007). Only France, which has both a small share of low-wage workers and high rates of unemployment, appears at face value to fit the standard inequality-unemployment trade-off. Indeed, from the mid-1980s, the national debate in France over the role of the French minimum wage in the "job deficit" in low-wage and less-skilled work (such as in retail, hotels, and restaurants) has been intense. In 1993 the French government introduced exemptions to employers' social contributions for low-wage jobs in an effort to counteract the potential negative effects of minimum-wage increases. The number of less-skilled jobs, which had been declining until then, began to increase again. Nevertheless, French unemployment remained high. However, as Robert Solow observed in the introduction to the French volume in the RSF series (Caroli and Gautié 2008), many macroeconomic factors are at play here, not simply the minimum wage.

Several factors might explain the lack of a clear-cut trade-off between wage inequality and employment outcomes. Some, but far from all, European employers have chosen high-road labor market strategies. As mentioned earlier, many employers in Danish food processing have responded to competitive pressures from globalization by increasing the capital intensity of their production facilities, increasing workers' productivity enough to justify wages above the low-wage threshold. Danish, Dutch, and British hospitals have upgraded the skills content of nursing assistants to include some of the responsibilities of more-skilled nurses. In Germany, the apprenticeship system trains many retail sales clerks in electronics to a level that improves firm sales enough to pay for higher wages. Moreover, the industry evidence suggests that in an important number of cases, employer strategies adapt over time to long-standing features of national institutions. In many European industries, employers have learned to live with legislated and negotiated costs that many U.S. firms would view as prohibitive.

Another potential factor is that government programs that partially fund or directly provide health insurance, pensions, parental leave, training, and other nonwage benefits may subsidize part of the high-road employment path, independent of individual employers' decisions about job design. As mentioned earlier, the biggest differences in low-wage work between the United States and the five European countries are not related to wages, but rather to a range of nonwage benefits, including health insurance, sick pay, vacation and holiday pay, parental leave plans, training, and other benefits. In the five European economies, the government assumes the financial responsibility for *some* of these nonwage benefits (health insurance, most notably), especially on behalf of low-wage workers and their employers. As a result, some employers of low-wage workers do not face the full cost of the nonwage benefits they provide workers.[26] The incidence of the costs of these subsidies depends on the structure of related national institutions. All employers, not just those who employ low-wage workers, may pay for these subsidies in the form of lower profits, driven by higher corporate taxes to support social spending on low-wage workers. Taxpayers more generally may bear the costs, with the exact incidence reflecting national tax systems.

Much greater wage compression in Europe (outside of the United Kingdom) may also act as an effective subsidy supporting the wage and nonwage benefits of frontline workers in Europe. Solidaristic bargaining strategies in Denmark and, to a lesser degree, in the Netherlands may function, in practice, as a subsidy for the wages and benefits of less-skilled workers. Solidaristic wage bargaining may involve paying less-skilled workers "too much," but also paying higher-skilled workers "too little."[27] Such an arrangement may allow employers to maintain relatively high rates of less-skilled employment without a strong negative impact on firm profits.

Similar arguments may explain why there is only weak evidence to support the general view that there is a systematic trade-off between employment levels and various nonwage dimensions of job quality. The introduction of and subsequent increases in the national minimum wage in the United Kingdom led some firms to cut some fringe benefits and to intensify work, and this response may have reduced any negative impact on employment (see Metcalf 2007; chapter 3). In some sectors, the German unions have conceded to wage cuts, declines in working conditions (including longer hours), and reductions in job security in order to save jobs. But Denmark, again, stands as a counterexample: the high level of job quality along all the key dimensions studied here does not seem to prevent Denmark from achieving the highest employment levels in our six countries.

CONCLUSION

The case studies show that stronger bargaining rights in some countries, more extensive labor market regulations in others, greater emphasis on equal opportunities for women, and the common but uneven influence of developments at the European Union level on employment models have differential effects on employers' ability or incentives to create and improve jobs at the bottom of the pay and skill spectrums. The case studies also demonstrate the substantial pressures on national employment models, pressures that have contributed to the deterioration of pay and working conditions for the most vulnerable workers in most of the six countries studied.

The effects of labor market institutions on the organization of work and on worker outcomes are changing as a result of the intensification of competition in all of the industrialized countries. Employer strategies in each country are affected by rising exposure to increasingly globalized markets for goods and services; by intensified competition in product and service markets; and in some countries by growing supplies of workers who are less able to defend themselves in the workplace, such as less-skilled immigrant and migrant workers and, in some countries, women.

Labor market institutions and laws governing the employment relationship are evolving in response to these changes in technology, globalization, competition, and labor supply. And despite a history of stronger unions and greater labor market regulation in Europe than in the United States, workers employed in low-wage or less-skilled jobs in some European countries have been susceptible to employers' efforts to reduce costs by reducing wages. Where such actions are not precluded by law or binding negotiation, some employers have taken steps intended to bypass the norms and regulations that characterize their nation's economic model (see the discussion of exit options in chapter 3). The result has been a sharply rising incidence of low-wage work in some, but not all, of the countries in this study.

In Germany, which lacks a national minimum wage, the declining strength of unions has led to soaring levels of low-wage work in the past few years. The rise in low-paid employment has been partly the result of outsourcing and subcontracting by employers, and partly the result of government policies explicitly designed to create low-wage jobs, most notably mini-jobs. The low-wage employment share reached an unprecedented level in Germany in 2005 (22.7 percent of the labor force), surpassing the share of low-wage work in the United Kingdom (21.7 percent) and approaching the U.S. level (25.0 percent).

Where unions remain strong, as in Denmark, a negotiated national minimum pay package still provides an effective floor. In Denmark, the effective minimum wage is close to the U.S. median wage—low-paid Danish workers earn about as much as the typical American worker, and there is relatively little low-paid work.[28] In France, the national minimum wage is set just below the low-wage threshold and rises annually based on a formula that takes into account increases in both consumer prices and blue-collar workers' wages. The incidence of low-wage employment in France (where unemployment is high) and in Denmark (where it is quite low) has remained far below that in the United States (11.1 percent in France and 8.5 percent in Denmark). In Germany, however, the weakening of unions and the lack of a legally mandated national minimum wage have enabled many employers to evade the norms of the German employment model and increase low-wage employment. In the face of weaker unions, a legislated national minimum wage set at or near the low-wage threshold could serve as a bulwark against an increase in working poverty.

Establishing a national minimum wage may not be sufficient to reduce the low-wage share, however, if the rate is fixed too low to set a meaningful floor. The relatively high low-wage share in the Netherlands despite a national minimum wage can be attributed in part to the "long tail" of the Dutch minimum wage, which authorizes the payment of subminimum wages to workers up to the age of twenty-four and has served as a catalyst for employers to replace older workers with younger ones. In the United States, the national minimum wage was frozen in nominal terms for ten years, from 1997 to 2007. The value of the minimum wage decreased over that period both in real terms and relative to the wages of other workers. Indeed, when the minimum wage rose to $7.25 an hour in 2009, the pay rate was still well below the low-wage threshold and still left a full-time, full-year worker in a three-person family below the official U.S. poverty line.

The analysis of the effects of labor market institutions is complicated by the fact that jobs are gendered. Low pay is strongly associated with women's employment and part-time jobs. The proportion of women who are low-paid is significantly higher than the proportion of men, although in countries experiencing increases in wage inequality, the incidence of low-paid work among men is also rising. Thus, the rise in women's participation in paid employment intersects with the gendered nature of jobs and with norms and expectations about responsibility for unpaid care work in the home that differ across countries. Labor market institutions reflect these national differences in expectations about the participation of women in paid employment, especially women with children. In some countries (Germany, for example), these institutions still reflect the expectation that men will be the sole breadwinner; in others (the United Kingdom and the Netherlands), national institutions reflect the view that women are more likely than men to work part-time; while in still others (France and Denmark), the institutions reflect the view that women as well as men may need or want to work full-time. Women's expectations and behavior are changing rapidly, and labor market institutions are evolving at different speeds, creating further complications for examining the effects of these institutions on employer decisions and worker outcomes.

Among our six countries, the more inclusive the labor market institutions (collective bargaining, minimum wages, nonwage benefits, and others), the lower the share of low-wage work in the national economy (Denmark and France). Wherever inclusiveness has been eroded by the proliferation of legal and extralegal exit options—which put some types of workers (part-timers and immigrant or migrant workers, for example) outside of the established inclusive system—low-wage work has increased sharply (the Netherlands and the United Kingdom in the 1980s and early 1990s and especially Germany since the mid-1990s).

The specific institutions and policies that yield an inclusive system vary substantially across countries. Denmark's famous "flexicurity" produces inclusiveness through national-level collective bargaining that covers about 90 percent of workers and features strongly solidaristic bargaining that channels resources disproportionately to low-wage workers. Generous out-of-work benefits reinforce the high wages and benefits, without employment protection legislation or a legal minimum wage. France generates inclusive outcomes through the legal extension of collective agreements, which cover 95 percent of workers, but a relatively high minimum wage is almost as important in reducing the share of low-wage work. Overall, state regulation plays a more significant role in France than in Denmark.

Similarly, where countries have chosen to give firms exit options that allow them to sidestep otherwise inclusive systems, the specifics have reflected national circumstances. In the Netherlands, employers, unions, and the government effectively negotiated a youth minimum wage below the national adult rate (which itself has also been frozen at several times), and this allowed a large increase in low-wage, part-time jobs in the 1990s. In Germany, a decline in union strength allowed many small and medium-sized firms to ignore industrywide collective agreements and accelerated the use of minijobs, posted workers, and other nonstandard work arrangements from the mid-1990s through the present. The level and changes over time in the share of low-wage work across the six countries closely track the level and changes over time in the degree of inclusiveness.

Some general lessons can be drawn from our industry case studies. One of the advantages of fieldwork, as compared to macroeconomic empirical work based on international indicators of institutions, is the light shed on the large potential gap between *formal* and *effective* regulations.[29] The distinction is of course particularly relevant for the low-wage segment of the labor market. Even in inclusive Denmark, some laws and regulations are not always respected in some industries (particularly the hotel sector). France, which has a labor market characterized by a high level of legislated (as opposed to negotiated) regulation, offers many examples of violations of the labor law, even in public hospitals.

If taking into account only formal rules and institutions may sometimes lead to an overestimation of the effective degree of inclusiveness of an institutional system, it may in other cases lead to an underestimation. Social norms also shape firm and worker behaviors. These norms may be particularly important in deterring opportunistic behavior by employers and may limit employers' use of exit options. As such, in some circumstances, social norms may also constitute an important dimension of institutional inclusiveness at a national or industry level. In the Danish call center industry, for example, something approaching a high-road strategy emerged despite the lack of formal agreements and regulations. In this case, the employer response did not seem to flow primarily from a culture of "social consensus" (as is often argued for the Scandinavian countries), but more from fear of retaliation from unions (even though union density is relatively low in this sector) and from concerns about being stigmatized in the eyes of both workers and consumers. Explicit "name-and-shame" campaigns, such as those in the U.S. hotel and retail industries, also illustrate how low-wage workers can use social norms to defend their interests.

The increase in the share of low-wage work in three of our countries at different times in the last thirty years has to do with both changes in institutions *and* changes in the behaviors within given institutions—a consequence of eroding social norms. Germany offers a striking example. The large changes in the regulation of the German labor market are quite recent: the so-called Hartz laws (which deregulated temp agency work, decreased the generosity of unemployment benefits, and led to other changes, as discussed in chapters 3 and 4) have been adopted only since the beginning of the 2000s. During the 1990s, however, changes in employer behavior within a relatively stable institutional environment played at least as big a role as the formal reforms that followed. In some sectors, for example, a growing number of employers withdrew from collective bargaining agreements, and more and more employers who had not been formally covered by industry agreements, but had opted to participate, discontinued their earlier practice. German unions, under pressure from rising unemployment, made major concessions in some sectors, including retail, cleaning subcontractors in the hotel sector (see chapter 7), and call centers (see chapter 10), which undercut pay and other terms, especially for new entrants. Changes in formal institutions are themselves often the consequence of changes in social norms.[30] Changes in social norms may simultaneously affect labor supply, as the trend increase in female labor market participation seems to illustrate; this change in participation rates may, in turn, affect norms or the effectiveness of institutions. As mentioned earlier, differences across countries in the commitment to equality and solidarity help to explain differences in minimum-wage policies, which have played a crucial role in the evolution of the low wages in the past two decades in France, the Netherlands, the United Kingdom, and the United States. In Germany, both the change in the macroeconomic context (the big rise in unemployment following reunification) and changes in social norms in the 1990s may have fostered the changes in the institutional system in the 2000s. As Robert Solow puts it, "It is still a matter of controversy among specialists whether the traditional system was unsustainable or simply unsustained" (quoted in Bosch and Weinkopf 2008, 9).

The decline in social norms and the retrenchment of protective institutions, at both the national and industry levels, may generate a high degree of dualism in countries where the institutional system used to be quite inclusive. This tendency toward dualism appears strongest in Germany (between regular employees and mini-jobbers across many sectors, for example, or between operators in in-house and outsourced call centers), but it is also visible in the Netherlands (between part-timers and full-timers) and France (between civil servants and contract workers in public hospitals).

Our research may also shed some light on the debate about the varieties of capitalism and national "models." Peter Hall and David Soskice's (2001, 5) distinction between "coordinated" and "liberal" market economies—based on an approach "locating the firm at the center of the analysis"—is of limited usefulness to help understand our results. Liberal market economies such as the United Kingdom and the United States do display a higher share of low-wage work, but there is a wide divergence of experience among coordinated economies such as Denmark and Germany. And France, where state regulation plays a crucial role, does not fit the typology very well. Our view is closer to the "employment regimes" perspective put forward by Duncan Gallie (2007), which points to the employment and industrial relation policies that underlie national institutional structures and distinguishes between three principal models: inclusive, dualist, and market regimes.[31] This framework appears to capture fairly well the low-wage labor market regimes we observe in our six countries. Denmark is inclusive, Germany is dualist, and the United States and, to a lesser extent, the United Kingdom are market regimes. France and the Netherlands, for their part, lie somewhere in between the inclusive and the dualist regimes. Nevertheless, as Gerhard Bosch, Steffen Lehndorff, and Jill Rubery (2009) have emphasized, a clear understanding of specific national outcomes requires moving beyond typologies, which are often too functionalist and too static and tend to overestimate institutional complementarities. National institutional arrangements, in practice, often display many conflicts, contradictions, tensions, and inconsistencies that can be brushed aside to fit into a particular typology.[32]

In a dynamic perspective, our research points to the fragility of national institutional models, and therefore to the potential volatility of national economic and social performance. During most of the 1980s, Germany had faster productivity growth, a lower unemployment rate, and a more compressed income distribution than did the United States, making Germany that decade's "model" economy in Europe. After reunification, however, from about the mid-1990s on, German performance deteriorated substantially. In the 1990s, the Netherlands saw an enormous increase in female employment rates and was consistently among the OECD countries with the lowest unemployment rate. Because of the relatively big rise in the share of low-wage work in the past decades, however, the Dutch model seems to have lost some of its luster. In the 2000s, high employment rates in Denmark, associated with high wages as well as a good performance along other dimensions of job quality, have made that country the reference economy for European economic and social policymakers. Is the Danish model sustainable? Will it succumb to external shocks or internal conflicts? Will other economic models that are currently performing poorly be better suited to the conditions of the next decade?

The rest of the volume is organized as follows. Part 1 (chapters 2 through 4) provides an overview of the extent and nature (including job quality) of low-wage work at the national level and tries to connect the observed outcomes with the national institutional systems. Chapter 2 reviews the main international differences and national trends in low-wage work and includes a comparison of job security, work intensity, and hours of work in each country. Chapter 3 analyzes the national pay-setting institutions, broadly defined, which are the primary determinants of wages in each of the six economies. Chapter 4 reviews the effect of national institutions on the supply side of the low-wage labor market. These first chapters serve as a background for reading part 2 (chapters 5 through 10), which presents the five industry case studies. Chapter 5 is an overview of the main industry-level findings. Chapter 6 examines retail, chapter 7 hotels, chapter 8 hospitals, chapter 9 food processing, and chapter 10 call centers.

We are very grateful to Rosemary Batt, Francine Blau, Richard Freeman, Caroline Lloyd, Philippe Méhaut, Jill Ruberg, Robert Solow, and Chris Warhust for extensive comments and suggestions.

NOTES

1. In this chapter, and throughout this volume, we use the term "high road" to refer to firms' labor market strategies, as distinct from product market strategies. As several of the case studies illustrate, firms can choose high-road product market strategies while simultaneously pur-

suing low-road labor market strategies (low pay, low skill, low training, and low productivity).

2. The five national volumes also include overviews of national institu-
    tions and macroeconomic policy and their impact on the prevalence of
    low-wage work.

3. Low-wage work is not synonymous with less-skilled work. In all six
    countries, some relatively high-skilled workers earn low wages and
    some less-skilled workers earn wages above our low-pay threshold. In
    Germany, more than three-fourths of low-wage workers are skilled.

4. All six economies are rich by world standards, but in 2005 the range in
    gross domestic product (GDP) per capita was not small between the
    lowest-income country (Germany at $29,758 per year) and the highest-
    income country (the United States at $41,789 per year) in the sample.
    See "Table 1: OECD Estimates of Labor Productivity for 2005" (Sep-
    tember 2006) at: www.oecd.org/dataoecd/30/40/29867116.xls (ac-
    cessed March 22, 2009).

5. The cross-country research design also included stratification within
    industries within countries—for example, food processing was gener-
    ally evenly divided between meat processing and confectionery.

6. The five national European volumes are: Bosch and Weinkopf (2008)
    on Germany; Caroli and Gautié (2008) on France; Lloyd, Mason, and
    Mayhew (2008) on the United Kingdom; Salverda, van Klaveren, and
    van der Meer (2008) on the Netherlands; and Westergaard-Nielsen
    (2008) on Denmark. On the methodological choices, see the introduc-
    tion by Robert Solow to each of the national monographs.

7. As mentioned earlier, throughout this volume we define low-wage
    workers as those with a gross hourly wage that is less than two-thirds
    of the median national gross hourly wage.

8. Apprentices are included in the calculations for the Netherlands,
    France, and the United Kingdom, but not for Denmark and Germany.

9. Aggregate differences in the incidence of low-wage work between the
    United States and Germany, the Netherlands, and the United Kingdom
    are even smaller when we control for differences in industry structure.

10. Across our six countries, it is often important to distinguish between
    immigrant workers—foreign-born individuals who move permanently
    (or with the intention of staying permanently) to a new country where
    they work—and migrant workers—foreign-born workers who work
    temporarily (or with the intention to work only temporarily) in a new
    country.

11. Note that, as also discussed later in the chapter, many migrant work-
    ers coming from eastern Europe are actually highly skilled but are do-
    ing low-skilled jobs, often because of language difficulties.

12. In 2004 ten new members joined the European Union: Cyprus, the

Czech Republic, Estonia, Hungary, Latvia, Lithuania, Malta, Poland, Slovakia, and Slovenia. Bulgaria and Romania joined in 2007. In 2007 twenty-seven countries were members of the European Union.

13. In Germany during the time period covered by most of the analysis in this volume, mini-jobs were jobs of less than fifteen hours per week, with earnings below 400 euros per month. Mini-jobs were exempt from employees' social security contributions and some other forms of taxation. Posted workers are those who work for a limited period outside the European Union member country where they normally work, while still employed by their original firm. They work under the labor standards of their country of origin unless the host country extends its minimum wage or its collective agreements to posted workers. For more detail see chapter 3, table 3.10.

14. The British national minimum wage was set below the low-pay threshold as we have defined it, and it remains below that level. The stabilization in the low-wage share in the United Kingdom is also a reflection of various institutional changes that were increasing low-wage work during the period of the study but that had worked their way through the system by the mid-1990s.

15. The 1999 EU Directive on Equal Treatment for Fixed-Term Workers also stipulates that fixed-term workers cannot be treated on less favorable terms than those for equivalent permanent workers. A similar directive, the EU Directive on Temporary Agency Work, was adopted in 2008 (after the period covered by this study). As noted earlier, however, some firms have adopted strategies that allow them to sidestep the full economic force of these protections.

16. The impacts are not limited to workers in directly affected sectors. Labor markets can transmit bargaining power effects to workers with similar skills in other sectors of the economy.

17. The rise since the early 2000s in the number of migrant workers (primarily from eastern Europe) has had a larger impact than immigration on the supply side of the European labor markets studied here, particularly Germany and the United Kingdom.

18. Compared to the other five countries, the immigrant-to-native employment ratio is particularly low in Denmark.

19. The effect of benefit systems on employment outcomes also depends on the strictness of the eligibility criteria, the strictness of the administration of those criteria, and the duration of available benefits. In all of the countries analyzed here, benefit eligibility rules tend to make it relatively less likely that some groups, especially immigrants, young people, and women, will be eligible for many forms of benefits, such as unemployment insurance.

20. Since 2004, the Hartz reforms in Germany have cut the generosity of

benefits for the long-term unemployed and increased the pressure on the unemployed to accept available jobs.

21. For international comparisons of intergenerational mobility, see Blanden (2005), Corak (2004), and Jäntti and others (2005).

22. If we were to use total hourly compensation, including government-financed benefits, rather than the gross wage to calculate wage inequality, measured inequality would be higher in the United States—and lower in Europe—than what we find in this volume. In addition, the share of low-wage workers, using a total hourly compensation measure, would be higher in United States and lower in Europe than what we calculate here.

23. Work organizations where work has been fragmented and workers have been consigned to routinized, repetitive tasks. In such work systems, there is little payoff to creative thinking or problem solving by front-line workers. Close supervision (either human via supervisor or electronic via monitoring), replaces intrinsic motivation and keeps workers on task. Communication is typically top down, and communication among workers serves little useful company purpose.

24. Functional flexibility refers to firm policies that adjust to demand fluctuations by redeploying workers to new tasks or product lines within the firm. By contrast, numerical flexibility refers to firm policies that adjust to fluctuations in product demand by reducing the size of, or average hours worked by, the firm's workforce.

25. In addition to industry case studies, this volume—as well as the national monographs underlying it—also includes background chapters focused on national-level institutions. These chapters, however, do not intend to address directly the issue of a possible wage-employment trade-off.

26. This is also true for the Earned Income Tax Credit (EITC) in the United States, though the fiscal size of the EITC is much smaller than the other nonwage costs discussed here in the European context.

27. Solidaristic bargaining may also be seen as a strategy to overcome the long-standing undervaluation of women's work. The argument that the "market" pay reflects productivity while collective bargaining "distorts" market outcomes may ignore the sources of social disadvantage that lead to a much wider distribution of earnings than is justified by differences in productivity. In this view, institutions such as collective bargaining act to counter the impact of social disadvantage on pay outcomes. In Denmark, for example, where solidaristic wage bargaining is important, prime-age women are not substantially more likely to be in low-wage work than men are. Solidaristic wage-bargaining may also reduce the scope for individual

rent-seeking and may also raise productivity, as is often argued in the case of Sweden.

28. The wage figures here refer to before-tax hourly earnings. Danish low-wage workers pay higher taxes than the median worker in the United States, so the after-tax wage of low-wage Danish workers is below that of the median U.S. worker. That said, Danish low-wage workers receive a range of government services in exchange for higher taxes, most importantly, health insurance. Danish low-wage workers also have statutory rights to paid vacation and holidays, paid sick days, and paid parental leave; these benefits are often not available to the median U.S. worker—or when available, not as generous (see chapter 2).

29. Moreover, these international indicators often fail to take into account the complexity of regulations and other institutional features (see Howell et al. 2007).

30. Of course, the relative power of social actors has a significant influence over the evolution of social norms.

31. Inclusive employment regimes "are those where policies are designed to extend both employment and common employment rights as widely as possible through the population of working age"; dualist regimes "guarantee strong rights to a core workforce of skilled long-term employees at the expense of poor conditions and low security of the periphery"; and market regimes are characterized by minimal employment regulations (Gallie 2007, 17).

32. National institutional arrangements often rely on equilibriums that reflect a temporary balance of power between social actors at a particular point in time. For an analysis that places a strong emphasis on "political equilibriums" to explain both national institutional arrangements and institutional changes, see Amable and Palombarini (2009).

REFERENCES

Amable, Bruno, and Stefano Palombarini. 2009. "A Neorealist Approach to Institutional Change and the Diversity of Capitalism." *Socio-Economic Review* 7(1): 123–43.

Appelbaum, Eileen, Annette Bernhardt, and Richard J. Murnane, eds. 2003. *Low-Wage America: How Employers Are Reshaping Opportunity in the Workplace.* New York: Russell Sage Foundation.

Blanden, Jo. 2005. "Intergenerational Mobility." PhD diss., University College London.

Bosch, Gerhard, Steffen Lehndorff, Jill Rubery, eds. 2009. *European Employment Models in Flux: A Comparison of Institutional Change in Nine European Countries.* Basingstoke, U.K.: Palgrave Macmillan.

Bosch, Gerhard, and Claudia Weinkopf, eds. 2008. *Low-Wage Work in Germany.* New York: Russell Sage Foundation.

Caroli, Ève, and Jérôme Gautié, eds. 2008. *Low-Wage Work in France.* New York: Russell Sage Foundation.

Corak, Miles. 2004. *Generational Income Mobility in North America and Europe.* Cambridge: Cambridge University Press.

Gallie, Duncan, ed. 2007. *Employment Regimes and the Quality of Work.* Oxford: Oxford University Press.

Hall, Peter A., and David Soskice. 2001. *Varieties of Capitalism.* Oxford: Oxford University Press.

Howell, David, Dean Baker, Andrew Glyn, and John Schmitt. 2007. "Are Protective Labor Market Institutions at the Root of Unemployment? A Critical Review of Evidence." *Capitalism and Society* 2(1): online. Available at: http://www.bepress.com/cas/vol2/iss1/art1.

Jäntti, Markus, Bernt Bratsberg, Knut Røed, Oddbjørn Raaum, Tor Eriksson, Robin Naylor, Eva Österbacka, and Anders Björklund. 2005. "American Exceptionalism in a New Light: A Comparison of Intergenerational Earnings Mobility in the Nordic Countries, the United Kingdom, and the United States." Working paper 781. Coventry, U.K.: University of Warwick, Economics Department.

Krugman, Paul. 1994. "Europe Jobless, America Penniless?" *Foreign Policy* (summer): 19–34.

Lloyd, Caroline, Geoff Mason, and Ken Mayhew, eds. 2008. *Low-Wage Work in the United Kingdom.* New York: Russell Sage Foundation.

Mason, Geoff, and Wiemer Salverda. 2008. "RSF Benchmarking Study: Low-Wage Employment in Western Europe and the United States." Report to Russell Sage Foundation, New York.

Metcalf, David. 2007. "Why Has the British National Minimum Wage Had Little or No Impact on Employment?" Discussion paper 781. London: London School of Economics, Centre for Economic Performance (CEP) (April).

Organization for Economic Cooperation and Development (OECD). 1994. *The OECD Jobs Study: Facts, Analysis, Strategies.* Paris: OECD.

Salverda, Wiemer, Maarten van Klaveren, and Marc van der Meer, eds. 2008. *Low-Wage Work in the Netherlands.* New York: Russell Sage Foundation.

Westergaard-Nielsen, Niels, ed. 2008. *Low-Wage Work in Denmark.* New York: Russell Sage Foundation.

PART I

Low-Wage Work and National Labor Market Institutions

CHAPTER 2

Low Pay, Working Conditions, and Living Standards

Geoff Mason and Wiemer Salverda

As a prelude to discussion of the role of industrial relations and wage-setting institutions in chapter 3 and the impact of labor market institutions on labor supply in chapter 4, this chapter describes the importance and characteristics of low-wage work and the living standards and working conditions of low-wage workers in the six countries. The chapter first examines how each country compares in terms of the incidence of low pay, the evolution of low-wage shares of employment, the characteristics of low-wage jobs and workers, and the chances of low-wage workers eventually succeeding in moving to higher pay brackets. The chapter then compares the six countries in terms of three elements of employment and work conditions that are important components of job quality for low-wage workers: job security, work intensity, and hours of work. Finally, we assess what being low-paid in each country means in terms of the purchasing power of low wages and living standards, taking account of employer- and state-provided nonwage benefits such as health and pensions, and the extent of any overlap between low pay and household poverty.

LOW PAY: DEFINITION, LEVEL, AND EVOLUTION

The specific definition of low-wage work that we adopt is work for which the pay is less than two-thirds of the gross hourly median wage. Compared to the frequently used quantiles of the distribution—say, the bottom 30 percent—which generate an incidence of low pay that by definition remains the same, the definition used here offers the possibility of change over time and enables us to link low-wage work to the density of the distribution. Taking the median as a base instead of the mean wage mitigates the effect of the few extremely high wages at the upper end of the distribution and possible measurement error at the lower end.[1] The definition is further based on *hourly* wages to enable coverage of part-time workers, whose importance differs significantly across countries and has been growing over time in most countries, sometimes very considerably. The hourly approach also permits a more precise treatment of full-time workers, whose hours vary substantially across individuals and countries as well as over time, in part because of the drastic shortening of the working week in some countries.[2] Finally, it should be stressed that this section considers only gross wages for the worker. Other wage concepts—such as wages received by workers net of taxes and contributions, and gross labor compensation paid by firms, including payroll taxes and employer contributions—are discussed later in the chapter, as are nonwage benefits. This approach also offers the practical advantages of being endorsed by the Organization for Economic Cooperation and Development (OECD) and the European Union, having been adopted in many data sets, and being easier to calculate in international comparison.[3]

As shown in the first row of table 2.1, the six countries differ greatly in the incidence of low pay. However, the pattern of difference coincides only partially with traditional expectations that the United States and the United Kingdom would have much higher rates of low-wage employment than the continental European countries, and that the incidence of low pay would be lowest in the Scandinavian countries. In fact, the United States does still have the highest rate of low pay and Denmark the lowest. As a result of recent rapid growth in pay inequality in Germany, however, that country comes very close to the United States in terms of the low-wage share of employment and now slightly exceeds the rate of low pay in the United Kingdom.[4] Between these extremes, France is fairly close to the low Danish level, while the Netherlands is in the middle, following rapid growth between 1985 and 1998.

Figure 2.1 shows the evolution of low pay in each country. Strikingly, the U.S. level was already high in the 1970s and has changed little since then. By contrast, other countries, such as the United Kingdom, the Netherlands, and Germany, have moved closer to the American level. On these data, the German incidence in particular has followed a striking upward trend, increasing from 14.4 percent in 1995 to 18.7 percent for full-time workers only. Using a different data set that includes part-time workers, the low-wage share reached 22.7

Table 2.1 Rate of Low Pay Among Employees[a] and Working-Age Population, 2003 to 2005

	Denmark	France	Germany	Netherlands	United Kingdom	United States
Percentage of employees below low pay threshold, head count	8.5%	11.1%	22.7%[b]	17.6%	21.7%	25.0%
Percentage of population below low pay threshold, head count	6.2	6.4	11.8	11.2	13.6	16.3
Year	2005	2005	2005	2005	2005	2003 to 2005[c]

Source: Authors' compilation based on, for Denmark—Centre for Corporate Performance (CCP): Integrated Database for Labor Market Research; for France—L'Institut National de la Statistique et des Études Économiques (INSEE): Enquête Emploi; for Germany—Deutsches Institut für Wirtschaftsforschung (DIW): German Socio-Economic Panel; for Netherlands—Centraal Bureau voor de Statistiek (CBS), Loonstructuuronderzoek; for UK—Office of National Statistics (ONS): Annual Survey of Hours and Earnings; for United States—Bureau of Labor Statistics (BLS) Current Population Survey; Ongoing Rotation Groups.

a. Excluding apprentices in Denmark and Germany.
b. 22.0 percent if low-pay thresholds are determined seperately for East and West.
c. Data were pooled to generate a sufficient number of cases to support the estimate.

Figure 2.1 Evolution of Rate of Low-Wage Employment, 1973 to 2005

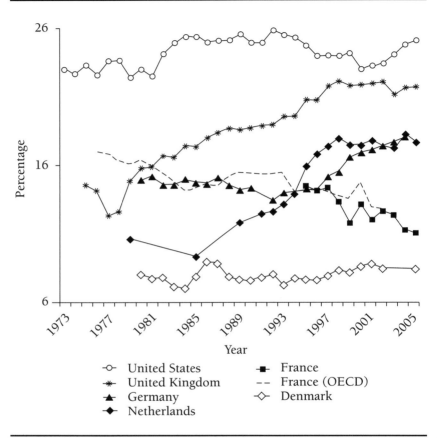

-o- United States   -■- France
-*- United Kingdom   -- France (OECD)
-▲- Germany   -◇- Denmark
-◆- Netherlands

Sources: See table 2.1 for Denmark, the Netherlands, and the United Kindgom; for France—see same table and authors, estimation from OECD, Earnings by decile limits database (courtesy OECD; for Germany)—Institut für Arbeitsmarkt- und Berufsforschung (IAB) and Bundesagentur für Arbeit (BA) (various years); for United States—authors' estimation from Mishel, Bernstein, and Allegretto (2007).
Notes: For some countries these data are not directly comparable with the estimated shares of low-paid employment in table 2.1, which cover part-time as well as full-time workers. In this chart the data for France (dotted line) are roughly estimated from OECD data on the earnings distribution of full-time workers only. For Germany the data refer only to full-time workers, excluding civil servants; the calculations were derived from the IAB regional sample (IABS-R01) and the BA employee panel by Thorsten Kalina. Similar data for the United States are not available. For the United States, the incidence was approximated by linear interpolation within the decile of the earnings distribution where the low-pay threshold is found (data from Mishel, Bernstein, and Allegretto (2007, table 3.4).

percent in 2005 (table 2.1). The Danish rate of low pay has remained consistently low, while the French level seems to have gradually fallen since the late 1990s.

Given that the low-pay thresholds are defined as a proportion of hourly median earnings, it is not surprising that many of the trends in the incidence of low pay shown in figure 2.1 are broadly reflective of trends in income dispersion in each country.[5] For example, the ratio of fifth decile (D5) to first decile (D1) earnings for full-time employees in the United States settles around the 2.0 to 2.1 level from the mid-1980s onward (figure 2.2, panel A). In the United Kingdom, the increase in the D5/D1 ratio between the early 1980s and mid-1990s mirrors the rising incidence of low pay during that period. The Dutch D5/D1 ratio rose in the early 1990s, as did the low-paid share of employment. In Germany, the rising trend in the D5/D1 ratio from 1995 onward is mirrored in the low-pay measure. In France and Denmark, the correspondences between trends in the D5/D1 ratio and the incidence of low pay are also apparent.

What stands out in particular from this and other measures of earnings dispersion shown in panel B (D9/D5 ratios) and panel C (D9/D1 ratios) is the relatively compressed wage structure in Denmark and the relatively wide dispersion of wages in the United Kingdom and—especially—in the United States. In France, Germany, and the Netherlands, earnings dispersion has converged in recent years to a position intermediate between Denmark and the United Kingdom. The rapid growth of D9 earnings relative to median earnings in the United States over much of the period since 1980 is striking and shows how stability in the incidence of low pay can easily coexist with widening dispersion of incomes as a whole.

PERSONAL AND JOB CHARACTERISTICS OF LOW-PAID EMPLOYMENT

In many respects, the groups most vulnerable to low-wage employment in each country are quite similar. Multivariate analysis indicates that the probability that an individual will be in low-paid employment is greater in all six countries for women compared to men; for youths up to age thirty compared to older persons; for the least educated compared to those with better education; for those working in service, sales, crafts, production, and elementary occupations compared to clerks (the reference occupation) and other occupations; for those working in trade or hotels and restaurants compared to manufactur-

Figure 2.2 Gross Earnings of Full-Time Employees, Decile Ratios, 1980 to 2005

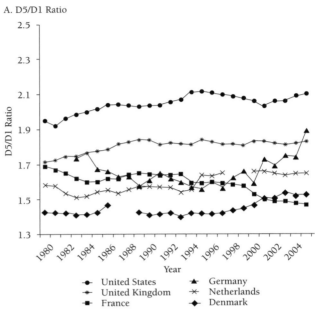

A. D5/D1 Ratio

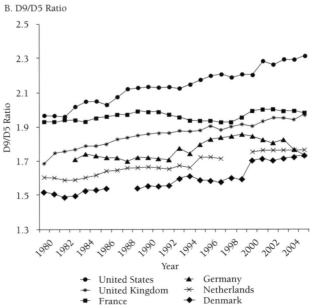

B. D9/D5 Ratio

LOW PAY, WORKING CONDITIONS, AND LIVING STANDARDS   41

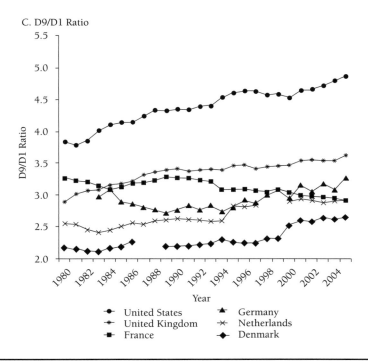

C. D9/D1 Ratio

Sources: Authors' estimates based on OECD earnings database and statistical supplements to OECD (1996, 2007a, 2009) for all countries except Denmark. Danish estimates are based on Statistics Denmark IDA (Integrated Database for Labour Market Research), courtesy of Niels Westergaard-Nielsen.

ing, utilities, and construction; and particularly for those already employed in a low-paid job in the previous year (see table 2A.1).[6]

However, there are some important intercountry differences in the quantitative importance of these effects. Women clearly suffer less relative to men in Denmark than elsewhere. At the same time, the age effect is strongest in Denmark, followed by the Netherlands and France. The educational effect is strongest in the Netherlands.[7] The occupational and industry effects are strongest in the United Kingdom. Unfortunately, occupational effects for the United States are not comparable to Europe. The impact of having been employed in a low-paid job in the previous year is strong everywhere and strongest in the Netherlands and the United Kingdom.

Other characteristics either are not universally significant in the multivariate analysis or do not work in the same direction in all countries. Temporary contracts significantly increase the probability of being low-paid in France, the Netherlands, and the United Kingdom, while part-time employment does so in the Netherlands, the United Kingdom, the United States, and Germany. Seniority of more than five years with the current employer significantly lowers the risk of being low-paid in France and Germany, but not in the United Kingdom, the Netherlands, or Denmark.

Further intercountry differences emerge in descriptive statistics derived from the European Community Household Panel (ECHP) and the U.S. Current Population Survey (CPS). For example, the incidence of low-wage employment among fifteen- to twenty-four-year-olds is highest in the Netherlands for both young men and women and lowest in the United Kingdom for young women and in the United States for young men (table 2.2). It is only in Denmark, however, that young people make up the majority of the low-paid. In terms of education levels, the incidence of low pay is highest for workers educated to the primary level in all countries, but primary-educated workers represent only a majority of low-wage workers in Denmark. In the other countries, a majority of low-wage workers are educated at least to the secondary level.

Immigrant status also increases the probability of being low-paid in most countries. Low pay tends to affect non-EU immigrants disproportionately in all the European countries except for the United Kingdom, where many immigrants are better educated than the majority of local workers. In the United States, the share of immigrants among the low-paid (19 percent) is much higher than in any of the European countries, in part because of higher employment participation among immigrants in the United States.[8]

Among adult workers the concentration of low pay—defined as the low-wage share within a category relative to the low-wage share for the economy as a whole—is highest for women in the United Kingdom and for men in the United States (table 2.2). For primary-educated workers, the concentration of low pay is highest in Denmark and the United States, while for secondary-educated workers it is highest in the United Kingdom. Although the concentration of low pay for tertiary-educated workers is relatively low in all countries, some well-educated and -skilled workers account for non-negligible proportions of the low-paid in all six countries (see Gautié, Westergaard-Nielsen, and Schmitt, this volume).[9]

Table 2.3 shows that, for the workforce as a whole, employment as a proportion of population is highest in Denmark (75 percent in 2005)

	Denmark	France	Germany	Netherlands	United Kingdom	United States
Incidence: The low-paid as a percentage of all employees in the category						
Total	12%	15%	23%	23%	22%	24%
Young women[a]	56	57	68	75	54	61
Young men[a]	68	56	71	75	44	51
Adult women[a]	7	17	26	22	26	21
Adult men[a]	3	8	10	8	8	12
Primary education[b]	38	19	48	48	33	60
Secondary education	9	—	21	27	26	25
Tertiary education	2	8	10	11	13	6
Nationals	12	15	23	22	22	22
Other EU	24	15	28	23	NA	NA
Non-EU or unknown[c]	36	23	25	33	19	33
Composition: Percentage of all employees in low-wage employment						
Total	100	100	100	100	100	100
Young women[a]	25	12	17	22	19	21
Young men[a]	37	18	18	22	15	19
Adult women[a]	24	46	43	37	51	38
Adult men[a]	13	24	22	18	15	22
Primary education[b]	56	84	37	9	46	28
Secondary education	40	—	52	75	25	64
Tertiary education	4	16	10	16	29	7
Nationals	97	96	91	99	98	82
Other EU	1	2	3	0	NA	NA
Non-EU or unknown[c]	2	2	5	1	2	18

(Table continues on p. 44.)

Table 2.2 (Continued)

	Denmark	France	Germany	Netherlands	United Kingdom	United States
Concentration: Incidence of low pay in the category as percentage of overall incidence						
Total	100	100	100	100	100	100
Young women[a]	474	369	296	331	247	258
Young men[a]	576	366	305	332	198	216
Adult women[a]	57	108	111	100	119	96
Adult men[a]	28	49	44	37	36	51
Primary education[b]	325	123[a]	204	213	151	254
Secondary education	77	—	90	118	120	105
Tertiary education	14	51	44	50	59	27
Nationals	98	100	99	100	100	94
Other EU	206	96	125	101	NA	NA
Non-EU or unknown[c]	303	148	107	146	88	141

Sources: Authors' analysis of European Community Household Panel Survey (ECHP) and Current Population Survey (U.S. BLS); see also Mason and Salverda (2008).

Notes: All employees, including apprentices and those working less than fifteen hours per week. See table 2A.2 for more detail.

a. Young men and women age fifteen to twenty-four; adult men and women age twenty-five to sixty-four.

b. Educational level was imperfectly observed for France. Similar data for 1995 indicate higher incidence of low pay among the least educated, as in other countries.

c. Non-nationals for the United Kingdom and foreign-born for the United States.

Table 2.3 Employment-Population Ratios, 2005

Employed persons in population	Denmark	France	Germany	Nether-lands	United Kingdom	United States
All persons age 15 to 64	75%	63%	66%	71%	73%	72%
Men age 15 to 24	66	33	45	62	60	55
Men age 25 to 49	88	88	84	88	88	88
Men age 50 to 64	73	58	64	66	73	74
Women age 15 to 24	58	26	40	62	57	53
Women age 25 to 49	80	74	71	76	75	72
Women age 50 to 64	61	50	49	46	57	62

Source: Authors' compilation based on OECD (2009).

and lowest in France (63 percent) and Germany (66 percent). These intercountry differences in employment rates primarily concern younger workers (age fifteen to twenty-four) and older workers (age fifty to sixty-four). For example, youth employment rates are much lower in France and Germany (even when apprentices are included) than in the other four countries, as are employment rates for older men. Among older women, employment rates in France and Germany are also well below the United States, Denmark, and the United Kingdom, but slightly above the Netherlands. In the prime-age category (age twenty-five to forty-nine), there are few differences between countries in employment rates for men, but employment rates for prime-age women range from 80 percent in Denmark to 71 percent in Germany.

Figure 2.3 relates important cross-national demographic differences in employment participation by age and gender to the incidence of low pay, distinguishing full-time, low-paid workers from part-timers. Looking first at the fifteen-to-twenty-four age group, the very low incidence of low-paid youth in France partly reflects the relatively low youth employment rate in that country. By contrast, high youth employment rates in Denmark and the Netherlands are strongly associated with low pay, and particularly so for part-time jobs in the Netherlands, where low-paid, part-time work accounts for roughly half of all youth employment. Students (including apprentices[10]) seem to be playing the most important role in Denmark, the Netherlands, and Germany, especially for part-time jobs of fifteen hours per week or less (table 2A.3). Clearly, the overlap between ed-

Figure 2.3 Employment Rates by Level of Pay and
           Working Hours, 2001

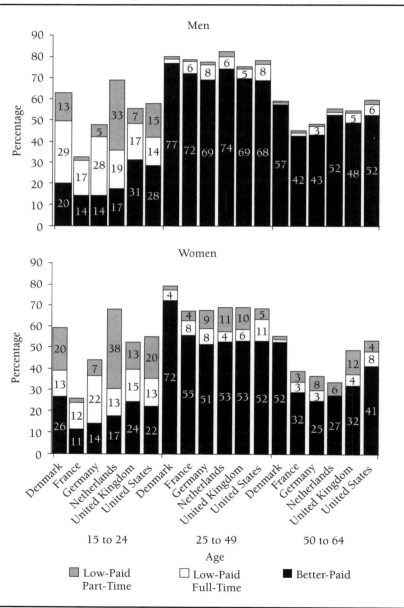

Sources: Authors' calculations from European Community Household Panel (ECHP) and CPS-ORG (U.S. BLS).

ucation and paid work is much less in France than in the other five countries. The relatively high proportions of low-paid full-time jobs among young men in Denmark and Germany partly reflect the prevalence of apprenticeship training in those two countries.

For men age twenty-five to forty-nine, there are few differences in the proportions in low-paid part-time jobs between five of the six countries. Denmark is the exception for its low share of low-paid employment in both part-time and full-time jobs. Denmark stands out even more clearly for its relatively low incidence of low pay among women age twenty-five to forty-nine. By contrast, there are relatively high proportions of low-paid, part-time jobs among women age twenty-five to forty-nine in the Netherlands, the United Kingdom, and Germany and among full-time women in this age bracket in the United States.[11] Turning to workers age fifty to sixty-four, the incidence of low pay is lower than among workers age twenty-five to forty-nine in all countries except for the United Kingdom, where older women are at comparatively high risk of low pay.

SECTORAL DISTRIBUTION OF LOW PAY

As noted earlier, persons working in the trade and hotel and restaurant industries run the highest risk of low pay in all countries, and to these can be added the agriculture and personal services industries (table 2A.4).[12] These industries also have the lowest levels of average pay within each of the national economies.[13] In all countries, hotels and restaurants lead the pack in terms of the concentration of low pay, but always with the proviso that the overall incidence of low pay is lower in Denmark and France than in the other four countries. In most of these low-paying sectors, the concentration ratio in the United States is similar to that in the EU countries—the exception being agriculture, which has a much higher concentration of low pay in the United States.

A shift-share decomposition of the gaps in low-pay incidence between each of the five European countries and the United States enables us to isolate the effect of intercountry differences in sectoral structure (table 2A.5). Some interesting conclusions can be drawn. In general, the overall lower incidence of low pay in Denmark and France compared to the United States is attributable primarily to differences in low-pay incidence across the board, while the differences in sectoral structure account for relatively little. By contrast, for Germany, the Netherlands, and the United Kingdom, the somewhat lower overall incidence of low pay compared to the United States is largely explained by lower shares of employment in low-paying industries in the three European countries than are found in the United States.

CHANCES OF ESCAPING FROM LOW PAY

Over time, low-wage workers can follow three possible employment and earnings paths. First, they can get stuck and remain low-paid for prolonged periods, even the rest of their working lives; second, they can move from low-paid employment to unemployment or inactivity, then perhaps return to low-wage work (the infamous "low-pay-no-pay" cycle); or third, they can succeed in using the low-wage job as a stepping-stone to better-paid employment. If all low-wage workers spent only limited periods of their working lives in low-wage work, low pay would not be a significant social problem. This is not the case, however, and indeed, a substantial number of workers follow all three paths. Therefore, it is important to examine the quantitative importance of the different paths of mobility and analyze how the characteristics of workers and their jobs systematically affect which kinds of workers end up where. Unfortunately, such an analysis encounters severe problems of (longitudinal) data availability and scientific method; an extensive literature has grown to deal with these. It is beyond the scope of the present chapter to discuss this literature in detail (see, for example, Lucifora and Salverda 2009). Suffice it to say that, although the study of earnings mobility has made considerable progress in recent years, it still focuses primarily on the national level, and international comparisons of the earnings mobility of low-paid workers are almost nonexistent. Here we aim to fill that gap for the six countries using comparative data and state-of-the-art methodology.[14]

The national monographs analyzed earnings mobility in different ways. The main results showed relatively high mobility rates out of low pay for Denmark, where many low-paid workers are young, and for France, especially among those with intermediate or higher educational qualifications. In Germany, the Netherlands, the United Kingdom, and the United States, mobility seems more limited, with a greater risk of cycling between low pay and no pay.

For the present comparison, we adopted a uniform approach that builds on analysis of the risks of being low-paid, taking into account the whole range of problems that usually trouble the analysis of mobility: selection bias, initial conditions, panel attrition (which plausibly has a greater nonrandom effect on the low-paid), and genuine state dependence. The approach here is well suited to analyzing the effects of a low-pay-no-pay cycle.

Table 2.4 presents the results based on data from the European Community Household Panel (ECHP) for the European countries and the Panel Study of Income Dynamics (PSID) for the United States, covering the period from the mid-1990s through 2001.[15] The results largely support those reported in the European monographs working from national data sources, but they enable us to make a more precise comparison. The results for the United States are a new contribution. U.S. outcomes largely fall within the range of European results. Clearly, there is less risk of remaining low-paid in Denmark and France (below 0.5) than in the other European countries (around 0.6); the risk in the United States lies between. In Denmark and France, low-wage workers have both a higher chance of moving to better pay and a higher risk of shifting out of waged employment—particularly in Denmark (0.229). The highest chances of moving up and out of low-wage work are in the United States, though the U.S. data are not strictly comparable since they refer to a two-year transition period and include transitions to self-employment (which are treated as non-employment in the ECHP data). Low-wage workers in the United States also have the greatest chances of falling back into low pay from better pay. At the same time, the United States has the lowest outflow from low pay into non-employment, which seems plausible (with the above caveats about differences between the U.S. and European data). The chances of remaining in non-employment are rather similar across all European countries, at about 0.8, and only slightly less for the United States.

The table also specifies the transition probabilities separately for women. In all countries, women are worse off compared to men, having higher chances than average of remaining in an unfavorable situation or falling back into low pay and lower chances of moving into a more favorable position. Only women's chance of moving from non-employment to a low-wage job is smaller. Gender differences for remaining in low-wage employment are small, though less so in the United States than in Europe, but gender differences seem larger for the probability of leaving low pay to enter non-employment (except in the United States) or to move up the earnings ladder.

Table 2.4 Predicted Year-on-Year Transition Rates Between
Low-Wage and Better-Wage Employment and
Non-Employment, 1995 to 2001

	Transition			
	Low Pay to Low Pay	Better Pay to Low Pay	Low Pay to Better Pay	Not Employed to Low Pay
Denmark				
Total	0.487	0.030	0.294	0.080
Females	0.502	0.035	0.265	0.081
Part-timers	0.484	0.081	0.227	
France				
Total	0.492	0.048	0.344	0.068
Females	0.505	0.055	0.289	0.060
Part-timers	0.492	0.054	0.227	
Germany				
Total	0.601	0.035	0.256	0.102
Females	0.615	0.048	0.220	0.099
Part-timers	0.592	0.051	0.227	
Netherlands				
Total	0.618	0.042	0.250	0.137
Females	0.623	0.060	0.215	0.120
Part-timers	0.638	0.071	0.200	
United Kingdom				
Total	0.580	0.061	0.276	0.112
Females	0.605	0.083	0.231	0.117
Part-timers	0.626	0.122	0.196	
United States				
Total	0.532	0.081	0.411	0.113
Females	0.568	0.100	0.354	0.120
Part-timers	0.556	0.098	0.360	

Sources: Authors' analyses of ECHP, as reported in Blázquez Cuesta and Salverda (2009), and authors' estimations on Panel Study of Income Dynamics (PSID) (Institute for Social Research).
Notes: Data are pooled over the period; "all employees" includes those working less than fifteen hours per week, except for France (where such employees represented 0.4 percent of all employees in 2001); "not employed" comprises self-employment, unemployment, and inactivity.

Transition			
Not Employed to Better Pay	Not Employed to Not Employed	Low Pay to Not Employed	Better Pay to Not Employed
0.214	0.800	0.229	0.083
0.203	0.788	0.248	0.099
		0.295	0.115
0.109	0.872	0.171	0.082
0.092	0.887	0.213	0.101
		0.227	0.102
0.122	0.842	0.145	0.070
0.106	0.851	0.168	0.086
		0.185	0.094
0.129	0.829	0.136	0.055
0.113	0.841	0.166	0.070
		0.164	0.077
0.166	0.791	0.148	0.069
0.137	0.800	0.169	0.083
		0.180	0.094
0.201	0.738	0.079	0.050
0.192	0.754	0.082	0.066
		0.079	0.054

The table also summarizes the prospects of mobility for part-time workers. At first glance, part-time workers seem less prone to remaining in low pay. However, they also have a substantially higher risk of moving from low pay into non-employment (except in the United States) and a lower chance of moving on to higher earnings. Part-timers also generally run a greater risk of falling back from better pay into low pay (particularly in the United Kingdom and the United States) or leaving better pay for non-employment (notably in Denmark). Compared to women, part-timers are often, but certainly not always, slightly worse off.

JOB QUALITY: TERMS OF EMPLOYMENT AND CONDITIONS OF WORK

JOB SECURITY

OECD measures of labor market regulation suggest that employment protection is considerably weaker in the United States, the United Kingdom, and Denmark than it is in France, Germany, and the Netherlands.[16] In the case of the United Kingdom and Denmark, this is reflected in lower average job tenure figures than are found in France, Germany, or the Netherlands (table 2A.9, columns 1 and 2). Equivalent data for the United States are not readily available, but it would be surprising if they were not closer to Denmark and the United Kingdom than the other three countries. Note, however, that British and American workers do not enjoy the degree of "protected mobility" found in Denmark, where low employment protection is supported by a generous income replacement system that subsidizes temporary layoffs by employers and offers training to the unemployed.

That said, if we look at another indicator of job security, such as possession of permanent rather than temporary employment contracts, then relatively low employment protection in the United Kingdom and the United States is associated with comparatively low levels of temporary employment in those two countries (table 2A.9, columns 3 to 5). This is in line with OECD analysis, which suggests that employers have fewer incentives to offer fixed-term contracts in countries such as the United Kingdom and the United States where employment protection for workers on permanent contracts is relatively weak (OECD 2004). By contrast, in the four continental European countries, high levels of employment protection are associated with relatively high shares of temporary employees among the workforce.

It is important to note, however, that the extent to which temporary status is associated with low pay, status and protection differs between countries, depending on institutions such as regulations and collective labor agreements. For example, Klaus Grunert, Susan

James, and Philip Moss (this volume) report that, in their samples of food-processing firms, temporary employment was used as a means of enhancing numerical flexibility in all six countries and was increasing everywhere except Denmark. In general, terms and conditions for temporary workers compared less favorably to those for permanent workers in the United Kingdom, Germany, and the United States than they did for permanent workers in Denmark and France, with the Netherlands somewhere in between these two groups of countries.

WORK INTENSITY

Low-paid workers are particularly vulnerable to deteriorating working conditions as many jobs have become more stressful and demanding in recent decades in both Europe (Green 2005) and the United States (Landsbergis 2003). In an analysis based on British data, Francis Green (2004) found that higher work intensity was associated, among other things, with technological changes and new forms of work organization requiring increases in task flexibility, with a decline in union power, and with increased use of temporary agency workers and contractors.

Using data from the European Working Conditions Survey (EWCS), Francis Green and Steven McIntosh (2001) developed a measure of "work effort" that comprises the average scores on questions relating to pressure to work at high speeds and to meet tight deadlines. By this measure, they found that Britain experienced a faster rise in work effort during the early 1990s than other EU countries. In their ranking, France and the Netherlands were not far below Britain in terms of the change in the levels of average effort during this period, whereas the increases in average work effort in Denmark and West Germany were much smaller.[17]

Pierre Boisard and his colleagues (2003) suggest that changes in employees' pace of work are governed by two groups of constraints: "industrial constraints" relating to the speed of production and quality standards, and "market constraints" deriving from increased pressure to adapt to customer demands. Their analysis of data from the 2000 EWCS suggests that the mix of such constraints encountered by workers varies markedly between occupational groups and sectors. Among the low-wage sectors covered in this book, food-processing employees were more likely to report industrial constraints, while hotel, retail, and health workers were more likely to report market or "demand" constraints, such as frequent interruptions of work in progress in order to embark on other unforeseen tasks.

Analysis of the most recent EWCS in 2005, combining data for Denmark, France, Germany, the Netherlands, and the United Kingdom, shows that workers in relatively low-paid occupations, such as service and sales workers and elementary occupations (such as cleaners and laborers), are the most likely to report having to work in tiring or painful positions for long periods of time and to have to stand or walk or engage in repetitive hand or arm movements while carrying out their jobs (table 2.5, rows 5 and 6). Sales and elementary workers in these five European countries, however, are no more likely than professional and technician-level employees to report that their health is jeopardized by their work because employees in white-collar occupations report relatively high levels of stress due to the pace of work and time pressures on the job (rows 7 and 8).

Unfortunately, available data on working conditions do not lend themselves to cross-country comparisons of work intensity levels for specific occupations, either within Europe or between European countries and the United States.[18] The available evidence suggests, however, that work intensity in the United States is at least as great as that found in Europe. Across the U.S. workforce as a whole, data from the General Social Survey (GSS) found that, over the period 1989 to 2002, some 30 to 40 percent of respondents reported that their work was "often" or "frequently" stressful.[19] As in Europe, physical strain and injury is more likely to be experienced by low-paid workers in the United States. Paul Landsbergis (2003) cites evidence that health impacts of job strain such as cardiovascular disease and high blood pressure are greater for blue-collar men than for men in better-paid occupations. In addition, some industries pose greater health risks than others for low-paid workers. For example, in the hotel industry, Niklas Krauser, Teresa Scherzer, and Reiner Rugulies (2005) found that occupational injury rates among workers were above average in relation to other service industries. Most room cleaners experienced severe back or neck pain that was strongly associated with physical workload, work intensification, and ergonomic problems. These findings are echoed in chapter 7 of this volume, where Achim Vanselow and his colleagues report evidence of physical injuries suffered by hotel workers on both sides of the At-

Table 2.5 Indicators of Work Intensity, Analyzed by Occupational Group, Denmark, France, Germany, the Netherlands, and the United Kingdom, 2005

	Profes-sionals	Technicians and Associate Professionals	Clerks	Service and Sales Workers	Craft and Related Trades Workers	Plant and Machine Operators and Assemblers	Elementary Occupations
Percentage of employees (weighted)[a] who . . .							
Work at very high speed for half of the time or more	41%	45%	47%	46%	60%	55%	47%
Rarely or almost never have enough time to get the job done	21	16	12	13	12	10	8
Work in tiring or painful positions for half of the time or more	13	19	16	22	44	27	36
Carry or move heavy loads for half of the time or more	5	8	8	19	41	25	31
Stand or walk for half of the time or more	42	47	26	72	84	57	82
Engage in repetitive hand or arm movements for half of the time or more	38	37	51	48	66	61	65
Consider their health or safety to be at risk because of work (percentage yes)	18	16	13	21	34	36	23
Believe their work affects their health (percentage yes)	26	26	21	25	38	39	26

(Table continues on p. 56.)

Table 2.5 *(Continued)*

	Profes-sionals	Technicians and Associate Professionals	Clerks	Service and Sales Workers	Craft and Related Trades Workers	Plant and Machine Operators and Assemblers	Elementary Occupations
How are working time arrangements set?							
They are set by the company with no possibility of changes	35	45	50	55	62	72	59
Workers can choose between several fixed working schedules	10	10	13	13	8	7	12
Workers can adapt their working hours within certain limits	36	32	28	18	12	14	19
Working hours are entirely determined by workers	20	13	9	14	18	7	10
Number of observations	686	972	733	821	615	217	630

Source: Authors' compilation based on Fourth European Working Conditions Survey, 2005 (European Foundation for the Improvement of Living and Working Conditions 2005).
a. Estimates are based on weighted data taking account of nonresponse rates in light of European Labor Force Survey data; weights also incorporate selection probability weighting that adjusts for the size of households.

lantic. In part, such injuries reflect work intensification as room attendants in all six countries have typically been required in recent years to step up the number of rooms they clean per shift.

Another source of high work intensity for low-paid workers is pressure to work unsocial hours such as evenings, nights, weekends, and public holidays. EWCS data for the five European countries under consideration show that workers in low-paid occupations are less likely than better-paid workers to be able to influence their own work schedules (table 2.5, rows 9 to 12). This is particularly important in the retail industry, where employers demand a high level of flexibility on hours of work from sales workers. In their comparison of retail firms in the United States and European countries, Françoise Carré and her colleagues (this volume) found that U.S. workers typically had less control over their work schedules, and less advance notice about their schedules, than did European workers, in large part because of the absence of collective labor agreements and other institutions found in Europe. However, the ability of European retail workers to influence their own work schedules is tending to diminish over time.

WORKING TIME

Long hours of work are another cause of physical strain and injury as well as mental strain and fatigue (Landsbergis 2003). In 2004 average annual hours worked per person engaged in work (both employees and the self-employed) in the United States were about 9 percent higher than in the United Kingdom and some 25 to 34 percent higher than in Denmark, France, the Netherlands, or Germany (table 2A.8, column 3). These differences have widened since the mid-1970s as France, Germany, Denmark, and the Netherlands have all shown a marked decline in average working hours relative to the United Kingdom and the United States (partly reflecting strong union pressure in the continental countries). Differences in average working time are associated with different rates of part-time employment (especially for women) and with working long hours to different degrees, as well as with differences in standard daily working time in each country. A measure of "usual weekly hours of work most frequently reported" for male employees in 2002 shows these figures to be lowest in France and Denmark out of the six countries (table 2A.8, columns 4 to 7).

One institutional reason why workers are less likely to work long hours in the continental European countries is the European Union's 1993 Working Time Directive, which limited working time to a maximum of forty-eight hours per week over a seventeen-week reference period. The United Kingdom is distinctive for having secured an opt-out from this legislation that allows British workers to agree not to be subject to the forty-eight-hour limit. Catherine Barnard, Simon Deakin, and Richard Hobbs (2004) report substantial use of the opt-out in sectors such as health care, hotels and restaurants, and manufacturing, and a 2001 survey found that an estimated 13 percent of all U.K. employees "usually" worked more than forty-eight hours per week (BMRB 2001). Food processing (Grunert, James, and Moss, this volume) offers a striking illustration: in some firms in the British sample, some workers were on the job seventy to eighty hours per week. Working long hours to this degree in the United Kingdom is not dissimilar from the United States, where some 9 percent of male employees reported usually working fifty to fifty-four hours per week in 2002 (table 2A.8, columns 7 and 8).

Another job quality indicator of interest concerns "involuntary part-time work," defined as: (1) individuals who usually work full-time but are working part-time because of economic slack; (2) individuals who usually work part-time but are working fewer hours in their part-time jobs because of economic slack; and (3) individuals working part-time because full-time work could not be found. There seems to be a marked contrast in this job quality indicator between, on the one hand, the United Kingdom and the Netherlands, where involuntary part-time employment rates are relatively low in spite of high part-time rates as a whole, and, on the other hand, the United States and Germany, Denmark, and especially France, where involuntary part-time employment is relatively high (table 2A.9, columns 6 to 8).

LOW PAY AND LIVING STANDARDS

What does being low-paid mean in terms of living standards in these different countries? In this section, we first consider a common measure of average living standards across the population as a whole and then present estimates of the purchasing power of wages at the low-pay thresholds in each country in terms of both gross pay and net (take-home) pay. In the next section, we go on to consider intercountry differences in nonwage benefits financed by the state or employers that also contribute to the living standards of low-wage workers (for example, health care and pension benefits).

Recent OECD estimates based on purchasing power parity (PPP) exchange rates indicate that average gross domestic product (GDP) per head of population in the United States is 20 to 40 percent higher than in the five European countries (table 2.6, row 4). Compared to Denmark, Germany, and the United Kingdom, the U.S. advantage in GDP per capita derives from both higher average labor productivity per hour worked (row 1) and higher average annual hours worked per person in employment (row 3). In two European countries (the Netherlands and France), however, productivity is much the same as in the United States, and the U.S. lead in GDP per capita over these two countries derives solely from longer hours worked relative to both countries, as well as a higher ratio of employment to total population compared to France (rows 2 and 3).

To compare the purchasing power of take-home hourly pay at low-pay threshold levels in each country, we convert the thresholds to a common currency and make rough adjustments for taxes and employees' social contributions to derive estimates of net hourly wages in each case (row 6). The results show that, in spite of the U.S. lead in average living standards for the population as a whole, the estimated purchasing power of take-home hourly pay at low-pay threshold levels in the Netherlands, Denmark, and the United Kingdom is, respectively, only 4 percent, 6 percent, and 7 percent lower than in the United States. In other words, the estimated purchasing power of net hourly wages at the ninth percentile of the wage distribution in Denmark, where the low-pay threshold is situated, is only 6 percent lower than that of net hourly wages at the twenty-fifth percentile of the American wage distribution, which corresponds with the U.S. low-pay threshold.

This narrowing of intercountry differentials in purchasing power at low wage levels—as compared to the differences in average living standards measured by GDP per capita—reflects the higher degree of compression in income distributions in the European countries relative to the United States (figure 2.2). It is only in France and Germany that the purchasing power of net wages at the low-pay threshold is appreciably lower than in the United States—partly owing to relatively high employee social contributions in both countries and the impact of reunification on Germany.[20]

Table 2.6 Measures of Labor Productivity, Living Standards, and Average Labor Costs

	Denmark	France	Germany	Netherlands	United Kingdom	United States
Productivity and living standards: PPP exchange rates: whole economy and population, 2006						
GDP per hour worked (U.S. = 100)	85	99	93	102	82	100
Employment/population ratio— all ages (U.S. = 100)[a]	108	83	99	106	99	100
Average annual hours worked per person in employment (U.S. = 100)	87	87	80	77	92	100
GDP per head of population (U.S. = 100)	80	71	73	83	75	100
Purchasing power at low pay thresholds: PPP exchange rates						
Year	2005	2005	2004	2005	2005	2003 to 2005
Low-pay threshold in U.S. dollars at PPP exchange rates (U.S. = 100)— gross hourly wages[b]	125	83	105/77[c]	112	94	100
Low-pay threshold in U.S. dollars at PPP exchange rates (U.S. = 100)— estimated hourly wages net of taxes and employee social contributions[d]	94	78	83/60[c]	96	93	100

Average labor costs at low-pay thresholds:
current exchange rates

Estimated labor costs at low-pay threshold in U.S. dollars at current exchange rates (U.S. = 100)—gross hourly wages[e]	190	97	119/86[c]	127	113	100
Estimated labor costs at low-pay threshold in U.S. dollars at current exchange rates (U.S. = 100)—gross hourly wages plus payroll taxes and employers' social contributions[f]	177	127	133/96[c]	137	114	100

Sources: Authors' compilation based on OECD, "Breakdown of GDP per Capita in Its Components," available at: http://stats.oecd.org/WBOS/Default.aspx?DatasetCode=DECOMP; and national labor force surveys in European countries (as reported in the national monographs) and Current Population Survey (U.S. BLS) in the United States. Exchange rates: OECD, "PPPs and Exchange Rates," available at: http://stats.oecd.org/wbos/Index.aspx?datasetcode=SNA_TABLE4.

a. Note that this refers to employment-population ratios for the entire population, not just the fifteen- to sixty-four-year-old population of working age.

b. PPP exchange rates for private consumption, domestic currencies (U.S. dollar = 1.00): Denmark kroner 9.09, France euro 0.94, Germany euro 0.91, Netherlands euro 0.91, U.K. pound 0.66.

c. Refers to West and East Germany, respectively.

d. Based on average tax rates at 67 percent of average wage for full-time workers, including employee social contributions in 2000 (Immervoll 2007; see also table 2A.6).

e. Market exchange rates, domestic currencies (U.S. dollar = 1.00): Denmark 6.00, France 0.80, Germany 0.81, the Netherlands 0.80, the United Kingdom 0.55.

f. Based on average payroll tax rates and employer contributions for full-time employees earning 67 percent of average wage, 2000 (Immervoll 2007; see also table 2A.6).

Conversely, when we compare low-pay threshold pay rates in terms of labor costs to employers, taking account of intercountry differences in payroll taxes and employer social contributions, then labor-cost levels in all the European countries (and especially in Denmark, where taxes are relatively high all the way down to the lower reaches of the income distribution) are well above that in the United States (table 2.6, row 8). One implication of this comparison is that employers in the European countries may be under greater pressure than employers in the United States to economize on the use of low-wage workers and to find ways of raising their productivity (for example, through up-skilling and more capital-intensive forms of work organization).

NONWAGE BENEFITS AND ENTITLEMENTS

Though wage earnings are at the core of the employment relationship and define low pay, there are other important conditions that contribute to job quality and living standards for the low-paid as for any other worker. These conditions can be offered by individual firms to their workers on the basis of rules and regulations or by society at large.[21] When we turn to consider the many such working and living conditions associated with low-wage employment in these economies the important differences between Europe and the United States emerge. Low-wage workers in Europe, be they many or few, seem to be relatively better treated than their U.S. counterparts. To assess these contrasts, we take into account both nonwage benefits and entitlements that are directly provided by employers and those that are funded primarily by general taxation or, in some countries, by employers' and employees' contributions.

Over recent decades, European Union directives on matters relating to work conditions have ensured that on a number of key dimensions, such as annual leave, sickness leave, and the entitlements of part-time and temporary workers, the five European countries have a lot more in common with each other than they do with the United States. In addition, some elements of what can be called the "social wage," such as affordable health care, are generally more available to European than to U.S. workers. With respect to other work conditions, however, such as working time and job security, there are differences between European countries, in enforcement as well as in the letter of regulations, and some of the European countries resemble the United States in some ways. The same is true of other elements of the social wage, such as private pension entitlements, which tend to be less available to low-wage workers than to higher-wage workers in some European countries, as is also the case in the United States.

ANNUAL LEAVE

Partly as a result of statutory minimum annual leave entitlements set out in European working time regulations, workers in all five European countries (including low-paid workers) enjoy substantially longer average periods of annual leave than do their U.S. counterparts (table 2A.7). The United States is distinctive in having no statutory minimum annual leave entitlement at all. In fact, many U.S. employers do offer paid vacations and public holidays to some employees, but low-wage workers and those working part-time or in small establishments tend to receive comparatively small amounts of paid leave or none at all (Ray and Schmitt 2007). Overall, about 23 percent of all private-sector workers in the United States do not receive any paid vacation or paid public holidays.

SICKNESS LEAVE

There are also clear U.S.-European differences in the availability of paid leave for sickness. This is an important consideration for workers in low-paid occupations, which have an above-average risk of on-the-job health hazards, such as having to use repetitive arm or hand movements, working in tiring or painful positions, or being required to carry or move heavy loads (EFILWC 2005; Krauser, Scherzer, and Rugulies 2005).

In all five European countries, employees are guaranteed cash sickness benefits for short- or long-term illness, with benefit duration of at least six months.[22] In France and Germany, provision is organized through social insurance funds to which both employers and employees contribute. In Denmark and the United Kingdom, sickness leave is based on a combination of statutory requirements of employers and tax-funded benefits (SSA 2007). (Where individuals do not qualify for mandatory sickness pay owing to a limited prior employment history or similar reasons, they are typically eligible for state-funded benefits.) In the Netherlands, firms are obliged to meet statutory requirements for which they can take out private insurance.

These minimum levels of provision are then enhanced in each European country in varying degrees through employer-specific, sick-pay schemes, which may be based on collective labor agreements.

Even though these European employer-specific schemes tend to provide less generous sick-pay arrangements for less-skilled workers, whose bargaining power is limited, the minimum levels of guaranteed sick-pay provision ensure that low-paid European workers are better off than the great majority of their counterparts in the United States. Vicky Lovell's (2004) analysis of employee benefits surveys from 1996 to 1998 shows that 48 percent of all U.S. workers (39 percent of full-timers and 84 percent of part-timers) had no paid sick-leave entitlement at all. This proportion increased to 77 percent for those in the bottom wage quartile.

In a study of nine European countries and Canada, Marco Ercolani, Tim Barmby, and John Treble (2002) found that there was no clear link between rates of sickness absence and the generosity of statutory sickness benefits across countries. In most of these countries, the highest rates of sickness absence were found, as expected, among less-skilled occupations with the highest exposure to health hazards. Although women tended to have higher rates of sickness absence than men, these gender differences were largely explained by differences in age distribution together with marital status. It seems likely that the higher absence rates for married women reflected their greater domestic responsibilities outside the workplace, an indication of the importance of paid sickness leave provision for workers in female-dominated, low-paid occupations.

ENTITLEMENTS OF PART-TIME AND TEMPORARY WORKERS

All five European countries have implemented European Union directives designed to ensure that pay and conditions for part-time employees are not less favorable than for comparable full-time employees (see Bosch, Mayhew, and Gautié, this volume). Thus, for example, employers are typically required to treat part-time employees in the same way as comparable full-timers with respect to:

- Hourly rates of pay
- Access to company pension schemes

- Entitlements to annual leave and maternity or parental leave on a pro rata basis

- Entitlement to contractual sick pay

- Access to training

These legal requirements have no parallel in the United States. The incidence of part-time working is relatively low in the United States, however, compared to the five European countries. A similar disparity exists in the case of temporary workers (those on fixed-term contracts), who, in Europe, are covered by a European Union directive designed to ensure parity with permanent workers employed by the same firm. Again, there is no parallel for this requirement in the United States, but the United States also has a relatively small proportion of temporary employees—in common with other countries where protection for permanent workers is itself relatively weak (OECD 2004; Bosch, Mayhew, and Gautié, this volume).

PENSION ENTITLEMENTS

Pension entitlements are generally regarded as part of the "social wage." In all six countries, they derive in part from occupational (employer-based) or personal (individual-based) pension schemes as well as from public-sector schemes. In each country, mandatory pensions comprise both "first-tier" universal benefits and "second-tier" benefits derived from social insurance schemes of different kinds (table 2A.10, columns 1 and 2). Estimates of formal gross replacement rates from these mandatory pensions (that is, gross pension entitlements as a proportion of gross preretirement earnings) show that the average drop in income postretirement for those relying on mandatory pensions is much lower in Denmark and the Netherlands than in the other four countries (table 2A.10, column 3).[23]

In France, Germany, the United Kingdom, and the United States, all mandatory second-tier pensions are public sector–based. By contrast, Denmark's second-tier provision is based on private but mandatory personal pensions and quasi-mandatory occupational pensions, while Dutch second-tier provision is based on quasi-mandatory occupational schemes that can be provided collectively or privately. The upshot is that 90 percent or more of the Danish and Dutch workforces are covered by such pensions, whereas in the other four countries all private pension schemes are voluntary and cover only 18 percent of the workforce in France, 51 percent in the United Kingdom, 56 percent in the United States, and 63 percent in Germany. In general, the workers who are excluded from private occupational schemes or who do not participate in private personal schemes in these four countries are likely to be lower-wage employees (OECD 2006b). Hence, low-wage workers in these countries tend to be dependent on mandatory pension schemes and suffer sharp drops in income postretirement. For workers earning 50 percent of average earnings in each country, these drops in income are only slightly cushioned by the workings of tax and benefits systems in France, Germany, the United Kingdom, and the United States (table 2A.11, column 4).

HEALTH CARE

Another key element of the social wage affecting comparisons of the living standards of low-wage workers in each country is access to public services such as health care. In France and Germany, the bulk of public health funding comes from taxes and compulsory social health insurance contributions from employers and employees. Users make only modest contributions to the costs of services, and there are some exemptions for low-income persons (NAO 2003). In the United Kingdom, the National Health Service (NHS) is largely funded out of general taxation and is free at the point of delivery (NAO 2003). In Denmark, health services are financed partly through local taxation and partly through block grants from the central government. The great majority of health services are free of charge for users.[24] In the Netherlands, a mandatory private health insurance system is funded by direct contributions, which are capped, income-related individual contributions to the tax authorities up to a certain income threshold, and by employers' contributions, which are taxed as income for employees. Private insurers are obliged to accept every resident in the areas in which they operate for a statutory package of provisions.[25]

By contrast, U.S. health care is primarily funded on a "voluntary" (that is, market-driven) basis by private sources, with the government providing essentially universal coverage to the elderly (through Medicare) and some provision for the poor (through Medicaid). One outcome is that private health insurance coverage is positively associated with income in the United States. For example, in 2004 only 24 percent of workers in the lower wage quintile were covered by private-sector, employer-funded health insurance, compared to 46 percent in the second wage quintile and 62 to 78 percent in the third to fifth wage quintiles (Mishel, Bernstein, and Allegretto 2007, table 3.12).[26] Thus, we conclude that low-wage workers in the United States are much less likely than their European counterparts to be able to gain access to affordable health care.

LOW PAY AND HOUSEHOLD POVERTY

The relative absence of welfare state provision in the United States also contributes to a greater overlap between low pay and household poverty than is found in Europe—which may be considered another important indicator of comparative living standards at low pay levels (for a fuller treatment, see Nolan and Marx 2009). Recent OECD (2006b) analysis applies the same definition of relative poverty internationally (50 percent of equivalized household income) to compare the incidence of "working poor" across countries. The results suggest that the proportion of the population in poor households containing at least one worker was 13 percent in the United States in 2001, about five percentage points higher than in the Netherlands and eight to ten percentage points above Denmark, France, Germany, and the United Kingdom (table 2.7, columns 1 to 3). If we look at the proportion of the population in poor households of all kinds, then the United States is also highest, at 17 percent, compared to 5 to 11 percent in the European countries (columns 4 and 5). In general, household poverty in Europe is more likely to involve jobless households than it is in the United States.[27]

SUMMARY AND ASSESSMENT

The most important comparative findings can be summarized as follows: First, the incidence of low pay in Germany is found to be surprisingly close to British and American levels, and major differences seem to occur within continental Europe—much more than between Europe and the United States and the United Kingdom. Second, this appears to be based on a differential evolution of the incidence of low pay: it has grown significantly in the United Kingdom, the Netherlands, and Germany during different periods of time over the last twenty years, while remaining low in Denmark and falling in France. Notably, the high level of low pay in the United States is not a recent phenomenon but can be observed over most of the last three decades. Third, there are many similarities between the six countries in terms of the groups that are most vulnerable to low-wage employment. Fourth,

Table 2.7 Proportion of the Population in Poor Households, 1984 to 2001

	With at Least One Worker[a]			All Households	
	1987[b]	1994	2001[c]	1994	2001
Denmark	—	1.9%	2.6%	3.8%	5.3%
France	1.1%	3.4	2.8	7.5	7.0
Germany	4.0	3.3	4.3	9.4	9.8
Netherlands	2.8	4.1	8.5	6.4	7.9
United Kingdom	6.9	3.5	4.7	10.5	10.7
United States	10.0	9.7	13.2	18.4	16.9

Source: Authors' compilation based on OECD (2006b) (statistical data underlying figures 2.9 and 2.10).
Note: "Poor" is defined as having income below 50 percent of the current median household income.
a. No minimum of hours and months worked in previous year.
b. France and Germany 1984; the United Kingdom and the United States 1986.
c. United Kingdom 1999, the Netherlands and the United States 2000.

part-time jobs turn out to be important for the international comparison of low-wage employment because their role can be very substantial, thus bearing out the relevance of an hourly definition of low pay. Fifth, not surprisingly, short-time, low-wage jobs (less than fifteen hours per week) are closely related to the countries' employment rates of youth and thus to aggregate employment rates. Finally, transition patterns between low-paid employment, better-paid employment, and non-employment are strikingly similar between Europe and the United States; the chances of escaping low pay are better in Denmark, France, and the United States than elsewhere, but the low-pay-no-pay cycle is an important phenomenon in many countries.

It might be expected that higher taxes and employees' social contributions in European countries would reduce the purchasing power of the take-home hourly pay of low-paid workers compared to the United States. Estimates presented in this chapter suggest, however, that this only applies to France and Germany—and even in those countries it could be argued that relatively high employee social contributions should be included in the estimates of total compensation, since these contributions generally go toward health care and pensions.

When we compare low-pay threshold pay rates in terms of average labor costs to employers, taking account of intercountry differences in payroll taxes and employer social contributions, then labor costs in all the European countries are well above those in the United States. One implication of this comparison is that employers in the European countries may be under greater pressure than employers in the United States to economize on the use of low-paid workers and to find ways of raising their productivity (for example, through up-skilling and more capital-intensive forms of work organization).

The most important differences between Europe and the United States in terms of the working and living conditions associated with low-wage employment emerge when we take into account both non-wage benefits and entitlements that are directly provided by employers and those that are funded primarily by general taxation or, in some countries, by employers' and employees' contributions.

Over recent decades, European Union directives on matters relating to work conditions have ensured that on a number of key dimensions of work conditions—such as annual leave, sickness leave, and the entitlements of part-time and temporary workers—the five European countries have a lot more in common with each other than they do with the United States. In addition, some elements of the social wage, such as affordable health care, are generally more available to European than to U.S. workers. And partly as a result of differences in social benefits systems, low pay in the United States is more likely to be associated with household poverty than it is in Europe (see Nolan and Marx 2009).

However, with respect to terms of employment and working conditions, such as working time and job security, there are differences between the European countries, in enforcement as well as in the letter of regulations. Some of the European countries resemble the United States when it comes to the working conditions experienced by many low-wage workers (for example, their degree of exposure to physical strain and injury in their jobs). There are also some similarities between the United States and European countries in relation to elements of the social wage, such as private pension entitlements, that tend to be less available to low-paid workers than better-paid workers in the United Kingdom, France, and Germany, as is the case in the United States. Private pensions have relatively wide coverage, however, in Denmark and the Netherlands (over and above publicly funded pensions).

With these important similarities and differences in mind, the next two chapters consider the institutional factors regarding pay setting and labor supply that may affect wage outcomes. The following six chapters compare the characteristics and dynamics of low-wage occupations and industries in detail.

Table 2A.1 Determinants of the Probability of Being Low-Paid, Age Fifteen to Sixty-Four, 1995 to 2001

	Denmark	France	Germany	Netherlands	United Kingdom	United States[a]
Female	0.195	0.458	0.475	0.430	0.412	0.456
Age thirty to forty-four	-0.619	-0.552	-0.308	-0.584	-0.313	-0.250
Age forty-five to sixty-five	-0.731	-0.422	0.005	-0.345	-0.186	-0.329
Secondary	-0.421	-0.090	-0.364	-0.402	-0.244	-0.342
Tertiary	-0.699	-0.389	-0.665	-0.835	-0.320	-0.629
Part-time job	-0.030	-0.017	0.077	0.220	0.170	0.130
Temporary contract	0.015	0.348	0.008	0.318	0.169	NA
Seniority of five years or more	-0.045	-0.223	-0.135	-0.035	0.002	NA
Legislators, senior officials[a]	-0.081	-0.090	-0.040	-0.053	-0.186	-0.181
Professionals	-0.171	-0.267	-0.126	-0.150	-0.356	-0.166
Technicians and associates	-0.069	-0.114	-0.008	-0.153	-0.180	-0.049

Service, shop, and market	0.450	0.455	0.307	0.283	0.529	0.319
Craft and related trades	0.219	0.246	0.239	0.130	0.211	0.202
Plant and machine operators	0.236	0.342	0.162	0.246	0.494	NA
Elementary occupations	0.360	0.527	0.310	0.334	0.620	NA
Trade, hotels, and restaurants	0.150	0.147	0.214	0.125	0.453	0.389
Transport, finance, and business services	0.081	0.015	0.058	0.098	0.061	−0.015
Public and personal services	0.140	−0.014	0.035	−0.003	0.041	0.110
Low pay in previous year	1.326	1.303	1.367	1.706	1.617	1.242
Constant	−0.313	−0.729	−0.769	−0.575	−1.379	−1.043

Sources: Analysis of European Community Household Panel (Blázquez Cuesta and Salverda 2009) and the Panel Study of Income Dynamics (Institute for Social Research).

Notes: Following Cappellari and Jenkins (2004), a multivariate five-equation probit model with endogenous selection and endogenous switching is estimated that corrects for selection bias, initial conditions, (nonrandom) panel attrition, and genuine state dependence (as visible in the large effect of low pay in the previous year). See also Blázquez Cuesta and Salverda (2009).

Data are pooled over the period; "all employees" include those working less than fifteen hours, except for France (where such employees represented 0.4 percent of all employees in 2001); bold values are significant at the 5 percent level; occupations are one-digit ISCO in ECHP and selected likewise in PSID as much as possible; temporary contracts and seniority not available for PSID; on-the-job training included in estimation but not available for France, the United Kingdom, and the United States.

Reference categories for dummy variables are: age under thirty; primary education; in full-time employment; permanent contract; seniority less than five years; clerical occupations (administrative for the United States); manufacturing, utilities, and construction.

a. The U.S. occupational classification differs strongly from EU countries; the CNEF classification was aggregated to its first digits, pooling 0 with 1 (because of similarities), and 6 with 9 and 7 with 8, respectively (because of small numbers of observations).

Table 2A.2 Concentration of Low Pay, by Job Characteristics, 2001

	Denmark	France	Germany	Netherlands	United Kingdom	United States
Total	100%	100%	100%	100%	100%	100%
Working hours						
Thirty-five hours or more	81	94	83	62	69	74
Fifteen to Thirty-five hours	83	132	121	110	173	224
Less than fifteen hours[a]	514		263	274	234	254
Seniority on job[b]						
More than two years	53	60	74	62	78	63
Two years or less	207	239	193	202	124	159
Type of contract[b]						
Permanent	70	77	85	81	96	
Short-term or fixed-term	488	311	26	335	179	NA
Casual	416		189	463		
Other	357			214		

Occupations						
Professionals, managers	26	33	51	51	29	32
Clerks	57	88	96	118	99	98
Personal services workers	164	214	197	181	211	216
Salespersons, sales and services	384	231	204	236	267	156
Building and craft	214	153	116	111	86	69
Metal workers and operators	117	93	100	106	81	80
Agriculture workers	130	211	194	191	174	216

Sources: Authors' analysis of European Community Household Panel Survey (ECHP) and Current Population Survey-Outgoing Rotation Groups (U.S. BLS), and Center for Economic Policy Research (CEPR); see Mason and Salverda (2008) for more.
Notes: "All employees" include those working less than fifteen hours per week.
a. The smallest jobs are a tiny fraction in France.
b. Excluding those working less than fifteen hours; U.S. data refer to 2002.

Table 2A.3 Students and Apprentices Among Young (Age Fifteen to Twenty-Four) Workers, by Length of Working Week, 2005

	Denmark	France	Germany	Netherlands	United Kingdom	United States
All hours	64%	20%	53%	60%	36%	37%
Less than fifteen hours	96	60	80	94	82	83
Fifteen to thirty-five hours	60	37	31	58	55	62
Thirty-five hours or more	39	16	52	23	15	15

Sources: Authors' calculations based on European Labour Force Survey (ELFS) and CPS (U.S. BLS).

Table 2A.4 Low-Wage Employment by Selected Job Characteristics, 2001

	Denmark	France	Germany	Netherlands	United Kingdom	United States
Incidence						
Total	12%	15%	23%	23%	22%	24%
Low-paying occupations						
Personal services workers	19	33	46	41	46	51
Salespersons, sales and services	45	36	47	53	59	37
Building and craft	25	24	27	25	20	16
Agriculture workers and laborers	15	32	45	43	38	51
Low-paying industries						
Agriculture	12	37	54	38	38	51
Trade	18	20	36	40	42	36
Hotels and restaurants	42	40	60	54	65	58
Personal services	23	32	37	38	28	39

(Table continues on p. 76.)

Table 2A.4 (*Continued*)

	Denmark	France	Germany	Netherlands	United Kingdom	United States
Concentration						
Total	100	100	100	100	100	100
Low-paying occupations						
Personal services workers	164	214	197	181	211	216
Salespersons, sales and services	384	231	204	236	267	156
Building and craft	214	153	116	111	86	69
Agriculture workers and laborers	130	211	194	191	174	216
Low-paying industries						
Agriculture	100	237	235	169	173	218
Trade	150	120	156	177	189	153
Hotels and restaurants	353	258	255	241	298	249
Personal services	198	205	158	160	126	168
Three broad sectors of the economy						
Goods production	81	92	81	83	69	72
Market services	135	114	138	134	133	126
Public services	80	90	79	70	73	71

Source: Authors' calculation of ECHP and CPS-ORG (U.S. BLS).
Note: Hours count (FTE) is based on hourly wages.

Table 2A.5 Low-Wage Employment Gaps Compared with the United States: Shift-Share Decomposition by Industries, 2001

	Total Difference	Due to Different Incidence	Due to Other Sectoral Structure	Interaction
Denmark	−11.7%	−10.4%	−2.4%	+1.1%
France	−8.1	−6.4	−3.2	+1.5
Germany	−0.3	+3.3	−3.6	−0.1
Netherlands	−1.0	+1.4	−2.5	+0.1
United Kingdom	−1.5	+0.3	−2.1	+0.3

Sources: Authors' analysis of ECHP and CPS-ORG; see Mason and Salverda (2008).
Notes: "All employees" include those working less than fifteen hours per week, except France, where no detail is available for this category, which is also a tiny fraction of employees.

Table 2A.6 Tax Rates at Different Wage Levels for Full-Time Workers, 2000 and 2006

	Percentage of Gross Wage, 2000			Percentage of Gross Wage, 2006		
	MW	67% AW	AW	MW	67% AW	AW
Average tax rates, including employee social contributions						
Denmark	NA	40.8%	44.1%	NA		
France	21.0%	25.7	28.8	16.7%	26.1%	29.1%
Germany	NA	38.1	44.5	NA		
Netherlands[a]	26.6	32.6	33.2	22.6	31.2	36.1
United Kingdom	11.7	22.2	25.5	12.7	23.7	26.8
United States	16.3	21.1	23.9	14.5	20.6	23.4
Payroll taxes and employer contributions						
Denmark	NA	0.7	0.5	NA		
France	23.0	41.2	41.2	17.6	33.3	42.3
Germany	NA	20.5	20.5	NA		
Netherlands[a]	15.0	16.1	10.7	14.7	15.8	15.0
United Kingdom	5.2	8.8	9.9	6.8	9.7	10.7
United States	8.2	8.0	7.9	8.2	7.9	7.8

Source: Private communication from the author. See Immervoll (2007), table 3.
Notes:
MW = minimum wage
AW = average wage
a. Minimum-wage amounts mentioned for the Netherlands were wrong, and in private communication we have obtained from the author an adapted data set that is used here.

Table 2A.7 Annual Leave and Public Holidays, Circa 2001

Country	Statutory Minimum Annual Leave Entitlement	Average Annual Leave Entitlement[a]	Statutory Paid Holidays per Year	Public Holiday per Year
Denmark	25	30.0	9	9.5
France	30	30.0[b]	1	11.0
Germany	24	29.1	10	10.5
Netherlands	20	31.5	0	8.0
United Kingdom	20	24.5	0	8.0
United States—employees in medium-sized and large private-sector firms	0	16.9[c]	0	10.0
United States—all workers	0	9.0	0	6.0

Sources: Authors' compilation. Columns 1 and 3 and estimates in columns 2 and 4 of row 7: Ra and Schmitt (2007); columns 2 and 4 excluding row 7: European Industrial Relations Observa tory (2001).

a. Average collectively agreed entitlement for EU countries; average vacation days in mediun sized and large private-sector firms for United States.

b. Source as in column 1 for France.

c. After ten years' service in medium-sized and large private-sector firms.

Table 2A.8 Average Annual Hours Worked per Worker, Part-Time Employment Rates, and Usual Weekly Hours of Work, Various Years

	Average Annual Hours Worked per Worker			Part-Time Employees as Percentage of Total Employment, 2004		Usual Weekly Hours of Work Most Frequently Reported[a]: Male Employees in Their Main Job, 2002			
	1984	1994	2004	Males	Females	Major Peak-Hours	Working Those Hours	Minor Peak-Hours	Working Those Hours
Denmark	1,502	1,495	1,454	12%	25%	37	53%	45	7%
France	1,651	1,582	1,441	5	23	35	42	39	14
Germany	—	1,536	1,443	7	39	40	37	38	19
Netherlands	—	1,362	1,357	15	61	40	40	38	17
United Kingdom	1,729	1,736	1,669	10	39	40	14	38	8
United States	1,869	1,864	1,824	8	18	40	63	50–54	9

Sources: Authors' compilation based on, for hours worked: OECD (2006a); part-time employment and usual weekly hours of work: OECD (2006b), including statistical supplement.

a. For example, for Denmark in 2002, the data show that the most commonly reported level of hours per week was 37 and that 53 percent of male employees reported working that number of hours.

Table 2A.9 Indicators of Job Quality and Security, 1984, 1994, and 2004

	Average Job Tenure[a]		Temporary Employment[b]			Involuntary Part-Time Employment[c]		
	1994	2004	1984[d]	1994[e]	2004[f]	1984[d]	1994	2004
Denmark	8.5	8.7	12.5%	12.0%	9.8%	12.7%	16.4%	13.4%
France	10.8	11.5	3.3	11.0	12.3	NA	31.5	24.2
Germany	10.1	10.8	10.0	10.3	12.2	5.7	7.0	13.8
Netherlands	9.1	10.6	7.5	10.9	14.6	11.2	5.2	3.9
United Kingdom	8.3	8.4	6.2	6.5	5.7	8.6	12.0	6.0
United States	NA	NA	NA	5.1	4.0	12.5	14.2	13.9

Source: Authors' compilation based on OECD statistical supplement (2006b), and, for U.S. involuntary part-time employment, Mishel, Bernstein, and Allegretto (2007), table underlying figure 4V.

Notes:

NA = Data not available

a. Data on average job tenure in current job with the same employer are expressed in numbers of years.
b. Temporary employment (including temporary agency workers) as a percentage of total employment.
c. Share of involuntary part-time employment among part-time employment.
d. Netherlands, 1985.
e. United States, 1995.
f. Germany, 2003; United States, 2001.

Table 2A.10 Types of Pension Provision and Formal Gross Replacement Rates from Mandatory Pensions, Recent Years

	First Tier: Universal Coverage, Redistributive[a] (Type of Scheme)	Second Tier: Mandatory Insurance	Gross Replacement Rates from Mandatory Pensions[b] (Percentage of Earnings for Average Earner)	Main Types of Private Pension[c] (Type of Scheme— Coverage: Percentage of Workforce)	Coverage by Private Pensions (Percentage of Workforce)
Denmark	Resource-tested + basic	Private	76%	Mandatory personal (more than ninety), quasi-mandatory occupational (more than eighty)	More than 90%
France	Resource-tested + minimum	Public	51%	Voluntary occupational (10%), voluntary personal (8%)	18%
Germany	Resource-tested	Public	40%	Voluntary occupational (57%), voluntary personal (13%)	63%

(Table continues on p. 82.)

Table 2A.10 (*Continued*)

	First Tier: Universal Coverage, Redistributive[a] (Type of Scheme)	Second Tier: Mandatory Insurance	Gross Replacement Rates from Mandatory Pensions[b] (Percentage of Earnings for Average Earner)	Main Types of Private Pension[c] (Type of Scheme—Coverage: Percentage of Workforce)	Coverage by Private Pensions (Percentage of Workforce)
Netherlands	Basic	Private	82%[d]	Quasi-mandatory occupational (more than ninety)	More than 90%
United Kingdom	Resource-tested + basic + minimum	Public	31%	Voluntary occupational (43%), voluntary personal (16%)	51%
United States	Resource-tested	Public	41%	Voluntary occupational (47%), voluntary personal (17%)	56%

Source: Authors' compilation based on OECD, *Pensions at a Glance,* 2007, table 1.1, "Retirement-Income Indicators" (p. 33), table II.2.1, and figure II.2.2.

a. Resource-tested pension schemes pay higher benefits to poorer pensioners than to better-off ones. Minimum pensions have a similar redistributive purpose but do not take account of any other income apart from pension income.

b. The gross replacement rate is defined as gross pension entitlement divided by gross preretirement earnings.

c. Occupational pension schemes are employer-based. Personal schemes are individual-based. Quasi-mandatory schemes are typically based on collective agreements. For the United Kingdom, voluntary private schemes refer to schemes whose members are contracted out of the state second pension.

d. This figure needs to be treated with caution. The maximum entitlement from the first and second pillars is 70 percent of earnings, but usually only after forty years of contributions. However, many employees do not achieve this level of entitlement.

Table 2A.11 Gross and Net Replacement Rates from Mandatory Pensions, Recent Years

	Gross Replacement Rates from Mandatory Pensions: Percentage of Gross Preretirement Earnings[a]			Net Replacement Rates from Mandatory Pensions: Percentage of Net Preretirement Earnings[b]		
	For Persons on 50 Percent of Average Earnings	For Persons on 75 Percent of Average Earnings	For Average Earner	For Persons on 50 Percent of Average Earnings	For Persons on 75 Percent of Average Earnings	For Average Earner
Denmark	120%	90%	76%	133%	102%	87%
France	64	51	51	78	65	63
Germany	40	40	40	53	57	58
Netherlands	81	82	82	97	104	97
United Kingdom	34	38	31	66	49	41
United States	44	46	41	67	58	52

Source: Authors' compilation based on OECD, *Pensions at a Glance, 2007,* "Retirement-Income Indicators," pp. 33, 35.
a. The gross replacement rate is defined as gross pension entitlement divided by gross preretirement earnings.
b. The net replacement rate is defined as the individual net pension entitlement divided by net preretirement earnings, taking account of personal income taxes and social security contributions paid by workers and pensioners.

NOTES

1. The U.S. mean is 29 percent above the median, as against 12 to 13 percent in Denmark, Germany, and the Netherlands, with the United Kingdom and France in between, according to the OECD earnings deciles data set (various years 1999 to 2005).

2. It should be noted, however, that measurement error may be increased, as hourly pay must be calculated from period wages and period hours.

3. Some American research (for example, Mishel, Bernstein, and Allegretto 2007) applies absolute poverty-level wages derived from household poverty levels. However, this wage measure complicates labor market analysis, as it corresponds with very different individual wage levels in the labor market. It is also extremely demanding in terms of data availability and treatment, especially in international comparison. For a discussion, see Lucifora and Salverda (2009).

4. However, relative to the working-age population, traditional expectations are warranted, as the United Kingdom and the United States have higher employment rates than Germany (table 2.1, row 2).

5. Wiemer Salverda and Ken Mayhew (2009) show that low-pay incidence correlates significantly to the D5/D1 inequality ratio across the United States and thirteen European countries.

6. The probit estimates shown in table 2A.1 are derived from an approach that is more uniform and developed compared to the national monographs and that uses comparable data as much as possible. Note that data are pooled over the 1995 to 2001 period to arrive at a sufficient number of observations of year-on-year transitions. This comes at a cost of having to disregard any changes over the period. It is often also a period of favorable job growth. For Europe, the European Community Household Panel (ECHP) data set was used, and for the United States the Panel Study of Income Dynamics (PSID) data set. (See note 15 for a caveat and further explanation.) We are grateful to Maite Blázquez Cuesta for her work on the model and on the ECHP and to Daniella Brals for her work on the PSID.

7. The education effect is small in France, but that finding may be related to problems with the French educational variable after 1997.

8. It is important to take into account that "foreign-born" is a broader definition than "foreign nationality," since a proportion of immigrants may become nationals of the host country. The population share of the former is twice that of the latter for the United States (12.8 percent against 6.6 percent), and more so than in the five European countries on average (9.9 percent against 5.7 percent). However, at half the level

of 19 percent, the U.S. immigrant share of low pay would still top all European countries. See OECD (2006c), *International Migration Outlook 2006*, chart I.4.

9. For further details of the concentration of low-wage employment analyzed by working hours, seniority, type of contract, and occupation, see table 2A.2.

10. The variable lumps both together; the numbers for thirty-five hours or more may indicate apprentices, and those for below thirty-five hours students in full-time education.

11. See table 2A.3 for further details on the concentration of low pay by part-time/full-time status and other job characteristics.

12. Within the trade sector, we are primarily concerned with retail trade, as can be shown using other sources but not with the ECHP, which, unfortunately, does not allow disaggregation between retail and wholesale activities.

13. See EU-KLEMS data on compensation of employees per hour. EU-KLEMS is a European Union–funded database for twenty-six countries that includes data on capital, labor, energy, materials, and service imports. Available at: http://www.euklems.net.

14. For an explanation of the approach, derived from Cappellari and Jenkins (2004), see Blázquez Cuesta and Salverda (2009).

15. To mimic ECHP as much as possible, we used the Cornell University Cross-National Equivalent File (CNEF) of the PSID. Unfortunately, important differences remain: the PSID is not available for 1998 and 2000, and as a result the transitions observed for 1999 and 2001 are two-year instead of one-year, as is the case with other years and with ECHP. Evidently, this may upwardly affect transition rates, and this is an important caveat to be kept in mind. Hourly wages for the PSID are defined on annual hours and earnings over the preceding year instead of usual monthly earnings and weekly hours, as for the ECHP. Part-time employment, though identically defined as less than thirty-five hours a week, is also derived from these annual hours (in combination with the part-time variable). Finally, the PSID has a different classification of occupations.

16. Note that the monographs for Germany (Bosch and Weinkopf 2008, 80), France (Caroli and Gautié 2008, 62), and the Netherlands (Salverda, van Klaveren, and van der Meer 2008, 108) cast some doubt on the practical significance of the OECD's EPL indicators (because they are based on formal provisions) and their use for cross-country and time-series comparison (because the underlying weighting of detailed provisions disregards diverging applications in practice). See also Bosch, Mayhew, and Gautié (this volume).

17. On complementary indicators such as occupational illness and work accidents, France scores quite badly compared to the other European countries; this may be an indication of higher work intensity and worse working conditions in many industries (Caroli and Gautié 2008, 56–57).

18. Even in the EWCS 2005, sample sizes in specific occupations such as elementary workers were as low as fifty-two in Denmark, seventy-five in Germany, and ninety-six in the United Kingdom.

19. See "General Social Surveys, 1972–2002: Cumulative Codebook 1972–2004," vols. 1–2, a biannual personal interview survey of U.S. households conducted by the National Opinion Research Center, available at: http://www.norc.uchicago.edu/projects/gensoc.asp.

20. Note that the impact of employee social contributions on workers' standard of living is not straightforward. Employee (and employer) contributions, which largely go toward health care coverage and pensions, are not simply reductions in earnings received by workers but may also reasonably be viewed as part of workers' current or deferred compensation and considered a component of what can labeled the "social wage." See the discussion in the next section.

21. Or, naturally, they can be offered voluntarily. We leave that category aside here for lack of systematic data.

22. Pure sickness benefit durations miss, first, that the start of sickness leave depends on varying preceding waiting periods, and second, that it is potentially followed by disability benefit (see also OECD 2003, tables A.2.1 and 3).

23. Note that "unfortunately, data on coverage of private pensions can be extremely difficult to obtain and is often difficult to compare because of institutional differences in the markets for long-term savings . . . and the estimates shown should be regarded as preliminary"(OECD 2007b, 77).

24. See Danish Ministry of the Interior and Health, "Health Care in Denmark," available at: http://www.im.dk/publikationer/healthcare_in_dk/all.htm.

25. See Dutch Ministry of Health, Welfare, and Sport, available at: http://www.minvws.nl/en/themes/health-insurance-system/default.asp.

26. Refers to private-sector wage and salary workers age eighteen to sixty-four who work at least twenty hours per week and twenty-six weeks per year.

27. The usual aggregate poverty rate for the United States, based on an absolute standard, seems lower but not fundamentally different. Estimates for 2001 vary between 11 and 12 percent, and those for 2007 between 13 and 16 percent. See "Official and National Academy of

Science (NAS) Based Poverty Rates: 1999 to 2007," available at: http://
www.census.gov/hhes/www/povmeas/altmeas07/nas_measures_histor
ical.xls.

REFERENCES

Barnard, Catherine, Simon Deakin, and Richard Hobbs. 2004. "Opting Out
of the Forty-Eight-Hour Week: Employer Necessity or Individual Choice?
An Empirical Study of the Operation of Article 18(1)(b) of the Working
Time Directive in the United Kingdom." Working paper 282. Cambridge:
University of Cambridge, Economic and Social Research Council (ESRC)
Centre for Business Research.

Blázquez Cuesta, Maite, and Wiemer Salverda. 2009. "Low-Wage Employment and the Role of Education and On-the-Job Training." *Labor* 23(s1,
special issue on "Training and Job Insecurity"): 5–35.

Boisard, Pierre, Michel Gollac, Antoine Valeyre, and Damien Cartron. 2003.
Time and Work: Work Intensity. Dublin: European Foundation for the Improvement of Living and Working Conditions.

Bosch, Gerhard, and Claudia Weinkopf, eds. 2008. *Low-Wage Work in Germany*. New York: Russell Sage Foundation.

British Market Research Bureau (BMRB). 2001. "A Survey of Workers' Ex-
periences of the Working Time Regulations." BMRB Social Research,
Employment Relations Series 31. London: Department of Trade and
Industry.

Bundesagentur für Arbeit (BA). Various years. Employee Panel [database].
Available at: http://www.iab.de/de/daten/forschungsdatenzentrum.aspx.

Cappellari, Lorenzo, and Stephen P. Jenkins. 2004. "Modeling Low-Pay
Transition Probabilities, Accounting for Panel Attrition, Nonresponse,
and Initial Conditions." Working paper 1232. Munich and Brussels: CE-
Sifo (Center for Economic Studies, Ifo Institute for Economic Research,
and CESifo GmbH).

Caroli, Ève, and Jérôme Gautié, eds. 2008. *Low-Wage Work in France*. New
York: Russell Sage Foundation.

Center for Economic Policy Research (CEPR). Various years. Current Population Survey Uniform Data Extracts–Job Tenure, and Outgoing Rotation
Groups respectively [database]. Available at: http://www.ceprdata.org/
cps/index.php.

Centre for Corporate Performance: Integrated Database for Labor Market
Research (CCP: IDA). Various years. [database]. Aarhus University, Denmark. Available at: http://www.asb.dk/article.aspx?pid=663.

Centraal bureau voor de statistiek (CBS) (Statistics Netherlands). Various
years. Loonstructuuronderzoek (Structure of Earnings Survey) [data-

base]. Available at: http://www.cbs.nl/nl-NL/menu/methoden/dataverza meling/loonstructuuronderzoek-art.htm.

Deutsches Institut für Wirtschaftsforschung (DIW) Berlin (German Institute for Economic Research). Various years. German Socio-Economic Panel Study (GSOEP) [database]. Available at: www.diw.de/de/soep.

Ercolani, Marco, Tim Barmby, and John G. Treble. 2002. "Sickness Absence: An International Comparison." *Economic Journal* 112(June): F315–31.

European Community Household Panel Survey (ECHP) [database]. Created by Eurostat. Available at: http://circa.europa.eu/irc/dsis/echpanel/info/data/information.html.

European Foundation for the Improvement of Living and Working Conditions (EFILWC). 2005. *Fourth European Working Conditions Survey, 2005.* Dublin: EFILWC.

European Industrial Relations Observatory. 2001. *Industrial Relations in the EU, Japan, and USA.* Available at: http://www.eurofound.europa.eu/eiro.

European Labour Force Survey (ELFS) [database]. Created by Eurostat. Available at: http://circa.europa.eu/irc/dsis/employment/info/data/eu_lfs/index.htm.

Green, Francis. 2004. "Why Has Work Effort Become More Intense?" *Industrial Relations* 43(4): 709–41.

———. 2005. *Demanding Work: The Paradox of Job Quality in the Affluent Economy.* Princeton, N.J.: Princeton University Press.

Green, Francis, and Steven McIntosh. 2001. "The Intensification of Work in Europe." *Labor Economics* 8(2): 291–308.

Immervoll, Herwig. 2007. "Minimum Wages, Minimum Labor Costs, and the Tax Treatment of Low-Wage Employment." Social Employment and Migration Working Papers 46. Paris: Organization for Economic Cooperation and Development.

Institut für Arbeitsmarkt- und Berufsforschung (IABS). IABS-R01 Employment Samples [database]. Available at: fdz.iab.de/en/FDZ_Individual_Data/IAB_Employment_Samples.aspx.

Institut national de la statistique et des études économiques (INSEE). Enquête Emploi [database]. Available at: http://www.insee.fr/fr/default.asp.

Institute for Social Research. Various years. Panel Study of Income Dynamics (PSID) [database]. Ann Arbor: University of Michigan. Available at: psidonline.isr.umich.edu.

Krauser, Niklas, Teresa Scherzer, and Reiner Rugulies. 2005. "Physical Workload, Work Intensification, and Prevalence of Pain in Low-Wage Workers: Results from a Participatory Research Project with Hotel Room Cleaners in Las Vegas." *American Journal of Industrial Medicine* 48(5): 326–37.

Landsbergis, Paul A. 2003. "The Changing Organization of Work and the Safety and Health of Working People: A Commentary." *Journal of Occupational and Environmental Medicine* 45(1): 61–72.

Lovell, Vicky. 2004. *No Time to Be Sick: Why Everyone Suffers When Workers Don't Have Paid Sick Leave.* Washington, D.C.: Institute for Women's Policy Research.

Lucifora, Claudio, and Wiemer Salverda. 2009. "Low Pay." In *The Oxford Handbook of Economic Inequality*, edited by Wiemer Salverda, Brian Nolan, and Timothy M. Smeeding. New York: Oxford University Press.

Mason, Geoff, and Wiemer Salverda. 2008. "RSF Benchmarking Study: Low-Wage Employment in Western Europe and the United States." Report to Russell Sage Foundation, New York.

Mishel, Lawrence, Jared Bernstein, and Sylvia Allegretto. 2007. *The State of Working America 2006–2007.* Ithaca, N.Y.: Economic Policy Institute and Cornell University Press.

National Accounting Office (NAO). 2003. *International Health Comparisons.* London: NAO.

Nolan, Brian, and Ive Marx. 2009. "Economic Inequality, Poverty, and Social Exclusion." In *The Oxford Handbook of Economic Inequality*, edited by Wiemer Salverda, Brian Nolan, and Timothy M. Smeeding. New York: Oxford University Press.

Organization for Economic Cooperation and Development (OECD). 1996. *Employment Outlook.* Paris: OECD.

———. 2003. *Transforming Disability into Ability.* Paris: OECD.

———. 2004. *Employment Outlook.* Paris: OECD.

———. 2006a. *Employment and Labor Market Statistics.* Paris: OECD.

———. 2006b. *Employment Outlook.* Paris: OECD.

———. 2007a. *Society at a Glance.* Paris: OECD.

———. 2007b *Pensions at a Glance.* Paris: OECD.

———. 2009. Labour Force Survey Database. Available at: http://www.sourceoecd.org/database/OECDstat.

Ray, Rebecca, and John Schmitt. 2007. *No-Vacation Nation.* Washington, D.C.: Center for Economic and Policy Research.

Salverda, Wiemer, and Ken Mayhew. 2009. "Capitalist Economies and Wage Inequality." *Oxford Review of Economic Policy* 25(1): 125–164.

Salverda, Wiemer, Maarten van Klaveren, and Marc van der Meer, eds. 2008. *Low-Wage Work in the Netherlands.* New York: Russell Sage Foundation.

U.K. Office of National Statistics (ONS). Various years. Annual Survey of Hours and Earnings (ASHE) [database]. Available at: www.statistics.gov.uk/StatBase/Product.asp?vlnk=13101.

U.S. Bureau of Labor Statistics. Various years. Current Population Survey.

CPS-ORG: Outgoing Rotation Groups [database]. Available at: http://www
.census.gov/cps.

U.S. Social Security Administration (SSA). 2007. "Social Security Programs
Throughout the World." Available at: http://www.ssa.gov/policy/docs/prog
desc/ssptw/.

CHAPTER 3

Industrial Relations, Legal Regulations, and Wage Setting

Gerhard Bosch, Ken Mayhew, and Jérôme Gautié

The preceding chapter summarized the main features of low-wage work across our six countries. In this chapter and the next, we explain the main institutional determinants of the size and structure of low-wage work, focusing on the national institutions involved in setting pay.

The overall incidence of low pay in the six countries and the results of the case studies suggest that pay-setting institutions play a central role in explaining international differences in low-wage work. By "pay-setting institutions" we mean the formal and sometimes informal mechanisms used to determine the wages (and benefits) received by workers in different industries and occupations within each country. More specifically, we mean collective bargaining arrangements, minimum wages, and other labor and product market legislation, regulations, and procedures that have an impact on wage determination.

These institutions, with their mutual linkages, may form "inclusive" or "exclusive" pay-setting systems. In exclusive systems, the pay and other terms and conditions of employees with strong bargaining power have little or no effect on employees with weaker bargaining power within a company, within an industry, or across industries. Inclusive systems extend the benefits of such bargaining power to workers who have relatively little bargaining power in their own right. The more inclusive the set of institutions, the better protected are those at the low end of the workforce. Inclusiveness does not depend just on the formal institutions but also on the extent to which the various players are committed to reducing inequality.

Our review of national pay-setting institutions has two main findings. First, the prevalence of low-wage work appears to be strongly related to the inclusiveness of national pay-setting institutions. The more inclusive the pay-setting institutions, the lower the prevalence of low-wage work. The most inclusive systems use centralized and co-ordinated national collective bargaining agreements to extend the wage gains of the most powerful, generally unionized, workers to those workers with less bargaining power, especially less-skilled and non-union workers. Some countries, meanwhile, provide a degree of inclusiveness through a national minimum wage that positions a wage floor below workers who would otherwise have little ability to secure higher wages. The least inclusive countries, such as the United States, rely on largely unregulated market forces to set wages, and in contrast to many European governments, in the past the U.S. government has not been committed to increasing the statutory minimum wage.

The second key finding is the important role played by employer "exit options"—the de jure or de facto exemptions, exceptions, or loopholes in otherwise inclusive pay-setting institutions. For example, where nonstandard work contracts or workers in small and medium-sized companies fall outside national collective bargaining agreements, employers are able to set low wages, even in countries with extensive collective bargaining. Lax enforcement of existing labor law, particularly in contexts where there is little or no union oversight, provides another exit option for firms seeking to cut labor costs. The most vulnerable workers in the five industries we studied were most affected by these exit options.

Gender, ethnicity, national origin, region of residence, and other factors all play a role in explaining differences in the wages paid across industries and occupations, but we concentrate here on institutional features that have an impact on workers' bargaining power and therefore help to determine what they earn—and also, potentially, other dimensions of their job quality. The most important of these institutions in most of our countries is the national system of collective bargaining. The national minimum wage is probably the next most important national pay-setting institution, particularly in countries where collective bargaining is limited in its reach. Employment protection legislation (EPL) and, more widely, the regulations concerning the rights attached to different employment statuses (permanent and temporary) also influence workers' bargaining power, as do product market regulations. Efforts to open product markets to national and international competition often increase competitive pressures on workers, especially by putting them in direct competition with workers from other countries or with companies not covered by collective agreements within the same country. Finally, two dimensions of wage setting at the level of the firm or organization have to be taken into account. The first relates to nonwage benefits, many of which are fixed in some countries by law or by collective agreement (and therefore are not dependent on employers' discretion). Such benefits constitute a kind of minimum "social wage" (see also chapter 2). The second dimension relates to institutions promoting employees' representation and voice at the organizational level.

The rest of this chapter looks at the inclusiveness of collective bargaining arrangements and national minimum wages; at nonstandard work arrangements and product market deregulation as opportunities for exit options from the generally more inclusive national pay-setting systems; and finally, at issues related to pay setting at the firm level through "social wages" and employee voice.

THE IMPACT OF COLLECTIVE BARGAINING ON PAY

THE ARCHITECTURE OF COLLECTIVE BARGAINING IN THE SIX COUNTRIES

The extent of the influence of collective bargaining on pay is usually measured by the coverage of collective agreements. The coverage rate refers to the share of workers who benefit from a collective agreement or from collective status.[1] The coverage rate must be distinguished from the unionization rate (or union density), which relates to the share of workers who are union members. As we see later in the chapter, the gap between the two may be quite important in some countries.

The well-known close relationship between the incidence of low pay and coverage by collective agreements (OECD 1997, ch. 3) can be observed in the six countries covered in this study (see figure 3.1).

Not only do the three countries with the lowest incidences of low pay (Denmark, France, and the Netherlands) have greater coverage than the countries with higher incidence (the United States, the United Kingdom, and Germany), but coverage in the former group has increased or remained stable since 1980, while it has decreased in the latter (see table 3.1). Historically, the United Kingdom and Germany had high levels of coverage (in the United Kingdom until the early 1980s and in Germany until the mid-1990s); after substantial transformations of institutions and of employer and state strategies,

Figure 3.1   Incidence of Low Pay and Coverage by
Collective Agreements, 2005

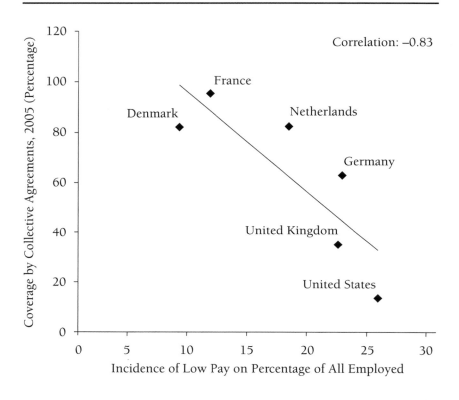

Sources: Low-pay incidence: Mason and Salverda (this volume); coverage: Visser
(2008, 27).

coverage subsequently declined in these two countries. Germany,
with its still relatively high coverage, seems to be nearer France and
the Netherlands than to the United Kingdom and the United States.
But the decline took place mainly in labor-intensive industries, such
as the ones studied in this volume, and as a consequence the German
industrial relations system has become less inclusive, which helps to
explain the strong growth of low-wage work.

The extent of collective bargaining coverage (see tables 3.2 and
3.3) depends on different institutional settings in different countries.
We can distinguish four types of institutional linkage:

Table 3.1 Collective Bargaining Coverage, 1980, 1990, and 2007

	1980	1990	2007	Change 1980 to 2007
United States	26	18	14	−12
United Kingdom	70	54	35	−35
Germany	78	72	63	−15
France	85	92	95	+10
Netherlands	76	82	82	+6
Denmark	69	69	82	+13

Sources: Authors' compilation. The Netherlands 1980 and Denmark 1980 and 1990: OECD (1997, 71), other data: Visser (2008).

Notes: The figures in this table are from the most reliable comparative data source available. National statistical sources may produce slightly different numbers. In France, the figure is only for workers covered by a branch collective agreement. If workers covered by a firm collective agreement, or benefiting from special status (mainly in publicly owned firms in utilities and transportation) are added, the coverage rate amounts to almost 98 percent in 2004.

1. *Low inclusiveness because of low trade union density:* In the two liberal market economies (the United States and the United Kingdom), coverage is mainly influenced by trade union density. Employers' associations at the industry and higher levels are weak and are mainly lobbying organizations rather than actors in the collective bargaining process. Shrinking trade union density, in the absence of other mechanisms to cover non-unionized workers (such as strong employers' organizations or extension of agreements by the state), has led to a decline in coverage in these two countries. Although British and American unions fail to extend the benefits of collective bargaining to non-union workers, these unions do succeed in improving the wages and work conditions of their members. Indeed, studying fifteen low-wage occupations in the United States, John Schmitt and his colleagues (2008, 339) show that "controlling for differences between union and non-union workers . . . unionization substantially improves the pay and benefits offered" to low-wage workers.

2. *High inclusiveness because of high trade union density:* As in the United States and the United Kingdom, union coverage in Denmark is mainly determined by trade union density, but density is high across the whole economy. More than 70 percent of the

workforce are union members, and density has remained fairly stable over recent decades. Because of strong union power, most firms that are not party to an agreement also pay the negotiated rates. As a result, collective bargaining coverage is even higher than union density. However, the state is not completely absent. High density in Denmark can partly be explained by the so-called Ghent system, in which the unions run unemployment insurance funds, financed mainly by the state. This, together with the fact that job protection is low, strongly motivates workers to join a union and to stay in it when they leave their jobs. The only workers who do not join a union are those with high individual bargaining power or young workers who are still pursuing an education and are not yet looking for permanent employment.

3. *High inclusiveness because of extended collective agreements and strong employer organizations*: In France and the Netherlands, trade union density has been falling, but without the same negative impact on coverage as in the United Kingdom and the United States. In fact, collective bargaining coverage has actually increased even as density has fallen, owing primarily to the increased involvement of employers' organizations and strong support by the state. In France, as in the Netherlands, nondiscriminatory agreements are legally required, so that negotiated agreements are extended to both unionized and non-unionized workers in any given company. In addition, because the state declares most agreements to be generally binding throughout the relevant sector, collective agreements have significant leverage.[2] In a small country such as the Netherlands, coordination between employers is easier than in bigger countries, while central agreements on wage moderation, which are attractive for employers, can only be implemented with high employer coverage or legal extension mechanisms.

4. *Low inclusiveness in spite of high employer density[3] and high coverage*: As in France and the Netherlands, high employer density is the major institution for achieving medium to high coverage in Germany. However, in contrast to France and the Netherlands, employer density in Germany is shrinking. Collective bargaining is still important, but the linkages between the well-organized industries and regions and the less-organized industries and regions have been broken. In contrast to past practice, employers'

Table 3.2 Collective Bargaining Coverage, Employers' Organizations, and Union Density, 2007

	Percentage									
	1 to 10	11 to 20	21 to 30	31 to 40	41 to 50	51 to 60	61 to 70	71 to 80	81 to 90	91 to 100
France	U							E		Cov
Netherlands			U					E	Cov	
Denmark						E		U	Cov	
Germany							E Cov			
United Kingdom			U	Cov, E						
United States	E	U, Cov								

Sources: Authors' compilation based on Visser (2008); European Commission (2006).
Notes:
Cov = bargaining coverage (nonstandardized)
E = employers' density: share in percentage of employers who are members of an employers' organization (private sector)
U = union density: share in percentage of employees who are union members

Table 3.3 Union Density, Employer Density, and Extension of Agreements

	Trade Union Density, 1980	Trade Union Density, 1990	Trade Union Density, 2007	Change 1980 to 2007	Employer Density, 1994 to 1996[a]	Employer Density, 2000[a]	Change 1994–1996 to 2000	Extension of Agreements by the State
United States	22%	16%	12%	−10%	0%	0%	—	No
United Kingdom	51	39	29	−22	54	40	−14	No
Germany	35	31	20	−15	72	63	−9	Few and decreasing
France	18	10	8	−10	74	74	—	Very high and stable
Netherlands	35	26	26	−9	79	85	+6	Very high and stable
Denmark	76	71	68	−7	39	52	+13	No

Sources: Authors' compilation. Trade union density: OECD (1997, 71), and Visser (2008); employer density: data for 1996 to 1997, Traxler (2004), and for 2000, European Commission (2004).

Note: The table measures net union density: trade union membership minus inactive members (retired, students, etc.).

a. Measured as employees covered by employer peak organizations.

organizations are now generally refusing to agree to the extension of agreements. As a result, there is no mechanism to extend coverage to industries with weak unions. Collective agreements on minimum pay levels are declared generally binding in only a few industries, so that decreasing employer density has directly reduced bargaining coverage.[4]

These four types of collective bargaining circumstances differ not only in their institutional linkages but also with respect to their institutional stability.

A precondition for high coverage as well as for inclusiveness within industries seems to be multi-employer bargaining at the industry or sectoral level. This gives employers' organizations an active role in collective bargaining, which they do not have if decentralized bargaining is dominant, as it is in the United Kingdom and the United States. Multi-employer bargaining makes the coordination of collective agreements between different industries easier. It also gives collective bargaining more stability because, to an extent, it takes wages out of competition within any given industry. It encourages the social partners to include new types of workers, new companies, and new industries in collective bargaining and to avoid fragmentation of bargaining if product markets are deregulated. In addition, because multi-employer bargaining aggregates the interests of employees and employers, the social partners are better able to negotiate other issues besides wages at the industry or national level and have a strong voice in negotiations with the government. One example is the strong involvement of the social partners in vocational training in Germany and Denmark (Bosch and Charest 2010).

The country monographs clearly show that the scope of multi-employer bargaining and its coordination is absolutely central to explaining the differences between the countries. In Denmark, the country with the lowest share of low-wage workers, unions have pursued a solidaristic wage policy, as in other Scandinavian countries. The Danes have successfully reduced wage differentials between industries and between different groups of workers (by gender, skill, and region) within industries, which was possible only because of the strength of the national umbrella union federation.[5] Furthermore, in 2005 the social partners agreed to introduce a high minimum wage for all industries.[6] This policy can be explained in part by Denmark's high trade union density. Unions have high shares of members from low-wage industries, and they push for more wage equality (European Commission 2008, 86).

Such strong intervention in the overall earnings distribution is not a feature in the other countries with multi-employer negotiations where unions are dominated by workers with strong bargaining power. In France, the Netherlands, and Germany, pay differentials between industries have remained high. In these three countries, unions have not pursued—or have not had the power to pursue—a solidaristic wage policy. In all three countries, unions in the typical labor-intensive low-wage industries have been too weak to negotiate wages much above a low floor. In many French industries, the national minimum wage is higher than the collectively agreed rate. In Germany, the collectively agreed rates in a number of industries are below the low-wage threshold. Multi-employer bargaining, however, has helped to reduce wage differences within industries and between regions. But in recent years the metal industries agreement has ceased to serve as the pattern agreement for the whole economy, diminishing the impact of bargaining on wage differentials.[7]

In the decentralized bargaining systems of the United Kingdom and the United States, there are virtually no higher-level or pattern agreements left. Until the 1980s, significant parts of the U.K. economy, including much of private manufacturing and even some private services, had multi-employer agreements. These agreements set minimum terms and conditions for the sector or industry concerned. Though they were not legally binding, in effect they did set floors. Such agreements disappeared in the 1980s, however, and bargaining is now confined to the company or even establishment level. Thus, a dramatic fall in union density was accompanied by a major change in the industrial relations architecture. Today coverage in the United Kingdom is only slightly higher than union density. The same is true in the United States, where the steady drop in union density since the mid-1970s has been entirely a function of the decline in private-sector union membership. Since the mid-1970s, public-sector unionization rates have held steady at just under 40 percent. Over the same period, private-sector density has fallen from over 25 percent to under 8 percent. Collective bargaining takes place mainly at the company level, and only employees at the relevant company are covered. Coverage is not extended by the state or by the membership of an employers' organization. Thus, falling trade union membership reduced not only coverage but also the indirect spillover influence of able 3.4 Centralization and Coordination of Collective Bargaining

	Centralization				Coordination			
	1970 to 1974	1985 to 1989	1995 to 2000	2007	1970 to 1974	1985 to 1989	1995 to 2000	2007
nited States	1	1	1	1	1	1	1	1
nited Kingdom	2	1	1	1	3	1	1	1
ermany	3	3	3	2	4	4	4	2
ance	3.5	3.5	3.5	3.5	4	4	4	4
etherlands	3	3	3	3	3	4	4	4
enmark	5	3	3	3	5	4	4	4

urces: Authors' compilation. For row 4 and columns 4 and 8, Russell Sage Foundation
untry studies (Bosch and Weinkopf 2008; Caroli and Gautié 2008; Lloyd, Mason, and
ayhew 2008; Salverda, van Klaveren, and van der Meer 2008; Westergaard-Nielsen 2008); for
other data, OECD (2006, 81).
otes: Based on the country studies, in the case of France we corrected the values of both the
ECD indicators. In France, the predominance of industrywide collective bargaining and the ex-
ence of tripartite national agreements point to a value of 3.5 instead of 2 for all three periods,
hile the high level of industry bargaining and its extension by the state points to a value of 3.5
stead of 2 for coordination.

collective bargaining on the economy as a whole.[8] Because fewer
companies are afraid of union organization campaigns, more companies are more willing than they used to be to pay lower rates.

Our analysis of multi-employer bargaining and pattern agreements
shows that inclusive industrial relations systems need some centralization and coordination between the social actors within and across
industries. The Organization for Economic Cooperation and Development (OECD) has developed indicators of centralization and coordination, and these statistics are a helpful addition to the existing
data on unionization. "Centralization" refers to the level of bargaining (establishment, firm, sectoral, regional, or national), whereas "coordination" denotes the degree of interconnectedness between different collective bargaining units. The indicators (see table 3.4) show
that in the three countries with a small incidence of low pay, centralization and coordination are greater than in the other three countries.[9] Germany has witnessed a decline of both indicators since the
end of the 1990s. Industry-level bargaining is still dominant and coordinated, but only in the core industries.

In summary, in Denmark, the Netherlands, and France, the industrial relations institutions interact in ways that work to increase or at

least sustain collective bargaining coverage, while in the United Kingdom and the United States, coverage depends mainly on one single factor: trade union density. In Germany, a system that historically promoted high levels of collective bargaining coverage has been weakened substantially in recent years.

The Impact of Collective Bargaining on Pay Levels in the Selected Industries

The chapters on the individual sectors consider this issue in some detail. In this section, we confine ourselves to some general illustrative comments since it was not possible to collect comparative data on trade union and employer density and coverage by collective agreements in all the industries and all the countries. The most important single message to emerge is that the impact of national bargaining institutions can vary from sector to sector within any country—even in the most inclusive systems. These variations may derive from the fact that some industries have specific collective agreement and pay-setting practices. Differences in the enforcement of legal or agreed rules, however, are also an important factor in explaining cross-industry diversity—beyond many other potential factors, such as differences in skills, productivity, and product market regulations.

In all the countries of our comparison, the degree of inclusiveness of pay setting in the food-processing industry closely follows the relevant national patterns (see Grunert, James, and Moss, this volume). Union density is low in both the United States and the United Kingdom, and coverage reflects this. By contrast, density is very high in Denmark. Union membership is significantly lower in both France and the Netherlands, but the two countries still manage to be inclusive owing to the legal extension of collective agreements to the whole sector. Union density is low in the German food industry, but there are significant differences in coverage between the subsectors analyzed in this study. In confectionery, a multi-employer national agreement still survives; no such agreement exists in meat processing. These differences within the German food sector are reflected in the different pay and conditions experienced by workers in the two subsectors.

This is not the case in the hotel industry (see Vanselow et al., this volume). Across all six of the national systems, hotel room attendants fare relatively badly. Even in inclusive countries, this industry stands as an exception in many ways. The unionization rate is particularly low in Denmark as compared to the other industries. In France, hotel employers have benefited for a long time from legal dispensations from some Labor Code rules that apply to all other workers, including the statutory national minimum wage. Moreover, in all the countries the problems facing hotel workers provide a striking example of the importance of enforcement at the workplace—even in Denmark, where room attendants, many of them foreign-born women, are often not unionized and often do not know their rights. Even where there is relatively high union density at the sectoral level, unions are generally weak at the level of the individual hotel.

In the case of retailing (see Carré et al., this volume), Germany and the Netherlands have at least as great an incidence of low-paid work as in the United States. In Germany, the high share of low-wage retail workers reflects the decreasing coverage by national agreements. In the Netherlands, extension agreements ensure high coverage, but employers partially evade the consequences of this by employing a high percentage of young workers who receive a special subminimum wage. In Germany, the extensive use of mini-jobbers serves a similar purpose. Youth minimum wages and mini-jobs are examples of the possible exit options for employers, which we discuss in more depth in the following sections. In the Netherlands, weak employee representation at the establishment level gives employers an unusual amount of discretion. In France, unions are very weak in the workplaces, and the statutory minimum wage plays a crucial role as a wage floor. In sharp contrast, union representation is rather strong in Denmark, and even retailers that do not sign the industry collective agreement usually adhere to its conditions.

The hospital sector (see Méhaut et al., this volume) arguably exhibits more diversity across countries than the other sectors studied in this volume. The public and private mix of both the funding and the provision of health care vary significantly across the six countries. Yet the distinction between inclusive and non-inclusive industrial relations systems matches quite well the relative incidence across countries of low pay in this sector. The United Kingdom, however, is an interesting special case: in Britain, sectoral institutional developments "break" the national pattern. Health-sector unions have been able to exert a degree of influence over the government as employer in a way that usually appears to be beyond British unions that deal with private-sector employers. British health-sector unions, for example, have managed to establish a national pay scale for frontline hospital employees, and unions have succeeded in exercising some muscle in changing human resource management practices. So far, these contract victories have not had a signifi ant impact on earnings, but they may be sufficient enough to do so in the future. The hospital sector in Germany may provide a microcosm of developments in other parts of that country's labor market. Collective agreements are becoming fragmented, and outsourcing of cleaning has become more common. The consequence has been some deterioration in the relative pay of the low-end employees.

For call centers (see Lloyd, Weinkopf, and Batt, this volume), a relatively new type of activity, the strength and inclusiveness of collective bargaining institutions reflects the specific arrangements of the industry in which the call center is located—for example, banking in Europe has been relatively well organized. The ability of unions to ensure that employers do not "escape" from existing agreements depends to a great extent on the national regulatory and institutional environment. In France and the Netherlands, industry agreements have been reached with subcontractors. Interestingly, union coverage is relatively low in the call center sector in Denmark, a fact that largely reflects the newness of this particular activity. Nevertheless, the incidence of low pay is low there, since even uncovered employers have little choice but to adhere to agreed wage rates because of the relative power of unions in the country as a whole. These factors lead to a very small number of low-wage workers in France and Denmark. In contrast, in the Netherlands, a low minimum wage for young workers and the low entry-wage levels set by the collective agreements for subcontractors and temporary work agencies have allowed a significant number of low-wage call center workers to emerge. Germany's lack of a minimum wage and the failure to extend collective agreements to new employers, particularly subcontractors, have also led to a high incidence of low pay in call centers. In the United Kingdom and even more in the United States, the coverage rate is very low among subcontractors.

REGULATING LOW WAGES: THE ROLE OF MINIMUM WAGES

Different Institutional Arrangements and Different Policies

The minimum wage takes different forms in the six countries studied.[10] In France and the Netherlands, collective agreements fix minimum-wage levels at the industry level, and these are then usually extended by the government to uncovered workers throughout the industry. These agreements not only set a minimum pay floor but also establish a complete pay scale with different rates for different types of jobs and employee characteristics (mainly skills and seniority) and, in many cases, additional industry-specific premiums and bonuses as well as some fringe benefits. In Germany, in a small number of industries such as construction, cleaning, and postal services, the government declares the minimum wage set in the industry collective agreement as binding within the industry, but generally does not extend other terms of the agreement.[11] In Denmark, the social partners agree on a national minimum-wage floor, which is enforced by unions and employers. Finally, the United Kingdom, the United States, France, and the Netherlands have legislated national minimum wage rates (NMW), often called "statutory" or "legal" minimum wages.[12] In France and the Netherlands, if the minimum pay rate set by the industry collective agreement is lower than the NMW, the latter must apply.[13]

Three characteristics of an NMW play key roles in shaping the wage distribution: its coverage, its level, and its implementation. We may define the legal (or "formal") inclusiveness of an NMW by the extent of its legal coverage. This coverage does not differ much across the four countries in this study with an NMW (see table 3.5), since almost all industries and firms are covered. But there are also some special rates for young workers that constitute legal exit options. In the Netherlands, these youth rates are very low, and in that sense the NMW in that country is less inclusive than it is in France, the United Kingdom, and the United States. However, the gap between formal regulations and reality may be important. Our industry case studies shed some light on the effective (as opposed to the formal) inclusiveness of the NMW. Among the occupations covered, housekeepers in hotels provide the most striking example (see Vanselow et al., this volume). Practices that are more or less illegal are common in all five European countries: undeclared work and target quotas for rooms per day to be cleaned that are not feasible in normal hours (that is, when the monthly wage is divided by the actual number of hours worked, the real hourly rate can be significantly below the legal NMW). Unpaid overtime (which is the most common way of circumventing the legal hourly minimum wage) is also a feature in other sectors in some countries (such as retail in France). Overall,

(*Text continues on p.110.*)

Table 3.5 Minimum-Wage Legislation

Does a legal NMW exist?

Denmark	Germany	France
No, but there is a national wage floor set by a collective agreement between unions and employers.	No, but there is a legal minimum wage in some industries (for example, construction). Collective agreements at the industry level set wage floors in industries with strong unions.	Yes. Introduced in 1950 and reformed in 1970 (with the introduction of the current SMIC), the NMW is indexed to consumer prices and must be raised annually—at least half the increase in the hourly wage rate of all blue-collar jobs. Minimum pay rates are set by industry collective agreements. Most industry agreements are declared generally binding.

Coverage

Denmark	Germany	France
Some firms do not implement the national wage floor, especially in low-wage sectors.	An increasing number of firms are withdrawing from industry collective agreements.	All sectors (except public services) are covered by SMIC. A special rate of 80 percent or 90 percent of NMW for, respectively, sixteen- and seventeen-year-olds can be paid, if

Netherlands	United Kingdom	United States
Yes. Introduced in 1968, the NMW is for adults only (over age twenty-four; later over age twenty-three) and linked to the average growth rate of collectively negotiated wages, but indexation has often been suspended by special legal measures. Since 1992, it can be suspended by the government if the ratio of welfare recipients to employment rises above a threshold level. Minimum pay rates are set by industry collective agreements. Most industry agreements are declared generally binding.	Yes. The NMW was introduced in 1999. The Low Pay Commission (which includes employer and union representatives) makes annual recommendations to the government regarding uprating. There is no automatic indexation. However, between 2000 and 2006, the NMW was uprated above increases in the average earnings index.	Yes. Introduced in 1938, the NMW is not automatically indexed to prices or wages. About thirty states have state minimum wages above the federal NMW.

Netherlands	United Kingdom	United States
All sectors are covered by NMW. Special rates for youth were introduced in 1974, starting at 30 percent of the adult minimum for age fifteen; up to 1993, it was not applicable to jobs	All sectors are covered with separate, lower "development rates" for sixteen- and seventeen-year-olds and for eighteen- and nineteen-year-olds. Enforcement is quite strict, although some	Applies to all firms with more than $500,000 annual business activity and to all employees, with very few exceptions. During the first ninety calendar days of

(*Table continues on p. 108.*)

Table 3.5 (*Continued*)

Coverage (continued)

Denmark	Germany	France
		they have less than six months' tenure. Apprentices and some trainees are not covered.

Percentage of employees at NMW (2005)[a]

Denmark	Germany	France
—	—	16.3%

NMW as a percentage of low-wage threshold (early to mid-2000s)

Denmark	Germany	France
88% (wage floor agreed to by the social partners)	—	95%

Gross (adult) NMW as a percentage of gross average wage (2006)[b]

Denmark	Germany	France
—	—	47%

NMW, at purchasing power parity, net of income tax and employee social contributions, U.S. dollars, 2006

Denmark	Germany	France
—	—	$7.68

Labor cost at NMW as percentage of average labor cost, 2006

Denmark	Germany	France
—	—	39%

Sources: Authors' compilation based on Eurostat (Allen and Regnard 2007); and Immervoll (2007), updated by the author.

[a.] The figures are not directly comparable between the different countries; in France,

Netherlands	United Kingdom	United States
of less than about thirteen hours per week.	agencies that employ migrant labor find ways of evading NMW legislation.	their employment, youths under the age of twenty must be paid no less than $4.25 per hour (the federal minimum wage was $5.85 per hour at the end of 2007). Some state-level minimum wages are above the federal level.

Netherlands	United Kingdom	United States
2.2%	1.8%	1.3%

Netherlands	United Kingdom	United States
84% (adult minimum wage)	79%	54%

Netherlands	United Kingdom	United States
43% (46% for full-time workers age 23 or older)	35%	33%

Netherlands	United Kingdom	United States
$7.05	$7.66	$4.40

Netherlands	United Kingdom	United States
43%	34%	33%

a worker is considered a minimum-wage earner if his or her basic wage (that is, with none of the premiums taken into account) is the minimum wage.
b. For the United States, average wage does not include supervisory and managerial workers. If included, the ratio would be even lower.

there may be a non-negligible number of workers earning less than the NMW, especially in countries where its level is high or enforcement is low.

In the mid-2000s, the level of the NMW differed substantially, both in absolute and relative terms, between France, the Netherlands, the United Kingdom, and the United States. At the beginning of 2007, the monthly purchasing power of an American full-time (adult) minimum-wage earner was notably lower than the purchasing power of his or her European counterpart: about 32 percent lower than in France, 37 percent lower than in the Netherlands, and 40 percent lower than in the United Kingdom (see Regnard 2007).[14] In 2006 in France and the Netherlands, the gross wage of a full-time minimum-wage earner was just under half of that of the average wage of a full-time worker (47 percent and 46 percent, respectively), and only about one-third of what was earned by a full-time minimum-wage earner in the United Kingdom and the United States (35 percent and 34 percent, respectively) (Immervoll 2007).[15] These contrasts are the consequence of very different policies during the past fifteen years or more. The NMW was frozen in nominal terms in the United States between 1996 and 2007, and it increased only a small amount in the Netherlands during the same period. As a consequence, the value of the NMW decreased in those two countries, in both real and relative terms.[16] By contrast, the increase in the NMW has been substantial in France and the United Kingdom (since its introduction in 1999). In France, the NMW (the so-called SMIC) is legally indexed to consumer prices and (partially) to the growth of the hourly wages of blue-collar workers. Thus, even without any specific government intervention, the purchasing power of minimum-wage earners is preserved and even increases over time.[17]

The level of the NMW in relative terms (that is, expressed as a percentage of the average or median wage) determines how hard it "bites." The share of employees receiving the minimum wage is highest in France (see table 3.5).[18] NMW policies may have a direct impact on the global incidence of low-wage work by reducing wage inequality, at least at the bottom of the wage distribution. There is indeed strong evidence that the introduction of an NMW (as in the United Kingdom) or the increases in its relative level (as in both the United Kingdom and France) reduce wage dispersion below the median and below the low-wage threshold.[19] Since the NMW has remained well below the low-wage threshold in the United Kingdom, its impact on the share of low-wage work so far has been limited (Lloyd, Mason, and Mayhew 2008). Its main benefit has been to cut off very low wages and increase wage compression within the low-wage sector. The story is different for France, where the low-wage threshold was only about 5 percent higher than the SMIC in the early 2000s, and where the share of low-wage work has been declining in the past ten years. In sharp contrast, the small increments in the nominal value of the minimum wage in the Netherlands played an important role in the rise in low-wage work there in the 1990s. In the United States, the real and relative decline of the minimum wage may have been a key factor in the increase in inequality in the bottom half of the wage distribution in the 1980s and 1990s (Di Nardo, Fortin, and Lemieux 1997; Manning 2003, ch. 12). Meanwhile, the absence of an NMW in Germany and the high differentiation of the NMW by age in the Netherlands explain the long tail in the income distribution down to very low rates of pay that are effectively cut off by the minimum wages in the United Kingdom and France. Note that collective bargaining and a statutory minimum wage can interact. Within Europe as a whole, there is evidence to suggest that strong collective bargaining institutions tend to push up the level of the statutory minimum wage when there is one (European Commission 2008).

THE IMPACT OF MINIMUM WAGES ON LOW-WAGE WORKERS

There is an extensive literature on the effect of an NMW on employment (see Card and Krueger 1995; Manning 2003; Ragacs 2004; Neumark and Wascher 2006; for the United Kingdom, see Metcalf 2007). One of the lessons of the "new minimum wage research" is that there is no simple relationship between minimum wages and employment. Theoretically, the relationship is indeterminate. Minimum wages may increase efficiency by reducing turnover or improving motivation. They may also increase incentives to work. Where there are monopsonistic labor markets, wages are below the competitive equilibrium. In these circumstances, a minimum wage compensates for the low bargaining power of labor and, by setting a higher wage, may even increase employment (Stigler 1946). For a long time, monopsony was seen as an exceptional situation. Alan Manning (2003, 360) argues, however, that "one should not get hung up on the prefix 'mono': no employer exists in isolation . . . and one should think of a model of oligopsony or 'monopsonistic competition.'" He adds: "There are many frictions in the labour market which give employers the power to set wages like mobility costs or lacks of transparency about labour market opportunities. If the market power of employers is strong then this explains the amazing wage differentials between workers doing equal work like the wage gaps between men and women, small and bigger firms, good or bad employers."[20]

Overall, there seems to be a "range of indeterminacy" (Lester 1964) in which minimum wages can be set without negative employment impacts. Reviews of the empirical research have come to the conclusion that the effect on the employment of adults has been in general negligible in countries where the NMW rate is rather low in relative terms (as in the United States or the United Kingdom). In the case of young people, there have been negative impacts in some cases (OECD 1998, 47; see also Neumark and Wascher 2006). But the negative impact on employment may be more sizable in countries, like France, where the level of the NMW is high compared to the median wage (for comparative evidence on France and the United States, see Abowd et al. 2000).

Potential negative employment impacts of minimum wages might be muted by subsidizing wages—notably through social contributions exemptions, as in France (Caroli and Gautié 2008) or in Germany with mini-jobs, which are exempt from social security contributions and income tax (see Bosch and Kalina 2008a, 48, 52).

Another possible way of muting the employment effects of rising minimum wages would be policies designed to improve productivity—policies such as investment in education and training, active labor market measures, support of lifelong learning, incentives for innovation, and the like.

Denmark, with its high collectively agreed national minimum wage of €12 per hour (about €14 if paid vacations are included), is a good example of such a proactive empowerment strategy (see Gautié et al., this volume). In Denmark, extensive training helps to raise the productivity levels of less-skilled workers to the level required by the minimum wage.[21] Less-skilled workers in Denmark (those with only a lower secondary education) receive more job-related training hours than is the case in any of the other five countries in our study (OECD

2007, table C5[1a]).[22] The highly skilled in Denmark also receive more training than elsewhere, but the gap between the skill levels is still lower in Denmark than in our other countries. Such institutional complementarities may help to explain why the "penniless/jobless" trade-off—depicted by Paul Krugman (1994)—does not necessarily hold in a cross-country comparison. In the mid-2000s, the wage distribution was much more compressed in Denmark than it was in the United States, but the employment rate (including the employment rate for less-educated workers) was nevertheless higher in Denmark than it was in the United States. In the United Kingdom, the evidence concerning the impact of the introduction of the NMW on firm-provided training is more mixed: training decreased in some firms (with a potential negative impact on future wages), while others appeared to react by investing more in their employees.

Aside from the potential negative impact on employment and hours worked, a high minimum wage may involve other costs for low-wage workers—mainly in terms of work intensification, reduced fringe benefits, or "deferred compensation." Research done for the United Kingdom Low Pay Commission indicates that some minimum-wage recipients have had to work harder to "justify" their higher wages, while in some cases other monetary rewards, like bonuses, have been reduced (Denvir and Lucas 2006). A small proportion of affected firms also reduced overtime rates (Low Pay Commission 2007). In addition, some employers reduced fringe benefits in order to compensate for the introduction of the NMW and subsequent increases. In France, the high level of the SMIC may have contributed to flatter wage profiles and, because of the subsidies to social contributions for low wages, to a low-wage trap.[23]

Nevertheless, from a dynamic perspective, an NMW can prevent a "race to the bottom" that might be encouraged by a variety of economic circumstances or institutional changes. The recent experience of Germany—which, despite recent debate (Bosch and Kalina 2008b), still has no NMW—provides a dramatic example here. In some sectors, such as meat processing (see Grunert, James, and Moss, this volume), a growing number of employers have withdrawn from sectoral collective agreements and taken advantage of the very high unemployment levels (partly caused by the low growth following the reunification), as well as the entry (more recently) of central and eastern European countries into the EU, to set very low wages (€4 per hour or even less). As a consequence, local workers are in danger of being undercut by "posted" workers (foreign workers who technically work under the labor law of their country of origin, not of the country where they are actually working) who are earning very low wages (see Grunert, James, and Moss, this volume; Bosch and Weinkopf 2008).[24] In hotels, hospitals (cleaning activities), and call centers, outsourcing to subcontractors has become a particularly intensive practice in Germany, as compared to the other countries, since the arrangement allows employers to escape the collective bargaining institutions. In one of the case study call centers, entry wages were set at €6 per hour for qualified workers. Such practices help to explain the significant increase in the number of low-wage workers in Germany. Overall, an NMW can be an effective counterbalancing factor to the consequences of the decrease in the inclusiveness of collective bargaining.

THE REGULATION OF NONSTANDARD WORK AND EXIT OPTIONS FOR EMPLOYERS

In recent decades, nonstandard forms of work, including part-time, temporary contracts, and temporary agency work, have been growing in most industrialized countries.[25] The likely causes of the rise in these forms of employment are the pay gaps between regular and nonstandard jobs because of different regulations, workers' changing preferences, the integration of women into the labor market, and a growing tendency for young people to mix school and work (see Gautié et al., this volume). Employers may also be consciously employing nonstandard forms of work in order to be able to adjust labor costs more quickly in response to fluctuations in demand without incurring the separation costs implied by strict employment protection legislation, as well as to reduce labor costs by employing cheaper workers.

Nonstandard jobs will be more attractive to employees if these new forms of employment provide the same pay, benefits, and social insurance coverage as standard employment. However, if these types of jobs are less protected, involve lower pay than regular work, and do not eventually lead to more standard employment, then workers will see them as second-best, and employers will view them as another exit option from inclusive labor relations systems (for a wider-ranging analysis, see Bosch 2004).

STRICTNESS OF EMPLOYMENT PROTECTION LEGISLATION FOR REGULAR AND TEMPORARY WORKERS

Since employment protection legislation (EPL) shores up the bargaining power of workers, it can influence wages as well as other dimensions of job quality. National regulations on temporary work not only affect the job security of workers holding these types of contracts but also determine the constraints on employers who would like to use these contracts.

As table 3.6 shows, the extent of EPL varies considerably across the six countries (see also Mason and Salverda, this volume, on job security). The EPL of regular workers is high in France, Germany, and the Netherlands, moderate in Denmark and the United Kingdom, and almost nonexistent in the United States. The differences between countries are even greater when it comes to the regulation of temporary forms of employment. France is clearly an outlier, with restrictions on the use of both fixed-term and agency work contracts that are severe and designed mainly to protect permanent workers by limiting the ability of firms to replace them with temporary workers. But as we see later in the chapter, the existence of many derogatory contracts, as well as enforcement problems, may make the level of effective protection significantly lower than suggested by the indicator, especially for low-wage workers. At the opposite extreme, the restrictions put on the use of temporary workers appear to be very weak in the United Kingdom and the United States. Note that for

Table 3.6 The Strictness of Employment Protection Legislation for Regular and Temporary Employment, 2003

PL Strictness	Denmark	France	Germany	Netherlands	United Kingdom	United States
or regular[a] workers	1.5	2.5	2.7	3.1	1.1	0.2
or temporary[a] workers	1.4	3.6	1.8[b]	1.2	0.4	0.3
rotection gap	−0.1	+1.1	−1.0	−1.9	−0.6	+0.1

ource: Authors' compilation based on OECD (2004).
. Regular means not on a temporary contract.
. This value of the EPL indicator for temporary work in Germany is notably overestimated since 004 (when temporary agency work was deregulated by the Hartz laws). The real value must be earer to 0.9 since then.

Germany the EPL indicator (dating back to 2003) is largely overestimated from the mid-2000s, since with the so-called Hartz reform the employment protection of temporary agency work has been completely deregulated.

If EPL for regular workers is low, then the incentive for organizations to employ temporary workers in order to save on separation costs is also low. There seems to be a positive correlation across countries between the strictness of the EPL concerning regular workers and the overall incidence of temporary employment (OECD 2004). In the early 2000s, the share of temporary employment in total employment was about 10 percent in Denmark, more than 12 percent in France and Germany, and only about 6 percent in the United Kingdom and 4 percent in the United States (see Mason and Salverda, this volume, table 2A.9). Therefore, the gap between the employment protection of permanent workers and nonpermanent workers is an important feature of the inclusiveness of a system. If a significant gap exists, high EPL for permanent workers may increase the dualism of the labor market by contributing to the growth of precarious temporary employment in which workers have little bargaining power and therefore experience a higher incidence of low-wage work.

The Issue of Equal Treatment of Nonstandard Forms of Work

Employers may also benefit from direct cost savings if the regulation of nonstandard work itself offers an exit option by allowing lower wages and benefits and less favorable terms and conditions of employment for workers hired under these arrangements. In the EU member states, firms must comply with European-level legal provisions promoting the "equal treatment" of and nondiscrimination against nonstandard work. Toward the end of the 1990s, the European Union adopted two such directives—the first on part-time work, the second on fixed-term contracts—and they are binding for all member states.[26] Agreement was reached on a third EU directive, on temporary agency work, in June 2008, but it has not yet been implemented in all EU member states.[27] These directives fix minimum requirements—which are below standards that already exist in some member countries such as France and Denmark—but have had an important impact on the legislation of other member states such as the United Kingdom. No specific regulations exist in the United

States concerning equal treatment for nonstandard work—only the general antidiscrimination laws apply. In some sectors, such as retail, part-time work is intensively used as an exit option by employers because its fringe costs are lower.

Table 3.7 provides an overview of the regulation and protection of nonstandard employment in the different countries. In the three countries generally seen as having high levels of EPL (France, Germany, and the Netherlands), the practical impact of EPL in most of the low-wage industries we studied is substantially less than OECD-style indicators might suggest. The regulations provide substantial leeway and even explicit loopholes. In some countries, the same is true of complementary provisions on equal treatment of nonstandard workers: there is a gap between the legal requirements and the day-to-day practices of employers, especially in the low-wage sector.

NATIONAL SPECIFICITIES

Nonstandard employment plays a crucial role in the low end of the French labor market. The "precariousness" issue has been prominent in public debate following the upward trend in the share of temporary forms of employment. Almost 30 percent of all unskilled blue-collar workers are employed on a temporary contract. In theory, these temporary contracts are highly regulated and well protected. In practice, two major caveats apply. First, in addition to the standard forms of the open-ended contract and the temp agency contract, which are relatively well-protected contracts, French law also permits a set of far less protective contracts, including "sporadic" permanent contracts, seasonal contracts, derogatory fixed-term contracts, and special contracts for labor market policy schemes, which provide little legal protection against dismissal or unequal treatment.[28] Employers in the five industries examined in this volume, especially in the food-processing, hospital, and hotel industries, make regular use of these alternative contracts. Second, employers do not always adhere to their legal obligations, especially where unionization rates are low, as in retail and hotels.

In the Netherlands, the gap in EPL between permanent and temporary employment also used to be quite high (although the true degree of formal protection for permanent employees is almost certainly overestimated by the OECD index). In 1998 the temporary work agency licensing system was abolished, and the number of

Table 3.7 Formal Regulation and Protection of Nonstandard Employment

Regulation and protection of part-time workers

Denmark	France	Germany
There are no restrictions on the use of part-time work, but there are incentives encouraging the use of full-time work. The EU Directive on Equal Treatment for Part-Time Workers applies.	There are no restrictions on the use of part-time work. The EU Directive on Equal Treatment for Part-Time Workers applies.	Many part-timers are employed under mini-job status. This applies to jobs paid €400 a month or less; workers do not pay social contributions or income tax and are not entitled to social insurance. Mini-jobbers are supposed to benefit from equal treatment (EU directive applies), but often this is not implemented at the workplace level.

Regulation and protection of temporary agency workers

Denmark	France	Germany
There are no particular restrictions. The EU Directive on Equal Treatment for Fixed-Term Workers applies.	There are major restrictions on the use of agency work. Equal treatment is imposed by the EU, and by law before the EU directive, in terms of pay (except seniority premiums, profit-sharing, and health plans specific to the firm) and other employment and work conditions, but it is not always implemented at the workplace level. There is a "precariousness employment bonus" of 10 percent of the wage.	Since 2004, restrictions on the use of temporary agency work have been abolished. Equal pay is enforced only as required by EU directive and by law, but deviation by collective agreement is possible. In practice, deviations predominate since Christian trade unions concluded agreements with lower pay rates.

Netherlands	United Kingdom	United States
The EU Directive on Equal Treatment for Part-Time Workers applies.	The EU Directive on Equal Treatment for Part-Time Workers applies.	There are no restrictions on the use of part-time work. Firms may legally discriminate against part-time workers with respect to pay and benefits.

Netherlands	United Kingdom	United States
The EU Directive on Equal Treatment for Fixed-Term Workers applies.	Restrictions on the use of agency work are very low. Equal treatment is now imposed by EU directive.	There are very few restrictions on the use of temporary workers. No equal treatment is imposed by law.

(*Table continues on p. 120.*)

Table 3.7 (*Continued*)

Regulation and protection of workers on fixed-term contracts

Denmark	France	Germany
The EU Directive on Equal Treatment for Fixed-Term Workers applies.	The "standard" fixed-term contract is highly regulated and well protected, providing equal treatment beyond the EU directive requirements. A "precariousness premium" (10 percent of the wage) is paid if the fixed-term contract is not transformed into an open-ended contract. There are many derogatory fixed-term contracts, which are less regulated and less protected.	The EU Directive on Equal Treatment for Fixed-Term Workers applies.

Source: Authors' compilation.

agencies increased rapidly. The 1999 Flexibility and Security Act was designed to increase the rights of fixed-term and agency work contracts at the same time as it slightly reduced the protection of permanent workers, but it did not impose full equal treatment. The Netherlands has become the "most temp agency work intensive country in Europe" (see Salverda, van Klaveren, and van der Meer 2008). Moreover, some sectors, such as food processing, make intensive use of foreign temps, mainly from eastern Europe.

As noted earlier, the share of temporary forms of employment is rather low and stable in the United Kingdom as compared to France, Germany, and the Netherlands. The relatively small use of temporary workers in the United Kingdom may be partially explained by the low level of employment protection for regular employment there. Nevertheless, within temporary work, the share of agency workers has increased substantially, while the proportion of workers em-

Netherlands	United Kingdom	United States
The EU Directive on Equal Treatment for Fixed-Term Workers applies.	The EU Directive on Equal Treatment for Fixed-Term Workers applies.	Very little restriction on the use of temporary workers. No equal treatment imposed by law.

ployed on fixed-term contracts, on a casual basis, or in seasonal work has gradually declined in the past decade. There is a clear "cost-saving" motive here. The status of agency work is particularly vulnerable in the United Kingdom, since there is no formal contract either with the agency or with the client organization. Agency workers do not usually benefit from pay parity and are not entitled to the full range of employment rights, including unfair dismissal protection, sick pay, and pension schemes provided by the firm. As in the Netherlands, some sectors, like food processing, have increasingly used foreign temps in the recent years. As for fixed-term workers and part-time workers, the United Kingdom had to change (with some delays) its national legislation in order to implement the EU directives. The new directive on temporary agency work will also require changes in legislation.

Germany allows important exceptions from equal pay for nonregular work. These exceptions may help to explain the high incidence of low pay, despite relatively high levels of coverage by collective agreements. The combination of high coverage and low inclusiveness warrants more detailed explanation. The ability of employers to avoid coverage by collective agreements has been substantially increased by the use of new partially regulated or almost entirely unregulated forms of work (mini-jobs, agency work, posted workers) or by outsourcing work to noncovered small and medium enterprises (SMEs) in the same or other industries. Most restrictions on the use of agency work were abolished by the Hartz laws in 2004. After this deregulation, the amount of temporary agency work grew dramatically—from about 300,000 jobs in 2003 to 850,000 in June 2008. Although the law still requires equal pay for agency workers, firms can sidestep this requirement through the use of collective agreements. Employers have exploited this loophole by reaching agreements with the Christian trade unions—employer-friendly unions which generally do not have members in the affected firms—to fix wage rates at between €5 and €7 per hour. Another striking illustration of the "protection gap" is provided by the case of mini-job positions in which the top earnings are limited to €400 per month. Mini-jobbers do not pay social contributions or income tax and are not covered by social insurance; instead, employers pay a flat-rate tax. Mini-jobbers are legally (or via collective agreements) entitled to equal treatment in terms of hourly wages, working time, holidays, sick pay, and other employment rights (and notably protection against dismissal), but in practice these rights are generally not protected. The number of mini-jobbers has increased dramatically in recent years: by the mid-2000s, mini-jobs made up about 15 percent of total employment and an even larger proportion in some low-wage sectors (25 percent in retail and 36 percent in hotels and restaurants).

Although EPL is low in Denmark, the country ranks high in terms of workers' perceptions of job security (OECD 2004). EPL probably has no significant impact on low-wage employers or workers. Several Danish policies that focus on "employment security" or "income security" in general rather than on "job security" with a particular employer may foster employer flexibility and worker mobility between jobs in a context where displaced workers receive fairly generous unemployment benefits. As a result, the Danish system offers a form of "protected mobility" to dismissed workers (the so-called flexicurity model), with generous income replacement payments providing workers with an alternative source of "bargaining power" (see also Gautié et al., this volume).[29] Overall, Denmark may be the country where the dualism between a well-protected segment and a much less protected segment is the least significant among the countries in our study.

This dualism also appears to be weak in the United States, though for very different reasons. EPL covering both permanent and nonpermanent work is low, and in contrast to Denmark, there are few other collective sources of bargaining power to compensate for the lack of job security. Except for workers in unions (about 13 percent of the workforce and less than 8 percent in the private sector) and usually well-paid professionals, who sometimes have individual employment contracts, the vast majority of workers, including probably almost all the low-waged, are employees "at will" with no legal guarantees of job security. "Equal treatment" relies mainly on a combination of federal, state, and local laws that prevent employers from discriminating in hiring, firing, promotion, pay, and in other ways based on race or ethnicity, gender, religion, national origin, or other worker characteristics, including, in some areas and contexts, sexual orientation. The United States has a limited requirement, in a restricted set of contexts, for advance notification of large-scale layoffs, but these notifications generally affect large manufacturing employers in well-paying industries.

PRODUCT MARKET REGULATION AND PAY SETTING

Labor standards often depend not only on employment regulations but also on the structure of product markets and their regulation. In public enterprises, unions often have an easier time organizing workers and negotiating collective agreements since governments are more open to unions and collective bargaining than are private employers. Often public enterprises were monopolies and price-setters, which allowed them to pay high wages and provide good working conditions. In addition, tariffs, conduct regulations, including restriction on prices and requirements to respect agreed wages (such as prevailing wage laws), and market entry regulations often created a supportive environment for collective bargaining and labor market regulation.

In the literature on institutional change, globalization is often regarded as a major driver of change in national models of employment (Streeck and Thelen 2005) and as a source of danger for labor standards. Globalization, however, affects national product and labor markets only if these markets are opened up without parallel protection of labor standards. The deregulation of product markets through free trade agreements or privatization and the opening of labor markets to immigration are important here.

THE FORMS AND INTENSITY OF DEREGULATION

Over the last two decades, many product market regulations have been weakened or abolished. This deregulation has sometimes been determined at the national level and sometimes at the supranational level by international agreements, such as those concluded in the World Trade Organization (WTO). Indeed, it is not too fanciful to describe product market deregulation as organized globalization via (self)-transformation of the national states. Deregulation of product markets has been a major preoccupation of the EU, with the aim of creating a single, competitive European market. The EU member states agreed to deregulate important industries like gas, electricity, water, communications (post and telephone), and transport. In most countries, public enterprises had dominated these industries. Because of EU directives, the member states were obliged to open entry to new competitors. In most cases, EU member states also privatized public firms or are planning to do so. In theory, the European market for the provision of services has been open for a long time. However, the possibilities were only rarely exploited before the early 1990s. Since then, and particularly since the 2004 entry of new central and eastern European member states, competition has become more and more common. The most recent initiative is the so-called Services Directive, or Directive on Internal Services of 2006. Since many service markets are highly regulated by licensing and other standards, the European Commission proposed in its first drafts of this directive to apply the principle of origin to all services with some exceptions—lawyers of course (who drafted the directive), but also the health sector.

There are tensions between product market deregulation and labor standards. In some cases, reregulation has taken place or agreement has been reached on provisions to support labor standards:

Table 3.8 Overall Indicator of Product Market Regulation for Six Countries, 1998 and 2003 (6 = High, 0 = Low)

	1998	2003
United States	1.3	1.0
United Kingdom	1.1	0.9
Denmark	1.5	1.0
Germany	1.9	1.4
Netherlands	1.8	1.4
France	2.5	1.7

Source: Authors' compilation based on Conway, Janod, and Nicoletti (2005, 59).

- *Posted Workers Directive:* Since services could be offered in other countries with the working conditions of the home country, this made it possible for foreign competitors to undercut terms and conditions. The Posted Workers Directive of 1996, however, allowed national governments to set minimum standards or to extend collective agreements such that national and foreign competitors would offer the same pay and benefits.

- *Services Directive:* Because of substantial opposition in many EU countries, the principle of country of origin for labor standards has been removed from the Directive on Internal Services of 2006, which means that it is now left to the states to require that local rates are applied.

- *Privatization:* In some countries, regulatory authorities have been established that have some power to enforce labor standards. In the German postal industry, new competitors have to be licensed, and the regulatory authority can require that they pay prevailing wages.[30]

The OECD has developed a wide range of indicators monitoring changes in product market regulations.[31] The results show that, over recent years, product markets have been deregulated substantially in the six countries in our study (see table 3.8; Conway and Nicoletti 2006, 42). In 2003 the United Kingdom had the least-regulated product markets, followed by the United States and Denmark, Germany, and the Netherlands, with France some distance behind (Conway and Nicoletti 2006, 47).[32]

THE IMPACT ON WORKERS

The key question is this: how have these changes in product market regulation affected labor standards? (See table 3.9.) In short, the impact has varied across the countries and has been filtered by the national institutions regulating the labor market. In the United States, the United Kingdom, and Germany, product market deregulation (broadly defined to include changes in trade and migrant worker policies) has been a major factor in bringing wages back into competition and increasing the incidence of low pay. In the United Kingdom, such forces were aided and abetted by industrial relations legislation (which made it more difficult for unions to organize and to pursue industrial action) and by widespread privatization in the 1980s and early 1990s. In the United States, deregulation of the trucking industry was a major reason for the breakup of employers' organizations and the collapse of one of the few multi-employer agreements—the National Master Freight Agreement—and substantial wage cuts in this industry (Belzer 2000, 110). The abolition of

Table 3.9 Product Market Deregulation and Labor Standards

United States	Fragmentation or disappearance of collective bargaining in deregulated industries. Lower threshold (minimum wage).
United Kingdom	Disappearance of industrywide bargaining in affected industries. Fragmentation or disappearance of collective bargaining in deregulated industries. Since 1999, lower threshold (legal minimum wage).
Germany	Threat to, fragmentation of, or disappearance of industrywide bargaining. No lower threshold. High percentages of low wages in newly privatized industries (postal services, etc.).
France	Low impact because of extension of industrywide collective agreements and legal minimum wage.
Denmark	Low impact because of high trade union density and high coverage by collective agreements and the national minimum wage set by the social partners.
Netherlands	Low impact because of extension of industrywide collective agreements and legal minimum wage.

Source: Authors' compilation.

Table 3.10 Freedom to Provide Services and Its Potential
             Impact on Labor Standards in the EU

United States	Does not apply.
United Kingdom	Minimum wage has to be paid to posted workers.
Germany	Legally binding minimum wages were introduced following the Posted Workers Directive in only a few industries (construction, cleaning, postal services). In some other industries since 2004, with the entry of the new EU member states, there has been substantial undercutting of local rates, especially in the food industry. Germany is a major target country for foreign providers since it does not have a statutory legal minimum wage.
France	Social dumping based on posted workers is limited by the legal extension of industrywide collective agreements and a statutory national minimum wage. There have probably been some problems with enforcement in some industries.
Denmark	Social dumping based on posted workers has been limited so far owing to high trade union density and high coverage by collective agreements.
Netherlands	Social dumping based on posted workers is limited by the legal extension of industrywide collective agreements and a statutory national minimum wage.

Source: Authors' compilation.

prevailing wage laws in the construction industry in many U.S. states had a similar effect on multi-employer bargaining and pay levels (Philips 2003).[33] In Denmark, the Netherlands, and France, deregulation of product markets has had less impact on wages and benefits since deregulation did not allow downward pressure on employment practices in affected firms and industries.

More or less the same principles apply to the opening up of European markets for services from other countries—posting is a form of temporary migration and influences labor supply (see also Gautié et al., this volume). Posted workers are officially employed by a foreign firm that delivers a service to a domestic client firm. The pressure on domestic wages depends heavily on the labor market regulations in the client firm's country (see table 3.10). The downward pressure is greater in countries, such as Germany, where there is neither a statutory national minimum wage nor legal extensions of collective agreements. For instance, posted workers are found in the German meat-processing industry, where they can be paid as low as €3 to €5 an hour.

Product market regulations do still play an important role in some of the industries under study here. Health and security requirements have been increasing in recent years in food processing, with some noticeable impact on work organization. The health sector is highly regulated in all the countries, but with national specificities—concerning, for instance, the share and role of nonprofit hospitals. Barriers to entry—based on urban land-use regulations—in French food retailing provide an important explanation for the relatively low number of employees in this sector (compared to the other countries), with some consequences in terms of high productivity and high work intensity (see Carré et al., this volume; Caroli and Gautié 2008, ch. 6). Conversely, deregulation played an important role in some industries. The deregulation of the financial sector and utilities was one of the driving factors behind the development of the call center sector. In Germany, the abolishment of the "master prerequisite" in the cleaning industry in 2004 induced a fierce competition that led to decreasing wages, work intensification, and an increase in the outsourcing of cleaning activities in hotels.[34]

PAY SETTING AT THE FIRM LEVEL

Pay setting in the firm is partly influenced by institutions outside the firm, including industrywide collective bargaining and minimum wages. Firms themselves are also institutions and differ as much as the external institutions that influence pay and working conditions. To varying degrees, governments require that firms pay, in addition to hourly gross wages, "social wages" (health insurance, paid leave, and pensions, for example) and that they implement regulations on working conditions, including equal treatment and health and safety standards. In addition, employee bargaining power is likely to be higher wherever workers have strong representation at the plant or firm level; strong representation is also crucial for the implementation of external and internal regulations. Virtuous circles between institutions inside and outside the firm might be mutually reinforcing and lead firms to follow high-road labor market strategies, including higher pay.

FROM DIRECT WAGE TO THE "SOCIAL WAGE"

Beyond direct compensation, workers may receive other benefits, such as paid vacations, paid public holidays, health insurance, paid sick days, pensions, and other forms of compensation (for a global overview, see Mason and Salverda, this volume). In the United States, many of these benefits are paid for privately, entirely at the discretion of employers, though private-sector workers are eligible, for example, for Social Security pension benefits as a result of their payroll tax contributions.

All European welfare states require firms to continue to pay their employees when they are sick. The cost of sick pay is often shared between firms and the state. In addition, in all European countries employment is directly linked with mandatory health, old age, unemployment, and accident insurance, to which both employees and employers make contributions. In some EU countries, some welfare entitlements are financed by the state (mainly in Denmark), and in some cases, such as the National Health Service in the United Kingdom, entitlements are linked with citizenship (or residence) status, not employment. These rights are mandatory and cannot be denied to the low-paid, which means that alongside the minimum hourly wage, there is also a "minimum social wage" that is often sizable.

In the United States, a considerable proportion of *average* labor costs (about 37 percent in 2000) are nonwage costs (EBRI 2006), though these are substantially lower for low-wage workers, who generally have lower levels of nonwage benefits such as health care and paid time off. This overall U.S. share is not far below the 43.3 percent nonwage costs in Germany or the approximately 45 percent rate for France, but many social benefits (holiday and sick pay, for instance) are not legally regulated in the United States. This allows employers to pay low-wage workers social wages below the average. The National Compensation Survey, for example, shows that low-paid and part-time workers are frequently excluded from nonwage benefits. Only 76 percent of employees in the United States receive paid holidays, and only 57 percent receive sick pay. Among employees earning less than $15 per hour, these percentages are even lower, at 67 percent and 46 percent, respectively. The figures for part-timers are 37 percent and 22 percent (U.S. Department of Labor 2006).

Thus, for the low-paid, the differences in social wages between the United States, on the one hand, and the five European countries, on the other, are significantly larger than the differences for private wages alone. If the low-wage threshold used in this volume had been computed on the basis of social rather than private wages, the proportion of low-wage workers would almost certainly be even higher than 25 percent in the United States, and the gap with the European countries would be wider.

If, as in Europe, the government sets a minimum social wage, all firms are generally obligated to pay it. By contrast, many U.S. employers, operating in highly competitive and price-sensitive markets, see little possibility of paying nonwage benefits above the minimum wage since their competitors are not likely to follow suit.

EMPLOYEE REPRESENTATION AND VOICE AT THE FIRM LEVEL

A high incidence of low-wage work reflects the low individual bargaining power of workers and often poor enforcement of existing laws and collective agreements. Collective-voice representatives, such as shop stewards or works councilors, are important for enforcement. Table 3.11 gives an overview of the regulation of workplace representation and figures 3.2 and 3.3 show the actual represenation at plant level. In the United States, low union density means that only about 13 percent of the workforce can rely on shop stewards for enforcement of contract terms and applicable labor law. Some non-union companies have established systems of employee representation, but these systems rest heavily on the goodwill of the employer. In Europe, various forms of employee representation exist, and the European Commission has set some rules that apply to all the members of the EU. The European Works Council Directive of 1994 obliges companies with 1,000 or more workers and at least 150 employees in at least two EU member states to establish European Works Councils (EWCs). Workers' representatives from all the member states in which the company operates meet with management, receive information, and give their views on current strategic decisions.[35] With its Directive 2002/14, the European Union generalized the obligation to inform and consult employees at the national level as well (European Commission 2006, 59). The directive affected only countries in which no general statutory legal systems existed, like the United Kingdom and Denmark.[36] In the United Kingdom, there is a somewhat greater presence of shop stewards and other union repre-

Figure 3.2 Trade Union or Similar Presence at the Workplace

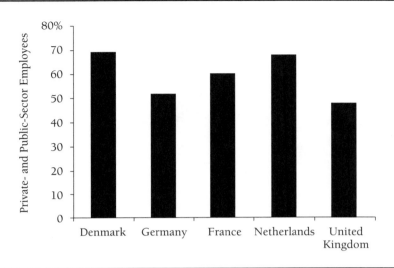

Source: Authors' compilation based on European Commission (2006, 71), which uses data from the 2002–2003 European Social Survey.

Figure 3.3 Workplace Representation by Sector and Country

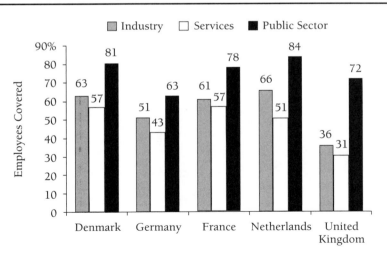

Source: Authors' compilation based on European Commission (2006, 72), which uses data from the 2002–2003 European Social Survey.

Table 3.11 Workplace Representation

	Workplace Representation	Scope of Participation of Workplace Representation	Representation at Firm Level
United States	Shop stewards—contractual rights.	Low	No representation.
United Kingdom	Shop stewards—contractual rights. New law: employee representation can also be non-union.	Low (mainly information and consultation)	No employee representation on the company board.
Germany	Works councils—strong rights in enforcing labor laws, collective agreements, and rights of co-determination. Shop stewards in big companies.	High (information, consultation, and codetermination)	In firms with 500 or more employees, employees elect one-third of supervisory board members; in companies with 2,000 or more employees, employees elect half of the board members.
France	Employee delegates (legally required in all firms with more than 10 employees) and works councils (legally required in all firms with more than fifty) who have information and consultation rights. Trade union delegates, but unions often weak and divided at firm level.	Medium (mainly information and consultation, some co-determination)	In private companies, up to one-third of board members can be elected by employees, but there is no legal obligation to do so. In privatized and public companies, employee representation on the board is legally required.
Netherlands	Works councils—strong rights in enforcing labor laws and collective agreements.	Medium (mainly information and consultation, some co determination)	Works council nominates board members (up to one-third). Very low threshold (companies with 100 or more employees and a turnover of €13 million or more)
Denmark	Shop stewards with strong rights.	High (information, consultation, and codetermination)	Employees elect one-third of board members in companies with more than 35 employees

Sources: Authors' compilation based on European Commission (2004, 2006); for employee representation on boards in Europe, database of Hans-Böckler Foundation, available at: http://www.boeckler.boxen.de/cps/rde/xchg/boxen/hs.xsl/2444.htm.

sentatives than in the United States (for example, for lifelong learning and for health and safety), but the power of such representatives is weak, and they are particularly sparse in the sectors covered in this book.

The dominant form of employee representation in Germany is the powerful works councilor. Works councilors are elected by all employees, not only by trade union members, and have strong rights of codetermination. In addition, employees are represented on the boards of medium-sized and large companies and have strong information and decision rights. Board representation is legally required, but works councils do not necessarily have to be established.[37] The German system of codetermination is strongly developed in medium-sized and larger companies but less so in smaller ones with high concentrations of low-wage workers. The increase in low-wage work in Germany was linked with a changing balance of workplaces from bigger to smaller establishments, reflecting mainly outsourcing and agency work. Despite strong works councilors in larger establishments, most low-wage workers do not have a collective voice at the workplace, and laws and collective agreements are often not enforced. Because of the greater presence of labor regulations in Germany as compared to the United States and the United Kingdom, non-enforcement makes a greater relative difference.

France has a dual system of workplace representation with works councilors and employee and trade union delegates. The rights of the two legal bodies, however, are low compared to Germany. Since unions are weak and often divided at the shop-floor level, reflecting low density and ideological divergences, there are problems, at least in small and medium-sized companies, with enforcement of regulations (Caroli and Gautié 2008). Representation at the board level is not required in private companies but is common in both public and privatized companies.

The Netherlands has works councilors, but with fewer codetermination rights than is the case in Germany (see table 3.11). Since the coverage of collective agreements, including small and medium-sized companies, is much higher than in Germany, there is less incentive for companies to relocate jobs to workplaces without works councilors. In addition, the threshold for board representation is much lower than in Germany, and this gives employees a stronger influence in medium-sized and smaller companies. There may also be a "small country" effect. Since most competitors know each other, free-rider strategies are less widespread than in the bigger, more anonymous German economy. There are indications, however, that works councilors are not adequately representing low-wage workers (Salverda, van Klaveren, and van der Meer 2008, 189).

Finally, in Denmark trade union representatives cover most companies in all industries and are major enforcers of collective agreements. In addition, trade union representation on the boards of even small companies helps to enforce labor standards across the economy (Westergaard-Nielsen 2008).

Overall, data from the European Social Survey on rates of workplace representation show higher rates of workplace representation for those countries with a smaller incidence of low pay (see figures 3.2 and 3.3). The differences are even more pronounced when the public sector is excluded.

CONCLUSIONS: INCLUSIVE VERSUS EXCLUSIVE PAY-SETTING INSTITUTIONS

This chapter has explored the influence of pay-setting institutions (broadly defined) on the incidence of low pay in the six countries represented in this study, both in their national economies and in the case study sectors. The distinction between the inclusiveness and exclusiveness of pay-setting institutions is of critical importance, particularly for the labor market fortunes of workers with little collective or individual bargaining power.

In the two "liberal market" economies (in the formulation of Hall and Soskice 2001), the United Kingdom and the United States, the pay-setting regime is less inclusive. Collective bargaining power is weak and does not extend much beyond union members. The national minimum wage is low relative to the average wage. Job security is also low. As a result, workers do well or badly primarily depending on their individual bargaining power, which almost by definition is slight for those occupying the lower reaches of the labor market. A critical difference between the United Kingdom and the United States is the impact of the state on the social wage. Low-paid workers in the United Kingdom can count on better benefits and working conditions than those available to their low-wage counterparts in the United States—paid holidays, paid sick days, paid parental leave, and health care, for example. Indeed, more than any other factor, the lack of a social wage separates the American low-paid from their counterparts in all of the other countries in this study. Furthermore, EU directives on equal pay have improved the position of fixed-term and part-time workers in the European Union and may do the same eventually for temporary agency workers.

In the "coordinated market economies"—Denmark, France, Germany, and the Netherlands—the role of institutions in determining wages is stronger.[38] However, the institutions and their interactions still differ substantially between these countries. All four countries have collective bargaining systems that are more inclusive than in the United States or the United Kingdom. A significantly larger percentage of workers are covered by collective bargaining agreements, this coverage being achieved in a variety of ways. In Denmark, high coverage simply reflects high union density. In France and the Netherlands, coverage is extended because of the importance of employers' organizations and the legal extension of collective agreements. A statutory national minimum wage also plays an important role—especially in France, where, without the SMIC, collective bargaining institutions would not have been sufficient to contain the incidence of low-paid work. In the Netherlands and France, the role of the state in the regulation of the low end of the labor market is more central than in Denmark. Germany, one of the prototypes of coordinated economies, still has high union coverage. Historically, Germany achieved high coverage rates through sector-level agreements combined with high levels of participation in employers' organizations. In recent years, however, coverage has declined as industrywide agreements have diminished in significance and employer density has declined. Unless the state intervenes to plug gaps in coverage and inclusiveness, the incidence of low pay is likely to increase; indeed, this is what has happened in Germany.

Product market, employment protection, and social security policies can shore up collective as well as individual bargaining power, but the case studies and the national-level evidence show that these same features of labor markets and social policy can also reduce inclusiveness and increase labor market dualism if some categories of employees are not covered. France provides a striking example of this in its treatment of some of its nonstandard workers. So does Germany in the case of agency workers, posted workers, and mini-jobbers. These nonstandard work arrangements, together with the outsourcing of jobs to companies not covered by collective agreements, offer many exit options for employers.

Inclusiveness also depends on the effective enforcement of collective bargaining agreements and national labor laws and regulations at the level of the individual company (Bernhardt, McGrath, and DeFilippis 2007). Here again we see considerable differences between countries. Germany is an example of a dual structure of enforcement (strong in big and medium-sized companies, which have robust works councils, and weak in small companies without works councils). Meanwhile, Denmark, the Netherlands, and, to a lesser extent, France have more comprehensive and less exclusive mechanisms of enforcement.

The fairly stable incidence of low pay in Denmark and France can be explained by the stability of their industrial relations architectures and underlying political coalitions. These two countries managed to keep the share of low-wage workers stable despite structural change and an increase in the number of more vulnerable service jobs. The increase of low pay in the Netherlands was mainly negotiated within an institutional setting that was also fairly stable.[39] Collective bargaining in the United States, the United Kingdom, and Germany is in transformation. Falling union density in the United States and the United Kingdom has led to further "exhaustion" of the already weak collective bargaining system. Although the German coverage of collective bargaining is still much higher than in the United States or the United Kingdom, Germany is losing ground because of the decline of industrywide agreements and the creation of new exit options for employers; the country appears to be drifting toward the liberal model. Because of the absence of increases in the federal minimum wage in recent years, the United States also provides an example of the deliberate neglect of institutional maintenance (Streeck and Thelen 2005). In sharp contrast, the introduction of the national minimum wage in the United Kingdom and its gradual increase provides an example of the successful revitalization of instruments for low-pay protection that had been removed by the Thatcher government.

In Germany, some exit options already existed before the rise in low-wage work in the 1990s, but they were used relatively infrequently. In some countries, such as France, legal exit options are more limited, but there are problems of enforcement. Within a given set of institutions, there always exists a margin of discretion that can be used for good or ill. Especially at the bottom of the labor market, a strong employee voice is necessary at the establishment level for the enforcement of collective agreements, minimum wages, and other employment protection regulation. Even when two countries have apparently equally strong wage-setting systems at the aggregate level, enforcement might differ substantially. Virtuous circles between institutions inside and outside the firm might mutually support each other and lead firms to follow high-road product and human resource management (HRM) strategies based on higher pay.

Such virtuous circles function only on the basis of a common understanding of their mission. Thus, for example, the equity norms shared by all the actors may emerge, which can then be used to settle distributional issues. Such mutually shared norms or beliefs of the main actors give specific institutional settings their stability. They have to be reaffirmed regularly to be kept alive and transmitted to new generations of actors. Pay-setting institutions not only embody social values but are reflective of historical compromises between different actors that might be subject to change. "Institutions frequently outlive their founding coalitions, and their endurance and robustness often involves a reconfiguration of their coalitional base in light of shifting social, political and market conditions" (Thelen 2004, 33). The result might be changes of institutions, but it is also possible for different strategies and outcomes to issue from the existing institutional setting. Changes in behaviors within a given set of institutions may in some cases be as important as changes in the institutions themselves.

Minimum wages—and even more so, minimum-wage policies that reflect social and political commitments to equality and solidarity—have played contrasting roles among the countries in our study. The potential negative impact of the relatively high minimum wages or high collectively agreed minimum rates in Europe—especially in Denmark—compared to the United States seems to have been successfully counteracted by linkages with institutions that provide high levels of productivity, such as more intensive training for the less-skilled. The impact of such institutional linkages needs to be further studied in order to avoid simplistic conclusions about the effect of minimum wages. Our country studies suggest no obvious causal relationships between wages and employment, while the link between the two variables seems to differ from country to country because of the diverging institutional architecture.

Whatever mix of institutions determines the extent of inclusiveness in any individual country, collective bargaining at a level above that of the company or organization is a common feature of inclusive systems. In achieving inclusiveness, the government cannot replace the social partners, but it must play a role if the incidence of low pay is to be small, a decent social wage is to be paid, and the consequences of low pay for the current living standards and prospects of its recipients are to be mitigated.

NOTES

1. Civil servants, for instance, benefit from a collective status.
2. Furthermore, in France, in spite of very low density, unions have considerable bargaining power since, at least in the public services, they can mobilize workers for industrial action.
3. Employer density can be defined as the share of employers who are members of an employers' organization.
4. In addition, inclusiveness within industries has been weakened by outsourcing to uncovered small and medium enterprises (SMEs) and by lower pay for certain types of work ("mini-jobs" and agency work). The state hesitates to interfere partly because Germany lacks a tradition of such intervention and partly because many political actors have welcomed the diminishing bargaining power of unions and the increase in low-wage work.
5. As a consequence, unions in the highly productive industries, such as manufacturing, have not pressed for wage increases that fully correspond to the growth of their productivity. Instead, the gains from productivity growth were relatively equally distributed across the economy. Therefore, in Denmark workers receive decent pay in industries that are typically low-wage in most other countries.
6. Overall, collective bargaining in Denmark is a powerful instrument for preventative intervention in the national earnings distribution, which eases the redistributive burden imposed on the welfare state. This preventative intervention not only supports the citizen status even of low-wage earners—who, like all workers, are taxpayers—but ensures that all workers, not just low-wage workers, are recipients of universal welfare transfers like child allowances.
7. In Germany and the Netherlands, the major coordination mechanism between industries (and regions in Germany) was provided by pattern agreements. The pace was set mainly by the metal industries agreement, and most other industries followed. The amount of low-wage work in Germany increased when the metal industries agreement became significantly less important in setting such a pattern because more and more employers' organizations refused to follow it and an increasing proportion of employees were not covered by any agreement at all.

8. Until the 1980s, many U.S. manufacturing companies followed the agreements of the Big Three (General Motors, Ford, and Chrysler) in the automobile industry. Today there is no pattern agreement left even within that industry—the Big Three have become relatively smaller and are under extremely high competitive pressures from other companies that are not covered by an agreement (Levy and Temin 2007).

9. Reflecting research carried out in connection with this project, in the case of France we have corrected the values of both the OECD centralization and coordination indicators. In France, industrywide collective bargaining is predominant, and there are also tripartite national agreements, which points to a value of 3.5 instead of 2 for all three periods, while the high level of industry bargaining and its extension by the state points to a value of 3.5 instead of 2 for coordination. Germany had high values on both indicators in the earlier years. Currently Germany is still in transition to a less regulated economy, since industry-level bargaining is still dominant and also coordinated, but only within the core industries. One sign of declining coordination is the divergence of wage movements across industries in Germany. A recent analysis of increases in real gross monthly wages in Germany showed that industries with a low-wage share below 50 percent of the average enjoyed wage increases of 12.6 percent between 1998 and 2005, compared with 6.3 percent in the rest of the economy (Bosch and Kalina 2008a).

10. At the time of writing, Germany was having a serious debate about the introduction of industry and national minimum wages (Bosch and Kalina 2008b).

11. These agreements may set different rates for different groups of workers—for example, for unskilled and skilled construction workers.

12. In recent years, the United States has also seen state-level minimum wages rise to levels that are higher than the federal minimum wage, but still low relative to the minimum-wage rates in the other five countries.

13. In France in 2005, in more than 50 percent of the industry collective agreements, the minimum pay rate was below the NMW and therefore not implemented (see Gautié 2008).

14. Monthly purchasing power is based on the monthly value of NMWs converted into dollars at the purchasing power parity (PPP) rate. Table 3.5 provides an estimate of the purchasing power of the *hourly net* (after-tax) NMW in 2006 (Immervoll 2007, updated). The gap between the United States and the three European countries is even wider.

15. The figure for the Netherlands, 46 percent, refers to employees who were age twenty-three or older and working full-time.

16. Another consequence of the long-term stagnation of the real value of the federal minimum wage has been the rise of state-level minimum wages (see Dube, Lester, and Reich 2007) and more locally oriented "living-wage campaigns" (see Pollin and Luce 1998).

17. Moreover, over the last thirty years—and notably since the end of the 1990s—French governments have increased the SMIC beyond these legal requirements. The hourly SMIC increased by 33.4 percent between 1999 and 2006 (19 percent in real terms). This resulted partly from the implementation of the law on the reduction of weekly working time (the so-called thirty-five hours law), when the government chose to maintain the monthly earnings of minimum-wage earners. In the United Kingdom, the NMW rose by 48.6 percent during the same period.

18. The figure for France is not directly comparable to the figures for other countries. It covers all those workers whose basic wage (that is, without taking into account any bonus or premiums, such as those for seniority) is the SMIC. But the total hourly compensation of many SMIC earners is much higher than the hourly SMIC: in 2002, for instance, 26 percent of SMIC earners had an effective total hourly compensation that was 30 percent higher than the SMIC (see Gautié 2008).

19. In the United Kingdom, the NMW has cut the gap between the fiftieth and the tenth percentiles of the wage distribution by five percentage points (Metcalf 2007). In the English care home workers sector, for instance, the introduction of the NMW caused significant compression at the lower end of the wage distribution (Machin, Manning, and Rahman 2003).

20. The idea that the monopsony power of employers may be widespread in advanced economies is also put forward by Christopher Erickson and Daniel Mitchell (2007, 163). They see "monopsony as a metaphor for the emerging post-union labor market." They argue that the employee voice needs to be restored to counter the undesirable consequences, such as wage inequality and reduced worker rights, associated with strong macroeconomic performance. Concerning the gender dimension, Jared Bernstein, Heidi Hartmann, and John Schmitt (1999) emphasize how much, in the United States, the national minimum wage is a working "woman's issue."

21. Taking initial education and training into account provides a more complete picture. Germany, for example, has much higher levels of initial vocational training than all the other countries, which partially compensate for this by investing in further training (Bosch and Charest 2009).

22. In Denmark, the training and education of adults is mostly financed by either enterprises or the state (Lassen et al. 2006).

23. There is also some evidence that the significant decrease in wage mobility at the bottom of the wage distribution during the 1970s was correlated with the large increase of the SMIC during this period (Gautié 2008).

24. On posted workers, see the discussion later in the chapter on product market deregulation.

25. By nonstandard work we mean work that deviates from a standard full-time, implicitly permanent job.

26. The EU Directive on Equal Treatment for Part-Time Workers (1997) requires equal hourly pay (including overtime pay), pro-rata entitlement to sick pay and maternity pay, equal treatment for holidays, maternity leave, parental leave, career breaks, redundancy provisions, pension schemes, and training. The EU Directive on Fixed-Term Workers (1999) stipulates that fixed-term workers should not be treated less favorably than equivalent permanent workers and that employers should be prohibited from abusing this form of employment by concluding a succession of such contracts without justification.

27. The 2008 Temporary Agency Work Directive stipulates that the basic working conditions of temporary agency workers should be at least as favorable as those that would apply if they had been recruited directly by the employer to occupy the same job. Exemptions are possible after consultation with the social partners or by collective agreements.

28. Derogatory fixed-term contracts are special fixed-term contracts that can be used on a permanent basis ("contrats à durée determinée d'usage")—that is, without complying with the rules governing duration and renewal that apply to the standard form of fixed-term contracts.

29. Generous unemployment compensation (particularly at low-wage levels) effectively subsidizes temporary layoffs by employers and increases the apparent fluidity of the labor market.

30. This requirement, however, has not been enforced. Therefore, a minimum wage was agreed upon in 2007. This industry-specific minimum wage has been extended by a decree of the Labor Ministry.

31. The summary indicator ("economy-wide product market indicator") is based on seventeen indicators summarizing information on 156 economy-wide or industry-specific regulatory provisions. These detailed indicators cover three broad regulatory domains: state control over business enterprises; barriers to entrepreneurship; and barriers to international trade and investment (Nicoletti, Scarpetta, and Boylaud 1999).

32. The United States had already started deregulation in energy, transport, and communication between 1975 and 1985. The United Kingdom followed suit between 1985 and 1995. Denmark and Germany deregulated these markets primarily between 1995 and 2003. France

started deregulation between 1995 and 2003, but has still not fully implemented the EU directives (Conway and Nicoletti 2006).

33. For a fuller discussion of the connection between product market deregulation and the labor market in the United States, see also Peoples (1998).

34. Until 2004, a master craftsman's diploma was an essential prerequisite for operating a cleaning company (Bosch and Kalina 2008a, 73) and served as a barrier to entry in the sector.

35. Of the estimated 2,264 companies covered by the legislation, some 828 (34 percent) have EWCs. Among multinationals employing 10,000 or more, 61 percent have EWCs; see European Trade Union Confederation, "European Works Councils," available at: http://www.etuc.org/a/125.

36. In this context, it is worth mentioning that the U.K. government was suspicious of the 1994 directive, and it was not until 2000 that the directive was implemented in Britain. The directive had an impact in the United Kingdom before 2000, however, because many big U.K. companies had subsidiaries in more than two other countries, and U.K. trade unionists in foreign-owned companies were keen to be represented in their European Works Councils.

37. Works councilors are to be found in nearly all big establishments (those with more than one thousand employees), but only in about 10 percent of small establishments (those with fewer than fifty employees).

38. In the Hall and Soskice (2001) typology, if the United States and the United Kingdom have usually been put forward as the reference models for liberal market economies, Germany, Sweden, and Japan serve as the reference models for coordinated market economies. According to Hall and Soskice, France does not fit the model for a coordinated market economy very well. Given the striking diversity among the group of countries serving as prototypes for this type of economy, some authors prefer to distinguish "corporatist" (Germany, Sweden) from "state-led" (France) varieties (Bosch, Lehndorff, and Rubery 2009; see also Appelbaum et al., this volume).

39. Using the Streeck and Thelen (2005) typology of change, we can categorize this as the "conversion" of a tool to guarantee a wage floor at least partially into a tool for wage moderation (see also Salverda, van Klaveren, and van der Meer 2008).

REFERENCES

Abowd, John, Francis Kramarz, David Margolis, and Thomas Philippon. 2000. "The Tail of Two Countries: Minimum Wages and Employment in

France and the United States." Discussion paper 203. Bonn: Institute for the Study of Labor (IZA) (September).

Allen, Tim, and Pierre Regnard. 2007. "Minimum Wages in the EU in January 2007: Statutory Minimum Wages in Euros Varied by One to Seventeen Across the EU." *Eurostat News Release* (85, June 18).

Belzer, Michael H. 2000. *Sweatshop on Wheels: Winners and Losers in Trucking Deregulation*. Oxford: Oxford University Press.

Bernhardt, Annette, Siobhan McGrath, and James DeFilippis. 2007. "Unregulated Work in the Global City: Employment and Labor Law Violations in New York City." New York: New York University School of Law, Brennan Center for Justice.

Bernstein, Jared, Heidi Hartmann, and John Schmitt. 1999. "The Minimum Wage Increase: A Woman's Issue." Issue brief. Washington, D.C.: Economic Policy Institute (September 16).

Bosch, Gerhard. 2004. "Towards a New Standard Employment Relationship in Western Europe." *British Journal of Industrial Relations* 42(4): 617–36.

Bosch, Gerhard, and Jean Charest, eds. 2010. *Vocational Training: International Perspectives*. London: Routledge.

Bosch, Gerhard, and Thorsten Kalina. 2008a. "Low-Wage Work in Germany: An Overview." In *Low-Wage Work in Germany*, edited by Gerhard Bosch and Claudia Weinkopf. New York: Russell Sage Foundation.

———. 2008b. "Germany: What Role for Minimum Wages on Low-Wage Work?" In *The Minimum Wage Revisited in the Enlarged EU*, edited by Daniel Vaughan-Whitehead. Geneva: International Labor Organization (ILO).

Bosch, Gerhard, Steffen Lehndorff, and Jill Rubery. 2009. *European Employment Models in Flux: A Comparison of Institutional Change in Nine European Countries*. London: Palgrave Macmillan.

Bosch, Gerhard, and Claudia Weinkopf, eds. 2008. *Low-Wage Work in Germany*. New York: Russell Sage Foundation.

Card, David, and Alan Krueger. 1995. *Myth and Measurement: The New Economics of the Minimum Wage*. Princeton, N.J.: Princeton University Press.

Caroli, Ève, and Jérôme Gautié. 2008. *Low-Wage Work in France*. New York: Russell Sage Foundation.

Conway, Paul, Veronique Janod, and Giuseppe Nicoletti. 2005. "Product Market Regulation in OECD Countries: 1998 to 2003." Working paper 419. Paris: OECD Economics Department (April 1).

Conway, Paul, and Giuseppe Nicoletti. 2006. "Product Market Regulation in the Nonmanufacturing Sectors of OECD Countries: Measurement and Highlights." Working paper 530. Paris: OECD Economics Department (December 7).

Denvir, Ann, and George Loukas. 2006. *The Impact of the National Minimum Wage, Pay Differentials, and Workplace Change*. Brighton, U.K.: Institute for Employment Studies.

Di Nardo, John, Nicole Fortin, and Thomas Lemieux. 1997. "Labor Market Institutions and the Distribution of Wages, 1973–1992: A Semiparametric Approach." *Econometrica* 64(5): 1001–44.

Dube, Arindrajit, T. William Lester, and Michael Reich. 2007. "Minimum-Wage Effects Across State Borders: Estimates Using Contiguous Counties." Berkeley: University of California, Institute for Research on Labor and Employment.

Employee Benefit Research Institute (EBRI). 2006. "EBRI Databook on Employee Benefits." Available at: http://www.ebri.org/publications/books/index.cfm?fa=databook.

Erickson, Christopher L., and Daniel J. B. Mitchell. 2007. "Monopsony as a Metaphor for the Emerging Post-Union Labor Market." *International Labor Review* 146(3–4): 163–187.

European Commission (EC). 2004. *Industrial Relations 2004.* Luxembourg: EC.

———. 2006. *Industrial Relations in Europe 2006.* Luxembourg: EC.

———. 2008. *Industrial Relations in Europe 2008.* Luxembourg: EC.

Gautié, Jérôme. 2008. "France: Towards the End of an Active Minimum Wage Policy?" In *The Minimum Wage Revisited in the Enlarged EU*, edited by Daniel Vaughan-Whitehead. Geneva: International Labor Organization (ILO).

Hall, Peter A., and David Soskice, eds. 2001. *Varieties of Capitalism: The Institutional Foundations of Comparative Advantage.* New York: Oxford University Press.

Immervoll, Herwig. 2007. "Minimum Wages, Minimum Labor Costs, and the Tax Treatment of Low-Wage Employment." Social Employment and Migration Working Papers 46. Paris: Organization for Economic Cooperation and Development.

Krugman, Paul. 1994. "Europe Jobless, America Penniless?" *Foreign Affairs* (summer): 19–34.

Lassen, Morten, John Houman Sørensen, Anja Lindkvist Jørgensen, and Rasmus Juul Møberg. 2006. "Skill Needs and the Institutional Framework Conditions for Enterprise-Sponsored CVT: The Case of Denmark." SP I 2006-121. Berlin: Social Science Research Center.

Lester, Richard. 1964. *The Economics of Labor.* New York: Macmillan.

Levy, Frank, and Peter Temin. 2007. "Inequality and Institutions in Twentieth-Century America." Working paper 13106. Cambridge, Mass.: National Bureau of Economic Research.

Lloyd, Caroline, Geoff Mason, and Ken Mayhew. 2008. *Low-Wage Work in the United Kingdom.* New York: Russell Sage Foundation.

Low Pay Commission. 2007. *National Minimum Wage.* Report. London: Low Pay Commission.

Machin, Stephen, Alan Manning, and Lupin Rahman. 2003. "When the Minimum Wage Bites Hard: The Introduction of the U.K. National Minimum Wage to a Low-Wage Sector." *Journal of the European Economic Association* 1(1): 154–80.

Manning, Alan. 2003. *Monopsony in Motion: Imperfect Competition in Labor Markets*. Princeton, N.J.: Princeton University Press.

Metcalf, David. 2007. "Why Has the British National Minimum Wage Had Little or No Impact on Employment?" Discussion paper 781. Washington, D.C.: Center for Economic and Policy Research (CEPR) (April).

Neumark, David, and William Wascher. 2006. "Minimum Wages and Employment: A Review of Evidence from the New Minimum Wage Research." Working paper 12663. Cambridge, Mass.: National Bureau of Economic Research (November).

Nicoletti, Giuseppe, Stefano Scarpetta, and Olivier Boylaud. 1999. "Summary Indicators of Product Market Regulation with an Extension to Employment Protection Legislation." Working paper 226. Paris: OECD Economics Department.

Organization for Economic Cooperation and Development (OECD). 1997. *Employment Outlook*. Paris: OECD.

———. 1998. *Employment Outlook*. Paris: OECD.

———. 2004. *Employment Outlook*. Paris: OECD.

———. 2006. *Employment Outlook*. Paris: OECD.

———. 2007. *Education at a Glance*, Paris: OECD.

Peoples, James. 1998. "Deregulation and the Labor Market." *Journal of Economic Perspectives* 12(3): 111–30.

Philips, Peter. 2003. "Dual Worlds: The Two Growth Paths in U.S. Construction." In *Building Chaos: An International Comparison of Deregulation in the Construction Industry*, edited by Gerhard Bosch and Peter Philips. London: Routledge.

Pollin, Robert, and Stephanie Luce. 1998. *The Living Wage: Building a Fair Economy*. New York: New Press.

Ragacs, Christian. 2004. *Minimum Wages and Employment: Static and Dynamic Non-Market-Clearing Equilibrium Models*. London: Palgrave Macmillan.

Regnard, Pierre. 2007. "Minimum Wages 2007: Variations from 92 to 1570 Euros." *Statistics in Focus: Population and Social Conditions* (71). Luxembourg: Eurostat.

Salverda, Wiemer, Maarten van Klaveren, and Marc van der Meer. 2008. *Low-Wage Work in the Netherlands*. New York: Russell Sage Foundation.

Schmitt, John, Margy Waller, Shawn Fremstad, and Ben Zipperer. 2008.

"Unions and Upward Mobility for Low-Wage Workers." *WorkingUSA: The Journal of Labor and Society* 11(3): 337–348.

Stigler, Joseph. 1946. "The Economics of the Minimum Wage Legislation." *American Economic Review* 36(3): 535–43.

Streeck, Wolfgang, and Kathleen Thelen. 2005. "Introduction: Institutional Change in Advanced Political Economies." In *Beyond Continuity: Institutional Change in Advanced Political Economies*, edited by Wolfgang Streeck and Kathleen Thelen. Oxford: Oxford University Press.

Thelen, Kathleen. 2004. *How Institutions Evolve: The Political Economy of Skills in Germany, Britain, the United States, and Japan*. Cambridge: Cambridge University Press.

Traxler, Franz. 2004. "Employers and Employers' Organizations in Europe: Membership Strength, Density, and Representativeness." *Industrial Relations Journal* 31(4): 308–16.

U.S. Department of Labor. 2006. *National Compensation Survey: Employee Benefits in Private Industry in the United States*. Washington: U.S. Department of Labor (March).

Visser, Jelle. 2008. "Institutional Characteristics of Trade Unions, Wage Setting, State Intervention, and Social Pacts (ICTWSS): An International Database." Amsterdam: Amsterdam Institute for Advanced Labor Studies (AIAS).

Westergaard-Nielsen, Niels, ed. 2008. *Low-Wage Work in Denmark*. New York: Russell Sage Foundation.

CHAPTER 4

The Impact of Institutions on the Supply Side of the Low-Wage Labor Market

*Jérôme Gautié, Niels Westergaard-Nielsen,
and John Schmitt, with Ken Mayhew*

The previous chapter focused on the impact of institutions on wage setting across firms and sectors, with an eye toward the impact of these factors on the industry- and economy-wide share of low-wage work. That chapter identified the degree of inclusiveness or exclusiveness of the national pay-setting institutions and the possibility for firms to opt out of these institutions as the key factors driving cross-national differences in the share of low-wage work.

In this chapter, we turn our attention to the supply side of the low-wage labor market. In crude terms, if the bargaining and regulatory structures analyzed in the preceding chapter are the primary determinants of the quantity of low-wage work, we find that the various institutions affecting labor supply play a large role in shaping the composition of low-wage work, which in most of our countries is disproportionately made up of women, young people, older workers, less-educated workers, and immigrants.[1]

If firms are to pay low wages to a portion of workers, they must have access to a pool of workers who are willing to work for low wages. In our six countries, the pool of low-wage workers consistently has three separate (frequently overlapping) features. The first is low levels of skills relative to the typical national worker. In most of our countries, low-wage work is heavily concentrated among less-educated (and less-trained) workers, younger workers with the least amount of on-the-job experience, and less-skilled immigrants.[2] The second feature of the pool of low-wage workers is that these workers can count on little or no financial support when they are not in work. Sometimes this lack of nonwork income reflects national policy— such as in the United States, which offers little or no support to out-of-work workers and their families. Sometimes the low level of non-work income is related to income support policies originally designed to support full-time male workers with long job histories; these policies tend to work against younger workers and women, who typically have less labor market experience and who tend to move in and out of the labor market too frequently to qualify for important forms of income support. Finally, the pool of low-wage workers also includes many workers—overwhelmingly women—who have substantial responsibility for child care and elder care. Women workers, whose responsibilities reduce their bargaining power relative to employers, frequently trade fewer hours or more flexible schedules for lower pay as part of a strategy to balance their market and nonmarket work responsibilities.

The chapter begins by showing that the difference in the incidence of low-wage work across countries cannot be explained by a simple market-driven supply-side story. Across our countries, for example, no simple correlation holds between the national share of low-wage work and either the share of less-educated workers or the size of the national immigrant population.

The next section presents the wide range of institutions that affect the labor supply decisions of vulnerable and potentially low-wage workers (women, younger workers, older workers, and immigrants); the income tax system, child care benefits, systems of student grants, and early retirement schemes are only a few examples. Differences across our six countries in these institutions explain part of the difference in both the overall *incidence* and the national *composition* of low-wage work. The following section analyzes the incentives and pressures on the unemployed to take low-wage jobs, taking into account both active and passive labor market policies as well as other forms of in- or out-of-work benefits.

THE SHARE OF LOW-SKILLED
AND IMMIGRANTS AND THE INCIDENCE
OF LOW PAY

Education, Training, and the Supply
of Low-Skilled Work

In the individual-level logistic regression analyses for all six countries in our study reported in chapter 2, we found that less-skilled

Table 4.1 Years of Schooling and Educational Attainment, 2004

	Average Years in Formal Schooling	Tertiary Qualifications	Upper Secondary Education	Below Upper Secondary Education	Total
Denmark	13.4	32%	49%	19%	100%
France	11.6	24	41	35	100
Germany	13.4	25	59	16	100
Netherlands	11.2	29	41	29	100
United Kingdom	12.6	29	36	35	100
United States	13.3	39	49	12	100

Source: OECD (2006).

workers have a higher probability of being in low-wage employment than do skilled or highly educated workers. Using national-level data, however, we found no evidence of a correlation between the size of the less-skilled labor force and the share of workers on low wages using our definition of low-wage work. Two common proxy measures of skill levels are average years of formal schooling and the proportion of the population holding qualifications above the upper secondary level. Table 4.1 shows that only one of the two countries with a relatively low incidence of low-wage employment (Denmark) is highly placed in terms of these two skill measures. The other country with relatively few low-paid workers (France) is second-lowest among the six countries in terms of average years of schooling and tied for lowest in terms of qualifications held above the upper secondary level. Conversely, the country with the highest incidence of low pay (the United States) is relatively highly ranked on both skill indicators.

Skills, however, are notoriously difficult to measure. Neither years of schooling nor formal qualification measures do justice to important institutional differences between these countries. The relatively high proportion of workers with upper secondary qualifications in Germany and Denmark, for example, reflects the strong apprentice training systems in those two countries. By contrast, in the United States the bulk of upper secondary qualifications are probably based on high school graduation rather than certified vocational skills. Literacy scores, available from the International Adult Literacy Survey (IALS) for the mid-1990s, may be a better measure of skills for our purposes. The IALS data cast doubt on skill rankings based on years of schooling and formal qualifications. For example, after defining a "low-skilled" category as all persons in the bottom quintile of literacy scores among IALS respondents across ten countries, Peter Mühlau and Justine Horgan (2001) estimated that some 23 percent of the U.S. working-age population are low-skilled by this definition, compared to 29 percent in the United Kingdom, only 15 percent in Germany, and 13 percent in the Netherlands.[3] Low levels of basic skills such as literacy may well contribute to the relatively high incidence of low pay in the United States and the United Kingdom, but the relatively strong performance of countries such as Germany on such skill measures has not prevented the low-paid share of the German workforce from approaching U.K. levels in recent years.

In addition, analysis of labor force data shows that high skill levels are not a sufficient condition to avoid low-paid employment. Although, as already noted, the probability of being low-paid is higher for less-skilled workers than it is for skilled workers in all six countries, four of the countries have nontrivial shares of low-paid workers who hold intermediate-level qualifications and, in some cases, even tertiary qualifications. In Germany, more than 75 percent of all low-wage workers are qualified to at least the craft apprentice level (Bosch and Kalina 2008). In the United Kingdom, one-fifth of workers holding National Vocational Qualification (NVQ) Level 3 (craft-level or upper secondary) qualifications are low-paid (Mason et al. 2008). In France in recent years, the incidence of low pay among the two most highly educated groups has increased, whereas it has decreased among the least-educated (Caroli, Gautié, and Askénazy 2008). In the Netherlands in the 2000s, the low-paid share of employment has increased among both the skilled and the less-skilled (Salverda 2008). In Denmark, low pay has become more concentrated among youth with secondary education, but there are low-paid among all skill groups (Westergaard-Nielsen 2008).

It is clear that differences in average skill levels between countries explain little of the differences in low pay between them. Nonetheless, analysis of income mobility in each country shows that skilled low-wage workers have a higher probability of moving up and out of low-wage employment in the future than do less-skilled workers (see Mason and Salverda, this volume). Thus, the most likely link between low skills and low pay is the relatively low mobility of the less-skilled, which, in combination with other factors discussed in this chapter, such as growth in immigration and the supply of student labor, may severely reduce the individual bargaining power of the majority of low-wage workers in some countries.

IMMIGRATION POLICIES AND THE IMPACT ON THE LOW-WAGE LABOR MARKET

In some countries, immigration may provide an important supply of less-skilled workers who, whether because of their legal status or language ability, may also have relatively little bargaining power.[4] By immigrants we also mean foreign migrant workers (workers who return to their country of origin after a certain period).[5]

The incidence of low-wage work among immigrants is indeed above the average in all six countries. The potential depressing effect on wages (and to a lesser extent, on employment opportunities) at the lower end of the labor market has been much debated in the United States, where the number of less-skilled immigrants has increased substantially over the last fifteen years (see, for example, Aydemir and Borjas 2007; Card 2005).

The stock of immigrants and the change in that stock differ substantially across our six countries (see table 4.2). First, in 2005, Ger-

Table 4.2 Share of Foreign-Born Population in Total Population and in Employment

	Share of Foreign-Born Population in Total Population		Growth in Share of Foreign-Born	Share of Employed Foreign-Born in Total Employment		Increase in Foreign-Born Compared to Native-Born
	1995[a]	2005[b]	1995 to 2005[a,b]	1995	2005	1995 to 2005
Denmark	4.8%	6.5%	35.4%	3.1%	5.8%	87%
France[a]	7.3	8.1	11.1	10.7	10.5	−1
Germany[b]	11.5	12.9	12.2	11.6	13.7	18
Netherlands	9.1	10.6	16.5	7.4	10.9	46
United Kingdom	6.9	9.7	40.6	7.0	9.8	41
United States	9.3	12.9	38.7	10.1	15.3	51

Source: OECD (2007a).
a. France, 1999.
b. Germany, 2003.

many had the same share of immigrants in its total population (12.9 percent) as the United States, with the Netherlands (10.6 percent) and the United Kingdom (9.7 percent) fairly close behind. France (8.1 percent) and Denmark (6.5 percent), meanwhile, had the lowest immigrant populations. The highest relative inflow of immigrants was found in the United Kingdom, the United States, and Denmark. In all countries except Denmark, immigrants had a higher employment rate than the native population. Immigrants were also more likely than natives to be self-employed. That said, the most dramatic increase in employment among the foreign-born was found in Denmark, where the foreign-born almost doubled their employment share between 1995 and 2005—albeit from a relatively low initial level. The employment share increased in all countries except France (where it has been essentially flat).

The size and growth of immigrant populations reflects, of course, the strictness of both de jure and de facto national immigration policies. Among the countries in our sample, France appears to have the strictest immigration policy. High and persistent unemployment there has contributed to the view that immigration represents an economic threat to native workers. As a consequence, the number of legal immigrants has grown slowly over the past three decades. Meanwhile, the United Kingdom has more actively encouraged immigration, particularly since the second half of the 1990s. The explicit aim of the British government has been to provide the economy with an available pool of labor for low-paid jobs—especially for sectors where recruitment difficulties threatened to induce wage inflation. In recent years, the large inflow into Britain of workers from the new eastern European member countries of the European Union has helped to reduce upward wage pressure in sectors such as hotels and food processing. British employers have often taken advantage of the country's limited regulation of temporary agency work (see Bosch, Mayhew, and Gautié, this volume) to recruit an increasing number of immigrant temps. This strategy has allowed employers to keep down both wages and the costs of fringe benefits. In recent years, German and, to a lesser degree, Dutch employers have implemented similar strategies, using both foreign temps and "posted workers" from eastern European countries (Bosch and Weinkopf 2008; Salverda, van Klaveren, and van der Meer 2008). National policies also shape shorter-term flows of migrant labor. Work permits in Germany and, to a lesser degree, the United Kingdom and the United States have contributed to significant increases in labor supply. Short-term migrant labor does not play a significant role in France, the Netherlands, or Denmark.

An important policy question is whether immigrants put downward pressure on wages, especially those of less-skilled workers. This does seem to be the case at the bottom of the wage distribution, even when immigrants have an intermediary level of education. Empirical evidence from the United Kingdom, for example, shows that many immigrants have to downgrade substantially upon arrival and accept work in occupations below their skill level, competing with unskilled natives and, especially, other immigrants (Dustman, Glitz, and Frattini 2008). According to Marco Manacorda, Alan Manning, and Jonathan Wadsworth (2007), because natives and immigrants are imperfect substitutes, the most sizable effect is on recent immigrants. In the medium run, however, the effects of immigration on natives may depend on institutional characteristics and therefore may differ between countries: according to Joshua Angrist and Adriana Kugler (2003), the negative impact on natives' employment may be significant in countries with restrictive institutions (high employment protection legislation [EPL] and high barriers to entry, for example), in particular because these restrictions may dampen the rate of job creation.

Employers take advantage of "holes" in the pay-setting and labor market institutions analyzed in the previous chapter, including the absence of equal treatment for temporary agency workers in the United Kingdom, Germany, and the Netherlands until the 2008 EU directive; the absence of a legal minimum wage in Germany; and the decrease in the coverage of collective agreements in Germany (see Bosch, Mayhew, and Gautié, this volume). The impact of immigration on the labor market is clearly mediated by these institutional contexts. Denmark provides an interesting illustration. The number of immigrants more than tripled between 1980 and 2004—reaching about 6 percent of the population in 2005—while the national incidence of low-wage work remained low. At the same time, the labor force participation rate of immigrants has been much lower than that of Danish natives—and their unemployment rate is twice as high. The main reason is that unions have maintained control over wage levels, including the right (held for more than one hundred years) to demand a contract on any work performed in Denmark. If the employer refuses to sign a contract, the unions have a right to take industrial action. In most cases, employers have found that it is cheaper to have a contract on the minimum tariff than to resist union pressure. As a result, the Danish unions have been able to police the wage levels at the lower end of the labor market. The contrast with the American experience is striking. In the United States, immigrants have much higher employment rates (both regular and nonstandard) and much lower wage rates than in Denmark.

The pattern of inflow of immigrants has altered the German labor market, moving Germany in the direction of the United States. In Germany, an increasing share of jobs are now performed by non-natives (though 92 percent of low-wage workers in Germany are not immigrants), with a simultaneous rise in the low-wage labor market within the least-regulated industries.

HOW NATIONAL INSTITUTIONS SHAPE THE LABOR SUPPLY OF VULNERABLE GROUPS

Women, young people, and older workers are the demographic groups most vulnerable to low-wage work (see Mason and Salverda, this volume). Members of these groups are more likely to fall victim to employers' "monopsony power" because they often lack alternatives to low-wage work owing to their low human capital (a relative lack of labor market experience for younger workers, reduced capacities or obsolete human capital for older workers) and other factors such as mobility costs (especially for women who may have child care or elder care responsibilities) and employer discrimination. The preceding chapter discussed the extent to which "collective" bargaining power may help to offset this potentially low "individual" bargaining power. The less inclusive the institutional system, the more likely it is that these individual differences in bargaining power will give rise to a dualistic labor market, resulting in a higher incidence of low-wage work among these disadvantaged groups.

When human capital (including mobility opportunities) is low, the main alternative to low-wage work is some form of public income support. Following Giuseppe Bertola, Francine Blau, and Lawrence Kahn (2007, 835), young people, older workers, and women can be labeled "secondary labor force groups" because their labor supply is more elastic (as compared to middle-aged males)—that is, "the value of their alternative uses of time is closer to that of being employed"— and as a consequence they are less "attached" to the labor market. In this section, we examine the role of institutions in shaping the "alternative uses of time" for the groups that experience a high level of low-wage work in most of our six countries.

WOMEN

In all six countries, women tend to be overrepresented among low-wage workers. But the ratio of relative concentration (adult women to adult men) differs across the countries (see table 2.2). The highest concentration is in the United Kingdom (about 3.3), followed by the Netherlands (about 2.7) and Germany (about 2.5), then France (2.2), Denmark (2.0), and, finally, the United States (1.9).

We have to disentangle the different factors that may affect the trade-off between low-wage work and nonwork—which is mainly a trade-off between paid work and home production for households at low income levels.

The basic facts are that women have increased their labor force participation rates substantially in recent years. Women's labor force participation rates are highest in Denmark (74 percent), followed by the United States and the United Kingdom (both 68 percent). The Netherlands (66 percent) in 2006 trailed closely behind, after a remarkable nineteen-percentage-point jump in female participation rates in less than two decades. Germany has also seen a large increase in female participation since 1990 (up nine percentage points) but still lags well behind the previous four countries. A similar situation holds in France, where female participation is up seven percentage points, but French women are still seventeen percentage points behind their Danish counterparts (table 4.3).

The labor force participation rates shown in table 4.3 do not tell the full story. Participation rates, on their own, do not tell us about the number of hours of paid work women perform, nor do they shed light on the pattern of participation over the life cycle.[6]

Women's normal work hours differ substantially between the countries (see figure 4.1).

Women in the United States tend to work forty to forty-four hours per week; a relatively small share work either fewer hours or longer hours. The same concentration is found in France and Denmark, though at a lower mean value that reflects lower maximum hours (thirty-five and thirty-seven, respectively) in both countries. Relatively few work part-time. German and British women tend to work

Table 4.3 Labor Force Participation in the Six Countries Among Sixteen- to Sixty-Four-Year-Olds

| | Women | | | Men | | |
	1990	2006	1990 to 2006	1990	2006	1990 to 2006
Denmark	72%	74%	2%	83%	82%	−1%
France	51	57	7	70	68	−3
Germany	53	62	9	76	74	−2
Netherlands	47	66	19	76	80	4
United Kingdom	64	68	4	84	80	−3
United States	66	68	3	83	81	−2

Source: OECD (2007a).

lower hours, and therefore we see more female part-time workers in these countries. Almost as many work short hours as work thirty-five to thirty-nine hours. The Dutch women are clearly working shorter hours than anywhere else. The lower the hours, the more marginal the workforce is likely to be. Since the hourly pay of part-time work

Figure 4.1 Number of Hours Worked by Women per Week

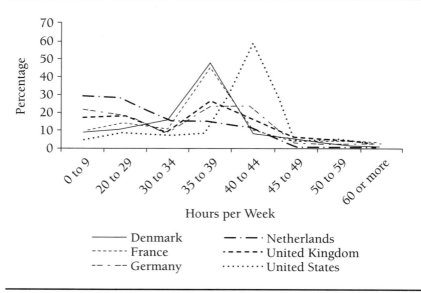

Source: OECD (2007b).

is also on average below that of full-time work, there is overall a negative correlation between the number of hours worked and the incidence of low wage. Women are least overrepresented among the low-wage workers in the United States, Denmark, and France, where they tend to work "normal" hours, as seen earlier.

The Tax System   National income tax systems have an important effect on women's incentives to work. Different countries tax couples in such a way that the second taxpayer in the couple is taxed differently from the first. Table 4.4 presents OECD data on income tax rates in our six countries for couples at different income levels. In all countries, the second earner actually pays a higher tax rate compared to a single earner. The difference means that there is a clear tax incentive not to work, or at least not to work as many hours, and this is especially true for low-wage earners (except in Denmark). The disincentives are clearly largest in Germany. Joint taxation in Germany, France, and, to a lesser degree, in the United States contributes to this situation. The difference in marginal taxation may actually encourage overtime work for men, which may compensate for fewer hours for women. The net result of these tax incentives is to diminish women's incentives to work and to push them toward a more marginal position in the paid labor market.

Employees' social contributions may also play a role in setting the reservation wage. In Bismarckian welfare systems, such as Germany, France, and the Netherlands, the entitlements of spouses and children to health insurance are typically derived from the entitlements of male breadwinners. Groups relying on these derived entitlements are more likely than they are in other systems to take low-wage jobs with reductions in or outright exemptions from employees' social contribution (such as "mini-jobs" in Germany; see Bosch, Mayhew, and Gautié, this volume) or even undeclared jobs. Whenever workers' individual bargaining power is weak, employers operating in these Bismarckian systems may take advantage of this legal or de facto exemption from social contributions (and income taxes) by lowering compensation.

Child Care Provision and Parental Leave   Looking at the participation rate over the life cycle, women are less likely to work when they have small children. This tendency is greater in the United States, the United Kingdom, Germany, and, to a lesser extent, France than it is in Denmark and the Netherlands. The reason is undoubtedly the

Table 4.4 Tax Incidence on Women's Wages

	Women Earning 67 Percent of APW, 2001			Women Earning 100 Percent of APW, 2000		
	Second Earner	Single	Ratio	Second Earner	Single	Ratio
Denmark	50%	41%	1.2	51%	44%	1.2
France	26	21	1.2	26	27	1.0
Germany	50	34	1.5	53	42	1.3
Netherlands	33	27	1.2	41	36	1.1
United Kingdom	24	19	1.3	26	24	1.1
United States	29	22	1.3	30	26	1.2

Source: OECD (2001).

much higher prevalence of relatively cheap child care in Denmark and the large number of low-hour, part-time jobs in the Netherlands (which allow women to combine paid work and child care responsibilities).

Large differences in the availability of paid and unpaid maternity, paternity, and parental leave undoubtedly influence women's labor supply decisions. The United States is the only one of our six countries where maternity leave is unpaid (and the right to maternity leave is limited to twelve weeks); moreover, because the U.S. Family and Medical Leave Act includes restrictions on establishment size (only establishments with fifty or more employees are required to grant unpaid leave) and job tenure (only employees with at least one year of tenure with their employer), many low-wage workers in the United States are not eligible even for unpaid leave (see Ray, Gornick, and Schmitt 2008). The other five countries have paid maternity leave of twelve to twenty-six weeks and even short periods of paid paternity leave. The United Kingdom also offers an additional entitlement to unpaid leave of another twenty-six weeks. In addition, the European countries are more generous when it comes to postmaternity and postpaternity leave, often referred to in Europe as "parental" leave. France, for example, provides a three-year entitlement, albeit it at a low replacement rate equal to about 26 percent (OECD 2007b) of an average manufacturing worker wage. Since 2007, Germany has replaced 67 percent of earnings (up to €1,800 per month) for up to fourteen months.

A long entitlement to a leave paid at a low level relative to the typical wage may render low-wage families unable to take advantage of long leave periods. At the same time, long and generous leaves made available exclusively to women or taken up overwhelmingly by women may inadvertently act to marginalize women in the labor market by reducing employers' incentives to hire women of child-bearing age or by taking women out of the labor force for prolonged periods of time precisely at the time in many workers' careers when they make their most rapid wage and occupation gains.

After the initial leave period, the availability of child care institutions matters. Denmark and France have a mixture of publicly provided, center-based care and family day care for the smallest children and preschool and kindergarten for the three-plus age group. Germany also offers publicly provided, center-based day care and kindergarten. The Netherlands has mainly privately provided child care centers and playgroups for children below age three and a half, and from then on publicly provided preschool. In the United Kingdom and the United States, the large majority of care for small children is paid for privately. The United Kingdom offers so-called reception classes for four-year-olds.

The level of government subsidies to child care (in the form of direct state payment or sliding-scale benefits) and the tax treatment of child care are also important. Child care subsidies work by reducing the relative price of child care and thereby increasing the return to market work relative to home production. In this respect, child care subsidies can be seen as a way of offsetting the negative effect on participation embedded in the tax systems discussed earlier.[7] Subsidies can also be seen as a mechanism to encourage low-wage working mothers to participate in the workforce. This effect is often reinforced by making the subsidy means-tested. In the absence of a generous subsidy for child care work, low wages, the availability of out-of-work supports, and the tax structure can combine to send a clear signal to mothers to decline paid work or to work only relatively short hours, as is the case in Germany and the Netherlands. However, in the United States, where women's employment rates are relatively high despite the absence of significant child care subsidies, low-wage mothers have a strong incentive to choose cheaper and usually lower-quality day care arrangements.

Finally, there is a public-good element in child care subsidies, where the public sector in some countries sets relatively high standards for the quality of child care. In order for low-income mothers to afford these services, there is clearly an argument for subsidizing child care facilities (Waldfogel 2006; Folbre 2001).

The OECD has estimated the generosity of child care in the different countries by how far (in standard deviations) a country lies above or below the OECD mean level of expenditures on child care (Immervoll and Barber 2005). According to the OECD, Denmark spends 2.5 standard deviations more on child care than the OECD average. France is about 0.8 standard deviations above the OECD average, while Germany is just a little above the OECD average. The Netherlands, the United Kingdom, and the United States all spend less than the OECD average. These numbers clearly reflect the high public-sector involvement in child care provision in the first three countries and the low involvement in the other three countries.

The accessibility of child care in each country, together with characteristics of the national tax and benefit system, has an important influence on the participation rates of women as well as on the types of jobs that women hold. In Germany and the Netherlands, which have social systems originally built on the "male breadwinner" model and only modest levels of publicly provided child care, many women accept mini-jobs (in Germany) or low-hour, part-time jobs (in the Netherlands). In the United Kingdom, the lack of publicly provided child care certainly contributes to the high share of part-time work among women. Partly as a consequence, Germany, the Netherlands, and the United Kingdom have the highest concentration of women in low-wage work.

The Marketization Issue   Families make joint decisions about the amount of labor to supply in the market. In deciding the number of hours that fathers and mothers in particular will work for pay, families weigh the hourly wage (net of taxes and subsidies) received by each member for an extra hour of paid work against the value of home production (child care services, for example) for each member. The tax wedge—the gap between a worker's gross pay and net pay—acts to lower the return of paid work relative to home production, thus discouraging work, especially among low-wage workers. The mechanism is explained in the accompanying box.

The total tax wedge is clearly lowest in the United Kingdom and the United States, suggesting that we should expect to see more market work in those countries than in the higher-tax-wedge countries of Denmark, France, Germany, and the Netherlands. Since many of the

The Marketization Trade-off:
An Illustration

Let us say that the household work in question is doing the family laundry. The value of that work is the cost of "outsourcing" the dirty clothes to a laundry service. The cost of the laundry service depends on the market wage for laundry workers, plus social contributions to be paid by the employer, plus any value-added or sales tax on the service, minus any subsidy for laundry workers or laundry services. At a laundry, the productivity is undoubtedly much higher than at home because the laundry has bigger and better washing machines, dryers, and presses. From a productivity standpoint, we should all send our dirty clothes to a laundry and use our time to work on what we do best. Using laundering machines in the household, of course, lowers the amount of time the household spends doing laundry in-house and helps to close at least part of the productivity gap between household and market production.

A concrete example of the choice facing a family illustrates the complexity of the family's labor supply decisions. If a Danish professional earns €40.00 per hour and is therefore paying a 61 percent marginal tax rate, that professional's after-tax earnings for his or her last hour of work each day is €15.60. The minimum wage rate in Denmark is about €14.00 per hour, to which must be added a value-added tax for services of 25 percent. As a result, for a professional to pay for an hour of service work at the Danish minimum wage rate would cost about €17.50, or more than his or her net wage from an hour of work at the professional rate. In other words, working one hour at a typical Danish professional wage buys only fifty-three minutes of assistance at the effective Danish minimum wage, disregarding capital costs.

In France, Germany, and the Netherlands, income taxes are clearly lower than in Denmark, but here the social contributions (paid by the employer or the employee) are particularly high, creating situations not unlike the case described here for Denmark.

low-wage jobs in the United States, for example, are low-wage service jobs in child care, food preparation, and other personal services, the tax wedge could have an important impact on the demand for low-skilled workers. But other factors are also at play.

One key factor is the degree of wage inequality. If the wage distribution is compressed, then the before-tax earnings of the professional (in search of outsourcing) and the (low-wage) worker hoping to do the outsourced work will be small, and for any given level of the tax wedge and relative productivity levels the amount of outsourced work will be smaller than if wage differentials were large. The greater the degree of wage dispersion, the more it pays for the high-income earners to outsource home work to lower-paid workers. Americans and, to a lesser extent, British professionals, who work in countries with a high degree of wage inequality, are more likely to choose to outsource household tasks than would be the case for professionals in Denmark, France, Germany, and the Netherlands, where hourly earnings are more compressed.

In this context, child care subsidies can work to counteract the disincentive effects of a large tax wedge. Child care subsidies in France and the Scandinavian countries, for example, are sufficiently large to induce women in particular to choose market work over child care.[8] Similarly, very few child care facilities are found outside the public and subsidized sector in these countries. In the United States, however, subsidies play little role in creating a market for child care services. The relatively low wage in the child care sector combines with the country's small tax wedge to ensure that generally private solutions to child care are found.

Another important area for outsourcing is food preparation. Time-use studies show that American women work more hours than their European counterparts, but that American women still have more leisure time than European women do because Americans spend less time on household production. According to Richard Freeman (2007) and Freeman and Ronald Schetkatt (2005), the biggest reason for the difference in time spent in household production is the difference in the degree of *marketization* in the United States and Europe. Americans move more activities from home production, including meal preparation, child care, and household cleaning and maintenance, to market production. Americans, for example, spend only four hours a week on cooking, compared to six and a half hours per week in Germany and the Netherlands. Not surprisingly, Americans simultaneously spend almost three times as much time eating out in restaurants.

Immigrant workers appear to play an important role in providing the relatively abundant, less-skilled labor that performs the marketized service-sector work. Consistent with this view, the United States and the United Kingdom clearly have more immigrant-friendly policies than do Denmark, France, and the Netherlands, where home production is more prevalent than it is in the United States. Germany falls somewhere in between these two sets of countries. The German immigrant population is similar in size to that of the United States, but marketization is not yet as extensive as it is in the United States, partly owing to the larger German tax wedge.

YOUNG WORKERS AND OLDER WORKERS

Young Workers   In all our countries, young workers are much more likely than the average worker to be in a low-wage job. The concentration index (the incidence of low-wage work among youth over the total incidence of low-wage work; see table 2.2) is highest in Denmark (about 5), followed by France (about 3.7), the Netherlands (about 3.3), and Germany (3), and it is lowest in the United States and the United Kingdom (both about 2.3).

Youths usually have fewer entitlements to income support than the rest of the population. The reduced entitlement may reflect their limited employment experience (unemployment insurance benefits typically depend on having made a stream of contributions) or the lower relevance for young people of some income support programs, such as sickness leave, incapacity or invalidity benefit, and early retirement. In some cases, government programs explicitly exclude young people, as in Denmark or France, where, for instance, the means-tested basic minimum income (Revenue Minimum d'Insertion, or RMI) is available only for those age twenty-five and older. Overall, the relatively limited access to income supports creates substantial incentives for the young to take low-wage jobs.

Across the six countries, students consistently are engaged in a higher-than-average rate of low-wage work. In Denmark and, to a lesser extent, the United Kingdom and the Netherlands, students are an important share of low-wage workers (see Mason and Salverda, this volume). The generosity and conditions of student grants play an important role in shaping the labor market experience of students. In the United Kingdom, for instance, publicly funded maintenance grants almost disappeared in the past decade (except for the poorest students), and this has induced a big increase in student work. In Germany, health insurance for students in mini-jobs is provided through their student status. In the Netherlands, a universal system of grants was put in place in the 1980s. Since students are allowed to combine their work earnings with their grants up to a threshold amounting to about 70 percent of the adult minimum wage, these grants effectively act as a subsidy enabling students to compete with working adults for low-wage, part-time jobs.

Denmark is the country in our sample where youth (and particularly students) play the biggest role in the low-wage labor market. Beyond the elements already mentioned, it is worth noting that access to further education in Denmark depends on grades from high school; if a student has poor grades, then access depends on work experience (although work experience now plays a lesser role). As a result, many students take jobs at the low end of the wage scale in order to improve their opportunities in the educational system. In any event, young people can receive welfare or unemployment benefits for only a short period, and students are not eligible for most transfer payments. A selection bias may also be at play in Denmark: since the Danish welfare system is quite generous, "only those who expect to move out of low-wage work relatively quickly accept low-wage jobs" (Westergaard-Nielsen 2008, 24).

Older Workers   The picture is more mixed for older workers. In the United States, many older workers have to take low-paid "bridge" jobs to retirement, or they combine retirement with employment because their pensions are low.[9] In Europe, pensions and other forms of financial support for older workers are generally more generous than they are in the United States. Low-wage jobs are often replaced by benefits such as early retirement schemes or incapacity benefits, which may act as a functional equivalent to an early retirement scheme.

In Denmark, an early retirement program was introduced as an option for all members of the national unemployment insurance system. Under the scheme, called a "post-employment wage," eligible workers are entitled, from age sixty through the regular retirement age, initially to receive a benefit equal to the unemployment insurance for the first several years, which is thereafter gradually reduced to the level of the regular retirement pension. In Denmark, the number of beneficiaries of invalidity benefits is also high (including many workers below the retirement age).

While access to invalidity benefits used to be stricter in France and Germany, publicly funded early retirement schemes (from the age of fifty-five) have also been used intensively in these countries in recent decades. In both countries, unions and employers have negotiated early retirement as part of restructuring packages. But in France, since the beginning of the 2000s, the new priority has been to curb the number of early retirees and to suppress the remaining publicly funded programs. The result has been an increase in the number of recipients of other benefits, such as long-term sick leave or a special unemployment allowance that has no job search requirement.

In 2006 the Netherlands abolished an early retirement program that until then had played an important role in the labor market.[10] Three years before, in 2003, the special unemployment allowance for those aged fifty-seven and a half or older was also ended. Over the last decade, the Netherlands has seen significant reforms to the various types of incapacity benefits (sickness benefit, comprehensive disability insurance, and others), whose beneficiaries had reached record levels owing to relatively easy eligibility criteria. Germany has also taken steps to reduce early retirement by raising the retirement age to sixty-seven (after a phase-in period that runs through the 2020s). Even though early retirement schemes were not implemented in the United Kingdom, the number of beneficiaries of the invalidity benefit system reached high levels there too.

Overall, while the existence and particulars of early retirement policies vary considerably across the six countries, these schemes help many older workers to avoid low-wage employment. Since, all else being constant, older workers tend to have less formal education than younger workers, we would expect older workers to be overrepresented among the low-paid. Country-level regressions (see Mason and Salverda, this volume), however, find that older workers are less likely than young workers to be low-paid, though older workers are generally more likely to be low-wage than prime-age workers are. Older workers, of course, tend to have substantial labor market experience and firm-specific human capital, but early retirement schemes (and functional equivalents) play some role in explaining the low incidence of low pay among preretirement-age workers. The United States, meanwhile, has little in the way of publicly funded early retirement plans—though rates of disability insurance have been rising in recent decades. As a result, the incidence of low-wage work among older workers is higher there than in the European countries (see Mason and Salverda, this volume). The low-wage bridge jobs to retirement that many older American workers take—often accepting wage and benefit cuts relative to the compensation they received earlier in their careers—were much less developed in the European countries until the mid-2000s, mainly because early retirement and disability programs were in place. But the thrust of policy in all the OECD countries has changed dramatically in the last decade and a half. Far from trying to get people to leave the labor force early, the emphasis now is on getting them to return to the labor force or to remain in it longer. European countries may see a rise in bridge jobs and accompanying low wages in the coming years, though public pensions in Europe may prevent these countries from reaching the American levels of such jobs.

INCENTIVES AND PRESSURES ON THE UNEMPLOYED TO TAKE LOW-WAGE JOBS

The supply of low-wage workers also depends on the pressure that labor market institutions put on the unemployed (and those out of the labor market) to accept low-wage jobs. The main determinants of the degree of pressure operating on potential low-wage workers are the benefit system (unemployment insurance, social assistance, in-work benefits) and active labor market policies (ALMPs), which seek to "activate" the unemployed as well as "marginally attached" and discouraged workers.

UNEMPLOYMENT BENEFITS

Unemployment benefits (UB) affect the reservation wage of the unemployed—and therefore their incentives to accept or refuse a low-wage job. The four most important features of any unemployment benefit system are: (1) the replacement rate, that is, the average share of the unemployed worker's on-the-job earnings replaced by unemployment benefits; (2) the administrative prerequisites for benefit receipt, including any employment or contribution history requirements; (3) the duration of the benefits; and (4) eligibility rules and monitoring, including the freedom to refuse a job offer and the criteria for what constitutes an "acceptable" job offer.

The generosity of the UB systems differs widely across countries. Table 4.5 shows large differences in the duration of unemployment insurance. The United Kingdom and the United States offer unemployment insurance (UI) for a maximum of six months; in Europe, Germany offers UI for up to twelve months, France for twenty-three

able 4.5 Unemployment Insurance (UI): Duration and
          Replacement Rates During the First Year, 2006

	Maximum Duration of UI (in Months)	Gross Replacement Rate of UI as Percentage of Previous Wage[a]	Gross Replacement Rate of UI as Percentage of Previous Wage[b]
?nmark	48	82.8%	69.9%
?ance	23	64.3	57.4
?rmany	12	40.1	37.7
?therlands	24	70.0	70.0
?ited Kingdom	6	18.8	12.5
?ited States	6	53.3	53.3

urce: Antoine Math's compilation from OECD data; see *Chronique Internationale de l'IRES*, 115
?008, 28), available at: http://www.ires-fr.org/Chronique-de-l-IRES-No115-numero.
te: Gross replacement rate = gross UI benefit during the first year/gross yearly wage.
For a forty-year-old single person with no children, earning 50 percent of the average full-time
?ge.
For a forty-year-old single person with no children, earning 75 percent of the average full-time
?ge.

months, the Netherlands for about twenty-four months, and Denmark for up to forty-eight months. Note that in the European countries (including the United Kingdom) the unemployed can usually get access to unemployment *assistance* (that is, a means-tested benefit) when their entitlement to UI is exhausted. Replacement rates of UI for a forty-year-old single person with full entitlements tend to be more generous in Denmark, France, and the Netherlands than they are in Germany and the United Kingdom, where they are even lower than in the United States (table 4.5).

Various characteristics of the national unemployment benefit systems, however, often make UB less relevant for the low-wage labor market. In all six countries, the existing UB systems reflect a strong historical emphasis on a "breadwinner" model built around beneficiaries who were assumed to be in stable jobs with long employment records. Low-wage workers often have more unstable employment. As a result, many features of the UB systems, such as minimum requirements for continuous employment or minimum earnings or contribution levels, work in practice to exclude many low-wage workers, who are often new entrants or re-entrants to the labor force (and therefore have no record of contributions to the UB system) or who have erratic employment histories that do not meet continuous-employment criteria or who have earnings or contributions records that fall below eligibility thresholds. Overall, UB systems are likely to be less generous for low-wage workers than the official replacement rates presented in table 4.5, which are relevant only for those who meet the administrative eligibility criteria.

SOCIAL ASSISTANCE AND IN-WORK BENEFITS

Other income replacement benefits (IRBs) also affect incentives to take a low-wage job. The first, and probably most important, of these IRBs are various types of social assistance schemes—that is, means-tested income supports: Kontanthjaelp in Denmark; unemployment social assistance (ASS), social assistance for lone parents (API), and basic minimum income (RMI) in France; in Germany, unemployment social assistance (so-called Unemployment Benefit 2) and Livelihood Assistance to Persons Outside of Institutions; general social assistance (ABW, which was replaced in 2004 by work and social assistance [WWB]) in the Netherlands; unemployment assistance and income support in the United Kingdom; and, to a lesser degree, Temporary Assistance for Needy Families (TANF) in the United States.[11] Many beneficiaries of these schemes are unemployed workers who have exhausted their eligibility for UI benefits but still have not found a job.

Over the last fifteen years, the potential negative impact of IRBs on the incentives to take a job has been a growing concern in the countries in our sample. To tackle this issue, a first strategy has been to reduce the generosity of the benefits (in terms of level, eligibility, and duration). The United States opened the way in the mid-1990s with "welfare reform," which required that many "welfare" beneficiaries work in return for benefits ("workfare"). The United States is also the only country in our sample to have introduced a maximum (cumulative) lifetime duration of social assistance (five years for the beneficiaries of TANF). More recently, in Germany the Hartz IV reforms merged unemployment assistance with social assistance to create a substantially less generous program for the long-term unemployed known as Unemployment Benefit 2.

Another policy strategy has been to "make work pay" by increasing the financial benefits of taking a job. Income tax credits are the most common in-work benefits. Such a scheme exists in the United States (the Earned Income Tax Credit [EITC]), the United Kingdom (the Working Family Tax Credit, the most generous in-work bene-fit—that is, a benefit conditional on employment—in the OECD countries, which was replaced in 2003 by the Working Tax Credit [WTC] and the Child Tax Credit), and in France (Prime Pour l'Em-ploi) and Germany (Eingliederungszuschuss); the latter two coun-tries offer benefits, so far, that are less generous or more narrowly tar-geted than the EITC and the WTC. Denmark recently introduced a version of an income tax credit, but with limited scope (only 2.5 per-cent of the wage, up to a maximum of €1,000, which was increased in 2008 to 4 percent of the wage and a maximum of €1,630, with fur-ther increases in a tax reform starting in 2010). Evaluations in the United States and the United Kingdom tend to show that such pro-grams increase incentives for job take-up for single parents and pri-mary earners in couples, but that they tend to reduce slightly the in-centives for secondary earners (especially with respect to the number of hours worked). Beyond in-work benefits, some other IRBs can be combined, under certain conditions, with earnings from work (for example, with means-tested unemployment assistance benefits and minimum incomes, such as Unemployment Benefit 2 in Germany and the ASS and the RMI in France).

In-work benefits may act as a subsidy to low-wage work. Depend-ing on program design, employers may have an incentive to lower wages or flatten wage profiles, with the knowledge that government-provided in-work benefits will make up the difference. High marginal implicit net tax rates may also make it difficult for workers to escape low-wage work by introducing a low-wage "trap." As a consequence, a legal minimum wage may be a useful complement to generous in-work benefits. In the United Kingdom, for example, the national minimum wage (NMW) was introduced simultaneously with the in-crease in the level of the national earned income tax credit (the Working Family Tax Credit, replaced by the Working Tax Credit).

Another possible trap is that workers and employers will collude at the expense of the government. In the United Kingdom, for exam-ple, in order to comply with the minimum wage (which is defined on an hourly basis), some British employers understate their workers' total hours of work but also understate the real pay of the worker (by a smaller degree), so that employees can benefit from higher in-work benefits (Ram, Edwards, and Jones 2004).

Overall, taking into account all the social benefits (including in-work benefits), what is the incentive to take a low-wage job in the different countries in our sample? The OECD provides comparative data on the so-called inactivity trap, based on the estimation of the marginal effective tax rate (METR) applicable to the after-tax earnings of those who move from social assistance to work.[12] In 2001, for example, a single person who moved from social assistance to a job with a wage equal to 67 percent of the average production worker wage, faced a METR of 83 percent in Denmark, 80 percent in Germany, 71 percent in France, 84 percent in the Netherlands, 70 percent in the United Kingdom, and only 29 percent in the United States. On the same basis, Stéphane Carcillo and David Grubb (2006, fig. 6) provide an estimate for 2004 of the financial incentive to work at the minimum wage in several countries, depending on the household structure. The gap between all three European countries in our sample with a statutory minimum wage, on the one hand, and the United States, on the other, is high. For a single person with no children, for instance, the net income from social assistance amounts to about 90 percent of the minimum wage in the Netherlands, 80 percent in the United Kingdom, and 60 percent in France, but only 20 percent in the United States.[13]

All in all, when taking into account out-of-work social benefits, the financial incentive to take up a low-wage job appears on average much stronger in the United States than it does in the European countries of our sample.

The Role of Active Labor Market Policies

Active labor market policies cover a wide range of policies running from placement and job search assistance (provided by the public employment services or mandated service providers) to training, job subsidy in the private sector, direct job creation in the nonprivate sector, and start-up incentives for the unemployed. Table 4.6 presents OECD data on ALMP public expenditures for our six countries. Denmark (1.85 percent of GDP) and the Netherlands (1.32 percent of GDP) spend substantially more on ALMPs than do the other countries in the table; Germany (0.97 percent) and France (0.90 percent) follow; and the United Kingdom (0.45 percent) and the United States lag far behind (0.14 percent). After we adjust these expenditures for the share of unemployed workers[14] in each country, Denmark (0.34 percent of GDP per percentage point of unemployment) and the Netherlands (0.28) still far outpace the remaining countries. Ger-

Table 4.6 Active Labor Market Policy Expenditures, 2005

	Total Expenditure (Percentage GDP)	Unemployment Rate (Percentage of Labor Force)	Total Expenditure/ Unemployment Rate
Denmark	1.85[a]	5.5[a]	0.34
France	0.90	9.3	0.10
Germany	0.97	10.6	0.09
Netherlands	1.32	4.7	0.28
United Kingdom	0.45[b]	4.8	0.09
United States	0.14[b]	5.1	0.03

Source: OECD (2008), appendix, table J.
a. 2004.
b. 2005 to 2006.

many (0.09) and France (0.10)[15], however, now fare no better than the United Kingdom (0.09) because the greater German and French expenditures must be spread across much larger shares of unemployed workers. The United States (0.03) continues to spend far less on ALMPs than the other countries, even after adjusting for its relatively low unemployment rate.

As we saw in the preceding section, Denmark and the Netherlands manage to provide extensive and generous UB and related benefits while maintaining unemployment rates as low as the much less generous United Kingdom and United States. The expenditure patterns shown in table 4.6 suggest that one reason why Denmark and the Netherlands achieve these results may have to do with both countries' strong emphasis on ALMPs.

ALMPs seek to overcome a host of problems in the low-wage labor market. Various ALMPs focus on closing skill deficits (through education and training); overcoming informational problems in the low-wage labor market (through the creation of centralized hiring halls, payment of recruitment bonuses, job search counseling, and assistance with job applications); and directly or indirectly creating more low-wage job opportunities (through job subsidies and public-employment creation).[16] Finally, ALMPs may also serve as a threat or an enforcer to discipline recipients of unemployment and other benefits because participation in ALMPs is often an eligibility condition for unemployment benefits.

More widely, ALMPs attempt to "activate" benefit recipients to find and take jobs by "making work pay," either through raising the costs and responsibilities involved in receiving government-provided benefits or by helping to overcome work-related costs (including child care, transportation, and taxes). In the last decade, the idea of "activation" has increasingly become the unifying principle across most ALMPs. As the OECD explains:

> Activation includes both the provision of employment services and obligations on individuals who are able to work, to look for jobs and participate in programs. Activation reforms can take two main forms: (i) limiting access to non-employment benefits by individuals who are considered able to work . . .; (ii) applying certain requirements, usually short of requiring full work-availability, to a significant proportion of all individuals on non-employment benefits." (Carcillo and Grubb 2006, 6)[17]

ALMPs initially developed as part of efforts to reduce the prevalence of long-term unemployment (the RESTART program in the United Kingdom, for example). Subsequently, governments began to employ ALMP-style strategies to reduce benefit rolls for means-tested income support ("welfare reform" in the United States) and disability-benefit programs.

Beyond the general principle of activation, different types of active labor market policies have different impacts on the low-wage labor market. In some countries, ALMPs are geared more toward a "work-first" strategy: job search assistance and monitoring that place pressure on the unemployed to return to work as quickly as possible. These approaches seek to reduce workers' scope to refuse a job offer, including broadening the definition of what constitutes a "suitable job." Among the European countries, the United Kingdom offers the best illustration of this approach. In 1996 the British unemployment benefit was replaced by the "job-seeker's allowance." Administrators at national Job Centres Plus became more aggressive in their efforts to persuade unemployed workers to accept jobs—withholding benefits sometimes when job-seekers refused an offer. The "New Deal" was introduced two years later. (Initially targeted only at youth, it was later extended to older groups of workers.) The New Deal is now compulsory for all young people age eighteen to twenty-four who have been on the job-seeker allowance for more than six months. Participants are given four months of intensive job search assistance, and if they do not succeed in getting a job during this period, they have to choose one of four options: education, a subsidized job with training, voluntary work, or environmental work (all at low or no pay). In recent years, the British government has also extended the New Deal to other categories and put greater pressure on recipients of incapacity benefits. Overall, ALMPs in the United Kingdom probably contributed to the downward pressure on wages by increasing the labor supply at the bottom end of the labor market.

Since the Hartz reforms adopted in the beginning of the 2000s, Germany has also put much more emphasis on forcing the unemployed to take jobs, notably by widening the definition of "suitable jobs" so that failure to accept a suitable job offer results in loss of benefits. At the same time, as mentioned earlier, the reform of unemployment assistance has left the program much less generous than it had been.

Other countries put less emphasis on job search assistance and monitoring and have so far kept a more traditional strategy focused on different kinds of job subsidies in the private sector and direct job creation in the public sector. This approach may also amount to promoting low-wage work by directly subsidizing it. The French government, for example, subsidizes a wide variety of specific jobs and workers on certain types of employment contracts that promote training in the private sector; over the last three decades, France has also provided temporary jobs in the public sector as a last resort. Beneficiaries of these programs are usually paid at the minimum wage (sometimes less when they work on special employment contracts designed to promote training). As a result, subsidized jobs through ALMP schemes have become an important segment of the low-wage labor market (especially for youth). Beyond these targeted schemes (mainly for youth and the long-term unemployed), a general public subsidy for low-wage jobs was also introduced in 1993.[18] The general subsidy consists in reducing employers' social security contributions. Since the subsidy decreases as the wage increases (from 26 percentage points of gross wage at the minimum-wage level down to 0 at 1.6 times the minimum wage and beyond), employers have an incentive to fix wages as low as possible and also to flatten wage profiles—which may contribute to a low-wage "trap." Until recently, the general approach in the Netherlands has been similar to that of France. The largest employment subsidy program is the WVA (Reduction of Employers Tax and Contribution), which provides substantial subsidies (€2,500 for workers earning less than 130 percent of the minimum wage) to firms that take on and train low-wage workers. Until 2005, the Netherlands also operated a program known as SPAK (Specific Tax Rebate), which sought to promote low-wage employment by subsidizing employers that hired workers earning up to 115 percent of the minimum wage.[19] On a financial basis, however, the largest ALMP was the WSW ("sheltered workplaces"), which, as a last resort, activated workers (often on disability) through public employment. Overall, as Peter Mühlau and Wiemer Salverda (2000) note, subsidies conditional on low wages may have actually ended up increasing, rather than decreasing, the prevalence of low-wage work in the Netherlands as employers restructured work in order to qualify for subsidies.

Denmark offers an alternative approach, both to the "work-first" strategy and to the de facto subsidy to the low-wage sector. Denmark stressed activation with its 1994 labor market reforms that require job-seekers on unemployment benefit to enter an ALMP program after one year of unemployment (after six months for young people).[20] It has never been proven, however, that ALMPs in Denmark have a generally positive impact on the probability of getting a job or on pay level once a job is located. More recent research in Denmark and elsewhere puts more emphasis on the threat effect of ALMPs. Exit rates from unemployment to employment, for example, appear to increase sharply as the one-year benefit deadline approaches (Rosholm and Svarer 2004). Nevertheless, training plays a crucial role in Danish ALMPs: public expenditures on training amounted to 0.53 percent of GDP in 2005, as compared to 0.29 percent in France and 0.25 percent in Germany (where the unemployment rate was twice as high; see table 4.6), 0.13 percent in the Netherlands, 0.09 percent in the United Kingdom, and 0.05 percent in the United States. In recent years, four out of five job-seekers in the activation programs have chosen educational courses; others take subsidized jobs. Workers involved in on-the-job training through an activation program work in either a subsidized job in the private sector—the employer receives half of the typical low-wage salary over a six-month period and the employee receives the regular rate of pay for the job—or a government job on a relatively low wage rate. About 20 percent of on-the-job training programs work in the private sector, and the rest are in low-wage public employment. But in both sectors, the wage rate of the collective agreement must apply, so subsidized jobs are not derogatory contracts that can be used to circumvent normal wage rates—in contrast to ALMP schemes in France, for instance. Overall, Danish ALMPs put less pressure on the unemployed to take low-wage work than the American, British, or German systems, and Denmark does not appear to subsidize low-wage jobs in the way that seems to be the case in France and, to a lesser extent, the Netherlands.

Overall, the social benefit systems and the active labor market policies differ markedly across our six countries. Denmark and the United States occupy two extreme positions. The "Danish model" relies on a generous social system and on an ALMP-based policy that focuses primarily on training. This approach could be labeled an "empowerment strategy" in that it aims to provide workers with both human capital and out-of-work income to foster their individual bargaining power in the labor market. Whether Denmark has gone too far in this direction is an open question. Some argue that social benefits in Denmark are too generous and may create unemployment traps for some groups (such as immigrants) and that the real impact of training on employment prospects and wages needs to be assessed.

Nevertheless, the Danish approach is completely different from the one taken in the United States, where the social system gives little support to those outside of employment. The social supports that do operate in the United States generally give strong incentives to take low-wage jobs, with a priority given to in-work benefits, especially the EITC. At the same time, ALMPs in the United States are weak and mainly based on a work-first strategy (the 1996 welfare reform) that considers any kind of job better than no job.

The other four countries in our study lie somewhere in between these two extremes. The Netherlands is closest to Denmark but has some features similar to the French system that act to promote low-wage jobs—through employment subsidies of different kinds. At first glance, the United Kingdom appears to share important characteristics of the U.S. model, including the emphasis on in-work benefits and the priority given to the work-first strategy, but a closer look suggests important differences. In the United Kingdom, for example, the minimum wage is much higher than it is in the United States, social benefits are more generous (including health insurance, child support, and housing benefits, for example), and expenditures on ALMPs are higher in the United Kingdom, especially for young people. In its own distinct way, the United Kingdom is, in this sense, more a part of the European "social model" than a representative of U.S.-style policies in Europe.

CONCLUSION

In most of our countries, low-wage work is disproportionately made up of women, young people, older workers, less-educated workers, and immigrants. In general, national social safety nets provide these groups with little or no financial support when they are not working, usually because most national welfare systems continue to reflect their roots in policies designed to support full-time male "breadwinners" and their nonworking families. Many low-wage workers— overwhelmingly women—also combine their low-wage employment with substantial responsibilities for child care and elder care. These extra-market responsibilities appear to reduce these workers' bargaining power relative to their employers and frequently lead them to trade reduced or flexible hours for lower pay rates.

The national differences in the incidence of low-wage work cannot be explained by a simple market-driven, supply-side story. There is no simple correlation across countries between the share of the less-skilled in the working-age population and the national incidence of low-wage work. Immigration has been important and increasing in recent years in countries such as the United States, the United Kingdom, and Germany, where the incidence of low-wage work has been high and rising in the past decade or so. Over the same period, however, Denmark has also witnessed a large increase in immigration without any visible effect on the incidence of low-wage work—but the employment rate of immigrants has remained particularly low. The impact of immigration does not appear to be automatic, but rather mediated through the national system of labor market institutions. The pay-setting institutions and other labor market regulations analyzed in the previous chapter and the availability of out-of-work income support play a particularly important role in this respect.

The take-up of low-wage jobs by potentially vulnerable groups (women, youth, and older people) depends on national tax and benefits systems. The lack of publicly provided child care contributes to the high share of part-time women workers in countries like Germany, the Netherlands, and the United Kingdom. In Germany and the Netherlands, joint taxation and derived social rights also encourage women to accept low-wage, part-time jobs—like the "mini-jobs" in Germany. In all countries, particularly in generous Denmark and France, students are less eligible for transfer payments and have to take low-wage jobs. The increase in the number of students and the parallel leveling or decrease in grants (as in the United Kingdom) have reinforced this trend. The picture is more mixed across countries for older workers. Until the beginning of the 2000s, they had been more protected from low-wage work in countries with higher pensions at low income levels and publicly funded early retirement schemes (or functional equivalents), such as Denmark, France, Germany, and the Netherlands, in contrast to the United Kingdom and, even more, the United States.

One key consequence of the labor supply institutions is that the social meaning of low-wage work differs substantially across the six countries. For example, Denmark's low share of low-wage workers and high concentration of low-wage work among young people suggests that low-wage work is mainly a transitory state in the first stage of the life cycle there. By contrast, in Germany, the Netherlands, and the United Kingdom, low-wage work is more widespread, and the concentration among women is particularly high. Both the overall share of low-wage workers and the low-wage gender gap are lower in France than in most of the rest of our six countries. The overall low-wage share is quite high in the United States, but the probability of being low-paid is more evenly distributed across sociodemographic groups in the United States than it is in the five European countries, and the incidence of low-wage work among older workers in the United States is notably higher than it is in other countries.

Active and passive labor market policies, as well as means-tested in- or out-of-work benefits, shape the incentives for the unemployed to take low-wage jobs. Two distinct institutional models stand out. On the one hand, in some countries (such as the United States, the United Kingdom, and, to some degree, Germany since the Hartz IV reforms), unemployment benefits are low and ALMPs are geared toward a work-first strategy—job search assistance and monitoring that place pressure on the unemployed to return to work as quickly as possible and therefore to accept low-wage work if available (with in-work benefits acting as an additional incentive in the United States and the United Kingdom). On the other hand, the Danish model relies on a generous welfare system, complemented by ALMPs based on training. The Danish approach is based on an empowerment strategy that aims to provide workers with both human capital and out-of-work income to foster their individual bargaining power in the labor market. France and the Netherlands are somewhere in between, with more generous out-of-work benefits than the United States, the

United Kingdom, and (in more recent years) Germany, but less active ALMPs than Denmark.

NOTES

1. Of course, the bargaining and regulatory institutions discussed in the preceding chapter and the labor supply factors discussed here interact with one another. In particular, some of the institutions related to labor supply discussed in this chapter—including unemployment insurance, social assistance, active labor market policies, and immigration policy—have an important impact on the bargaining power of low-wage workers relative to their employers.

2. An exception with respect to less-skilled workers is Germany, where skilled workers are an important share of low-wage workers.

3. These rankings do not change if analysis is confined to native speakers in each country.

4. Of course, immigrants often have levels of education that are above the national average. For evidence of a bimodal distribution of immigrant educational qualifications in the United Kingdom and the United States—with immigrants overrepresented at both the low end and high end of the education distribution—see Schmitt and Wadsworth (2007).

5. In some countries, such as the United Kingdom and Germany, the inflow of mainly migrant workers from eastern Europe under various statuses (temp agency work, posted work, and so on; see Bosch, Mayhew, and Gautié, this volume) has been important from the beginning of the 2000s.

6. Note that for women age twenty-five to fifty-four, the differences in participation rates between countries are much lower and France and Germany get much better scores: in 2006 this rate amounted to 85.1 percent in Denmark, 81.2 percent in France, 80.3 percent in Germany, 78.4 percent in the Netherlands, 77.9 percent in the United Kingdom, and 75.5 percent in the United States (see also Mason and Salverda, this volume).

7. Child care subsidies might also offset the rise in child care workers' wages in response to higher demand for child care workers.

8. Note that at least some portion of the women who choose market work over unpaid child care in the home are choosing to work in the paid labor market as child care providers.

9. "Bridge" jobs are lesser-paid jobs that older workers take after leaving their "career" job (for this distinction, see Ruhm 1990).

10. The reform faced strong opposition, and as a result, workers are allowed to use their "life course scheme"—their tax-deductible individual saving accounts—to retire early.

11. Note that unemployment assistance benefits are usually included in passive labor market policies (PLMPs), while other means-tested benefits (social assistance) are not. The merger of unemployment assistance with social assistance in Germany explains the big increase in the beneficiaries of PLMPs counted by the OECD (more than 53 percent between 2004 and 2005).

12. METR = 1 − [increase in net income/increase in gross work activity earnings].

13. Net incomes are calculated taking into account incomes taxes and secondary benefits adjusted to each situation. Data include: unemployment assistance, social assistance, minimum income or lone parent benefits (depending on the situation), income tax (net of any tax credits), employees' social security contributions, housing-related cash benefits, family benefits, and in-work or employment-conditional benefits. They exclude unemployment insurance benefits.

14. This measure, though convenient, may not be ideal since ALMP to some extent reduces the number of unemployed by moving them out of the unemployment statistics.

15.` This amount does not take into account the public budget dedicated to the exemptions of employers' social security contributions at low wage levels, which are the main "employment subsidies" in France.

16. As mentioned earlier, income tax credits, which are not taken into account in the ALMP expenditures, are important low-wage job subsidies, at least in the United Kingdom and the United States and, to a lesser degree, in France.

17. The 2005 OECD *Employment Outlook* provides greater detail: "Key examples of activation programmes are requirements on unemployed people to attend intensive interviews with employment counsellors, to apply for job vacancies as directed by employment counsellors, to independently search for job vacancies and apply for jobs, to accept offers of suitable work, to participate in the formulation of an individual action plan and to participate in training or job-creation programs. The main target groups for activation programs are recipients (or claimants) of income-replacement benefits which are conditional on availability for work. This includes most recipients of unemployment benefits. Comparable availability-for-work conditions often apply to lone-parent and social assistance benefits. Participation in employment services can also be made obligatory for disability beneficiaries, but the services involved are relatively specific" (OECD 2005, 175).

18. The general scheme is based on employers' social security contributions. Before exemptions, the employers' social contributions amount to 40 percent of gross wage. At minimum-wage levels, the exemptions reach a maximum and amount to about 26 percentage points (in

2005)—that is, the employer pays only 14 percent of the gross wage, while the state pays the remaining 26 percent to the social security system.

19. The employment effects of SPAK, which was abolished in January 2006 for budgetary reasons, were, at best, mixed (see Mühlau and Salverda 2000) and deadweight losses were over 90 percent.

20. For youth under twenty-five, the UI runs for only six months. After this period, a young unemployed person must take an education course of at least eighteen months, if he or she has no qualification, or undergo job training.

REFERENCES

Angrist, Joshua, and Adriana Kugler. 2003. "Protective or Counter Protective? Labor Market Institutions and the Effect of Immigration on EU Natives." *The Economic Journal* (June): F302–F331.

Aydemir, Abdurrahman, and George Borjas. 2007. "Cross-Country Variation in the Impact of International Migration: Canada, Mexico, and the United States." *Journal of the European Economic Association* (June): 663–708.

Bertola, Giuseppe, Francine D. Blau, and Lawrence M. Kahn. 2007. "Labor Market Institutions and Demographic Employment Patterns." *Journal of Population Economics* 20(4, October): 833–67.

Bosch, Gerhard, and Thorsten Kalina. 2008. "Low-Wage Work in Germany: An Overview." In *Low-Wage Work in Germany*, edited by Gerhard Bosch and Claudia Weinkopf. New York: Russell Sage Foundation.

Bosch, Gerhard, and Claudia Weinkopf, eds. 2008. *Low-Wage Work in Germany*. New York: Russell Sage Foundation.

Carcillo, Stéphane, and David Grubb. 2006. "From Inactivity to Work: The Role of Active Labor Market Policies." Working paper 36. Paris: OECD Directorate for Employment, Labour, and Social Affairs.

Card, David. 2005. "Is the New Immigration Really So Bad?" Working paper W11547. Cambridge, Mass.: National Bureau of Economic Research (August).

Caroli, Ève, Jérôme Gautié, and Philippe Askénazy. 2008. "Low-Wage Work and Labor Market Institutions in France." In *Low-Wage Work in France*, edited by Ève Caroli and Jérôme Gautié. New York: Russell Sage Foundation.

Dustman, Christian, Albrecht Glitz, and Tommaso Frattini. 2008. "The Labor Market Impact of Immigration." *Oxford Review of Economic Policy* 24: 477–94.

Folbre, Nancy. 2001. *The Invisible Heart: Economics and Family Values*. New York: New Press.

Freeman, Richard. 2007. *America Works: Critical Thoughts on the Exceptional U.S. Labor Market.* New York: Russell Sage Foundation.

Freeman, Richard, and Ronald Shettkat. 2005. "Marketization of Production and the EU-US Gap in Work." *Economic Policy* 20(41): 5–50.

Immervoll, Herwig, and David Barber. 2005. *Can Parents Afford to Work? Child Care Costs, Tax Benefit Policies, and Work Incentives.* Paris: Organization for Economic Cooperation and Development.

Manacorda, Marco, Alan Manning, and Jonathan Wadsworth. 2007. "The Impact of Immigration on the Structure of Male Wages: Theory and Evidence from Britain." Discussion paper. London: London School of Economics, Centre for Economic Performance (CEP) (September).

Mason, Geoff, Ken Mayhew, Matthew Osborne, and Philip Stevens. 2008. "Low Pay, Labor Market Institutions, and Job Quality in the United Kingdom." In *Low-Wage Work in the United Kingdom*, edited by Caroline Lloyd, Geoff Mason, and Ken Mayhew. New York: Russell Sage Foundation.

Mühlau, Peter, and Justine Horgan. 2001. "Labor Market Status and the Wage Position of the Low-Skilled." Working paper 5. Amsterdam: European Low-Wage Employment Research Network (LoWER) (July).

Mühlau, Peter, and Wiemer Salverda. 2000. "Effects of Low-Wage Subsidies: The Example of 'SPAK' in the Netherlands." In *Policy Measures for Low-Wage Employment*, edited by Wiemer Salverda, Brian Nolan, and Claudio Lucifora. Cheltenham, U.K.: Edward Elgar.

Organization for Economic Cooperation and Development (OECD). 2001. "OECD Tax Models: Taxing Wages" (database). Paris: OECD.

———. 2005. *Employment Outlook.* Paris: OECD.

———. 2006. *Education at a Glance.* Paris: OECD.

———. 2007a. *International Migration Outlook.* SOPEMI 2007 ed. Paris: OECD.

———. 2007b. *Family Database.* Chart LMF 7.1. Paris: OECD.

———. 2008. *Employment Outlook.* Paris: OECD.

Ram, Monder, Paul Edwards, and Trevor Jones. 2004. *Informal Employment, Small Firms, and the National Minimum Wage.* Report for the Low Pay Commission (September). Available at: http://www.lowpay.gov.uk/lowpay/research/pdf/t0NTAVZ4.pdf.

Ray, Rebecca, Janet C. Gornick, and John Schmitt. 2008. "Parental Leave Policies in Twenty-One Countries: Assessing Generosity and Gender Equality." Working paper. Washington, D.C.: Center for Economic and Policy Research (CEPR) (September).

Ruhm, Christopher J. 1990. "Bridge Jobs and Partial Retirement." *Journal of Labor Economics* 8(4): 482–501.

Rosholm, Michael, and Michael Svarer. 2004. "Estimating the Threat Effect of Active Labor Market Programs." Working paper 2004-6. Aarhus, Denmark: University of Aarhus, School of Economics and Management,

Salverda, Wiemer. 2008. "Low-Wage Work and the Economy." In *Low-Wage Work in the Netherlands*, edited by Wiemer Salverda, Maarten van Klaveren, and Marc van der Meer. New York: Russell Sage Foundation.

Salverda, Wiemer, Maarten van Klaveren, and Marc van der Meer. 2008. *Low-Wage Work in the Netherlands*. New York: Russell Sage Foundation.

Schmitt, John, and Jonathan Wadsworth. 2007. "Changes in the Relative Economic Performance of Immigrants to Great Britain and the United States, 1980–2000." *British Journal of Industrial Relations* 45(4, December): 659–86.

Waldfogel, Jane. 2006. *What Children Need*. Cambridge: Cambridge University Press.

Westergaard-Nielsen, Niels. 2008. "Low-Wage Work in Denmark." In *Low-Wage Work in Denmark*, edited by Niels Westergaard-Nielsen. New York: Russell Sage Foundation.

PART II

Industry Case Studies

CHAPTER 5

Institutions, Firms, and the Quality of Jobs in Low-Wage Labor Markets

Eileen Appelbaum

The case studies in this volume suggest that European employment models are under considerable pressure. Efforts to reduce wages have led some employers to take advantage of various loopholes that can enable them to escape the institutions and social norms that govern the employment relationship in their countries, leading to what one observer has come to call "varieties of institutional avoidance"—in a play on the term "varieties of capitalism." The United Kingdom, for example, moved some considerable distance toward the United States during the Thatcher years. More recently, the national employment models in the Netherlands and Germany have also begun to fray, a development most evident in hotel and retail employment. These efforts at institutional avoidance have been most successful in Germany, where the low-wage share has soared and now exceeds rates in the United Kingdom and is fast approaching those of the United States.

Despite strong competitive pressures in every country, however, and the desire of many employers to reduce wages, institutions still matter. Where unions retain much of their traditional strength and influence, where employment regulations provide workers with protections against layoffs, or where a national minimum wage provides an effective floor, employers have seen these escape routes closed off. In Denmark, employers voluntarily comply with union agreements. A high reservation wage combined with extensive union coverage in the Danish economy means that a company that rejects the extension of collectively bargained wages will face problems recruiting and retaining workers, as well as a union campaign of disapproval that might damage its reputation with customers. In the Netherlands, access to quality health care is enshrined in the nation's constitution. Under the pressure of an aging population and rising health care costs, the reform of the financing mechanism for hospitals has forced the health care system to evolve. The adaptation involved further integration of the health care system, however, and a rethinking of the training, qualifications, and allocation of nursing staff to preserve the quality of care.

The institutional frameworks governing employment relations in all of the high-income economies has come under intense pressure as the effects of increased globalization, heightened capital mobility, new intra- and inter-firm relationships, and advances in information and communication technologies have strengthened the position of employers relative to workers. The case studies in this volume document employers' efforts to evade institutional constraints, as well as to reshape national labor market institutions, so as to increase their ability to lower wages and reduce employment security. In countries where labor market institutions have been inadequate to protect workers' interests (as in the United States and the United Kingdom) or where workers' interests have more recently come under attack and been weakened (as in Germany and the Netherlands), the result has been a deterioration in the quality of jobs that do not require a university degree, an increase in the incidence of low-wage work, and a widening of the earnings gap between high- and low-paid workers. At the same time, the industry case studies provide evidence of the continuing role played by strong unions, binding minimum wages, undiluted social norms, and strong regulations governing employee layoffs in closing off this low-road behavior, as well as evidence of push-back against the efforts of some employers to drive down wages and degrade working conditions in less-skilled jobs.

The chapters in this volume provide an analysis across the six countries of competitive industry dynamics, current employer strategies, and national institutions as they affect the pay and working conditions of cleaners and nursing assistants in hospitals, call center operators, room attendants in hotels, process operatives in food processing, and cashiers and stock or sales clerks in retail. This chapter contrasts the employment conditions faced by similarly situated workers in these same jobs in different countries. The chapter seeks to underscore the influence of variations in national labor market institutions on worker outcomes. The two main goals in what follows are, first, to provide concrete examples of the interaction between institutions, firm strategy, and worker outcomes that are instructive to an American reader and of interest to Europeans as well, and second, to call attention to the evidence that points toward a convergence to low-road models of employment across countries with a wide range of institutional settings.

NURSING ASSISTANTS AND CLEANERS IN HOSPITALS

Health care systems in general and hospitals in particular have come under substantial cost pressures as a result of aging populations and advances in medicine that enable more people to live longer with chronic conditions that require care. Hospitals are having a difficult time delivering high-quality care while covering these costs as a result of reimbursement formulas in the United States and all five European countries that base payments on the illness and not on the condition of the patient. Public budgets that support hospital care—ranging from a low of 57 percent in the United States to a high of 96 percent in Denmark—are under pressure. Hospital administrators are engaged in wide-ranging efforts to improve productivity and reduce costs. Despite the similarity in cost pressures on hospitals, we observe wide differences among countries in the nature of the work and pay of less-skilled workers in hospitals.

Employer-sponsored health insurance is the main way in which non-elderly Americans gain access to the health care system in the United States. Rising health care costs put U.S. companies that provide health insurance at a competitive disadvantage; not surprisingly, some are cutting back health benefits. In 2006 just 61 percent of the non-elderly population had health insurance through an employer, down substantially from 2001. Medicaid and other public programs covered 16 percent, and another 5 percent bought insurance privately. But 18 percent of non-elderly people—46.5 million U.S. adults and children—had no health care coverage, private or public, despite the fact that over 80 percent of them lived in families in which someone worked (Henry J. Kaiser Family Foundation 2008).

Health care reform is on the agenda in the United States, but not much attention has been paid to how to recruit, train, and allocate the nursing staff that will be required to care for all of the people who would suddenly have access to health care. We examine differences in pay, training, and allocation of tasks among nursing staff across the countries in some detail, not only because there are sharp differences, but because there may be useful ideas about the health care workforce that should enter health care reform discussions in the United States.

The Incidence of Low-Wage Work in Hospitals

One part of the strategy of U.S. hospitals to reduce costs has been increased reliance on certified nursing assistants with minimal—usually just six weeks—of formal training to toilet and bathe patients and monitor temperature and blood pressure. In some cases, nursing assistants are expected to draw blood, apply sterile dressings, or prepare patients for intravenous procedures—responsibilities for which they are generally not adequately trained. The use of low-paid nursing assistants rather than higher-paid licensed practical nurses or fully qualified registered nurses to perform these more-skilled tasks is motivated by hospitals' drive to cut costs. Hospitals increasingly rely on immigrant women to fill these jobs, as the low pay offered by employers makes the jobs unattractive to native-born and longtime residents of the United States. The result is a chronic labor "shortage" and high rates of staff turnover at the wages offered for this kind of work.

European hospitals are more limited in their ability to substitute lower-paid workers for more highly skilled and paid workers. In the five European countries, the quality of health services is a significant issue, either as a social norm or as an electoral issue. Service delivery in hospitals is highly dependent on a skilled workforce. In addition, the EU Transfer of Undertakings (TUPE) regulations of 1981 limit employer options by requiring employers to transfer employees on existing terms and working conditions along with the "undertaking" when work is contracted out (Earnshaw, Rubery, and Cooke 2002).

As reported by Philippe Méhaut and his colleagues (this volume), 38 percent of nursing assistants in hospitals in the United States are low-wage, compared with 21 percent in the United Kingdom, just 9 percent in Germany, and between 0 and 5 percent in the Netherlands, France, and Denmark. Cleaners in hospitals fare worse than nursing assistants, especially in Germany and the United Kingdom, where much of this work is subcontracted to private cleaning companies. In 2006 the incidence of low-wage work among cleaners was 50 percent in the United States, 55 percent in the United Kingdom, and 20 percent in Germany. German hospitals appear to ignore the TUPE regulations. Work is subcontracted to private cleaning companies under the conditions of the cleaners' union contract, at wages far lower than those set by the hospital workers' contract.

In the United Kingdom, subcontractors that provide cleaning services to public hospitals are bound by the TUPE regulations but have made extensive use of a loophole. The regulations apply only to workers who were transferred when the work was originally subcontracted. New hires can be paid less. The result has been a proliferation of two-tier wage contracts and a run-up in the incidence of low-wage work among hospital cleaners. The strength of the public-sector unions that represent hospital workers has recently been reasserted, however, and the public-sector wage agreement is being extended to employees of companies that provide outsourced hospital services. This agreement, only recently implemented, has not yet affected the earnings data reported here. Going forward, we can expect a reduction in the incidence of low-wage work among cleaners in U.K. hospitals.

TRAINING, SKILLS, AND QUALIFICATIONS

Training, skills, and qualifications of nursing assistants vary widely across Europe and differ markedly from the United States, where certified nursing assistants typically receive six weeks of training. There is a strong tension in all countries between efforts to increase the skills, responsibilities, and wages of less-skilled workers, such as nursing assistants, on the one hand, and the inappropriate substitution of poorly paid and trained workers for skilled nurses as hospitals endeavor to cut costs, on the other. In Denmark, tasks have shifted from higher to lower levels in the nursing skill hierarchy. This shift has been accompanied, however, by the upgrading of skills for all groups. Since 1992, a certificate has been required to obtain a job as a hospital nursing assistant. A thirty-four-month training program, including fifty-six weeks of theoretical training, is required for the certificate. France has been eliminating nursing assistants who lack qualifications. Vacancies are filled with qualified nursing assistants, and a strong vocational program has been developed to train and upgrade the skills of unqualified nursing assistants already on hospital staffs. The United Kingdom is similar to the United States in the high use it makes of minimally qualified nursing assistants. Nursing assistants are encouraged, however, to take the National Vocational Qualification (NVQ) Level 2 in care, which is an assessment of an individual's competence based on national occupational standards. Recently, some of these nursing assistants have also obtained NVQ Level 3 skills in order to qualify for new intermediate positions, such as a junior doctor's assistant or assistant practitioner. But inadequate training budgets, the limited availability of these types of posts, and hospitals' unwillingness to pay higher wages for credentials have limited this opportunity for nursing assistants in the United Kingdom.

Recruitment problems in Germany for both qualified and unqualified nursing staff led, in 1963, to the introduction of one year of vocational training followed by a state examination for nursing assistants. The training program led to higher wages for qualified nursing assistants, reducing the incidence of low-paid work. Historically, the nature of union bargaining in the hospital sector created a relatively small wage gap between nursing assistants and nurses, leading hospitals to reduce their use of nursing assistants relative to qualified nurses. Even as the union structure has changed in recent years, wage differentials have remained low. The ratio of nursing assistants to nurses continues to decline and is currently one nursing assistant for every twelve qualified nurses. More recently, some hospitals have taken advantage of the "mini-jobs" to use a small number of low-paid staff to wash patients on large wards.

Reform of the training system for nursing staff is both more recent and far more extensive in the Netherlands. A five-level vocational training and educational structure was introduced in 1996–97 that gives employed nurses options for paid vocational training and education leading to advancement. These are organized into various work-school combinations, including apprenticeships, and do not require that an employee leave paid employment and return to school—a high barrier in the U.S. context—in order to move to a more-skilled and better-paying job. A nurse 1 receives one year of training to become a "helper" and is mainly employed in home care services. A nurse 2 receives one year of vocational training to become a "qualified helper" and is employed primarily in homes for the elderly and sometimes in nursing homes. A nurse 3 receives three years of training at a higher vocational level to become an "assistant nurse." The training includes an initial six-month job preparation period in a training hospital that provides a mix of theory and practice followed by practical training and an average of four hours a week of instruction. These nursing assistants are mainly employed in nursing homes. Training for a nurse 4, or "general nurse," requires four years of education and training. It builds on the earlier vocational training of lower-level nurse positions. Alternatively, a nurse can obtain a four-year educational credential and enter nursing as a nurse 4 from the educational system. A nurse 5 is a "nurse manager" who takes medical actions, coordinates total patient care, and manages lower-level nursing staff. This position requires four years of university training. Until 2004, employers could tap into a sectorwide training fund. Now employers must provide their own training budgets, and spending on training has declined. The fall in training negatively affects career opportunities but also undermines the health care sector's ability to fill vacancies as the workforce ages and employees retire.

Germany and the Netherlands make little to no use of nursing assistants in hospitals. Cost pressures associated with the system of flat-rate reimbursements to hospitals for patient care have led the Netherlands to develop an integrated health care system of hospitals, nursing homes, elderly or residential homes, and home care services. The care of acutely ill patients in hospitals requires skilled nursing care in the Dutch view, and nursing assistants are generally not employed there. In Germany, the low number of nursing assistants reflects a continuation of two long-standing factors. German hospitals have traditionally employed low levels of nursing staff, both qualified nurses and nursing assistants, and small wage differentials between nurses and nursing assistants favor the employment of relatively more nurses. The flat payments for patient care have led hospitals to decrease nurse staffing levels and decrease the number of nursing assistants even further in Germany.

JOB BOUNDARIES IN NURSING CARE IN HOSPITALS

The greater training and skills of nursing assistants in Germany, France, and Denmark compared with the United States, the narrower wage differentials between nursing assistants and nurses, and the lower ratio of nursing assistants to nurses have also led to differences in job boundaries. Nursing assistant jobs overlap substantially with nurses' jobs in Germany, France, and Denmark, where nursing assistants have qualifications and are able to carry out more-skilled nursing tasks. This is true to a lesser extent in the United Kingdom as well. On the other hand, less-skilled tasks, such as bathing patients, are fully integrated into nurse jobs in Dutch hospitals, where there are virtually no nursing assistants; to a great extent, the same is true in German hospitals as well. In France and Denmark, these less-skilled tasks are mainly done by skilled nursing assistants. Thus, despite the similarity in the range of tasks to be carried out by nursing staff in hospitals in every country, the actual division of tasks between nurse and nursing assistant jobs varies considerably.

CALL CENTER OPERATORS

The emergence of call centers as a form of employment is rather recent, dating only from the 1980s and accelerating in the 1990s. Call centers are not an industry; rather, they are a new form of organizing customer sales and service in various industries through technology-mediated channels. Companies in financial services and utilities—the sectors examined in this study—were among the first to set up in-house call centers as a cost-effective way to handle their customer sales and service inquiries. Historically, call centers in these sectors were regulated or public-sector industries in all six countries, paid relatively high wages, and in most cases had high levels of union membership and bargaining coverage. Regular employees working in these centers still tend to have better pay and benefits than call center workers generally, even in the United States. Companies can also outsource this work to lower-cost subcontractors, who have expanded rapidly in the last decade in all six countries. They provide an easy avenue for employers to escape the constraints of sectoral or company bargaining agreements—an avenue that German employers in particular have pursued. Call centers also cut costs and manage demand fluctuations and asocial work hours through the use of part-time and temporary workers, particularly agency workers—a practice particularly noteworthy in the Netherlands and the United Kingdom. Companies in the United States and the United Kingdom also have the option of offshoring this work to low-wage, English-speaking countries—an option generally not available to Dutch and Danish employers owing to language barriers. Offshoring is only beginning as a possibility in France.

THE INCIDENCE OF LOW-WAGE WORK IN CALL CENTERS

The incidence of low-paid work in call centers varies widely both within and across countries. In in-house call centers in finance and utilities in each country, pay tends to be set by collective bargaining agreements or by company or industry norms. As a result, nearly all of the directly employed workers in the in-house case study organizations were paid above the low-pay threshold. Subcontractors also serve these industries and tend to have greater leeway in setting pay and benefits. Subcontractors are more likely to set wage rates below the low-pay threshold. Differences in pay levels between in-house call centers and subcontractors within countries are substantial in Germany and the Netherlands. The outsourcing of call center work can increase the incidence of low-wage work among call center operators.

Two of the most important reasons for differences in the incidence of low-wage work across countries are differences in the inclusiveness of collective bargaining systems and differences in the existence and level of a national minimum wage. In France, collective agreements are negotiated at the industry level, with mandatory extension to almost all employers in the industry. Collective agreements cover 81 percent of all call centers, including two-thirds of subcontractors. Together with a relatively high national minimum wage and wage protection for agency workers, this system of collective bargaining has effectively prevented French employers from embarking on low-road labor market strategies. Denmark's formal institutional framework is far less inclusive than France's. Nevertheless, high union density, the strength of trade unions, and the threat that they will make life difficult for employers that defect from traditional arrangements are factors that have similarly deterred employers from degrading call center operators' pay and working conditions.

Formal institutions in the Netherlands appear similar to those in France, but there are important differences. The Dutch minimum wage is much lower than the French, particularly for younger workers. And while employers are governed by sectoral collective bargaining agreements, these agreements set low levels of pay in entry-level jobs, in jobs for young workers, and in temporary agency work. As a result, even in-house centers have a relatively high incidence of low-wage work, and low wages apply broadly in agreements that cover subcontractors and agency workers. Dutch call center employers make extensive use of contingent workers. In contrast, low-wage work in German call centers is largely concentrated among subcontractors. Eastern Germany now provides a way for firms in western Germany to subcontract some call center work to low-wage parts of the country, and this has proven attractive for less-skilled tasks and for work at asocial evening and weekend hours. About half the call center workers in both Germany and the Netherlands work part-time. In the United Kingdom, the national minimum wage provides a floor for subcontractors and agencies, while tight labor markets have moderated the incidence of low-paid call center work.[1]

The result is a wide variance across countries in the incidence of low-wage work. The incidence of low pay is highest in call centers in the Netherlands (41 percent) and Germany (36 percent), compared with 28 percent in the United Kingdom, 19 percent in the United States, and only 5 percent in Denmark and 4 percent in France.

BUSINESS STRATEGY AND WORK ORGANIZATION

Despite the use of common technology, employers face hard choices in organizing call center work. On the one hand, the computer and information technologies with which operators work facilitates the use of electronic algorithms in interactions with customers. This approach requires few worker skills, limits employee discretion in interactions with customers, and maximizes the number of calls handled. Conversely, the technology may also be used to enable operators to customize products and services for customers and to negotiate sales and service contracts. In this setting, operators require literacy, numeracy, and communication skills as well as knowledge of the company's products and procedures. Employers that focus on maximizing short-run profits usually target high-volume, low-cost approaches to customer interactions that rely on less-skilled, low-paid workers and on the use of electronic algorithms to provide customer service. In contrast, employers that compete on the basis of quality and customer loyalty and take a longer-term approach to profit maximization need more highly skilled workers, want to invest in training, and may need to pay higher wages to attract and retain employees.

Both approaches to customer service and work organization can be found in call centers within each country, reflecting in part the legacy of the industry in which the call center originated as well as the business strategy adopted by the employer. Nevertheless, the evidence suggests that the institutional framework has had important influences on the organization of work.

In the Netherlands, the United Kingdom, and the United States, employers are more likely to fragment work, design jobs that are narrow in terms of tasks undertaken, organize work into separate departments, have employees adhere to "scripts" in dealing with customers, and engage in performance monitoring linked to individual employee targets and rewards. In the United States and the United Kingdom, weak employment security regulations and the lack of sectoral collective bargaining coverage have enabled employers to shut down traditional customer service operations and locate call centers in remote areas with a new workforce, to make greater use of agency workers, and to operate with few limitations on how work is organized. Despite company benefits and pay rates in the finance and utility industries that are often well above the low-pay threshold in both countries, poor job quality leads to high turnover rates. In the Netherlands, employers have been able to evade sectoral collective agreements that set minimum pay rates for jobs by employing temporary and contingent workers. The extensive use of part-time, temporary, and agency workers with high turnover rates is possible because employers are able to fragment tasks, script employee interactions with customers, and use technology to monitor workers.

In contrast, employers in Denmark, France, and Germany are more likely to utilize call center operators who are knowledgeable about their products and services, who can handle a broad range of customer inquiries, and who are capable of exercising discretion and judgment. They make little use of electronic monitoring, an onerous work practice in most call centers in the United States. Field research for this volume found no use of electronic monitoring of individuals in German centers, no use of it for performance management in France, and only rare use of it to reward individual performance in Denmark. Strong collective agreements and employment security and dismissal regulations in these sectors have limited the ability of employers in Germany and Denmark to lay off existing staff and set up new operations elsewhere. German employers have frequently been required to set up in-house call centers with existing skilled customer service employees. Unions and works councils have played an important role in securing broader jobs, reducing time on phones, and increasing the frequency of breaks for operators. Despite this, employers in Germany have succeeded in outsourcing a range of operations, as well as evening and weekend work, to lower-cost subcontractors that are generally not covered by union contracts, employ large numbers of part-time women workers, and pay substantially lower wages. Highly unionized Danish banking employees effectively enjoy lifetime employment and were often relocated along with the work when managers closed branches and established call centers. In France, call centers established by banks and utility companies typically carry out all of the activities previously done by advisers in branch offices. French unions have been involved in developing career paths for call center operators. Under these circumstances, Danish, French, and German employers have incentives to organize call center work to encompass a broad range of skills and tasks.

HOTEL HOUSEKEEPERS

Workers who clean hotel rooms do not face direct threats of offshoring and automation, which would seem to increase the scope for national labor market institutions to affect work and pay in these jobs. Yet institutions such as collective bargaining, minimum wages, and employment protection legislation have not generally led to much variation across countries in the nature of the job performed by room attendants. In all six countries, room attendants work at the bottom of each national labor market. Stronger industrial relations systems have not had much impact, although the existence and level of a national minimum wage or negotiated pay packet can make a difference.

The hotel industry is shifting from small, independently owned hotels to large international corporate chains concerned about share prices. Mergers and acquisitions have led to a proliferation of brands but a decreasing number of companies. Consolidation has intensified competition among chains in both the mid- and upper-market segments. Competitive strategy consists of increasing the number of features and complimentary items for guests (for example, coffee makers, hair dryers, trouser presses, TVs, DVDs, play stations, sauna robes) while simultaneously cutting costs. The result is an intensification of work for room attendants, who not only must do more work to clean each room but are often now required to clean more rooms during normal working hours.

In addition to requiring more work during each shift, hotels have turned to flexibility to achieve cost-cutting targets. In all six countries, the goal of hotel management is to be able to respond to fluctuations in occupancy rates by having the flexibility to pay cleaners only when rooms need to be cleaned. In the United States, employers achieve this kind of flexibility by simply not calling workers in to work when occupancy is low. Workers with low seniority face fluctu-ating weekly hours and pay. Some hotels in the United Kingdom of-fer only part-time jobs, while others use a core group of full-time room attendants supplemented by casual part-time or temporary workers. In German hotels, there has been a great increase in the use of short-term, short-hour workers who hold the mini-jobs created by national policy. French hotels make significant use of "extras"—room attendants who work only a few hours a day. Both Dutch and Danish hotels increasingly rely on part-time workers, although in Denmark these are largely young workers. In the Netherlands, hotels use "minimum-term" workers, or so-called zero-hour contracts. Workers have a job, but work only when needed and are paid only for the actual hours they work. Some German, Dutch, and British hotels make use of high levels of outsourcing to contract cleaning firms that pay workers on a piece-rate basis—that is, a fixed amount for each room cleaned. These practices have contributed to the rise in low-wage employment in Germany and the Netherlands.

WORK AND WORKFORCE CHARACTERISTICS

Women, often ethnic minorities or migrants, are the primary work-force among room attendants, and they often work part-time. In the United Kingdom and Denmark, hotels rely heavily on students, who make up between 15 and 20 percent of room attendants. The work is arduous and physically and psychologically demanding: a room cleaner must not only be able to do hard physical work but be incon-spicuous to guests. Managers often prefer immigrant workers, view-ing them as more willing to put up with these conditions without complaint.

Despite differences in institutions, the work of room attendants is remarkably similar in each of the countries. Room attendants typi-cally work alone to clean a target number of rooms, following strict operating procedures and being monitored by supervisors. The work involves lifting and shifting beds and other furniture. Downtime has been eliminated, and room attendants often work through scheduled breaks to complete the assigned work.

Although it would be possible to modernize and improve the qual-ity of room attendants' jobs, the work has changed little over time. Surprisingly few hotels allow room attendants to work together in teams to make the heavy labor more manageable; few hotels have in-

troduced beds that can be raised by pedals; and few provide ergonomic training to reduce injuries to workers or are concerned
about the health threats posed by the use of strong chemical detergents and cleaners.

Mobility to higher-paying jobs is limited by a lack of training, lack
of opportunities for immigrants to learn the language, and little opportunity to gain experience in other hotel jobs. New workers typically learn the job by shadowing an experienced worker. It is not unusual for a hotel to staff from a single immigrant group; these room
attendants speak to each other in their native tongue and have little
opportunity to learn the language of their new home. Opportunities
for advancement within housekeeping departments are inherently
limited by the structure of such departments—many room cleaners
and few supervisors. A few hotels in France and the United States experimented with combining room attendants' jobs with reception activities, but these were isolated examples. In most hotels, the expectation is that room attendants will not be promoted, and they are
denied access to training in customer relations. For immigrant workers, a job cleaning rooms rarely functions as a path into the larger labor market or to greater social inclusion in society. These workers
have few opportunities to acquire the language and other skills required to move to other jobs.

The Incidence of Low-Wage Work in Hotels

Although room attendants' jobs pay at or near the bottom of the pay
scale in every country, regardless of the market segment served by the
hotel, differences in institutions do result in wide variances in the incidence of low-wage work. In Denmark and France, where the wage
floor is close to the low-wage threshold, the share of room attendants
whose pay falls below that threshold is far smaller than it is in the
other countries. The share of low-wage work for all workers in hotels
is 20 to 25 percent in France and Denmark but rises to between 45
and 71 percent in the other four countries. Low-wage work is even
more prevalent among room attendants, reaching 72 percent in the
United States, 86 percent in Germany, and 89 percent in the United
Kingdom. Unions make a difference. In the United States, the union
wage premium for hotel workers is 17 percent, and it is even higher
in cities with high union density. In Denmark, the only country with

sizable union membership in hotels, union wages are 14 percent higher than wages for non-union workers.

Despite these differences, the European case studies mainly demonstrate the failure of industrial relations systems to make a difference to the earnings of hotel room attendants. The industry serves as an exemplar of the various ways in which low-wage work has been able to increase despite the institutions intended to limit its spread. The wage-bargaining system in the United Kingdom, as in the United States, is fragmented and decentralized, with few workers covered by collective labor agreements (CLAs). Germany and the Netherlands, in contrast, have sectorwide labor agreements that are extended to cover some or even all workers in non-union hotels. Despite high levels of union coverage, however, the lack of a strong union presence in the workplace leads to weak enforcement of contracts. Outsourcing of room cleaning to cleaning firms further undermines pay and working conditions because enforcement of labor agreements is especially weak among subcontractors, even in Denmark. Outsourcing and the use of agency temps has substituted contingent workers earning piece rates for permanent, full-time room attendants, leading to a further intensification of work and reduction in pay, even in France. Moreover, examples of violations of minimum-wage laws or CLAs are evident in every country. Piece-rate workers with daily targets set too high are especially susceptible to underpayment for the hours they work. Finally, hotel employers' associations in Denmark and Germany are establishing new ways for individual employers to avoid the extension of sectorwide collective agreements and encouraging decentralization and fragmentation of wage bargaining.

Turnover is high among hotel room attendants, but few hotels appear to feel any pressure to improve wages or working conditions in order to increase recruitment and retention. The United States and the United Kingdom already have established migrant labor markets that supply hotels with workers. The United Kingdom has opened its borders to workers from EU accession countries, and British hotels have become dependent on these workers to fill low-paid jobs. The other four European countries are scheduled to do the same in 2009. The part-time hours in hotel housekeeping jobs make this work an option for the increasing number of women workers—including single mothers subject to some form of "workfare"—who need to find a way to meet the demands of both paid work and unpaid care responsibilities.

PROCESS OPERATIVES IN FOOD MANUFACTURING

If the hotel sector is a low-skill industry in which national employment models have little effect on worker outcomes, food processing provides a counterexample of an industry in which industrial relations and legislation continue to exercise a significant influence on the extent of low-wage work.

Food processing is an important manufacturing sector in all of the countries in this study, accounting for a significant share of manufacturing output and employment. However, a combination of increased pressure from retailers (who are using the new power of their centralized buying and distribution networks to demand lower prices from manufacturers), increased international competition from low-wage producers, and changing consumer tastes and lifestyles now makes it difficult for large multinational food processors, as well as small and medium enterprises (SMEs), to operate profitably. The industry has consolidated in most countries through mergers and acquisitions, and companies have responded to heightened competition by choosing either to rely on quality and innovation or to specialize in basic products. The two strategies are not mutually exclusive, and many firms pursue both. Cost cutting is generally not viewed as sufficient for survival. Most European producers, for example, also see creating more value for consumers as essential for business success. The two food-processing sectors examined in this study, meat processing and confectionery, have evolved differently, and firms in the two sectors often adopt different business strategies. In most countries, confectionery is less dependent on the distribution of products through big retailers, such as supermarket chains, and the sector is more profitable than meat processing. One caution: in food processing high-road product market strategies do not necessarily translate into high-road labor market practices.

BUSINESS STRATEGY

France, with its unique food culture, is the leading food manufacturing country in Europe. Although meat processing remains quite fragmented and continues to be dominated by small producers, there has been considerable consolidation in the confectionery sector. Large firms, including multinationals, produce branded products that differentiate the product, communicate to consumers about intangibles (such as quality of ingredients or production process), command price premiums, and protect producers from undue pressure from retailers. Other firms specialize in high-volume, low-quality production, manufacturing food products for other firms or for retailers' private labels. A third group of firms pursues both strategies and tries to achieve economies of scale by producing for large retailers while also diversifying into high-value-added products produced in small batches and distributed through other distribution channels. Finally, France has many small businesses producing for niche markets.

Food processing is a major industry in Denmark, accounting for 22 percent of industrial production and 16 percent of exports. Meat processing is dominated by a few firms and is highly export-oriented: 85 percent of pork products are sold abroad, despite the fact that food processing is not a low-wage sector in Denmark. The negotiated minimum hourly wage for an adult slaughterhouse worker is about €15, but piece-rate agreements bring this up to €30 on average. Confectionery is lower-paid than meat processing, but the negotiated minimum wage of €12.40 per hour is still far above the low-wage threshold. The Danish food-processing sector relies on research and innovation, subsidized by the government, to develop the new products and production processes that enable it to remain competitive in world markets. The Danish Meat Research Institute works to improve product quality, food safety, and automation.

The use of technology in meat processing and confectionery to raise productivity and reduce unit labor costs is increasing. Pressure from food retailers on manufacturers to reduce costs has driven the adoption of automation in Germany, the Netherlands, and the United Kingdom. In France and Denmark, the use of technology is more often motivated by a commitment to producing higher-quality or more diverse foods that require both the attention of skilled workers (thus justifying the higher wages paid to food-processing workers in these countries) and a greater amount of processing, which provides additional scope for automation. Extensive use of automation, as in both Denmark and the Netherlands, requires workers with very different skill sets. Very low wages in some countries impede the introduction of technology to produce basic products, despite the ease of automating tasks, since it may be cheaper to use labor-intensive production processes than to purchase more sophisticated equipment.

INSTITUTIONS AND WORKER OUTCOMES IN FOOD PROCESSING

Worker outcomes in food processing vary widely across countries. Meat processing in both Germany and the United Kingdom is characterized by small and medium-sized firms that sell their products through supermarkets and by weak unions and a lack of industry-wide collective agreements. Meat producers are subject to intense cost pressures from retailers and respond with measures to undermine worker pay and benefits. Weak unions and employment regulations facilitate employers' increased use of temporary workers, who receive relatively low wages, as well as the use of part-time hours during slack periods, annual hours contracts in which workers are employed seasonally, and flexible shift work with hours varied at the employers' convenience. These practices have not only reduced workers' incomes but eroded the traditional system of mutual obligation between employer and employee. Migrant workers are widely used to staff temporary agency jobs in both the United Kingdom and Germany. In Germany, the unequal treatment of migrants is sanctioned through the "country of origin" principle, in which these workers are employed under the legal regulations of their home country.

Employers in Denmark and France have the least incentives to substitute temporary agency workers for regular employees because union contracts and regulations limit the extent to which agency workers can receive lower pay, benefits, status, or legal protections. For the same reasons, Danish and French employers also make little use of migrant workers. Because meat-processing plants in Denmark largely rely on export markets with high standards for quality, skilled permanent employees are an important asset. In addition, the strength of unions means that workers can effectively resist the substitution of temporary agency workers for regular employees. French firms make greater use of temporary agency workers than do Danish firms, hiring them through temp agencies and, in rural areas, as lower-paid seasonal workers. The high national minimum wage in France, however, limits the extent to which pay falls below the low-wage threshold. Moreover, French firms recruit from these temp pools for regular employees.

Dutch food-processing firms fall somewhere between the U.K. and German cases, on the one hand, and the Danish and French, on the other. Dutch firms can pay temporary agency employees less, and hence they have an incentive to make use of them. However, temporary workers are hired through agencies, and the terms on which they can be hired are regulated by law. Further, temp agency workers are included in the CLAs for the food-processing sector.

There is a danger that competition with low-wage countries will lead food-processing companies to make greater use of outsourcing and low-wage immigrants and temporary workers and to adopt strategies based on deteriorating working conditions. Germany and the United Kingdom have advanced the farthest down this path. National policies in Denmark, France, and the Netherlands—minimum-wage legislation, regulation of working conditions, and strong unions or CLAs—limit the ability of firms to choose this path in these countries. Moreover, firms may resist this tendency by using automation to increase productivity and research and technology to develop innovative products for local and export markets. This approach is easier in France, where there is a strong food culture, and in Denmark, where subsidized research institutes are fixtures of the food-processing industry.

GENDER AND PAY IN FOOD PROCESSING

In France and Denmark, food processing is generally *not* low-paid. Yet, in France, there are significant inequalities, with women's wages lower than those of men due to occupational segregation and the greater use of women in seasonal work. Wages in confectionery, which employs a greater proportion of women, are lower despite the fact that production is more capital-intensive and value-added per employee is higher than in meat processing. In Denmark, there are essentially no low-wage adult workers in meat processing and only 5 percent in confectionery, but 80 percent of those on low wages are women. Moreover, pay in confectionery is less than half that in meat processing. In the United Kingdom, one-third of all workers in food processing—but over half of all women—have earnings below the low-wage threshold. On average in U.K. food processing, women earn 84 percent of what men earn.

In Germany and the Netherlands, however, despite the high concentration of women in confectionery—women make up half of the confectionery workforce in the Netherlands but only one-quarter in meat processing—wages are higher for confectionery workers. In

Germany, close to half of meat-processing operators, but fewer than 30 percent of confectionery workers, are low-paid. The explanation lies in the early industrialization of confectionery production in both Germany and the Netherlands. In both countries, the sector has a long tradition as a manufacturing industry, with strong brands, strong unions, and industrywide CLAs and pay structure. In this industry, in these two countries at least, industrial relations appear to trump gender relations.

CASHIERS AND STOCK/SALES CLERKS IN RETAIL

The retail sector in the United States and Europe relies heavily on women and young workers, employed part-time, to staff stores. Although this is done, in part, to meet peak periods of demand and facilitate evening and weekend operating hours, it also provides employers with a workforce that is in a weak bargaining position. In retail, this weakness is exacerbated by a decline in union strength and the weakening of labor regulations—in Germany, the exemption of mini-jobs from social insurance contribution; subminimum wages for young workers in the United Kingdom, Denmark, and the Netherlands; and a declining value of the minimum wage in the United States. Extensive use of part-time staff increases the potential for retail employers to evade the national institutions that protect low-wage workers.

High-road product market strategies based on the nature of the goods sold and the services provided do not necessarily translate into high-road labor market practices and may not affect wages or job quality. On the contrary, higher-quality customer service may be "financed" through lower pay and benefits as low-wage employers can more readily afford additional checkout cashiers and sales staff. Moreover, what constitutes customer service in food and electronics retailing—the two retail segments studied—differs across the countries. In U.S. food stores, quick checkout and bagging are key to customer service. French hypermarkets, however, offer full-service departments for specialty cheeses or fresh fish. Customer service in British supermarkets relies on the availability of staff on the sales floor to answer basic questions and ensure minimum wait time at the checkout. In consumer electronics, the level of service is related to the complexity of the products. Some stores sell TVs and standard electronic products "off the shelf," while others sell more sophisticated products that require a high level of customer service.

The retail sector in every country has been affected by the diffusion of information technology and the spread of big-box discount chains that rely on advances in logistics to compete with traditional retailers. Retailers have responded by developing options that enable them to drive down wage and benefit costs and deploy workers only when needed, paying just for actual hours worked. These downward pressures on wages have been contained in France, where zoning regulations that limit store size as well as regulations governing store-opening hours are a barrier to entry for the large discount stores. In general, however, across the countries studied, retail stores increasingly combine technology-enhanced high performance with deteriorating wages and working conditions. Yet, despite the similarities in the market pressures and technologies confronting the retail sector in every country, national institutions continue to make a difference, although not always in the expected direction.

WORK ORGANIZATION AND WORK SCHEDULES

Sales jobs in retail can be divided into individual, limited tasks that are closely supervised, or the jobs can be organized so that sales staff are self-directed and perform a variety of tasks. In the United States, especially in big-box stores, jobs are fragmented and workers perform either a range of low-skill tasks—checkout, stocking, and bagging—or more-skilled but still limited tasks in meat preparation, fish, or bakery departments. Cashiers in both French and U.S. supermarkets are closely monitored and timed, though French consumers expect to weigh their produce and bag their orders themselves. Alternatively, sales staff may perform a wide range of tasks, from answering customer queries and ordering merchandise to ringing up sales and stocking shelves. In Germany, where retail apprenticeships are still common, well-trained sales workers perform diverse tasks requiring a range of skill and including tasks that are performed by managers in the United States and the United Kingdom. The availability of a skilled and functionally flexible workforce has the potential to create higher-quality jobs. France, the Netherlands, and Denmark are somewhere in between the German pattern and the U.S. and U.K. patterns. The Netherlands and Denmark offer vocational training and an intermediate-level qualification to sales clerks, and store size in both countries also influences the division of labor. Dutch and Danish supermarkets are generally smaller than those in other countries, and most are discount stores offering low prices and relying on self-service. Although formal jobs are narrowly defined, in practice the small space combines with short staffing to create the expectation that everyone will chip in and do everything.

Part-time jobs are prevalent in retail, with the share of part-time ranging from one and a half to twice the national average for part-time work. France and the United States have the lowest shares of part-time workers in retail, at 28 and 32 percent, respectively. Employers utilize workers, mainly students or mothers who need regular schedules, on short-hour contracts with predictable hours to meet known peak demands. Other part-time workers, however, have variable working hours and feel the pressure to meet unpredictable fluctuations in demand.

In the United States, full-time workers may not be guaranteed full-time hours. Nominal full-timers may be guaranteed a regularly scheduled thirty-two hours, and they can then be required at the employer's discretion to fill in as needed above that number of hours to meet fluctuations in demand. This enables employers to meet variations in demand without having to pay the overtime premium for additional hours worked. In general, U.S. workers have less control over, and less advance notice of, work schedules than is the case in Europe. The requirement of a time-and-a-half pay premium for hours worked over forty per week is, in this regard, the only legal constraint on management in the United States.

The scheduling situation in the United States contrasts with the situation in Europe, where unions, works councils, and regulations on store-opening hours all play a role in constraining management's ability to impose work schedules arbitrarily. German and Danish CLAs require that stores set work schedules four to six months in advance. In the United States, schedules are typically set three days to two weeks in advance. Codetermination laws in Germany, Denmark, and the Netherlands require retail employers to negotiate with works councils over work schedules. In France, a collective bargaining agreement specifying a minimum of twenty-six hours for part-time retail workers has been extended nationally. Finally, limits on store-opening hours and shift differentials in pay for working evening and weekend hours constrain employers' ability to set work schedules, although these limits have begun to erode.

The Incidence of Low-Wage Jobs in Retail

Nearly half (49 percent) of retail workers in the United Kingdom are paid wages below the national low-wage threshold—a higher proportion than in any other country. In the United States, about two-fifths (42 percent) of retail workers are low-wage. What is surprising, however, is that the share of low-wage workers in retail is as high or higher in Germany (42 percent) and the Netherlands (46 percent) as it is in the United States. The high minimum wage in France and strong unions in Denmark limit the extent of low-wage employment in retail in those countries to 18 and 23 percent, respectively. High union density in Denmark raises most workers in retail above the low-wage threshold. By contrast, unionization in the United States is now limited to only a few companies, and hard-pressed unions have accepted two-tier contracts that pay newly hired workers less than workers already on the job. Moreover, in the United States it is still legal to pay part-time employees an hourly wage that is less than what is paid to full-time workers, a practice that has been outlawed in the EU.

Despite higher productivity levels in food retailing, wages are higher and the incidence of low pay is lower in electronics—where men are the predominant workforce—than is the case in food retailing, where women predominate. This gender gap is probably due to the persistent effects of past gender discrimination in pay, to the glass ceiling in retailing (management positions go mainly to men), and to the use of sales commissions in electronics (which boost total compensation).

Youth subminimum wages, established either by law or by collective agreement, are widely used in Denmark, the Netherlands, and the United Kingdom. In the United Kingdom, the youth subminimum wage of a sixteen-year-old is 62 percent of the adult minimum wage; in the Netherlands, it is 35 percent. These large age differentials have created strong incentives for employers to hire very young workers and students. In the Netherlands, price wars in the middle of this decade led retailers to replace adult women with very young workers. In Germany, widespread use of mini-jobs in retail accounts for the large share of low-wage employment in the sector. By 2007, one-quarter of jobs in retail were mini-jobs, and nearly nine out of ten mini-jobbers (87 percent) were paid below the low-wage threshold.

Strong vocational systems in Germany, the Netherlands, and Denmark actually aid and abet employers' use of low-paid workers by ensuring that employers have access to skilled workers who are willing to take these jobs. In Germany—where access to child care is limited and schools and family life are still largely organized on the assumption of a male breadwinner with a stay-at-home wife—women with care responsibilities and access to social benefits through their husband take these mini-jobs. In Denmark and the Netherlands, part-time jobs in retail are filled by trained young people subject to sub-minimum wages.

These country-specific "exit options" for employers weaken the impact of the institutions that historically ensured a high degree of social inclusion, and they lead to the marginalization of various groups of workers. These generally legal loopholes undermine the capacity of collective bargaining and apprenticeship or vocational training to maintain job quality and compensation standards for all workers. Conversely, recent increases in the U.K. national minimum wage (too recently enacted to be reflected in the data reported here) have raised wages in retail and reduced the incidence of very low pay in the sector.

CONCLUSION

The comparative case studies in this volume of the effects of labor market institutions and firms' business strategies on frontline workers in five industries across six countries demonstrate both the continuing influence of these institutions and the substantial pressures on national employment models. It is important to recognize, however, that even where institutions have bent under the weight of changing technology, heightened global competition, and intensifying cost pressures, with the result that the incidence of low-wage work has increased, these institutions are evolving. This evolution itself is influenced by a country's institutional heritage and legacy. Across the industries analyzed in this study, in countries experiencing high or rising shares of low-wage work, there is evidence of pushback from workers and unions to the deterioration of pay and working conditions. The experience of these same industries also suggests the emergence of an incipient backlash against rising inequality: workers and unions are renewing their efforts to use the legislative process to level the playing field with employers.

Currently, the incidence of low-wage employment among Dutch call center subcontractors, for example, is quite high. Nevertheless, the collective bargaining agreement that covers subcontractors is a recent development and holds the potential for higher negotiated wages for these workers in the future.

Recent investments in child care in Germany and the Netherlands will improve mothers' access to quality care for their children and may reduce the willingness of women with skills and qualifications to accept marginal part-time jobs in retail.

The work of cleaners in U.K. hospitals has been outsourced and privatized. Two-tier wage contracts, common among cleaning subcontractors, have led to a precipitous decline in the wages of these workers and a sharp rise in the incidence of low-paid work. The public-sector unions, however, still strong in the United Kingdom, have recently succeeded in gaining an agreement that requires cleaners in hospitals to be paid at public-sector wage rates for this subcontracted work.

In the United States, unions have made passage of the Employee Free Choice Act, which would make it more difficult for employers to prevent workers from organizing a union, their top priority as they seek to increase union density.

And in the Netherlands, union leaders have responded to the protests of young workers, and to the downward pressure on adult wages, by seeking to limit the youth subminimum wage to workers under age eighteen.

Labor market institutions are in flux. The worldwide recession that began in the fall of 2007—after the research for this volume had been concluded—raises serious questions about the direction these changes were taking. New policies to address the rise in unemployment and new rules of the road for the global economy may help to level the playing field for workers and employers; new institutions for the twenty-first century may again yield broadly shared prosperity and a reduction in income inequality and low-wage work.

NOTE

1. The English language may also make it easier for companies in the United States and the United Kingdom to offshore the least-skilled portion of call center activities, reducing the national share of low-wage work in the sector in both countries.

REFERENCES

Earnshaw, Jill, Jill Rubery, and Fang Lee Cooke. 2002. *Who Is the Employer?* London: Institute of Employment Rights.

Henry J. Kaiser Family Foundation. 2008. "Health Insurance Coverage in America, 2006" (June 20). Available at: http://facts.kff.org/chartbook.aspx ?cb=50 (accessed June 23, 2008).

CHAPTER 6

Retail Jobs in Comparative Perspective

Françoise Carré, Chris Tilly, Maarten van Klaveren, and Dorothea Voss-Dahm

Retail businesses and retail jobs have much in common in the United States and western Europe in terms of core tasks, workforce, and competitive trends.[1] Yet, despite all these common features, we see significant variation in job quality as we look across the United States and the five European countries studied here. Retail workers toil at varied levels of pay, and with varying employment status and conditions. Table 6.1 charts three of these variations. Retail's low-wage share—the percentage of retail workers falling below the low-wage threshold of two-thirds of the national median—ranges widely, from less than one in five in France to nearly one-half in the United Kingdom. Average retail labor turnover in the United States is more than double that in France and Germany. The share of part-time workers differs considerably, from less than one-third in France to more than two-thirds in the Netherlands.

A variety of factors might explain cross-national differences in wages, job quality, and employment status. These differences could result from compositional differences (for example, the mix of small, large, and super-sized stores). Alternatively, or in addition, differences in market structure (degree of oligopoly power, exposed versus sheltered markets, and so on) could be important. Indeed, zoning limits on store size—which are still very important in France but have been weakened in other countries—play a role, as do store hours regulations. Nonetheless, a particularly compelling possible explanation may be found in differences in labor market institutions. And indeed, despite labor and product market deregulation, the five European countries jointly still diverge substantially from the United States in their portfolio of institutions (see Mason and Salverda, Bosch, Mayhew, and Gautié, and Gautié et al., all this volume).

In particular, the European countries generally have more inclusive institutions that protect those at the low end of the workforce

Table 6.1 Cross-National Variation in Selected Retail Job
Characteristics

	Percentage of Retail Workers with Hourly Wage Falling Below Two-Thirds of Economy-Wide Median, 2003	Annual Labor Turnover, 2002	Percentage of Part-Timers Among Retail Workers, 2006
Denmark[a]	23%	36%	50%
France	18	20	28
Germany	42	20	47
Netherlands[a]	46	27	70
United Kingdom[a]	49	26	51
United States[ab]	42	50	28

Sources: Authors' compilation based on, for percentage falling below two-thirds of the median: Denmark—Westergaard-Nielsen (2008, 72); France—Askenazy, Berry, and Prunier-Poulmaire (2008, 220); Germany—Voss-Dahm (2008, 258); Netherlands—van Klaveren (2009); United Kingdom—U.K. Office of National Statistics, Annual Survey of Hours and Earnings (2005); United States—authors' calculation from March Current Population Survey (U.S. BLS 2005a). Turnover in European Union countries: Eurostat calculation on EU Labour Force Survey on behalf of IAQ (Eurostat, various years), Germany from BA-Beschaeftigtenstatistik; Turnover in United States: Job Openings and Labor Turnover Survey (U.S. BLS 2005b). Percentage part-timers in European Union: Eurostat (various years); in United States: Current Population Survey, March (U.S. BLS 2007a).
a. The percentage falling below two-thirds of the threshold is calculated in 2002 for Denmark and the Netherlands, and 2005 for the United Kingdom and United States.
b. The percentage of part-timers among U.S. retail workers is calculated for 2007.

(see Bosch, Mayhew, and Gautié, and Gautié et al., this volume). Except for the United Kingdom, all the countries have multi-employer bargaining in place that covers most or all workers in retail, regionally or nationally, and that, in France and the Netherlands, is supported by the mandatory extension of agreements through the state. France, the Netherlands, and the United Kingdom have statutory minimum wages. In Germany, over 80 percent of all retail employees have two to three years of vocational training; Denmark and the Netherlands also provide vocational training for substantial numbers of retail workers.

Although institutions are central to job quality, firm strategies, as embedded in national institutional contexts, also contribute to differences across and within countries. At the national level, much literature stresses the "high-road" versus "low-road" distinction in firm product market strategies.[2] High-road firms emphasize higher quality and more rapid innovation, whereas their low-road counterparts aim at price competition. Many analysts have argued that better jobs will go hand in hand with such high performance (Huselid 1995; Osterman 1994). However, in a seminal 1997 article, Thomas Bailey and Annette Bernhardt found a contrary pattern in U.S. retail: high-road productivity in service was not linked to greater job quality. The retailers they studied upgraded productivity with information technology–based automation (see also Bernhardt 1999; Abernathy et al. 2000), and in some cases they also provided better, more customized service. These changes had little effect, however, on wages (which remained low), work organization, or opportunities for upward mobility. Importantly, they also noted, in U.S. retail high-road approaches coexist with numerous low-road market options coupled with low-quality jobs—a more predictable scenario.

There has also been important international comparative work on retail jobs, but to date, such research has not emphasized the distinction between inclusive and exclusive labor market institutions that is central to this volume (see Bosch, Mayhew, and Gautié, this volume). In their comparison of U.S. and French retail, Jean Gadrey and Florence Jany-Catrice (2000, 26) found that U.S. retail offers "higher quality and more services for the same average basket of goods sold," and that it "finances" the additional value-added by providing lower compensation to workers. In other words, they concluded, going even further than Bailey and Bernhardt (1997) to challenge the predicted relationship between high performance and job quality, the U.S. high-road service advantage *depends* on low compensation. More recently, Jany-Catrice and Steffen Lehndorff (2005) have offered an ambitious six-country (Denmark, Finland, France, Germany, Portugal, and Sweden) comparison focusing on how institutions shape nationally specific patterns of fragmentation of work and working time in retail and suggesting some of the institutional effects we explore further in this chapter.

Our analysis posits a set of relationships between markets, institutions, and firm strategies that we think plays a determining role in job quality, without presuming the specific nature of these relationships (figure 6.1). Though this general model places both the management's market strategy and the human resources (HR)/labor deployment strategy of the firm at the center, in practice most variation in market strategy takes place *within* countries, so our comparative lens leads us to focus more on HR strategy. We pay particular atten-

Figure 6.1 Analytical Map of Determinants of Job Quality

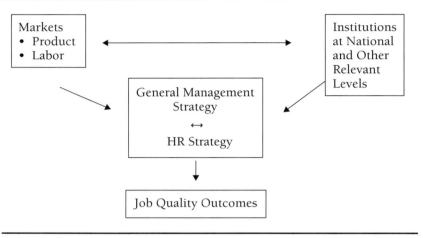

Source: Authors' illustration.

tion to the effects of national institutions, including both direct constraints on human resource strategy and indirect effects through adjustment of labor or product markets. We scrutinize the use of "exit options" that consist of gaps or weaknesses in institutions bolstering job quality or that result from deliberate top-down changes in regulation (see also Bosch, Mayhew, and Gautié, this volume). The retail sector has frequently taken the lead in demanding, creating, or exploiting such exit options.

Based on this scheme, we trace the conditions that give rise to the variation in job quality and employment patterns for the six countries under study, focusing on (and contrasting) food and consumer electronics retail. We examine whether the high-road competitive strategy is bundled with good jobs, and whether in fact job qualities are bundled into uniformly good and bad jobs. We highlight outcomes in two target occupations: cashiers and stock clerks/salespeople. Because the food retail subsector is much larger than consumer electronics, much of our explanatory discussion focuses on food stores, though we highlight salient contrasts with consumer electronics stores as appropriate.

We start the chapter by noting shared industry characteristics and trends. We then briefly lay out the fieldwork methodology. The bulk of the chapter consists of findings about variation in job quality and characteristics. In closing, we comment on trends and variation in job outcomes as well as prospects for change in retail job quality.

INDUSTRY OVERVIEW AND SHARED TRENDS

Despite national differences (treated later in the chapter), the retail industries of the six countries under study have much in common. Indeed, the core tasks performed by clerks and cashiers in retailing are quite similar in all developed countries: workers must take goods from the stockroom to the shop floor, replenish shelves, answer customer questions (and in some cases solicit customer purchases), ring up sales, and receive payment. Another commonality is that retail hours invariably extend beyond standard daytime shifts to include evening hours, weekends, and sometimes nights. The intensity of retail sales also varies by season, shaped as it is by school and vacation schedules, holiday gift-giving, seasonal food demands (summer picnics, holiday dinners), and so on. Retailers in the United States and western Europe have responded to nonstandard operating hours and seasonal swings by making substantial use of part-time labor (Tilly 1996; Jany-Catrice and Lehndorff 2005). In the European countries, as in the United States, stores rely heavily on women and young people to fill part-time slots.

Retail sectors in the United States and western Europe are similar in other ways as well. All have recently been rocked by three new forces that cut across national borders. The first is the diffusion of intricate information technology for supply-chain management and optimal staff scheduling. The second is the spread of aggressive discount chains that take advantage of the logistical technologies to mount a formidable competitive challenge to mainstream retailers. Big-box chain Wal-Mart is the example best known to U.S. consumers, but Germany's Aldi and Lidl, among others, have also grown rapidly by implementing variants of this model. Moreover, all of these countries are experiencing a set of institutional changes in the labor market that we can characterize as "neoliberal"; these changes are weakening workers' representation and increasing flexibility in labor regulations, including, in many cases, the relaxation of labor regulations for particular subsets of workers (Streeck and Thelen 2005). In the United States, such shifts have included a sharp decline in union density and significant erosion of the real value of the minimum wage, both of which changes have reduced job quality for low-wage workers in general and for retail workers in particular (Carré, Holgate, and Tilly 2006). Indeed, in all the countries under study, retail seems to be a laboratory for changes in labor market institutions; the sector often leads with experimentation in this regard. It currently seems to stand out everywhere as a sector where the relaxation of regulation, combined with a vulnerable workforce, enhances retailers' ability to bypass features of national institutions that protect low-wage workers. Numerous work sites also render regulatory monitoring and enforcement difficult.

Overall the industry structure is relatively similar across the six countries (see table 6.2). Productivity levels are comparable. In terms of establishment sizes, the United Kingdom shows a very high upper quartile (indicating a greater share of large establishments), but it bears mentioning that all of these countries have roughly the same set of store formats: hypermarkets (typically called "superstores" or "supercenters" in the United States) at the large end, and convenience stores and "mom-and-pop" shops at the low end. In general, the concentration ratios indicate that smaller countries have more concentrated retail sectors. The low level of concentration in food retail in the United States stands out, as does Denmark's particularly high level in consumer electronics.

Another cross-national commonality is a set of *differences* between the food and consumer electronics subsectors. Food retail makes up the biggest share of retail employment, though it is smaller in the United States than elsewhere (see table 6.2; the sales figures are similar). Food stores are also much larger than electronics outlets, and food sales are more strongly dominated by a small number of firms, except in the United States. Given the greater complexity of high-end electronic products, electronics stores have more staff devoted to active selling. Nonetheless, sales per employee are comparable between food and consumer electronics retail for the three countries for which such subsectoral measures are available: France, the Netherlands, and the United States (van Klaveren 2007).

METHODOLOGY

In each of the six countries, a research team conducted case studies of large retail companies in food and consumer electronics. These two subsectors were chosen to provide contrasts in gender and in the knowledge content required for selling. European case studies were conducted between March 2005 and September 2006, and U.S. studies between May 2005 and April 2007. In principle, a case consisted of interviews with company-level executives plus a store visit that included interviews with store managers, frontline workers, and (where relevant) union or works council representatives. In practice, the degree of access varied by company, although most of the cases conformed with this ideal profile. Worker interviews and focus groups zeroed in on our two target jobs of cashiers and stock clerks/salespeople, although teams sometimes interviewed other employees (such as supervisors) as well.

The number and composition of cases is detailed in table 6.3. The U.S. sample was designed to be twice as large as the others because it represents in some sense the "baseline" for international comparisons and the industry is larger. Researchers' initial goal was to conduct equal numbers of case studies of food and electronics retailers in each country. The teams had difficulty gaining access to consumer electronics chains. In the countries that came up short on electronics companies, however, a number of the food retailers also sold electronics. In these cases, researchers attempted to learn about and interview those in sales positions in the electronics departments of the stores as well as food retail workers. There was some unplanned heterogeneity across country samples. For example, the German researchers were not able to gain access to discounters, whereas the other country teams were able to include them; the U.S. sample, unlike the European ones, included two chains in the electronics category that principally sold office equipment and supplies. Nonetheless, the samples are quite strongly comparable across countries. In addition to these case studies, each team reviewed descriptive data from standard national data sources about the quality and characteristics of retail jobs.

VARIATION IN JOB QUALITY OUTCOMES

Despite broad similarities in tasks, in technological and market changes, and in the proclivity to experiment with exit options, retail industries across the countries displayed striking and important differences in major indicators of job quality. Relying on national patterns and case study findings, we review each dimension of job qual-

Table 6.2 Various Industry Characteristics by Country

Variable	Yardstick	Denmark[a]	France[b]	Germany	Netherlands	United Kingdom	United States
Value-added per hour worked	Euros, 2005 (PPP conversion)	21.94	29.55	26.36	23.43	24.59	25.41
Establishment size (frequency distribution by number of employees)	Lower quartile, 2002	3	3	6–19	3	4	3
	Median, 2002	5	8	20+	6	7	6
	Upper quartile, 2002	10	21	20+	10+	116	12
Food							
Percentage of retail jobs	2003	26	34	29	32	36	16
Average store size	Employees per establishment, 2003	14	95	27	36	39	26
Share of top five firms in sales	Percentage of sales, 2005 to 2006	95	85	69	88[c]	75	31

Electronics

	2003					
Percentage of retail jobs	2.9	3.5	3.0	3.4	3.0	3.4
Average store size	Employees per establishment, 2003					
	6	5	NA	8	14	11
Share of top five firms	Percentage of sales, 2005 to 2006					
	71	42	47	51	44	44

Sources: Authors' compilation. Value-added from from EU KLEMS (2005). Establishment size from: Denmark—Danmark Statistik (2002); France—INSEE (2003); Germany—Statistisches Bundesamt (2001); Netherlands—CBS (2002a); United Kingdom—Annual Business Inquiry (U.K. ONS 2002); United States—Economic Census (U.S. Bureau of the Census 2002). Percentage of retail jobs and average store size calculated from: national case study chapters and Eurostat (2003); United States—2003 Current Employment Statistics (U.S. Bureau of Labor Statistics, various years) and County Business Patterns (U.S. Bureau of the Census 2003). Share of top-five in food: Denmark—Esbjerg et al. (2008, 143); France—Askenazy et al. (2008, 214); Germany—Metro-Group (2006, 16); Netherlands—van Klaveren (2009); United Kingdom—Burt and Sparks (2006); United States—Economic Census (U.S. Bureau of the Census 2002) (figure for top four firms only). Share of top-five in electronics: Denmark—figure for 2003, Esbjerg et al. (2008, 146); France, Germany, and United Kingdom—figures for 2007: MNE Database (AIAS 2007); Netherlands—van Klaveren (2009); United States—Economic Census (U.S. Bureau of the Census 2002) (figure for top four firms only).

a. Number of Danish food establishments from 2006.

b. French electronics sales and number of food establishments from 2004.

c. Superunie buying group is counted as one; if Superunie is broken up, the top five share is 71.

Table 6.3 Sample Structure of Retail Case Studies in the Six Countries

	Food Retail Cases	Consumer Electronics Cases	Comments
Denmark	5	3	Three food retail cases also sol electronics.
France	6	2	Two food retail cases also sold electronics
Germany	4	4	
Netherlands	4	4	
United Kingdom	4	4	
United States	10	6	Two food retail cases also sold electronics.

Sources: Authors' compilation based on: Denmark—Esbjerg et al. (2008); France—Askena Berry, and Prunier-Poulmaire (2008); Germany—Voss-Dahm (2008); Netherlands–van Klaver (2008a); United Kingdom—Mason and Osborne (2008); United States—Carré and Tilly wi Holgate (2007).

ity in turn: work schedules; work organizations and tasks; turnover and vertical mobility; and compensation.

Work Schedules

In retail, work schedules are a primary dimension of job outcomes. The volume of hours (relative to desired hours), schedule predictability, and degree of worker control over schedules were significant differentiators of job quality in every country in the study. In the Dutch case studies, for instance, many workers complained of unilateral employer decisions concerning working times and days off, while British employees lamented being given insufficient hours of work, having little schedule flexibility to meet their needs, and being required to work evenings and weekends. Schedule patterns are also closely linked to workforce demography: women and young workers, in particular, concentrate in part-time jobs—in some cases because these hours fit their preferences, and in other cases because they are trapped in them. In this section, we first summarize common features of work schedules across the six countries. We then explore the U.S.-Europe differences—above all in workers' degree of control over scheduling—followed by a brief discussion of differences among the five European countries.

Common Features of Retail Work Schedules   As in the United States, the retail workforce in Europe is disproportionately (and increasingly) part-time (table 6.4). The proportions of part-time workers are even higher in case study stores, which are generally larger than the typical retail establishment. For example, in the U.S. case studies, part-timers made up 50 to 80 percent of the store workforce (with the exception of one chain with smaller stores and one electronics chain that relied on a commission workforce)—well above the 28 percent industry average.

Although part-time employment is widespread for retail as a whole, the rate of part-time employment differs markedly across the two retail subsectors, as the last two rows of table 6.4 indicate. Whereas the food retail workforce uniformly shows a higher rate of part-time employment than the already high retail average, consumer electronics equally uniformly has a lower proportion of part-time workers—in some countries, even lower than the economy-wide proportion. As we will see when we examine other job characteristics, this heralds a general pattern: within retail, consumer electronics retailing offers more "standard" and, by a number of criteria, better jobs than the food retail subsector. Because case studies in a number of countries revealed continued pay and working conditions disparities coupled with declining emphasis on electronics knowledge for jobs in electronics retailing, this differential seems to a considerable extent unlikely to result from skill differences. Instead, the most likely explanation is the much higher concentration of women in food retail than in consumer electronics stores (not shown). Indeed, as Florence Jany-Catrice, Nicole Gadrey, and Martine Pernod (2005) argue in the case of France, managers discount the soft skills required in frontline retail work in part precisely because they are skills tied to standard female socialization.

Table 6.5 demonstrates that high concentrations of women and younger workers in the retail workforce are associated with the high proportion of jobs that are part-time. In each of the six countries, the retail workforce is disproportionately female (though in the United States the overrepresentation is almost nonexistent).[3] Workers under

Table 6.4 Part-Time Employment in Retail Trade by Country (Headcount), 2006 (Denmark, the Netherlands, and the United Kingdom) and 2007 (France, Germany, and the United States)

	Denmark	France	Germany	Netherlands	United Kingdom	United States
Part-time in retail employment	49.7%	27.7%	52.0%	69.8%	50.2%	27.9%
Part-time in total employment	23.6	17.2	25.8	46.2	25.5	18.6
Ratio: retail part-time percentage to total part-time percentage	2.1	1.6	1.8	1.5	2.0	1.5
Ratio: food part-time percentage to retail part-time percentage[a]	NA	1.8	1.3	1.1	1.3	1.4
Ratio: electronics part-time percentage to retail part-time percentage[a]	NA	0.6	0.4	0.5	0.6	0.8

Sources: Authors' compilation based on: European Union: part-time in total employment from European Commission (2007); part-time in retail from authors' calculation of European Union Labour Force Survey (Eurostat, various years); retail subsectors from Danmark Statistik (2002) and Askenazy, Berry, and Prunier-Poulmaire (2008, 220); Annual Survey of Hours and Earnings (U.K. ONS 2006); van Klaveren (2008b). All of Germany's statistics from BA Beschaeftigtenstatistik (BA 2007). United States: part-time in retail from Current Population Survey microdata (U.S. BLS 2007b); subsector part-time imputed by combining Current Population Survey data for 2004 (U.S. Bureau of the Census 2004) with 2007 Current Employment Statistics data (U.S. BLS, various years); part-time in total employment from Employment and Earnings Online, Table A-18 (U.S. BLS 2008b).

a. Ratios of food and consumer electronics retail part-time percentages from 2004 data, except France (2003) and the Netherlands and the United Kingdom (2005).

Table 6.5 Women and Younger Workers Employed in Retail, by Country, 2006 (Headcount)

	Denmark	France	Germany	Netherlands	United Kingdom	United States
Share of females in retail	57.0%	63.3%	70.6%	60.9%	61.5%	49.4%
Share of females in total	46.4	46.3	45.4	44.9	46.7	48.1
Ratio: retail percentage female to total percentage female	1.2	1.4	1.6	1.4	1.3	1.0
Share under age twenty-five in retail	48.5	19.3	15.6	44.7	34.0	28.6
Share under age twenty-five in total	13.6	8.9	10.7	15.3	14.0	13.6
Ratio: retail percentage under twenty-five to total percentage under twenty-five	3.6	2.2	1.5	2.9	2.4	2.1

Sources: Authors' compilation based on: European Union: shares in retail from authors' calculations of European Union Labour Force Survey (Eurostat, various years); shares in total from European Commission (2007). United States: female shares from Current Employment Statistics (U.S. BLS, various years); young workers from Current Population Survey, March (U.S. BLS 2006).

age twenty-five are likewise universally overrepresented in retail. When we compare the representation of women and young workers in food retail, with its higher rate of part-time employment (and lower-paid jobs), and consumer electronics, with the opposite characteristics, we generally find larger female and young worker percentages in the former (not shown).

The heavy reliance on part-time work offers three main advantages for retailers. First, part-time work allows businesses to match staffing to peak days and hours, reducing "excess" labor. This matching is particularly valuable in the context of new "just-in-time" inventory management systems. Adopting the terminology of Jany-Catrice and Lehndorff (2005), part-timers in all six countries include both "gap fillers" and "time adjusters." Gap fillers are those employees who work on short-hour contracts and are deployed on regular schedules, working predictable time slots accordingly. Time adjusters, on the contrary, are deployed at variable times and have variable total work hours. Although in general both groups are disproportionately young and female, the gap fillers are particularly likely to be active students or women with young children, with schedule constraints in other parts of their lives. It is the time adjusters who bear the main burden of long opening hours and demand fluctuations and who feel the pressure to work overtime. In all six countries, the use of time adjusters acts as a functional equivalent of the use of temporary workers, which is more prevalent in other industries. The research teams found small numbers of temp workers in retailing, or none at all, though seasonal workers (for example, to cover the Christmas rush) are common.

Second, the classical argument for the high productivity of workers with short hours in repetitive work holds sway with retailers. As a manager in German food retailing noted: "The productivity of people with short working hours is simply higher. After five or six hours, an individual worker starts to run out of energy and to slow down, while two workers can complete a lot of work in four hours each."

The third advantage to retailers of widespread part-time employment is that it opens up exit options that allow them to evade normative, legal, or collective bargaining standards for compensation, fringe benefits, and social insurance. The specifics vary. In the United States, part-time employment itself represents an exit option, because in much of retail part-timers are paid lower wages and receive fewer or no benefits. A U.S. supermarket cashier noted: "Some people, they work over thirty-two hours, but they're just not considered full-time. And that makes them so mad." An HR officer at the same chain concurred: "There's probably plenty of thirty-plus hours part-time employees that just are not full-time because the stores are not able to make anybody wholesale full-time if they want to, because of the expense of the benefit packages." In Germany, a key exit option is the "mini-job," a short-hour part-time job often paid below the collectively bargained scale, in violation of the law. In Denmark, the Netherlands, and the United Kingdom, a lower statutory or collectively bargained wage scale for younger workers has opened up an important exit option. In France's highly inclusive employment relations system, there are few formally specified exit options, though as a practical matter legal and collectively bargained requirements are less rigorously enforced in small retail enterprises.

We discuss further the impact of these varied exit options later in the chapter, but here it is important to point out that the high concentration of women and young people has helped to make exit options a viable option for firms. Generally these groups are weakly organized and poorly represented through unions and works councils; employers are thus able to execute exit options with little public fuss. We note that, unlike in another low-wage industry, hospitality, immigrant labor is not commonly used to facilitate exit options in retail. Immigrant labor (by which we mean foreign-born or noncitizen workers) is not widespread, ranging from 4 to 13 percent of the retail workforce in the six countries. There is some immigrant overrepresentation in U.K. retail compared to the workforce at large, but underrepresentation in Denmark, Germany, and the United States.[4]

U.S.-Europe Differences in Work Schedules   Despite these common features of retail jobs in the United States and the five European countries, the United States also stands apart in a number of ways. Given the importance of work schedules as a job quality parameter, these U.S.-Europe contrasts are quite noteworthy. In U.S. case studies, full-time workers increasingly are not guaranteed full-time hours; in a number of the food and electronics chains, full-timers were guaranteed only thirty-two or thirty-five weekly hours out of the forty that traditionally and legally constitute a full-time schedule. This system turns full-time workers into another group of "time adjusters" while minimizing the risk of incurring the overtime pay premium. This practice was not encountered in European cases. Some

European retail full-timers did flex their hours upward from a full-time base, particularly consumer electronics employees motivated by commissions, as well as, more generally, German full-timers who had been socialized by that country's strong vocational education system. Indeed, even in the relatively liberalized U.K. labor market, seven out of eight case study firms use overtime rather than temporary workers to handle demand variations.

U.S. workers have less individual and collective choice, control, and advance notice of work schedules than their European counterparts. A single U.S. schedule regulation affects decision terms for management: virtually all retail frontline and first-level supervisory workers are hourly workers subject to the federal overtime pay provision of time and a half for work over forty weekly hours. This cost differential further contributes to the use of part-time time adjusters and affects managerial scheduling decisions in other ways (for example, overtime hours are rarely authorized). With regard to notification of work schedules, U.S. retailers typically inform workers of their work schedules three days to two weeks in advance; there is generally shorter notice and more schedule variation in food retail than in consumer electronics. The combination of lean staffing with high turnover and unreliability among short-hour part-timers frequently presents managers with the need to change staffing and adjust schedules on short notice; the virtual absence of collective bargaining clauses (owing to low union representation) and lack of mandates on schedule notification enable them to do so.

In contrast, the most extreme European cases are Germany and Denmark, where retail collective agreements require retailers to post schedules twenty-six and sixteen weeks in advance (though case studies revealed that breaches of these mandates were rather common, especially in smaller retailers). German, Danish, and Dutch codetermination laws also require retail employers to negotiate scheduling with their works councils (Tijdens 1998; Voss-Dahm 2003). In response to worker preferences on scheduling options and notification, German and Dutch works councils have used their legal rights to negotiate scheduling options in grocery stores to achieve compromises over flexibility for management and workers. In this context, German and Dutch retailers use sophisticated software to work out schedules that conform to worker preferences (Voss-Dahm 2000), whereas U.S. retailers press new employees to list the maximum possible hours of "availability" and penalize employees who do not agree to cover varied hours and shifts with fewer hours and promotion opportunities. Recounting how one part-timer quit, a U.S. electronics department manager noted that "[another part-timer's] availability opened up, so I started giving him more of the hours because he was a better associate for that, and the other gentleman, his hours dropped. . . . He ended up probably catching on and he just quit, just stopped showing up." Workers' main recourse is to swap shifts with coworkers, subject to management approval (also a common strategy in European stores).

In the United States, store managers (and to a lesser extent supervisors and full-time workers) are acutely aware of the difficulty of scheduling and often must solve scheduling problems by working extremely long hours themselves, ranging up to sixty or seventy hours per week. (In the European countries, store managers also report long hours, but not to the same degree; compare Denmark, where even in food retail, with its longer hours, managers report working "only" forty-five to fifty hours per week.) Above the store level, however, U.S. higher-level managers and executives expressed little concern about scheduling. In contrast, in many European companies, especially in Germany and the Netherlands, the difficulty of organizing satisfactory employee work schedules was a topic of discussion up to the executive level and even on corporate boards.

In the countries with more corporatist labor relations and robust unions in the workplace—Denmark, Germany, and the Netherlands—work hours are further shaped by both store hour regulations and collectively bargained shift premiums. Danish, Dutch, and German stores are barred from opening most Sundays. Interestingly, even in France, which puts fewer restrictions on store hours, hypermarkets typically are open 9:00 AM to 10:00 PM Monday through Saturday, but only a few Sundays a year (except in tourist areas), and super-discounters and consumer electronics stores operate even fewer hours. Danish, German, and Dutch retail collective bargaining agreements stipulate premium payments for overtime hours, night work, and work on Saturday, Sunday, and public holidays. Moreover, such premium payments are also prevalent in France and the United Kingdom, in both union and non-union settings. In contrast, in the United States, restrictions on store hours historically were imposed at the state and local levels, and most were already gone by the late 1980s. The U.S. cases show companies (including unionized ones) decreasing or eliminating pay differentials for off-shifts and Sundays.

Even in the countries with strong unions, however, the bite of working time regulation seems to be weakening. Some regulations, like shift differentials, already exempt some vulnerable groups, and now these regulations are coming under further attack. With the liberalization of opening hours in the Netherlands in 1996 and Germany in 2006, employers have begun to press for reduced premiums for nonstandard work times. In the Netherlands, as early as 1998 retailers negotiated the elimination of premiums for Saturdays and work between 6:00 and 8:00 PM. Yet, in a slight countertrend, a 2008 employers' effort to reach a new collective bargaining agreement and remove the remaining premiums foundered. In Germany, unions successfully resisted employer efforts to reduce shift differentials in 1999, but with opening hours now less regulated, employers have made the abolition of premiums their main demand, triggering a series of hard-fought strikes. Note also that the Dutch differential for work after 8:00 PM is available only to those who work more than twelve hours per week; most younger workers are thus excluded. And though German mini-jobbers are entitled to shift premiums, firms tend to withhold these premiums from them.

Despite these recent shifts, U.S. retail workers continue to have fewer tools to exert control over their schedules than do their European counterparts. The long reach of collective agreements and the presence and legally specified role of works councils, as well as differing norms, are the main explanations for these U.S.-European differences. The continuing (though diminishing) relevance of opening hours restrictions in some European countries also limits schedule variability.

Differences in Work Schedules Within Europe   The five European countries themselves differ in their work schedule patterns, as our discussion of work schedules has already revealed. These differences result from a combination of differences in labor supply (themselves provoked in part by differences in family and welfare state policies; see Gautié et al., this volume) and divergences in employment-related institutions. As table 6.5 shows, Danish and Dutch retailers—motivated in part by lower bargained or legislated rates of pay for young workers—have extraordinarily high levels of youth employment. In France and Germany, in contrast, there is more reliance on women workers, whereas U.K. retailers have more equal shares of women and men. In each country, a specific history underlies the demographic pattern. For example, in Denmark working women have shifted from part-time to full-time work since the 1970s, supported by government-sponsored child care and a tax system that assesses each spouse separately. In response, retailers have turned to youths for part-time staffing. In the Netherlands, on the other hand, the influx of women that took off in the 1980s was reversed when the price war that began in 2003 put pressure on wage costs. Retailers responded by availing themselves of the statutory youth subminimum wage enacted in the 1970s. Adult women complained that they were "bullied away" and replaced by cheaper young workers, many of whom (50 percent) were students whose income was made viable by a generous state student grant system. In France, for decades, large majorities of women have preferred full-time work, bolstered by a universal child care system. Thus, as interviews by the French team clarified, French retailers' reliance on women to cover part-time jobs traps many women in unwanted part-time schedules (though, notably, the overall rate of part-time employment, both in retail and throughout the economy, is considerably lower in France than in the other European countries).[5]

In fact, France is something of a special case—with the state playing a particularly prominent role in typical French fashion. On the one hand, French law has set the full-time workweek at 35 hours. On the other hand, pressed by unhappy women workers, French retail food unions have won a minimum part-time hours threshold of twenty-six hours (but with exceptions for students and those who "voluntarily" choose to work less). In combination, these provisions reduce the part-time/full-time hours gap to its lowest level across the six countries. With this minimum hours requirement, combined with a mostly adult workforce, only 16 percent of French part-timers work less than twenty hours per week; the other European countries range from 53 percent (Germany) to a staggering 77 percent (Denmark). The United States falls between France and the rest of Europe, with 34 percent of part-timers clocking less than twenty hours.[6]

In summary, work schedules are a critically important element of job quality in retail. Above all, the degree of predictability and workers' leverage over schedules affect the job experience. In most of the European countries, unlike the United States, collective bargaining and legislation reinforce workers' influence over their schedules. However, retailers in Europe—whose use of part-timers is already pervasive—are also experimenting with institutional loopholes as they recruit particularly vulnerable populations (women, young people). One consequence is the activation of exit options from regulating institutions, ranging from German mini-jobs to U.K., Danish, and Dutch youth subminimum wages. Interviews and focus groups conducted by the national teams confirmed that in some cases these options dovetail with workforce preferences. In particular, school-enrolled youths and some women take "gap filler" jobs precisely because they want short, fixed work hours. The overrepresentation of women and younger workers, in turn, implies that other institutions—notably government support for child care, the tax treatment of married couples' earnings, and student grants—modulate the industry's labor supply.

Work Organization and Task and Skill Composition

Though sales activities as a whole have much in common, the task and skill profiles of workers vary depending on the retail firm's business strategy. If retailers adopt a self-service strategy, customer advice and service are reduced to a minimum. If retailers follow a service strategy that includes lots of personal assistance to customers, then demands on the availability and skills of staff are much higher. Thus, the market segment in which companies position themselves is a crucial factor in determining the task and skill profile of retail workers.[7] The actual composition of individual segments varies from country to country, a pattern that can be attributed to differences in national consumption patterns as well as different notions of what constitutes service and different paths taken in the adoption of advanced technology.

Given this background, it could be argued that institutional factors have little or no direct influence on the mix of tasks and skills in sales work. Indeed, our findings confirm a close connection between business strategy and job profile. Nevertheless, analyses of the case studies also show institutional influences through product market regulations or training institutions on the task and skill composition of sales workers.

With regard to notions of customer service, we found varying task and skill profiles within countries, but importantly, we found some differences between countries as well. Virtually across the board in U.S. food retailing, quick checkout is part of the service pledge and affects how often employees are shifted from other departments to the "front end" (checkout). Likewise, in most U.S. food stores, simple service tasks like bagging are a central function in customer service, a priority that boosts the share of workers with narrow task profiles. Nevertheless, some service-oriented U.S. food retailers offer a wide selection of fresh and ready-to-eat products that are actively sold by sales staff and thus require special and often craftlike skills in storing or preparing fresh food.

Taking the consumer electronics subsector into consideration brings in an even greater diversity of job requirement profiles. Some stores concentrate on selling mass-market products "off the shelf" (TVs, small electronics), retail work that has only limited and clearly decreasing skill requirements over time. Others focus on specialized items, such as expensive, technically sophisticated home entertainment systems. Some large stores—having earlier implemented a move away from sales staff with technical knowledge—have developed "within-store" units that offer customization of home entertainment or office systems where specialized staff provide intensive consultation and coordinate installations. In some ways, this market innovation represents the completion of a cycle of skill elimination, then recreation, albeit for a subset of sales positions.

Adding Europe to the picture reveals other within- and between-country differences in food retailing. Service-oriented British supermarkets tend to focus on labor-intensive customer service features like the availability of sales staff to answer customer questions or short wait times at checkout. In the European case studies, employee bagging was found in the United Kingdom but not in Denmark, France, Germany, or the Netherlands. Within-country differences are large in France. There, as in other countries, small-scale discounters follow a pure self-service concept that sharply contrasts with that of French hypermarkets, which traditionally offer specialty cheeses or fresh fish at full-service counters, leading to a more heterogeneous and, in some parts of the store, sophisticated task and skill structure.

A comparison of French and German product market regulation, such as zoning or price regulations, reveals how the pattern of the task and skill structure in a country is influenced, at least indirectly, by institutional factors. In France, barriers to entry for large stores that include zoning regulations (1973 and later), periodic freezes on the authorization of large stores (1993 to 1996), and store size limits (1996) set obstacles to the expansion of sales space. As a result, established French hypermarkets, with their high-service approach and high product variety, face limited competition and are able to dominate. In contrast, Germany, which has no such regulations, has one of the highest selling-space-per-inhabitant ratios in Europe (EHI 2006, 91, 92). Winners in the expansion of selling space are low-price discounters like Aldi and Lidl, which have increased their market share at the expense of other formats with a more variegated range of items and a differentiated job profile of sales workers.

The picture seems to be rather mixed when we look at frontline activities. What can be observed with regard to activities that are related to the commercial handling of goods? In particular, is technology an equalizer of task and skill demands in sales jobs across countries? Retailers have long found ways to speed up and automate goods handling by using information and communication technologies (Moss and Tilly 2001). In the near future, RFID (radio frequency identification) technology promises to trigger a surge in rationalization, which will lead to the elimination of active goods scanning by employees, both in the receiving department and at checkout.[8] Work intensity at checkouts can already be considerably reduced by automated "self-checkout" counters at the retailers that use them. The use of advanced technology in goods handling and customer self-service, described as "lean retailing" (Abernathy et al. 2000), offers retailers ways to achieve high productivity with low labor costs. In such a system, knowledge demands on employees are low. In extreme cases, sales staff are left with little work to do beyond simple, routine activities such as shelf stocking. This scenario can clearly be linked with the high-performance-business–low-wage system that Bailey and Bernhardt (1997) have described for general merchandise.

With regard to the distribution of highly automated high-performance-business systems, we found substantial within-country differences rather than clear differences between countries.[9] Germany stands as an example of within-country differences in Europe. One company investigated in Germany stood out as a world leader in the use of labor-saving RFID technology. Conversely, in another German company, automatic goods ordering had been rejected for strategic reasons, so that replenishing the range of products was a standard task for sales staff.

Task- Versus Function-Centered Work Organization   It is insufficient to state a connection between business strategy, customer segmentation, and segmentation of the workforce in order to explain the varied pattern of tasks and skills in retailing. Such a statement understates management's leeway in bundling single tasks into actual jobs (Autor, Levy, and Murnane 2003, 132). As will be clear from what follows, there is some evidence that these management decisions are influenced by labor market institutions, particularly training institutions.

In general, there are two polar ways to bundle tasks into jobs. On the one hand, sales jobs can be organized on the basis of a strict division of labor. Then sales staffs perform individual, easily delimited *tasks* that are generally assigned to them by supervisors. On the other hand, jobs can be organized so that sales staffs perform many distinct tasks with a high degree of self-direction. Their job is to fulfill a *function* within the work process. According to Marsden (1999, 37), function-oriented work organization systems are based on "the employee's output or contribution to the collective effort of production or service provision."

In the countries under study, we found nationally specific patterns of work organization (see figure 6.2). In the United States and the United Kingdom, particularly in the big-box formats in food retailing, the dominant form of work organization is based on a strict division of work, with most workers performing rather narrowly defined tasks while only a few (full-time) workers or supervisors have knowledge about processes and products. High employee turnover can be regarded as a fundamental reason for this choice of work organization. Individual tasks are isolated from each other and can therefore be quickly learned and easily monitored. However, the easy substitutability of workers is not the only important argument in favor of a task-centered work organization system, with a correspondingly low level of individual freedom of action. Employees' skill and qualification levels also play a crucial role in the choice of work organization. Entry skill requirements in U.S. supermarkets are minimal. A U.S. grocery manager stated laughingly that the qualification for getting hired is "having a pulse," while others spoke of being able to "pay attention." Nevertheless, the U.S. and U.K. case studies show that task-centered work organization can be accompanied by some degree of horizontal task variability. In British supermarkets, when lines form at the checkouts, employees from the sales departments are instructed by their supervisors to go to the checkouts. Sales assistants in a U.K. discount retailer commented: "We go where we are needed;

Figure 6.2 Pattern of Work Organization

Type of work organization	Task-centered work organization	⟷	Function-centered work organization	
Position of country	United States United Kingdom	France	Netherlands Denmark	Germany
Type of training system	No retail-specific training institutions	⟷	Retail-specific training institutions	

Source: Authors' analysis based on Marsden (1999).

it could be on provisions [for example, dairy or produce], or it could be queue-busting on the checkout, or we could be doing replenishment. . . . The guidelines are all laid out so we follow them." Similarly, sales workers in the United States are deployed to different departments (except specialized departments) when the workload requires such a move, particularly in consumer electronics, where it is the norm. The reason for this ad-hoc adjustment to staffing requirements lies both in the cost-cutting strategies adopted by retail companies, which have reduced staffing levels to a minimum, and in temporary losses of employees due to high labor turnover.

The counterexample to the United States and the United Kingdom is Germany. There, most employees have completed vocational training, even in large food stores and in consumer electronics retailing in general. Ordinary sales assistants take responsibility for the whole distributive process—that is, for ordering goods, taking goods from stocks onto the shop floor, stocking shelves, merchandising products, and giving advice to customers. Hence, tasks are vertically integrated, and salespeople have a reasonable range of discretion; they do not receive daily instructions from supervisors. At the same time, tasks are narrower from a horizontal perspective. Sales assistants take care only of a particular part of the merchandise; they do not change between departments, and they never work at checkouts. They are expected to optimize the assortment of products in order to improve sales and profits. If this requires changing assortments, adding new products, or revising merchandising, they must coordinate these changes with team leaders. Though the potential of vertically integrated tasks for job quality is obvious, there are special constraints too, such as the delegation of responsibilities for tight cost control downward from managers. A comment by a German supermarket manager illustrates the reliance on trained workers: "I can put pressure on the permanent workers. They have the basic knowledge for me to be able to discuss particular developments, objectives, and plans with them. They have a background in retailing and know what it's all about." Thus, vertical integration of tasks within a cost-cutting environment constitutes an attempt to "exploit awareness," that is, to make use of, but not necessarily reward, worker attention and skill (Lehndorff and Voss-Dahm 2005). With their specialized skills, German retail workers are more likely than in other countries to have internalized the belief that what they do at work contributes to firm performance.

In the United States, we found other means of stimulating worker engagement. U.S. consumer electronics stores in particular orchestrate a process that includes "fun" experiences linked to achieving sales. Managerial prompts are key. In some big-box stores, the duty manager holds regular, sometimes daily, motivational meetings around team coordination and store performance results.

Comparison with Dutch and Danish supermarkets shows that store size also influences the strictness of the division of labor in day-to-day operations. Typically, Dutch and Danish supermarkets are small in terms of sales space; to a considerable extent, they are positioned as discount or near-discount stores offering mass-consumption goods at permanently low prices and on a self-service basis. Most supermarkets employ many young people in marginal part-time jobs; measured in full-time equivalents, however, the number of employees per store is rather small. Although formally these young people perform narrow tasks, in practice, "everyone is trained to do everything" to maintain the efficiency of the work processes. In some stores, managers assign tasks; in others, peer groups of workers flexibly organize themselves. Characteristically, a Dutch supermarket manager explained: "We maintain clear policies to keep lines short through the flexible opening of new checkouts. If necessary, we ask staff from counters and from the ranks of experienced stockers to join. Yet we don't feel the need to formalize or reward these practices."

The influence of store size on the degree of division of labor is also evident in the case of consumer electronics retailing. In particular, in smaller stores, sales assistants usually take care of the whole sales process, giving advice to the customer, operating the cash register, and then taking "ownership" of the customer's after-sales service arrangements. However, larger stores show more specialization: cashiers run cash registers without engaging in the sales process.

The task profile at checkouts in large stores is a special case. Cashiers' tasks are in some countries monitored for speed, pushing the worker to perform. In the United States, managers periodically post individual scanning results on a public wall in the work area for all staff to see and, in at least one case, on public display within the store. This places lateral pressure on workers, most of whom would prefer to quit the job if their scan rate falls below standards rather than be fired or passed over for raises. At first glance, the case of French supermarkets seems similar because supervisors provide weekly individual scanning results to cashiers. But there are substantial differences in the speeds that cashiers must attain; in U.S. case studies, we found items-scanned-per-minute targets of twenty to twenty-five, even in a discount chain, but at hard discounters in France target scan rates were up to forty to forty-five. In France, such rates, combined with poor checkout counter design, clearly contributed to high rates of stress and work-related injuries.[10] As a cashier in a classic hypermarket noted, "It's really tiring. The job is repetitive and insignificant. I no longer look at what I do. I can escape or daydream at times. I'm used to the motions and think of nothing."[11]

In contrast with both the United States and France, German and Dutch laws ban individual reporting of scan rates, owing to privacy considerations. In the Netherlands, before individual scan rate reporting was prohibited, it was attempted as part of a drive for faster performance. Food retailers found that it led to increased error rates, however, because the checkout speed was already quite high, and thus they had no problem accepting the legal limitations.

Training Institutions and Their Impact on the Qualification Level   We have argued that skill formation affects how tasks emerging from company business strategies are bundled into jobs. Therefore, sector-specific training institutions should matter. The basic principles of skill formation differ widely in the six countries. Low-skilled and semi-skilled employees dominate retail employment in the United Kingdom and the United States, and there is no notable vocational training system for retail frontline jobs. In France as well, no countrywide vocational training system exists in retailing that "produces" skills tailored to the retail trade, but in the country as a whole a consistently strong emphasis is put on general education. Almost half of retail employees have a French Baccalauréat degree.[12]

Because of the absence in these three countries of a vocational training system tailored to the needs of retail firms, more emphasis is put on job-specific training. For example, food retailers in France provide extra training to specialist staff working on counters such as fresh fish, meat and cheese, and baked products. Here induction training takes longer than it does for ordinary sales workers, and continuing training is more common so as to incorporate new products or, in the case of fresh food, hygiene regulations. In consumer electronics too, retailers tend to invest in in-house training, given that they sell expensive and more complex products. Ongoing training is typically organized using a "snowball" model: internal trainers are trained in new products through seminars or training modules delivered via the Internet, and then they pass this information on to colleagues at training and work meetings. In addition, training by suppliers plays a much more prominent role in consumer electronics than in food retailing.

In Germany, vocational training institutions continue to offer apprentice training and continuing training programs specialized for retail trade. The role of vocational training institutions—which are governed by unions, employers' representatives, and federal authorities—is to provide training curricula that fit the needs of retail companies as well as to issue standardized certificates. In general, training includes theoretical study in school and practical learning in firms. Despite a decline in total retail employment, the number of newly concluded training contracts in retail has not declined in the last fifteen years. The footprint of vocational training institutions is obvious: 81 percent of all retail employees have completed a two- or three-year vocational training program. Denmark and the Netherlands also have traditional vocational training institutions. About one-third of Danish retail workers have vocational training certificates. In the Netherlands, where an industry-based vocational training system was established later than in Denmark, only about 15 percent have such a certificate.

The Netherlands and, even more so, Denmark show that changes in the workforce composition alter both the qualification structure of a sector and the role of training institutions. In both countries, the growing number of young people working as sales assistants for a limited period of time has led to a shift in training patterns. In food retailing in particular, young people are given on-the-job training, using "e-learning" modules and quick instruction by experienced workers. Even though firms could make use of the sector-specific vocational training systems, they do not use these "higher-level institutions" (Marsden 2000, 344) for the bulk of new recruits. The consequences of this shift in pattern are twofold. First, the core of trained workers in food retailing will decrease over time. Second, the competition between a short-term pattern of skill formation and the traditional policies oriented toward the long term that are associated with vocational training will lead to an "exhaustion" of training institutions—defined by Wolfgang Streeck and Kathleen Thelen (2005, 29) as a gradual breakdown of these institutions over time through depletion.

Norms with Institutional Weight and Their Implications for Worker Experience   Beyond the task structure per se, worker experience with workload and pressure is also susceptible to social norms regarding customer service. These factors affect work organization and worker experience, even though the task structure is heavily marked by companies' choice of market segment. For example, European cashiers in food retailing sit to do their work, whereas companies in the United States mandate that cashiers stand. In Denmark, France, Germany, and the Netherlands, sitting is reinforced by national ergonomic standards and the labor inspectorate.

Work organization also responds to customer service expectations, but these expectations turn out to be malleable "upward and downward." As already noted, with the partial exception of the United Kingdom, European food customers expect to weigh produce and bag groceries. In the United States, bagging is considered an integral component of customer service, except at self-checkout counters. Also in the United States, produce displays are expected to be very attractive even in midrange stores, an expectation that generates tasks that are not present in other countries.

Workforce Turnover and Vertical Mobility

Mobility in retail jobs has two key dimensions: vertical mobility and labor turnover—"moving up or moving on," in the felicitous phrase of Fredrik Andersson, Harry Holzer, and Julia Lane (2005). Given a retail job pyramid with many entry-level jobs and few higher positions, opportunities for upward mobility are more limited than in many other industries. This presents retailers with several options: (1) tolerating high turnover in some jobs, (2) recruiting significant numbers of workers who do not aspire to mobility, or (3) creating some opportunities for growth even *within* an entry-level job (through enriched content and opportunities for compensation growth). As we will see, retailers in the six countries use all three solutions, but to varying degrees. We start by examining turnover—because retail is distinctive in its high level of employee turnover—and then turn to upward mobility.

Turnover   Labor turnover has several important effects on various dimensions of job quality, making it an important job characteristic in its own right. First, high turnover can depress productivity by creating a workforce dominated by workers who lack experience and firm-specific knowledge. Second, elevated turnover in low-end jobs results in very few workers actually exercising the option to move up. Conversely, high turnover in mid- and upper-level jobs opens up space for upward mobility for those who remain. Finally, when turnover is high, it is relatively easy to achieve a norm shift about what constitutes an acceptable job or schedule. The expectations of newer cohorts of workers can be ratcheted down. For example, a participant in a focus group of cashiers in one of the Dutch supermarket cases stated, "Working part-time is the normal state of affairs in this job," adding, "Yet, it's quite difficult to build a decent living for yourself based on this work." Managers at a U.S. electronics chain that eliminated commission payments several years ago acknowledged that the action had been very demoralizing for employees, but current salespeople were content; one commented, "I like not working on commission," and another, newer hire exulted over a 3 percent raise in his hourly rate after ninety days on the job, oblivious to the absence of commission pay.

We found considerable differences in retail labor turnover across countries. The United States has by far the highest churning rates (50 percent per year, thirteen percentage points higher than the U.S. economy-wide average), with Germany and France (both 20 percent) at the bottom (see table 6.1). Quantitative data and the case studies themselves suggest three reasons, or sets of reasons, for these variations in churn. The first two stem from the observation that sep-

Figure 6.3 Scatter Plot of Labor Turnover and
Unemployment Rate, with Fitted Line from the
Five European Countries

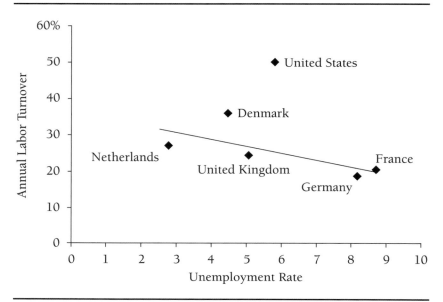

Sources: Authors' compilation. Comparable unemployment rates (2002) from OECD
(2003). Turnover rates (2002): see table 6.1.

aration rates are typically higher where unemployment is lower
(hence, other jobs are more available) and the workforce is younger.
As shown in figures 6.3 and 6.4, with the exception of the United
States, the correlation between the turnover rate and both unemployment and the percentage of the workforce under twenty-five is
quite strong.[13]

The roles of age and unemployment are mediated by a third factor—actually a set of factors—that we call "context," comprising institutions, labor market conditions (including the *interaction* of age
structure and unemployment), and firm strategy. As can be seen in
figure 6.4, retail turnover in Denmark is slightly above the five-country
fitted line based on age structure, whereas Dutch turnover falls somewhat below it. This corresponds well with what managers and workers say about young people's behavior as retail workers: Danish interviewees described young workers as "transitional," whereas their

Figure 6.4 Scatter Plot of Labor Turnover and Percentage
of Young Workers, with Fitted Line from the
Five European Countries

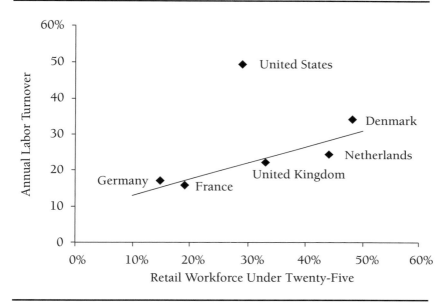

Sources: Percentage under twenty-five (2006) from European Union Labour Force
Survey (Eurostat, various years) and Current Population Survey (U.S. BLS 2008b).
Turnover rates: see table 6.1.

Dutch counterparts commented that many young workers, particularly immigrants, were "stuck." This difference, in turn, can be linked
to the disparities in labor market opportunities between the two
countries, but also to Denmark's famed system of "flexicurity," which
enhances labor market mobility.

The largest discrepancy from the dominant turnover pattern, however, arises in the United States, which has a far greater separation
rate than would be expected based on either the age mix or the unemployment rate. Interviews with U.S. retail managers and executives revealed a corporate strategy so pervasive that it has become in-
stitutionalized: these managers literally "tuned" turnover levels. On
the one hand, because pay raises, particularly in retail food, are
closely linked to seniority, managers sought to keep labor churning
high enough to maintain low average wages. "Your [average pay] rate
constantly goes up," a supermarket manager explained. "You have to

cycle in the lower end to balance the rate out." On the other hand, they sought to ensure that enough of the desirable workers were retained and groomed for internal promotion. In the European countries, this two-sided strategy can be recognized as well, but European retailers tend to emphasize the retention side quite a bit more, tilting toward better jobs overall rather than a large "turnover pool." As we explored earlier, longer job tenure may be a side effect of higher commitment to developing employee skills, whether through an apprenticeship system that offers a strong platform for doing so (Denmark, Germany, the Netherlands) or through a high wage floor that obliges retail managers to keep productivity high (France).

Also, analysis of institutional factors and corporate strategies leads us to look beyond the age profile of the retail workforce as proximate cause to consider underlying influences on this profile. France and Germany, the two countries in our sample with the lowest retail turnover rates and the lowest percentages of young workers in retail, are also the two countries with the *highest* proportions of women workers in retail. These high concentrations of women, in turn, are closely tied to France's family policies that support female labor force participation and German policies that promote mini-jobs with tax advantages that are particularly beneficial to married women. Alternatively, an older workforce could be the *result* rather than the cause of a lower propensity to quit. This alternative reminds us to look at nondemographic influences on turnover. Earlier, we cited the vocational training system and a high minimum wage as incentives for retailers to strive to hold on to workers; it is equally reasonable to argue that German workers' strong vocational training and French workers' high relative wages induce these workers to stay in retail jobs. Indeed, as a rule, churning can be brought down with higher wages and benefits, and even in the United States selected retail companies reduce turnover this way. Segmentation offers compensation opportunities to one slice of the workforce, with the part-time/full-time distinction serving as a key divider in the United States: in one U.S. grocery chain that provided detailed statistics, the turnover rate for part-timers was twelve times as high as for full-timers.

Vertical Mobility   Despite the varying contexts for upward mobility across countries, we found some commonalities. The available evidence from the six countries indicates that retail management posts are predominantly filled by promotion from within. However, especially in food retail, the odds of promotion for shop-floor workers are low given high ratios of workers to managers, as noted earlier. Given the flat employment structure of stores, management is virtually the only path for advancement. Moreover, in most countries a gender gap can be seen, again notably in food retail: women are broadly under-represented in management ranks. For the United States, earlier analyses of the U.S. research team (Carré, Holgate, and Tilly 2006) showed that women are more underrepresented in retail manage-ment (including food and consumer electronics) than in the econ-omy as a whole.

The U.S. case results connect these gender-specific results to broader mobility patterns. At most food retailers, company policies require every new employee to start in a part-time position; as a result, all full-timers come from within. Even up to the position of store man-ager, promotion from within predominates. Yet the cases highlighted that moving up into management is nonetheless difficult, especially for women, and that recruiting managers from outside is a growing practice. Many U.S. retailers, especially in consumer electronics, re-ported that they were moving away from the model of promoting al-most exclusively from within. At one electronics chain, the percent-age of store-level sales managers hired from within had dropped from between 90 and 95 percent to 50 percent over the past ten years. Var-ious forces may work in this direction. Cost-cutting pressure may have the unintended consequence of discouraging or thwarting in-ternal upward mobility: smaller pay increments and increased work-loads make supervisory and management positions less attractive. Perhaps the most important driver of outside recruiting has been the evolution of store management—especially in consumer electronics, but also in supermarkets—into an increasingly numbers-driven job that relies more on generic management skills. Recruitment thus is now more focused on professional and educational credentials than on company-specific knowledge.

The forces identified in the United States also are relevant in de-termining vertical mobility patterns in European countries, though other factors—notably those related to working time and commuting issues—come to the fore as well. In German food retail, promotion opportunities are limited and gendered segmentation patterns and processes are especially evident. Segmentation in career opportuni-ties starts as early as the selection process for vocational training po-sitions. Managerial positions at the store level are predominantly occupied by men, and the more companies use potential consideration for management positions as a criterion for allocating initial training slots, the more disadvantaged female applicants are. This mechanism works in step with the widely held view among male managers that investing in women's advancement is a waste of resources. Moreover, willingness to work long hours (over forty-five per week) and to be geographically mobile is an essential precondition for promotion from within. These two constraints, which are not directly linked to the business processes at stake, are also reported in the Netherlands and the United Kingdom. Though not explicitly excluding women, such demands are undoubtedly at odds with the preferences of large majorities of women and effectively prevent many women from building a career in retail. Closer analysis of the German interviews reveals that many women in the target jobs consciously refrained from efforts to get promoted in order to maintain a work-life balance and avoid the onerous management responsibilities linked to escalating performance benchmarks—akin to U.S. retailers' reports of worker reluctance to take on increasingly demanding management jobs. In some Dutch supermarket cases too, frontline workers refused increased responsibilities, especially if accepting them implied leaving their peer group. Notably in the Dutch and British cases, part-time workers gave few signs of concern about the lack of upward mobility opportunities; instead, they tended to emphasize positive aspects of the social life at work. As the U.K. retail team noted, such satisfaction may merely reflect workers' ability to remain positive in the face of limited options.

In European consumer electronics stores, though similar constraints on promotion apply as in food, opportunities for upward mobility and employee orientation toward seeking promotion appear stronger, perhaps because of the sector's growth. There is some evidence that this may also be the case for female salespersons, though patterns and processes seem to remain gendered to a certain extent. The influence of the peer group is most likely smaller, but it may be replaced by another factor that reduces the appeal of upward mobility: the large share of commission earnings. In both the English and French cases (as well as in a U.S. case with commission pay), there were reports that sales assistants in electrical goods stores were unwilling to take up career opportunities because, as long as they were successful at selling, their commission earnings could raise their total earnings close to the earnings of team leaders, or even managers, while they remained unburdened with the responsibilities of the latter.

The Danish case stands in contrast to the others. In Danish food retail, unlike food stores in the other five countries, channels of upward mobility seem relatively open. In the food chains studied, the Danish researchers found high degrees of internal mobility, with many promotion opportunities for motivated and qualified workers. Career seekers, starting as apprentices or trainees, did have opportunities to realize their ambitions. Because the food retailers faced strong competition from other industries in the labor market, they offered comprehensive training programs. Conversely, while researchers in other countries have found greater opportunities to ascend in consumer electronics retailing than in food retailing, in Denmark employees of specialty stores (including consumer electronics) find it difficult to advance beyond the level of full-time salesperson. The Danish team identified the career-seeker category as mainly male.

COMPENSATION

The retail trade is consistently a low-wage sector in all countries in this cross-national study. It is also an industry in which national institutions matter. However, the impact of institutions on lifting wages differs considerably. Before probing such institutional effects, we start this section by examining the gender pay gap and the related wage gap between food and electronics retailing. We then explore the role of national institutions in two countries with comparatively low shares of low-wage workers in retailing, France and Denmark. In contrast, the three other European countries give insight into the dynamics that drive an increase in low-wage work—specifically, the use of exit options. Strikingly, the lightly regulated United States, with the lowest rate of collective bargaining coverage, has the same incidence of low-wage work in retailing as Germany, which, despite its tradition of strong representative structures, has allowed numerous low-paid jobs to be created through the mini-job option.

The Gender Wage Gap in Retail   The mean gender pay gap in wholesale and retail is especially large in Germany and the Netherlands—according to WageIndicator data, 22 and 21 percent, respectively—while in the United Kingdom and France it is 16 percent (Chubb et al. 2008; van Klaveren, Tijdens, and Sprenger 2007).[14] In comparison, the U.S. wage gender gap is relatively moderate, though still significant: women in frontline retail jobs in 2004 earned 12 percent less than their male counterparts (Carré, Holgate, and Tilly 2006). Danish women's disadvantage in hourly compensation was even smaller, at 10 percent.[15] Gender sorting across retail subsectors and the wage penalty due to interruptions in paid employment play a role, as do the constraints on the vertical mobility of female retail workers. Within countries, the gender gap is likely to be smaller where wage-leveling institutions such as unions are stronger. At a unionized U.S. grocery chain, a woman cashier approvingly noted, "You get your pay raises per hour, hours worked. So that's fair. I know in some businesses you hear how men make 20 percent more than a woman in the same job." We discuss the gender wage gap later in the chapter as it arises in analyzing various aspects of compensation.

Pay in Food Versus Electronics Retail   In all countries, the share of low-wage work is much higher in food retailing than in consumer electronics (table 6.6), and the company case studies conform with this pattern of disparity. Significant differences between food and consumer electronics retail productivity in all countries would be one possible explanation, but the data, limited as they are, do not appear to bear this out. Indeed, food retailing has 6 percent higher productivity than electronics in the United States, 22 percent higher in Denmark, and 19 percent higher in the Netherlands.[16] The obvious alternative to explain pay differentials would be a historical gender bias in pay structure. This is a likely factor because men make up the majority of the workforce in consumer electronics and women constitute the majority in retail food. In 2004 the share of women in retail food sales occupations varied in Europe between 68 percent in Denmark and 85 percent in the Netherlands, while it was 53 percent in the United States; in consumer electronics, the European share of females varied between 17 percent in Denmark and 40 percent in France, while it was 30 percent in the United States. Gender patterns may play out indirectly as well: consumer electronics retailers may have to compete with information technology—another male-dominated sector—to attract knowledgeable salespeople and technicians. In a later section, we further scrutinize the food-electronics pay gap in an analysis of the practice of commission pay.

Table 6.6 Retail Workers with Wages Below Each National Low-
Wage Threshold, by Subsector, 2003

	Denmark	France	Germany	Netherlands	United Kingdom	United States
All retail workers	23%	18%	42%[a]	46%	49%	42%
Food retail	29	26	29[b]	57	64	35
Consumer electronics retail	15	3	27[b]	19	—	18

Sources: Authors' compilation based on: Denmark—Esbjerg et al. (2008, 141); France—Askenazy, Berry, and Prunier-Poulmaire (2008, 220); Germany—Voss-Dahm (2008, 258); Netherlands—Structure of Earnings Survey (CBS 2002c); United Kingdom—Annual Survey of Hours and Earnings (U.K. ONS 2005); United States—Current Population Survey microdata (U.S. BLS 2005a).
Notes: Low-wage threshold is two-thirds of the national median gross hourly wage. All Danish and Dutch figures are for 2002. U.S. figures and U.K. figure are all for 2005; the U.K. food figure is for 2001.
a. Full-time and part-time workers.
b. Full-time workers only.

National State and Labor Relations Institutions with a "Bite" Some national institutions set effective barriers against firms' drive to lower wages and depress working conditions. U.S. law does not mandate hourly wage parity for part-time and full-time workers, while in Europe, under pressure from EU guidelines, part-timers are entitled to the same hourly wages as full-timers if they perform the same jobs, and all those working over a minimum threshold (usually twelve hours per week) must be covered by national social security systems. The lack of quasi-mandated universal health and pension coverage (except for limited Social Security) also makes the U.S. situation exceptional (see Mason and Salverda, this volume). U.S. retailers have greater incentives to use "part-time" as a status (to ration access to employer-sponsored benefits) than is the case in European countries. "The fringe costs associated with part-time associate versus full-time associate are dramatically different," a U.S. grocery chain executive remarked.

The differential bite of national institutions becomes particularly clear when we contrast the U.S. situation to the two countries with the lowest incidence of low-wage work in retail, France and Denmark. In France, the high value of the national minimum wage (SMIC) relative to the national average pulls up the retail wage distribution and contributes to the lowest incidence of low wages in retail of all the countries in the study. The national minimum wage is well above contractual wage levels in retail and provides a floor that lifts most workers above the low-wage threshold, despite reports of frequent minimum-wage violations. In contrast, the real value of the U.S. minimum wage has been set relatively low. Retail entry-level wages are pegged close to it—barely above it in many cases—so the U.S. minimum wage does influence retail wages but does little to raise them.

France's SMIC is a far more potent tool than collective bargaining. In fact, despite the significant indirect impact of national union federations on wages, via setting the national minimum wage level, the direct impact of collective bargaining on retail wages is limited because the workplace weakness of French unions in retail renders France's mandatory contractual extension of pay provisions ineffective in the sector. Moreover, some retail firms pursue anti-union policies, as the director of a franchise store indicated: "An employee who joins a union has to be fired immediately. We find a virtual fault as justification." Product market regulations play a complementary role in limiting low wages. Regulations limiting store size and expansion constrain big-box competition and make comparatively high wage levels (and a smaller share of low-wage employment) possible.[17]

Strong union representation in Denmark, expressed in collective bargaining agreements that enforce significant wage compression, contributes to the low level of low-wage retail employment in Denmark. Collective bargaining coverage was 69 percent in the period 2004 to 2006 (Tijdens et al. 2007), and even those retailers that have not signed on to the collective labor agreement adhere to its conditions.[18] Furthermore, the Danish social partners (which include the Danish Employers' Federation) have agreed that no member firm will pay less than €12.00 ($16.20) gross wage per hour (Westergaard-Nielsen 2008, 38). Although it is true that, in spite of the absence of a legal mandate, the social partners have set a relatively high wage floor, it is important to keep in mind that even for workers at this wage level the income tax rate in Denmark is a high 44 percent (Westergaard-Nielsen 2008, 44).

In contrast, in the United States, retail collective bargaining coverage is the lowest of any of the six countries (less than 6 percent in 2007; U.S. Bureau of Labor Statistics 2008a). Unionization clearly has an impact on compensation for U.S. retail workers, but the union threat effect is minimal. Furthermore, U.S. workers lack access to other worker representation structures, such as works councils, that could affect wages. Though in decades past U.S. retail unions won significant gains for their workforces, in their current weakened state unions at many companies have been compelled to accept slower wage increases, lower wage ceilings, and benefit cutbacks, sometimes in more dramatic increments than their non-union counterparts. Such concessions often take the form of "two-tier" contracts specifying inferior terms for new hires.

The cases of Germany and the Netherlands—with a share of low-wage work that is about the level of that in the United States (Germany) or even slightly higher (the Netherlands)—show that the existence of collective bargaining institutions does not necessarily raise relative wages. In Germany, the high level of low-wage work in retailing partly results from a continuously decreasing coverage rate of collective agreements in recent years, with only about half of all retail employees still covered by collective agreements in 2006 (a twelve-point drop from 2003 in West Germany). Even the administrative extension of collective bargaining agreements in the Netherlands, which compels similar or identical agreements across the industry, is not, by itself, sufficient to yield a low incidence of low-wage work given the high percentage (44 percent) of workers under age twenty-five who get youth subminimum wages. In both countries, retail firms dispose of viable exit options, to which we now turn.

Exit Options and Weak Enforcement Dampen the Effects of Protective Institutions   Exit options, and the uses that retailers make of them, serve as gate openers for excluding certain groups of workers from the prevailing wage level of an industry. Consequently, they widen the wage dispersion within the sector. The impact of exit options on the pay structure can be "self-energizing" and grow over time if firms follow cost-cutting strategies in reaction to fierce competition. If certain groups in the labor market relevant for the sector receive lower wages than others, they may be substituted for those who are better-paid. Just as there are country-specific options for employers to achieve flexibility and cost control within the national regulatory environment, there are nationally specific "Achilles' heels" for worsening compensation. In addition to exit options, which are primarily aboveboard means to bypass national (and sometimes sectoral) institutions, the countries in our study also display some degree of weak enforcement of regulations, with further implications for compensation.

Youth subminimum wages are the most salient manifestation of an exit option in retail. Such subminimum wages are more broadly used in food than in consumer electronics retail. They exist in Denmark, the Netherlands, and the United Kingdom: in the Netherlands and the United Kingdom, they have a legal basis, though they differ widely in size and impact (in the United Kingdom the youth subminimum wage of a sixteen-year-old is 62 percent of the adult minimum wage, and in the Netherlands it is 35 percent); in Denmark, this subminimum wage is set in collective agreements. Youth subminimum wages are consistent with the United Kingdom's low regulation model, whereas in the other two countries they offer exits from institutional arrangements (relatively high collectively bargained wages). Youth minimum wages in Denmark and the Netherlands have played a significant role in staffing decisions, cost control, and ultimately the share of low-wage work in retail. They have created strong incentives to use very young workers and students in both countries. In the Netherlands, the statutory youth subminimum wage introduced by the government in the 1970s led to the replacement of adult women with very young workers in food retail when price wars flared between 2003 and 2006. More Dutch retail workers fell below the low-wage threshold than in any country but the United Kingdom (table 6.6). Prodded by the protests of young members and the downward pressure on adult wages, Dutch union leaders recently requested that adult wages be paid from the age of eighteen. In Denmark, the impact of the youth subminimum wage is mitigated by other institutional features that regulate compensation even in the presence of a high share of young workers. The retail subminimum wage, while about 30 percent lower than the (bargained) adult wage, is still high. As noted earlier, the national agreed-upon wage floor is high, and wage compression prevails in bargaining; retail labor agreements have high coverage and are adhered to by nonsignatory employers in many cases.

Though a national minimum wage, if high enough (as in France), can lift the retail wage distribution and limit the incidence of low-wage work, its effectiveness is limited in cases where it is set relatively low and in an environment with weak workplace-level unions. For example, in the United Kingdom, the national minimum wage (NMW) is still low relative to the median wage. Furthermore, British retailers reacted to increases in the NMW by reducing bonuses and shift pay differentials—leaving retail workers at low relative earnings levels. An executive of a food chain commented that "we pay just a tad over the minimum wage. . . . We used to [go] higher than that, but you know how it's hiked up. . . . we would probably have been around fifteen to twenty pence above it." Furthermore, as noted earlier, the country also has a youth subminimum wage and a relatively high share of young workers (33 percent under age twenty-five in 2006)—higher than in France though not quite as high as in the Netherlands and Denmark. The result, in combination with the very limited grip of collective bargaining, is an even higher incidence of low-wage work than in the United States.

In Germany, the increasing use of mini-jobs—short-hour, part-time jobs with a maximum monthly income of €400 ($637 in 2008)—accounts for the relatively high incidence of low-wage jobs in retail.[19] Nearly nine of ten mini-jobbers (87 percent) receive hourly wages below the low-wage threshold, whereas only one-third of full-time employees (34 percent) in German retail were low-paid in 2004. The pay difference is connected with the special national regulation of mini-jobs. By law, mini-jobs should provide a subsidy to job-holders by exempting them from tax and mandatory social security contributions. But in practice, and contrary to the law, most mini-jobbers never receive this subsidy because retail firms appropriate the benefit by offering lower wages—without being penalized by the state. The case study material indicates that married women, socially protected by their husband's entitlements, and young workers in mini-jobs may not object to unequal wages because, in the absence of mandatory social contributions, their wage level seems sufficient. In companies where works councils strongly represent employees' interests, however, it has proven possible either to prevent the use of mini-jobs altogether or at least to monitor developments closely in order to forestall a differentiated pay policy.

The case of German mini-jobs illustrates how the self-reinforcing effects of exit options can result in a wider deterioration of income opportunities. Mini-jobs fit retailers' needs for "gap fillers" to cover peak times and do not cut off access to trained personnel thanks to the presence of a high percentage of skilled women among mini-jobbers. Women often agree to work these marginal part-time jobs because they see a mini-job as a means to combine work and family responsibilities (in the absence of other viable options), and social norms still accommodate a secondary earner role for trained women. When combined with easy access to the mini-job option and an overall declining coverage rate of collective agreements on pay, the apprenticeship system, an institution that is geared to developing skills, upholding wage levels, and equalizing male and female earnings potential, does not forestall the growth of low-wage jobs as effectively as in the past. Thus, the case of Germany shows that occupational skills do not necessarily protect workers—especially female workers—from low wages. Furthermore, the extension of mini-jobs not only is a gateway for low-wage work within retail but also has become a driving force for the degradation of female employment in Germany as a whole. Ironically, mini-jobs were established and accepted, respectively, by the two institutions that in other contexts have done the most to bolster earnings: the German state imposed the mini-job option, and in some big retail companies works councils agreed to the establishment of mini-jobs, partly in the hope of protecting core worker employment conditions by sacrificing the "peripheral" newer hires.

In retail, exit options that are aboveboard means to lower pay coexist with opportunities for outright violation of employment standards. With multiple and scattered workplaces, it can be difficult to monitor and enforce labor standards, particularly if there are weak or no institutions of worker representation at the work sites. To varying degrees, case studies report instances of minimum-wage or overtime pay violations.

The Role of Commission Pay and the Gender Composition of Consumer Electronics   Consumer electronics retail has historically relied on commission pay, a practice that highlights gender-patterned behavioral expectations and appears congruent with the relatively high proportion of men in the sector (relative to the food sector). For example, German managers reportedly expect male workers to negotiate for themselves more than women would, even in an environment with union collective bargaining and works councils. Pay is also higher and the share of low-wage work is substantially smaller in consumer electronics than in food retail. We expect that commission pay plays a role in this difference. To the extent that male workers concentrate in parts of retail where commission pay is in effect, they stand to benefit from higher compensation. Commission pay is not always associated with higher pay, however, as we will see in the Netherlands.

Electronics retailers in Denmark, Germany, France, the Netherlands, and the United Kingdom very much rely on commission pay to drive motivation; such reliance is less common in the United States. Pay based on individual sales levels motivates a sales process that entails greeting customers, offering detailed product information and advice, and securing after-sales service contracts. (In France, salespeople collaborate in the scheduling of floor staff to match customer flow and limit staff competition over customers and the risk of alienating clients.) These service attitudes are needed both in consumer electronics retail and in some food stores. If these attitudes are explicitly rewarded in consumer electronics but not in food retail, it may indicate that they are assumed to be "natural" for women—and therefore not skills worthy of compensation—whereas soft skills like service and team orientation are criteria of pay systems in male-dominated consumer electronics.

Collectively bargained pay can coexist with commission pay, but with divergent outcomes across countries. In two German retailers, the collective agreement set a bonus level on top of base pay, but there was also the expectation that individuals would negotiate additional bonuses. These could be substantial, reaching as much as 25 percent of collectively agreed basic pay, according to one store manager. In the German cases, collective voice appeared to increase the relative share of fixed (guaranteed) pay in total compensation. In one case in which neither a collective agreement nor a works council was present, the fixed pay was one-third lower than in settings with bargaining. But commission pay can also undermine collectively bargained base pay—although its record is mixed enough that we would not consider it an exit option. The Dutch study found that commission pay is accompanied by lower collectively bargained wages because social actors have the perception that individuals can improve their compensation with commission.[20]

However, commission pay, while still prevalent in European countries, is under pressure, owing to falling margins on major video and audio consumer items as well as personal computers; these pressures are felt mostly in the United States and, to some degree, in Denmark. Some Danish case studies included reports by management that a slowdown of sales growth had raised questions about continuing with commission pay. More importantly, major big-box U.S. consumer electronics retailers moved away from commission pay in recent years in order to cut costs. It was possible to implement the change quickly—even abruptly—because there was no consultation with any representative bodies; unions and works councils are absent in U.S. consumer electronics retailing.

The U.S. cases reveal that the removal of commission pay is associated with declining pay levels for sales staff and with a growing share of part-timers. The fixed pay rates do not end up being commensurate with what could be achieved under commission pay. The removal of commission pay generates motivational issues for the sales workforce that management must address. Some U.S. electronics companies have developed bonus schemes for hourly wage workers, based on sales, profits, or other success indicators at the level of the department, store, or company.[21] It remains to be seen whether the removal of commission pay will result in a decline in male representation in consumer electronics retailing.

In sum, national institutions that set basic conditions for pay directly affect the incidence of low-wage work in retail. National institutions such as collective bargaining or a national minimum wage raise the wage floor when they are geared to do so, as in Denmark or France. However, we find that exit options from the institutional framework—such as a youth subminimum wage or mini-jobs—allow a significant number of low-wage jobs to be created even in settings with collective bargaining, apprenticeship, and other institutions geared to maintaining job quality and relatively higher compensation.

CONCLUSION

The leading question of this chapter has been: what aspects of the national institutional settings in which retail jobs are embedded make these jobs better or worse? To answer this question, we have explored how job quality outcomes in the United States, with its thinner web of formal regulatory mechanisms, diverge from those in European countries, as well as examining differences among the latter.

Concerns about the role of institutional settings are particularly salient because, as noted at the outset, retail leads other industries in experimenting with changes that affect the labor market and job quality. Pressures on job quality have been high in all countries alike as retailers have adopted supply-chain management strategies based on advanced technologies, along with employment strategies aimed at cutting costs. Yet the consequences of these pressures are not easy to predict given the different institutional traditions and recent changes in the countries under study. There is significant variation in the trade-offs faced by retailers, in the timing and extent (though not the main direction) of changes in retail jobs, and in the principal dimensions of job outcomes across the six countries. Specifically, across countries, retailers have faced different intensities of pressures to cut costs and have adopted service and labor deployment strategies that reflect direct and indirect effects of features of their national institutional environment and customs. In all countries, pressures to fend off competition from low-cost retail models have translated into market strategies that go in two opposite directions: increasing service and customization and, conversely, pushing for self-service. Concurrently, there have been consistent attempts to cut labor costs. Across countries, retailers have availed themselves of existing exit options from particular features of their institutional environment and also have led the push for introducing *new* exit options. These efforts have resulted in varied patterns of exclusion and different work conditions across countries as each national web of institutions offers differing options for exit. Thus, while retailers' uses of exit options dilute the impact of institutional factors that traditionally ensured a high degree of social inclusion for many European countries, they have done so in ways that are somewhat unique to each nation.

RETAIL JOB QUALITY: TREND AND VARIATIONS

In general, retail jobs have gotten worse across the countries in our sample in recent years. In the United States, jobs at most retailers have slipped in terms of scheduling options and opportunities for promotion and pay progression. In European countries, compensation and working conditions also have come under great pressure from cost-cutting strategies. We observe the weakening of uniform standards and a trend toward fragmentation of pay and working arrangements in all countries. Corporate strategy has played a part in these downward pressures on retail job quality. However, we do not principally attribute this trend to a "Wal-Mart effect" outside the United States, despite Wal-Mart's large global footprint (Brunn 2006). Instead, we see it as the result of two other main trends.

First, there has been a general liberalization trend in labor and product market regulations within all countries in the study. There is great variation across countries in the policies that are implemented and in how they are implemented. In fact, some exit options, such as the youth subminimum wage in the Netherlands and mini-jobs in Germany, are nationally specific. Conversely, we note that the impact of exit options can be significantly mitigated with renewed state policy. Recent U.K. national minimum wage increases have raised the wage floor in retailing and eliminated the very lowest pay levels.

The second trend is that retailers have adjusted by shifting to the heavier use of part-time workforces with weaker bargaining power (for example, mothers with young children, low-skilled young workers), who then bear the brunt of the adjustment and the sharp edge of cost-cutting management approaches. For European retailers, part-time employment has been closely related to several exit options (such as mini-jobs and a youth subminimum wage). The significant use of part-time workers is emblematic of practices that segment employment and the workforce, and it has also been associated with thwarting union organizing.[22] Furthermore, social norms for what constitutes an acceptable job or schedule have changed: the expectations of newer cohorts of workers have been diminished, an easy transition to achieve with high turnover and young hires.

Why are some countries' retail job outcomes better than others along certain dimensions, even given this broad negative trend? We observe that some historical institutions continue to have a strong effect on job quality. We call them institutions with "a bite." We can illustrate their impact best by looking back at key findings on schedules, work organization, mobility, and compensation.

In terms of institutions that affect *work schedules*, the primary contrast between the United States and European countries is the nearly complete lack of government regulation of hours of operation and worker schedules in the former. The United States has led the way in 24/7 store operation. The only significant remaining regulation on work schedules is the overtime premium. In contrast, unions, works councils, and store hours regulations all play a role in store and worker schedules in the European countries. German and Danish regulations require that work schedules be set far in advance (four to six months), a mandate that would be considered unmanageable by U.S. retailers. In France, the combination of a thirty-five-hour full-time workweek with a (nationally extended) labor agreement specifying a minimum of twenty-six hours for part-timers has narrowed the hours gap between part- and full-time work.

In the absence of hours regulation, and with a minimal union threat effect, social norms regarding reasonable workload and hours can erode. Witness U.S. food retailers that are progressively eliminating the Sunday (or nonsocial hours) wage premium. In contrast, in all European countries hourly wage premiums are common and are typically mandated by collective labor agreements, though employers are seeking to chip away at them.

The *organization of tasks* is clearly affected by the interactions of national institutions, social norms, policies affecting the reproductive sphere, and the labor market context. The education and training system, primarily the vocational education system, plays a role in Germany and, to some degree, in Denmark and the Netherlands, facilitating a broader job profile than in other countries. However, rather than ensuring that graduates of the vocational system all have good-quality jobs, the combination of vocational education and exit options results in retailers having access to skilled secondary part-time workers—in Germany women with family responsibilities who end up in mini-jobs, and in Denmark and the Netherlands (trained) young people subject to youth wages.

Workforce turnover and upward mobility affect managerial choice of work organization and, conversely, are affected by job quality and workforce expectations. As we noted at the outset, labor turnover rates are far higher in the United States than in the other countries, especially given the middling concentration of young workers in the retail sector. U.S. retailers' human resource strategies rely much more than those of their European counterparts on labor churning to keep average wages low. Vertical mobility patterns do not show readily explicable cross-national differences; instead, the strongest finding across all countries is that significant barriers impede women's movement into management.

The institutions with the most influence over *compensation* vary across countries. In some nation-states, state regulation, rather than industrial relations, has the most significant impact. In France and the United Kingdom, the state-set minimum wage has more impact on retail wages. In France, as noted, the high minimum-wage floor essentially reaches the "ceiling" for many frontline retail jobs, significantly boosting wages (it is superseded by higher wages in some large companies). In the United States, in contrast, the minimum wage has historically set a low floor for the industry. On the other hand, state policy may enable retailers' use of exit options, as with Germany's state-imposed mini-jobs.

Worker representation institutions also continue to have an impact on compensation. In Denmark, high union density and unions' commitment to wage compression lift most jobs above the low-wage threshold. In contrast, in the United States, because unionization and collective bargaining are by now limited to a few companies (where wages are higher), the union threat effect is negligible in most retail settings. In U.S. unionized settings, hard-pressed unions have accepted two-tier structures that offer lower wages and benefits to new hires while protecting incumbents.

Reproductive institutions also have a bearing on compensation by shaping retailers' exit options. In some European countries, a large pool of mothers with constrained child care access find part-time work in retail close to home a primary alternative. In contrast, U.S. women with school-age children increasingly work full-time.[23] The labor market context also shapes options for low-wage workforces. In Danish and Dutch cities, the tightening of local labor markets has resulted in a rise in wages for young workers—a primary target group for part-time hiring.

INSTITUTIONS AND GENDER PATTERNS

In all six countries, gender segregation of jobs remains a constant, and the same is true of gender-specific patterns of mobility and compensation. In all six countries, it is difficult for women to break through the glass ceiling into management, especially in food retail. Women are also mostly excluded from electronics retail's big-ticket sales, which are often linked with commission pay. Equalizing institutions, such as those that ensure skill acquisition and credentialing for women as well as men (the German apprenticeship system, for example), are important, as is wage compression implemented through collective labor agreements. However, such institutions have encountered significant obstacles to their effectiveness when combined with exit options that build on women's secondary earner status in the household and labor market. Similarly, when exit options have fostered the competition of one vulnerable worker group against another, women have sometimes been relegated to secondary earner roles. In the recent price war in Dutch food retail, stable women workers were replaced by very young workers paid at the subminimum wage.

Institutions that regulate the reproductive sphere also make a difference. In some countries, accessible child care can sometimes enable women with family responsibilities to access better job quality outcomes and avoid marginalization in very short part-time jobs. For example, in France, the historical preference for full-time work—understood to be supported by the strong provision of child care options—has prompted policy action to set a minimum number of part-time hours.

PATTERNS AND PROSPECTS FOR RETAIL JOBS

Taking a step back from the details of job quality, what can we say about the overall production models in retail in these countries? With shared market pressures and similar technologies, retail industries in all of our study countries have moved in the same broad directions, developing options for using cheaper labor and deploying it only as needed. Across the full set of countries, the emerging combination of technology-enhanced high performance with low wages and worsening working conditions conforms with Bailey and Bernhardt's (1997) finding for the United States. In this sense, one may argue for a finding of broad convergence of intensified use of exit options to cut labor costs—though, as these country case studies indicate, not of shared consequences for job quality. Yet even while there has been convergence of competitive pressures, ownership structure, and store formats, retail, an industry historically very local in character, retains national peculiarities, with consequences for job quality.

In all countries, there are questions about the sustainability of the strategies adopted by retailers to cut costs and maintain market share. For example, in Denmark and the Netherlands, competition for young or transitional workers with attitudes suited for retail work and a high level of general skills may drive wages up, undermining the cost containment lever this workforce provides. Even in the United States, retailers are caught in a bind between service and efficiency goals, on the one hand, and on the other, a workforce characterized by high turnover, low skills, and low commitment. Of course, change in state policy can alter worker decision terms and corporate strategies relatively quickly. In Germany and the Netherlands, recent increases in child care investment could alter the character of the labor supply of married women. In the United States, meanwhile, there are growing pressures to raise the minimum wage.

Yet, because the six countries started in different places with respect to compensation, working conditions, and regulatory institutions for both product and labor markets, working in retail pays differently and is a different experience across countries. In the United States, there has been a continuous, and rather uniform, erosion of compensation and working conditions. In European countries, the movement has been neither as continuous nor as uniform. New regulatory initiatives, such as higher minimum wages, have partially reversed trends toward falling compensation. Rather than uniform degradation of retail jobs, European countries have tended toward fragmentation via exit options: mini-jobbers in Germany, youths earning extra-low wages in the Netherlands, and involuntary part-time workers in France have taken the main hit. In all six countries, the retail industry has been a leader in such fragmentation and in experimentation with nonstandard hours, segmented work arrangements, and a variety of other exit options from the institutions that safeguard job quality. Because of this trajectory of experimentation, retail developments may well forecast the consequences of similar scheduling, recruitment, and compensation changes being considered in other industries. Alternatively, significant but hitherto unforeseen changes in the policy environment and the strengths of social movements might throw retail—with its emblematic "low-quality" jobs—into serving as a testing ground for novel collective action and regulatory strategies to bolster job quality for low-wage workers.

We thank our retail research colleagues on the Danish, French, and U.K. teams for providing details on data and field results as well as comments. We thank Brandynn Holgate, Karina Rozas, and Fabián Slonimcyk for assistance with statistics. The chapter benefited from comments from Eileen Appelbaum, Larry Hunter, Thomas Kochan, and Richard Murnane, as well as from Jérôme Gautié, John Schmitt, the authors of the overview chapters in this volume (chapters 1 to 4), the national team coordinators, participants in Russell Sage Foundation meetings, and three anonymous reviewers.

NOTES

1. In this chapter, we draw extensively on research summarized in the retail chapters of the "Low-Wage Work in Europe" national monographs

(Askenazy, Berry, and Prunier-Poulmaire 2008; Esbjerg et al. 2008; Mason and Osborne 2008; van Klaveren 2008a; Voss-Dahm 2008). See also Carré and Tilly, with Holgate (2007) for U.S. research. Unattributed interview quotes come from these chapters or the underlying case studies.

2. The high-road/low-road terminology is often applied to other dimensions of firm behavior as well, but here we focus on the product market.

3. Because overrepresentation is relative to the average gender distribution in employment across industries, the U.S. situation may be due to the fact that other large industries besides retail also have a significant female presence.

4. In the United States, the immigrant share in retail (13 percent), and in cashier/stocker jobs in particular (12 percent), is lower than for the private sector as a whole (18 percent) (authors' calculation from March 2007 Current Population Survey). The Danish figure of 4 percent (Esbjerg et al. 2008, 157) compares to 5.8 percent of foreign-born workers for total employment (Gautié et al., this volume). Germany's 5.5 percent share relates to 7 percent non-German citizens in the German workforce. In the United Kingdom, the figures of 8 percent immigrants among cashiers and 9 percent among sales assistants compare to 6 percent in the U.K. labor force (Mason and Osborne 2008, 135–36, compared to Gautié et al., this volume). For privacy reasons, exact figures are missing for France and the Netherlands, but case study data suggest for both countries an overrepresentation of immigrant workers or workers from ethnic minorities in low-end food retailing, notably in the large cities.

5. The cultural norm for women's employment in France has historically been full-time work. Survey-based studies have reported women workers' dissatisfaction with "constrained" part-time work, particularly in a context of high unemployment (Galtier 1999; OECD 1993). The French study's fieldwork interviews with workers and union representatives revealed dissatisfaction among part-time women workers (Askenazy, Berry, and Prunier-Poulmaire 2008).

6. European data are from the 2006 Labor Force Survey; U.S. data are from the 2007 Current Population Survey (CPS).

7. On strategic segmentation in the call center sector, see Batt (2000).

8. RFID technology can be used to track and monitor individual products by means of radio signals, thereby accelerating distribution processes. Thus, with RFID technology, there is no need to search for product codes and then scan these codes at close range by means of scanners.

9. These within-country differences are partly due to a research design

that split the company samples between "high-end" and "low-end" service levels, although there is no perfect match between service level and degree of use of highly automated high-performance-business systems.

10. The high scan speed may be partly driven by the small number of checkout counters derived from store size constraints. Short lines may be difficult to deliver in spite of the high speed of individual cashiers. Also, the French retail study found significant differences in aggregate retail food productivity between France and the United States (Askenazy, Berry, and Prunier-Poulmaire 2008).

11. French cashiers do not bag, and they rarely weigh and price bulk fresh fruits and vegetables—customers do it themselves and affix a machine-generated tag—whereas U.S. cashiers typically bag (or are assisted by baggers) and invariably identify and weigh produce.

12. The Baccalauréat is the national diploma that students have to earn at the end of high school in order to gain access to tertiary education.

13. The five-country correlation coefficients (omitting the United States) are -0.72 and 0.91, respectively.

14. French figure calculated by Ministry of Labor, DARES, from 2006 data of DADS (Déclaration Annuelle de Données Sociales).

15. Authors' calculations from 2006 data in StatBank Denmark, "Labor Market Table ATR1," available at: www.statbank.dk.

16. We have data for three countries only. The U.S. and Danish figures are sales per employee-hour because value-added data are not available for these subsectors. The U.S. figure uses sales from the 2002 Economic Census, employment and weekly hours from Current Economic Statistics (U.S. Bureau of Labor Statistics), and an economy-wide average of weeks per year from Hyde (2007) and Raines (2007). The Danish figure uses data from StatBank Denmark, except hours per full-time equivalent (FTE), which are from the European Foundation for the Improvement of Living and Working Conditions, and the economy-wide average of weeks per year, which is from Hyde (2007). The Dutch figures are from Industrial Board for Retail Trades (2005), 8 (based on value-added per hours worked per year).

17. Other European countries have store size regulations, but they are less stringent and in flux; these regulations have the greatest impact in France.

18. The law mandates only that the collective labor agreement (CLA) be in force if 50 percent of the workers in a workplace are members of the main union.

19. The share of mini-jobs in retail employment increased by 20 percent from 1999 to 2007, from 21.7 percent to 23.3 percent—to the point where every fourth job in retailing in 2007 was a mini-job.

20. Unemployment insurance benefits are based on the fixed part of pay

only. Thus, low bargained wages have an impact on unemployment benefits.

21. Interestingly, some U.S. *food* retailers are also experimenting with such schemes, and with individual one-time bonuses (in the form of gift certificates or cash cards) given at the discretion of the manager. This kind of experimentation does not seem to take place in many European grocery stores. However, several large French food chains have a CLA that includes a bonus based on store and chain performance.

22. Particularly because it is combined with the problems of union organizing in numerous small workplaces, short-hour, part-time work has had this effect (for a discussion of Germany, the Netherlands, and the United Kingdom, see Dribbusch 2003).

23. This trend is not due, however, to greater child care availability or affordability in the United States.

REFERENCES

Abernathy, Frederick H., John T. Dunlop, Janice H. Hammond, and David Weil. 2000. "Retailing and Supply Chains in the Information Age." *Technology in Society* 22(1): 5–31.

Amsterdam Institute for Advanced Labour Studies (AIAS). 2007. Multinationals Enterprise (MNE) Database. Amsterdam.

Andersson, Fredrik, Harry J. Holzer, and Julia I. Lane. 2005. *Moving Up or Moving On: Who Advances in the Low-Wage Labor Market?* New York: Russell Sage Foundation.

Askenazy, Philippe, Jean-Baptiste Berry, and Sophie Prunier-Poulmaire. 2008. "Working Hard for Large French Retailers." In *Low-Wage Work in France*, edited by Ève Caroli and Jérôme Gautié. New York: Russell Sage Foundation.

Autor, David H., Frank Levy, and Richard J. Murnane. 2003. "Computer-Based Technological Change and Skill Demands: Reconciling the Perspective of Economists and Sociologists." In *Low-Wage America: How Employers Are Reshaping Opportunity in the Workplace,* edited by Eileen Appelbaum, Annette Bernhardt, and Richard J. Murnane. New York: Russell Sage Foundation.

Bailey, Thomas R., and Annette D. Bernhardt. 1997. "In Search of the High Road in a Low-Wage Industry." *Politics and Society* 25(2): 179–201.

Batt, Rose. 2000. "Strategic Segmentation in Frontline Services: Matching Customers, Employees, and Human Resource Systems." *International Journal of Human Resource Management* 11(3): 540–61.

Bernhardt, Annette. 1999. *The Future of Low-Wage Jobs: Case Studies in the Retail Industry.* Working paper 10. New York: Columbia University, Teachers College, Institute on Education and the Economy (IEE) (March).

Brunn, Stanley D. 2006. *Wal-Mart World: The World's Biggest Corporation in the Global Economy.* New York: Routledge.

Bundesagentur fuer Arbeit (BA). (Federal Employment Service). 2005. BA Beschaeftigtenpanel (BA Employee Panel) [database]. Nuernberg, Germany: BA.

———. 2007. BA Beschaeftigtenstatistik (BA Employee Statistics) [database]. Nuernberg, Germany: BA.

Burt, Steve, and Leigh Sparks. 2006. "Wal-Mart's World." In *Wal-Mart World: The World's Biggest Corporation in the Global Economy,* edited by Stanley D. Brunn. New York: Routledge.

Carré, Françoise, Brandynn Holgate, and Chris Tilly. 2006. "What's Happening to Retail Jobs? Wages, Gender, and Corporate Strategy." Paper presented to the annual meeting of the International Association for Feminist Economics and the Labor and Employment Relations Association. Boston (January 5–8).

Carré, Françoise, and Chris Tilly, with Brandynn Holgate. 2007. "Continuity and Change in U.S. Retail Trade." Report to Russell Sage Foundation, New York.

Centraal Bureau voor de Statistiek (CBS, Statistics Netherlands). 2002a. Statline Database: Bedrijfsgrootte (Company Size). Voorburg, Netherlands: CBS. Available at: http://statline.cbs.nl/StatWeb/?LA=en.

———. 2002b. Statline Database: Enquete werkgelegenheid en lonen (Survey Employment and Wages). Voorburg, Netherlands: CBS. Available at: http://statline.cbs.nl/StatWeb/?LA=en.

———. 2002c. Structure of Earnings Survey Microdata [database]. Voorburg, Netherlands: CBS.

Chubb, Catherine, Simone Melis, Louisa Potter, and Raymond Storry. 2008. *The Global Gender Pay Gap.* Brussels: International Trade Union Confederation (ITUC).

Danmark Statistik. 2002. Statbank Denmark Data [database]. Copenhagen: Danmark Statistik. Available at: http://www.dst.dk/HomeUK.aspx.

Dribbusch, Heiner. 2003. *Gewerkschaftliche mitgliedergewinnung im dienstleistungssektor: ein drei-laender-vergleich im einzelhandel (Union Membership Promotion in the Service Sector: A Three-Country Comparison).* Berlin: Ed. Sigma.

Esbjerg, Lars, Klaus G. Grunert, Nuka Buck, and Anne-Mette Sonne Andersen. 2008. "Working in Danish Retailing: Transitional Workers Going Elsewhere, Core Employees Going Nowhere, and Career Seekers Striving to Go Somewhere." In *Low-Wage Work in Denmark,* edited by Niels Westergaard-Nielsen. New York: Russell Sage Foundation.

EU KLEMS Project. 2005. "Productivity in the European Union: A Comparative Industry Approach [database]." Available at: www.EUKLEMS.org (accessed July 2007).

Europaeisches Einzelhandelsinstitut (European Retail Institute) (EHI). 2006. "Handel aktuell 2005–2006." Köln: EHI.

European Commission. 2007. Employment in Europe [database]. Luxembourg: Office for Official Publications of the European Commission.

Eurostat (Statistical Office of the European Communities). Various years. European Union Labour Force Survey [database]. Luxembourg: European Commission. Available at: http://epp.eurostat.ec.europa.eu.

Gadrey, Jean, and Florence Jany-Catrice. 2000. "The Retail Sector: Why So Many Jobs in America and So Few in France?" *Service Industries Journal* 20(4): 21–32.

Galtier, Bénédicte. 1999. "Les temps partiels: Entre emplois choisis et emplois 'faute de mieux.' (Part-Time Work: Between Chosen Jobs and Jobs 'for Lack of Anything Better')" *Economie et Statistique* 321–22: 57–77.

Huselid, Mark A. 1995. "The Impact of Human Resource Management Practices on Turnover, Productivity, and Corporate Financial Performance." *Academy of Management Journal* 3(38): 635–72.

Hyde, Phil. 2007. "Americans Have the Shortest Vacation in the Developed World." *The Timesizing Wire,* available at: http://www.timesizing.com/1vacatns.htm (accessed November 2007).

Industrial Board for Retail Trades (HBD). 2005. *Arbeidsmarkt in de detailhandel 2005 (The Labor Market in Retailing).* The Hague: HBD.

Institut National de la Statistique et Etudes Economiques (INSEE). 2003. Trade Database. Paris: INSEE. Available at: http://www.insee.fr/en.

Jany-Catrice, Florence, Nicole Gadrey, and Martine Pernod. 2005. "Employment Systems in Labor-Intensive Activities: The Case of Retailing in France." In *Job Quality and Employer Behavior,* edited by Stephen Bazen, Claudio Lucifora, and Wiemer Salverda. Basingstoke, U.K.: Palgrave Macmillan.

Jany-Catrice, Florence, and Steffen Lehndorff. 2005. "Work Organization and the Importance of Labor Markets in the European Retail Trade." In *Working in the Service Sector: Tales from Different Worlds,* edited by Gerhard Bosch and Steffen Lehndorff. London: Routledge.

Lehndorff, Steffen, and Dorothea Voss-Dahm. 2005. "The Delegation of Uncertainty: Flexibility and the Role of the Market in Service Work." In *Working in the Service Sector: Tales from Different Worlds,* edited by Gerhard Bosch and Steffen Lehndorff. London: Routledge.

Marsden, David. 1999. *A Theory of Employment Systems: Micro-Foundations of Societal Diversity.* Oxford: Oxford University Press.

———. 2000. "A Theory of Job Regulation, the Employment Relationship, and the Organization of Labor Institutions." *Industrielle Beziehungen (Industrial Relations)* 7(4): 320–47.

Mason, Geoff, and Matthew Osborne. 2008. "Business Strategies, Work Organization, and Low Pay in U.K. Retailing." In *Low-Paid Work in the*

United Kingdom, edited by Caroline Lloyd, Geoff Mason, and Ken Mayhew. New York: Russell Sage Foundation.

Metro-Group. 2006. *Metro Handelslexikon (Metro Commerce Lexicon)* 2006–2007. Düsseldorf: Metro-Group.

Moss, Philip, and Chris Tilly. 2001. *Stories Employers Tell: Race, Skill, and Hiring in America.* New York: Russell Sage Foundation.

Organization for Economic Cooperation and Development (OECD). 1993. *Employment Outlook.* Paris: OECD.

———. 2003. *Employment Outlook.* Paris: OECD.

Osterman, Paul. 1994. "How Common Is Workplace Transformation and Who Adopts It?" *Industrial and Labor Relations Review* 47(3): 173–88.

Raines, Laura. 2007. "All Work and No Play?" *Atlanta Journal-Constitution,* "Career Center" page, May 18, available at: http://jobnews.ajcjobs.com.

Statistisches Bundesamt (Federal Statistical Office). 2001. Fachserie 6. Reihe 4. Jahreserhebung zum Einzelhandel (Annual Survey for the Retail Trade) [database]. Wiesbaden, Germany: Statistisches Bundesamt.

Streeck, Wolfgang, and Kathleen Thelen. 2005. "Introduction: Institutional Change in Advanced Political Economies." In *Beyond Continuity: Institutional Change in Advanced Political Economies,* edited by Wolfgang Streeck and Kathleen Thelen. Oxford: Oxford University Press.

Tijdens, Kea. 1998. *Zeggenschap over arbeidstijden: De samenhang tussen bedrijfstijden, arbeidstijden en flexibilisering van de personeelsbezetting (Control over Working Hours. The Relationship Between Opening Hours, Working Hours and Flexible Staffing).* Amsterdam: Welboom.

Tijdens, Kea, Reinhard Bispinck, Heiner Dribbusch, and Maarten van Klaveren. 2007. "Exploring the Impact of High and Low Bargaining Coverage Across Eight EU Member States." Paper presented to the eighth European Congress IIRA. Manchester, U.K. (September 3–7).

Tilly, Chris. 1996. *Half a Job: Bad and Good Part-Time Jobs in a Changing Labor Market.* Philadelphia: Temple University Press.

U.K. Office for National Statistics (ONS). 2002. Annual Business Inquiry (ABI) [database]. London: ONS.

———. 2005. Annual Survey of Hours and Earnings [database]. Newport, South Wales: ONS. Available at: http://www.statistics.gov.uk/StatBase/Product.asp?vlnk=13101.

———. 2006. Annual Survey of Hours and Earnings [database]. Newport, South Wales: ONS. Available at: http://www.statistics.gov.uk/StatBase/Product.asp?vlnk=13101.

U.S. Bureau of the Census. 2002. Economic Census [database]. Washington: U.S. Bureau of the Census. Available at: http://www.census.gov/econ/census02.

———. 2003. County Business Patterns [database]. Washington: U.S. Bureau of the Census. Available at: http://www.census.gov/econ/cbp/index.html.

U.S. Bureau of Labor Statistics (BLS). Various years. Current Employment Statistics [database]. Washington: BLS. Available at: http://www.census .gov/ces.

——— 2004. Current Population Survey microdata, March [database]. Washington: BLS. Available at: http://www.census.gov/cps.

———.2005a. Current Population Survey microdata, March [database]. Washington: BLS. Available at: http://www.census.gov/cps.

———. 2005b. Job Openings and Labor Turnover Survey [database]. Available at: http://www.census.gov/jlt/, Table 7, June.

———. 2006. Current Population Survey, March [database]. Washington: BLS. Available at: http://www.census.gov/cps.

———. 2007. Current Population Survey microdata, March [database]. Washington: BLS. Available at http://www.census.gov/cps.

———. 2008a. "Union Members in 2007." News release (January 25).

———. 2008b. Employment and Earnings Online (January): Table A–18. Available at: http://www.bls.gov/opub/ee/empearn200801.pdf.

Van Klaveren, Maarten. 2007. "RSF European Retail Studies: Overview Benchmarks in Six Countries" (unpublished tabulations). Amsterdam: Amsterdam Institute for Advanced Labor Studies (AIAS).

———. 2008a. "Retail Industry: The Contrast of Supermarkets and Consumer Electronics." In The Dutch Model of Low-Wage Work, edited by Wiemer Salverda, Maarten van Klaveren, and Marc van der Meer. New York: Russell Sage Foundation.

———. 2008b. "The Position, Design, and Methodology of the Industry Studies." In Low-Wage Work in the Netherlands, edited by Wiemer Salverda, Maarten van Klaveren, and Marc van der Meer. New York: Russell Sage Foundation.

———. 2009. Low Wages in the Retail Industry in the Netherlands. Working paper. Amsterdam: Amsterdam Institute for Advanced Labor Studies (AIAS).

Van Klaveren, Maarten, Kea Tijdens, and Wim Sprenger. 2007. "Dicht de loonkloof! Verslag van het CLOSE-onderzoek (Close the Gender Pay Gap! Report of the CLOSE Research Project)." Eindhoven/Amsterdam: STZ Consultancy & Research/Amsterdam Institute for Advanced Labour Studies (AIAS).

Voss-Dahm, Dorothea. 2000. "'Service-Sector Taylorism' and Changes in the Demands on Working-Time Organization: The Example of the Retail Trade." Paper presented to the international conference on "The Economics and Socioeconomics of Services: International Perspectives." Lille/Roubaix, France (June 22–23).

———. 2003. "Zwischen kunden und kennziffern: leistungspolitik in der verkaufsarbeit des einzelhandels" ("Between Customers and Indicators: Performance Policy in Retail Sales Work"). In Dienstleistungsarbeit: auf dem boden der tatsachen: befunde aus handel, industrie, medien und IT-

branche (Service Work: Grounded in Fact: Findings from Retailing, Manufacturing, the Media, and IT Industry), edited by Markus Pohlmann, Dieter Sauer, Gudrun Trautwein-Kalms, and Alexandra Wagner. Berlin: Ed. Sigma.

———. 2008. "Low-Paid but Committed to the Industry." In *Low-Wage Work in Germany,* edited by Gerhard Bosch and Claudia Weinkopf. New York: Russell Sage Foundation.

Westergaard-Nielsen, Niels. 2008. "Statistical Analysis and History of Low-Wage Work in Denmark." In *Low-Wage Work in Denmark,* edited by Niels Westergaard-Nielsen. New York: Russell Sage Foundation.

CHAPTER 7

Working at the Wage Floor: Hotel Room Attendants and Labor Market Institutions in Europe and the United States

Achim Vanselow, Chris Warhurst, Annette Bernhardt, and Laura Dresser

In the face of global competition and continued pressure on wages from less-developed countries, a popular prescription for industrialized nations is to differentiate themselves by pursuing a knowledge-based, high-skill economy (see, for example, Reich 1991; Florida 2002; EC 2004a). But it is instructive to remember that in both Europe and the United States many labor-intensive service jobs remain firmly rooted in place. Whether cleaning hotel rooms, caring for the elderly, or washing hospital linen, millions of workers are effectively sheltered from the threats of offshoring and automation because the work they do must be performed on-site, by human beings.

This rootedness would seem to open the door for national labor market institutions to make themselves felt in the workplace. If employers cannot relocate or automate frontline jobs, there is at least the potential for the state and trade unions to mediate the organization of work and production and, by extension, the quality of jobs. Such possibilities are important for researchers trying to understand how local and national labor markets operate in a global economy, as well as for policymakers looking for levers to fight the growth of low-wage work.

In this chapter, we report on a multi-year, cross-national study of economic restructuring in the hotel industry—a sector in which growing competition and consolidation across the globe has put intense pressure on labor costs even as the actual jobs remain place-bound. In the first phase of the project, researchers in the United States found that hotels were the archetypal low-wage service industry, dominated by room attendants working for low pay under arduous conditions with few opportunities for job mobility (Bernhardt, Dresser, and Hatton 2003). Unions were able to have an impact on wages and other job outcomes, but only in those cities where they had been able to build significant density over many years. Not surprisingly, given the free market model in the United States, the state itself left few traces on job quality.

The project then turned its eye toward five European countries, with the intuition that perhaps their stronger, more developed industrial relations and regulatory systems would result in substantially better outcomes for frontline workers. Researchers in Denmark, France, Germany, the Netherlands, and the United Kingdom replicated the U.S. hotel research, but in the context of very different systems of labor market regulation (Dutton et al. 2008; Eriksson and Li 2008; Guégnard and Mériot 2008b; Hermanussen 2008; Vanselow 2008).

In fact, things do not seem that much better on the other side of the Atlantic. As we document in this chapter, the surprising finding is that room attendants in all six countries appear to be working right at the bottom of their respective labor markets, with strong similarities in job content and working conditions across countries. Unpacking why historically strong industrial relations systems are failing the room cleaners in this industry and identifying the public policies that do have an impact on job quality for low-wage workers are the central goals of this chapter.

We begin by describing the intensive employer case studies and industry research that generated the data for our analysis. We then outline the impact of economic restructuring on the job quality of room attendants in all six countries, identifying which developments and outcomes are similar and, importantly, which are different. Our focus then shifts to explaining these outcomes through an in-depth discussion of industry drivers, employment regulations, and industrial relations systems. We conclude with a discussion of the implications both for future research and for strategies to improve job quality in the hotel industry.

RESEARCH DESIGN AND METHODS

To illuminate cross-country differences and similarities in room attendant jobs in the hotel industry, this chapter summarizes and synthesizes results from hotel industry research in six countries— Denmark, France, Germany, the Netherlands, the United Kingdom, and the United States. Although there were slight variations in research design across these countries, the research was disciplined and unified by the same goal: to examine whether European hotels have responded differently than their U.S. counterparts to similar economic pressures, and with what consequences for room attendants. Specifically, in each country researchers set out to identify the ways in which low-wage jobs in the hotel industry were being transformed, the effects of those transformations on workers, and the impact of national institutional context on firm strategy and worker outcomes. In each country, researchers studied the background and context of the hotel industry and then turned their attention to eight case study hotels to gather information on the jobs of room attendants in each site.

The approach to the case studies in each country was very similar. The research for the eight case study hotels was primarily qualitative, consisting of interviews and focus groups with room attendants, their supervisors, and other hotel management such as general, human resources, and operations managers; managers of outsourcing and temporary work agencies were also interviewed. The interviews focused on changes in business strategy, the organization of work, wages and compensation, training and promotion opportunities, and worker characteristics. For each hotel, these qualitative data were complemented, wherever possible, by financial statistics on hotel performance. To set the case study hotels in context and develop a stronger understanding of the overall industry trends, industrywide data were also collected to determine developments and trends over the last ten years or so. Supplementary interviews were also conducted with a range of industry experts, such as trade union officials and representatives from employers' organizations and professional bodies. The number of interviews conducted in each country is shown in table 7.1.

Throughout the chapter, we focus on the workers who do the hands-on work of cleaning hotel rooms. The job title of the target occupation varies by country: the terms "room attendants," "valets," and "room cleaners" are used in most of our European countries, and "housekeeper" is the title used in France and the United States (a title that, outside of the United States and France, could denote the supervisors of room attendants). For ease, "room attendant" is used in this chapter to denote those workers who clean and "make up" guest rooms and often the surrounding corridor areas in hotels for the use of guests.

In each of the European countries, and reflecting the polarization

Table 7.1   Overview of European and U.S. Hotel Industry Studies

Country	Number of Case Study Hotels	Total Number of Interviews Conducted	Primary Source of Analysis
Denmark	8	44	Eriksson and Li (2008)
France	8	65	Guégnard and Mériot (2008)
Germany	8	52	Vanselow (2008)
Netherlands	8	49	Hermanussen (2008)
United Kingdom	8	81	Dutton et al. (2008)
United States	8	111[a]	Bernhardt, Dresser, and Hatton (2003)

Source: Authors' compilation.
a. The initial U.S. research focused on a broader set of frontline workers, including food and beverage workers in hotels. The research reported in this chapter draws exclusively on room attendant interviews, of which there were 111.

of consumer demand in the industry (Mintel 2004), case study hotels were either upper- or midmarket in terms of product offerings, and they focused on the business market. All case study hotels also claimed to offer "quality" service. Although the grading systems are not uniform across countries, the upmarket segment of four- and five-star hotels typically offered high-quality services that were personalized and labor-intensive. The midmarket segment of two- and three-star hotels tended to be "no-frills," offering fewer and less personalized services. Consideration was also given to location: all case study hotels were based in or around major cities. Hotels could be independents or part of corporate chains. Although the hotel industry in each country is numerically dominated by small establishments—the stereotypical "bed-and-breakfast" in the United Kingdom, for example—all participating hotels in all countries were establishments with at least ten employees because it is the larger hotels that drive competition in the industry.

There are several important differences between the U.S. and European research designs. First, the European selection criteria were slightly broader than those of the United States. In the United States, with the research focus on the effect of unions and union density on job quality, the eight case studies came from four cities (two each with high and low levels of hotel unionization); in each city, one union and one non-union property were the subject of the case studies. Further, the European research occurred between 2004 and 2006, while the U.S. fieldwork was conducted in 2001 (and largely completed before the U.S. hotel downturn after 9/11). We therefore revisited U.S. data and industry informants to update our industry understanding. Although the labor market was relatively strong in the United States during the 2001 fieldwork, in Europe the situation from 2000 to 2005 was more mixed. With the exception of the United Kingdom, unemployment increased in all of our European countries during that time period. By 2005, the unemployment rate was highest in France and Germany (9.5 to 9.7 percent) and lower, at 4.7 to 4.8 percent, in Denmark, the Netherlands, and the United Kingdom. Although still relatively strong, the comparable unemployment rate for the United States also rose during this period, ending at 5.1 percent in 2005.

INDUSTRY DEVELOPMENTS

As services come to dominate economies and many locations attempt to present themselves as tourist and conference destinations, hotels have become a major employer with high job growth rates (ILO 2001). Worldwide employment in hospitality and related industries is estimated to be 192 million, or one in eight workers (Leidner 2004).[1] Employment in the hotel industry in our six countries is also significant. In the United States, 1.8 million workers are employed in hotels, in the United Kingdom 315,000, in Germany 277,000, in France 177,000, and in the Netherlands 44,000 (U.S. BLS 2008; Dutton et al. 2008; Vanselow 2008; Guégnard and Mériot 2008b; Hermanussen 2008). In Denmark, 80,000 workers are employed in hotels and restaurants (Eriksson and Li 2008).

Employment data for the industry are uneven in quality, as are the data specific to room attendants. Even so, a consistent picture emerges of room attendants in all six countries: women (particularly part-time) dominate, and ethnic minorities, migrants (legal and illegal), young people, and students feature strongly (Bernhard, Dresser, and Hatton 2003; Dutton et al. 2008; Eriksson and Li 2008; Guégnard and Mériot 2008b; Hermanussen 2008; People 1st 2006; Vanselow 2008). Many of these workers (with the exception of students) have relatively low educational attainment. Reliance on women, immigrants, and workers of color has also long been a feature of the hotel industry, in both Europe and the United States. Historically, room cleaners in the United States were African American women; in recent decades, there has been a shift to Hispanic and

Asian immigrant women. Before the current wave of Polish migrant workers, London hotels often employed Afro-Caribbean women from British Commonwealth countries. French hotels still employ workers from former North African colonies. The share of immigrants in the German hospitality industry is three times higher than in the economy as a whole. And in Copenhagen, over 80 percent of room attendants are immigrants. What is significant about these workers, as we shall see later, is that they often have limited bargaining power and limited workplace opportunities.

Importantly, a number of key developments in the ownership, organization, and operation of hotels have made the industry a competitive battleground. First, the hotel industry is fragmented and marked by segmentation. A wide range of accommodation is provided through large and small hotels, inns, hostels, time-shares, and long-stay apartments. They are offered by private, family-run businesses as well as by publicly traded corporations. Most of these establishments are categorized by a quality star-rating system, which, though not uniform internationally, differentiates lower, midmarket, and upmarket service provision. Typically, the more stars awarded to a hotel, the more services it offers—and the higher the price of its rooms.

The industry is also marked by fluctuating product demand. This fluctuation is most obviously seasonal, with demand typically peaking between April/May and September/October (EC 2006a). The industry is also vulnerable to political events and economic cycles. The global mini-recession and travel safety worries after 9/11 badly affected the hotel industry worldwide. In all of the countries in our study, hotels suffered a drop in profits from 2001 to 2003 (BTE 2005; *Caterer and Hotelkeeper* 2003, 2005; EC 2006a; Mandelbaum 2007). With greater supply than demand, competition became more acute, resulting in "price wars" as some hotels discounted room rates, particularly in the upmarket segment. It is for this reason that the larger, corporate hotel chains tend to concentrate in large city locations, where they hope for more market stability (Leidner 2004), and many mid- and upmarket hotels have expanded their range of services to include leisure, fitness, and conferencing facilities in an attempt to increase their market size with supplementary customer bases. Nevertheless, it is still the sale of beds that provides the most revenue for hotels; more recently, the profitability of the industry across the United States and Europe has improved with higher occupancy and increased revenue (BTE 2005; *Caterer and Hotelkeeper* 2005; Deloitte 2007; Mandelbaum 2007). As one industry consultant stated, after "three years of bad news," there is now "solid evidence of recovery" (Jonathan Langston, quoted in BHA 2005, 13).

Most establishments are still small and independent—family-run hotels such as "mom-and-pop" motels and "bed-and-breakfasts." Little has changed in terms of the structure and type of these providers. Although they might be celebrated for their uniqueness, or at least their local idiosyncrasies, through which they avoid the blandness of much standardized hospitality (see Ritzer and Lair 2009), these small accommodation providers also often rely on the underpaid or unpaid labor of small entrepreneurs and family members (ILO 2001; Leidner 2004).

Most guest rooms and the bulk of employment, however, are provided by larger establishments. Significantly, the industry is increasingly dominated by larger corporate concerns—the focus of our research here. Hotel ownership is shifting from small, independent owners to international and publicly owned chains. Furthermore, this ownership is becoming consolidated through mergers and acquisitions among a decreasing number of international chains with increased vertical and horizontal integration. In Germany, where the hotel industry has long been regarded as a weak performer with high costs, the international chains have been predatory, buying smaller competitors; one family-run hotel owner in our research reported that she was regularly approached by different chains to sell her business. Properties are also becoming larger: in the EU, the average establishment size grew from 45.3 to 51.8 beds between 1995 and 2004 (EC 2006a).

This consolidation has occurred across market segments. In Europe, for example, Accor offers the Ibis chain of hotels in the midmarket segment and Sofitel in the upmarket segment. Branded budget hotels positioned in the midmarket, offering low, fixed room prices, have grown particularly strongly over the past decade. There has also been the development of hotel resorts and boutique hotels, which have deepened the industry's fragmentation and segmentation and further intensified competition. Indeed, the International Labor Organization (ILO 2001, 42) notes that there are now "more and more hotel brands under fewer and larger corporate umbrellas" and that the "forces of consolidation are . . . gathering momentum." Some industry analysts even predict that "eventually five mega-hotel companies will control the worldwide hotel business" (Watkins 2000, 2). Major international hotel chains—such as Accor, Best Western, Hilton, Marriott, and Starwood—are growing and reshaping the dynamics of this once very local industry.

Despite its difficulties in the early 2000s, the hotel industry has continued to attract investment, leading to significant increases in competition in all of our countries. The number of available beds, for example, rose by 12.5 percent between 1995 and 2004 across the old EU-15 (EC 2006a). The result was overcapacity in the industry as hotels struggled to maintain occupancy rates in relation to the expanded availability of beds. Even in France, where construction was curbed during this period, the earlier overinvestment of the late 1990s caused the number of beds to rise during this period.

In response, hotels have recently focused on customer relationship management (particularly for marketing and sales), managed most obviously through the Internet (EC 2003; O'Connor and Murphy 2004). This technology not only enables hotels to make more sophisticated assessments of customer spending patterns but can yield cost savings by establishing direct contact with these customers (by cutting out travel agent commission fees, for example). As such, it is another development that reflects the dual competitive strategy evident across the industry of raising service quality while also cutting costs.

Given the industry's star-rating system, the desire for improved quality quickly translates into the delivery of a greater quantity of services provided. The result is a steady upward trend in the features and amenities provided in guest rooms. Hotels now provide banquet facilities, gyms, gambling machines, and meeting rooms, even in the midmarket segment. Hotels regularly provide extra pillows (four or even eight instead of two per bed), in-room coffee pots, thicker mattresses, and a broader array of soaps and personal care items. For room attendants, this "amenity creep" leads directly to increasing workloads because each of these features and complimentary items requires attention and maintenance.

This emphasis on improving the quality of service through the addition of new amenities and facilities has not been matched by increased resources; in fact, the opposite is happening as hotels simultaneously seek to reduce costs. Functional departments within hotels are recast as cost-driven "profit centers" with tightly constrained budgets. A number of hotel operations have been outsourced, or temporary agency staff are hired for functions such as food and beverage, payroll, IT services, security, leisure services, and housekeeping (Burgess 2007; *Caterer and Hotelkeeper* 2002, 2003, 2005; Hemmington and King 2000; Lai and Baum 2005; Nickson 2007). Sometimes the goal of this externalization is to bring in needed expertise (for example, IT specialists). But more often, according to Tomás Espino-Rodríguez and Antonia Ma Gil-Padilla (2005), the goal is to reduce costs. While there are seasonal swings of demand for hotel accommodation, daily and weekly changes in demand can be just as erratic. Hotels therefore seek to vary the staff headcount in order to reduce idle time and, by extension, the wage bill. Pei-Chun Lai and Tom Baum (2005) estimate that by using temporary agency staff, London hotels can save £1,000 ($550, 2005 dollars) in overhead costs per room attendant per year.

Fragmented, segmented, and highly sensitive to fluctuating demand, hotel industry ownership is becoming more concentrated, driven by international chains. With recent overcapacity in the industry, hotels are embarking on a dual strategy to attract more guests and improve profitability—increasing quality while reducing costs. The outcomes of this strategy, as we shall see, have important effects on the job quality of room attendants.

CROSS-COUNTRY VARIATION IN JOB QUALITY OUTCOMES FOR ROOM ATTENDANTS

The broad industry trends just described form a shared backdrop against which hotels in each of the six countries make decisions about how housekeeping is organized and managed, with direct consequences for the jobs of room attendants. In what follows, we take a tour of the major dimensions of job quality and summarize both the similarities and differences identified across the countries under study.

WORK ORGANIZATION AND CONTENT

What is remarkable about room attendants' jobs is the similarity in work content and work organization across countries, as well as how little the work has changed over time. All hotels require room attendants to clean and make up rooms. A small army of cleaners with trolleys loaded with detergents, mops, and cloths descend unseen on each room to vacuum and dust, clean bathrooms, make beds, change linen, and replenish soaps and shampoo. Room attendants also regularly "deep-clean" by cleaning or replacing shower curtains and carpets, and some room attendants clean areas around guest rooms such as corridors. This work is routine and repetitive, and it is essential to the functioning and reputation of hotels. "Every day's the same, every room they open is trashed in the same way, and they've got to bring it back to the standard you expect," said one U.K. general manager. And much of this work is deliberately unseen—"the hidden job," according to French managers—and is scheduled around the exit and entry schedules of guests.

Despite managerial rhetoric about teamwork, room cleaning was typically organized as a one-person job in our case studies, as it is across the industry generally (Mitchell 2007). Supervisors or head housekeepers allocated each attendant a target number of rooms to clean during a shift, with performance individually assessed. For some attendants, working alone was isolating. "It's a very solo job," said one U.K. manager. "You are working on your own most of the time, and it doesn't fit with a lot of people's personality." But for other attendants, the isolation was more positively perceived as autonomy: there is, one said, "nobody on your back saying, 'Right, you need to do this, and you will need to do that.'" Nevertheless, it was a responsible autonomy, with room attendants having to adhere to strict, pre-specified standards, usually in the form of rule-based operating procedures that were monitored and enforced with inspection checks by supervisors.

Across all hotels, the work was often hard labor, involving lifting and shifting heavy beds and other furniture. As one U.K. room attendant explained, "You think when you come in it's just like housework, but it's not. It's a lot more than housework because you are not pulling out units every day in your house." Rooms are designed primarily for guest satisfaction rather than ease of cleaning, with the result that room attendants are constantly bending up and down and contorting their bodies into tight spaces. Not surprisingly, back injuries and pains and strain injuries are common, more so than in many manufacturing jobs (U.S. Department of Labor 2001; Unite-Here 2006). Some hotels are experimenting with ergonomic training and the introduction of beds that can be raised by pedals, but in the main, housekeeping departments remain stubbornly labor-intensive, prone to health and safety threats because of heavy lifting and the regular use of strong chemical detergents and cleaners (Malik 2006).

Because it is viewed as akin to a "domestic" task, room cleaning is often undervalued, even by some attendants. One commented that "you don't need skills to dust or hoover." Another stated that "it's common sense mostly, common sense and basic housework, what you would do at home." Room attendants "don't need any special skills," a French manager said. And a head housekeeper in the United Kingdom explained that "most people know how to make a bed, and obviously, being a housewife, you know how to clean toilets, so it [is] basically an easy option." For these reasons, employers feel little need to provide extensive training and expect that any training that is required has mostly already been undertaken prior to job entry, in the home (Wood 1992).

Having able and willing workers was essential for our case study managers, who often complained that local workers had "attitude" problems. Workers from foreign countries, by contrast, were regarded as good-quality workers. "The Polish immigrants are . . . all very good," said one U.K. hotel owner, continuing bluntly: "[They] make British people look sick." U.S. managers likewise expressed a preference for immigrant workers: "They're quiet and do the work," said one. German managers also claimed that migrant women were more willing to put up with arduous working conditions.[2] Such claims raise an important point about room attendants. While typically regarded as unskilled, they are in fact required to possess specific attributes: the capacity for hard physical work, endurance, reliability, close attention to detail, and being inconspicuous to the customer. These attributes were once ascribed to a worker's personality rather than skill set, but this may be changing as employers increasingly talk of skill shortages in the industry (see Grugulis, Warhurst, and Keep 2004).

Opportunities for Upward Mobility

In all of the countries studied, room attendant jobs rarely served as launch pads for upward mobility. As one Dutch head housekeeper succinctly explained: "Careering is limited. Hotels don't have a broad range of jobs. Moreover, the knowledge and capacities of the room attendants often don't reach. That's a pity."

In part, the issue was lack of training. New room attendants typically learned on the job by shadowing existing workers and starting with lower room quotas. But if housekeeping departments were under pressure and supervisors were also having to clean rooms, it was not uncommon for new workers to jump in and start work without training. In addition, room attendants received little career development training. The hotel industry in Europe has the lowest incidence of employer-paid training for incumbent workers (standing at just 12 percent of workers), and most of what is provided is directed at management and professional employees (Parent-Thirion et al. 2007). The head of human resources in one U.S. hotel acknowledged that "this industry doesn't focus on mobility. We've done a really poor job of recognizing talent and building our own." Some European hotels did offer language lessons for their migrant and immigrant workers, and career training programs were available in a number of unionized U.S. hotels. Such training was not always easy to access, however, because of high workloads. "You don't get much time during the day here," explained one room attendant. "The head of housekeeping did say that if you are going to do that [learning], she would try and give you less rooms, but that's not guaranteed, you know, that goes by how the business is."

Equally important is the flat organizational structure of the hotel industry. Housekeeping departments in bigger hotels typically have a large pool of room cleaners, a few supervisors or assistant housekeepers, and then a head housekeeper. Consequently, the potential for promotion within these departments is inherently limited. As a Danish room attendant explained, "To move up, you have to do something else than this." But the other main department in hotels, food and beverage, is similarly flat and usually does not offer better jobs. The one source of good jobs within hotels, the front desk, has historically been closed to room attendants, who typically are not offered the requisite career ladders and skills training. We did find several hotels—for example, in France and the United States—that were experimenting with multitasking: room attendants combined cleaning with reception activities and thereby gained the experience that might enable them to make the leap to front-desk jobs. Such examples, however, were few and far between; more often, room attendants were not expected to be promoted and were therefore exempted from customer relations training.

As a result of such practices, many room attendants become trapped in their jobs. Especially for women with child care responsibilities, relocating to find a better job in another hotel can be unfeasible, because of longer commuting times or because relocating jeopardizes carefully coordinated child care arrangements (see also SCER 2006). For migrants, the job that is initially viewed as a stepping-stone into the host country's labor market becomes a millstone. Lack of contact with guests, the scarce provision of language classes, and the clustering of migrants in hotels by nationality provides them with little possibility of acquiring the necessary language skills. "If she can't speak very good English or understand, what else can she do really?" asked a U.K. contract cleaning company manager. At best, room attendants may hope to move from insecure, contingent jobs to stable, direct employment with hotels.

WORKLOAD

Being a room attendant has become more demanding over time. Across all countries in our study, there was evidence of work intensification driven by cost pressures: room attendants were required to either clean more rooms in each shift or clean more items in each room—or both.

With some variation, the average cleaning time in our case study hotels was fifteen to twenty minutes per room, which represents a marked decline over the past several decades that is widely recognized in the industry. "They are expected to do the work in their own hours, so the usual eight to ten rooms then become twelve rooms, but they still do it within the hours that they're allocated to work," one U.K. human resource manager admitted. "When I started this job in 2000," said a supervisor in a Dutch hotel, "I had three minutes per room more at my disposal. We do the same now—or even more—in less time, but the limit is reached. We still have to deal with human beings and not robots."

The concurrent standardization of cleaning, drawing on predefined procedures and regularly monitored by supervisors, has been a key enabler of intensification (Sandoff 2005). "Hotels are undergoing the same industrialization process now that the manufacturing industries underwent decades ago," said a German trade unionist. Work intensification has become a key issue for U.S. unions, which are increasingly bargaining over room-cleaning quotas as a core contract goal (Bernhardt, Dresser, and Hatton 2003).

Room attendants in our study were often unable to take legally required breaks because of work pressures. "I usually don't take my last break because of the amount of rooms we have," said a U.K. room attendant. A Dutch housekeeping manager stated bluntly that she had changed the work schedule to eliminate downtime: "Now the room attendants can finish their work without a pause, and they carry out the same amount of work in three hours that they formerly did in four." When they were able, room attendants in many of our case study hotels reported that after meeting their own cleaning targets, they would often help coworkers who had a particularly heavy workload on a given shift.

Another source of intensification was the dramatic growth in room amenities over time. Particularly in the upmarket hotels but also in the midmarket hotels, guest rooms were stocked with an ever-expanding list of amenities, such as shampoos, trouser presses, TVs, DVDs, play stations, hair dryers, sauna robes, sewing kits, notepads, pens, and a full-service tea and coffee station. In some upmarket hotels, over one hundred such items may be present in a single guest room, and all of them have to be maintained, replenished, and presented according to standard operating procedures. Supplying extra pillows and sheets and larger mattresses is becoming a similarly widespread practice; all these items take time and strength to clean and arrange. "It's not just physically, it's mentally [tiring] as well, because you need to remember everything," one U.K. housekeeper explained.

As noted earlier, a key force driving work intensification across the industry has been the recasting of housekeeping and other hotel departments as "profit centers." Within our hotels, the result was that individual departments struggled to deliver quality standards within ever-tighter quarterly budgets. Reducing the number of room attendants while raising cleaning and room presentation standards inevitably resulted in increased workload, if not plain understaffing. "We always run lean," said a U.S. manager.

The Use of Nonstandard Work Arrangements

Up to this point, the picture of room attendants that we have drawn across our six countries is one of similarity in terms of work content, lack of upward mobility, and work intensification. A further point of similarity lies in the managerial quest to reduce labor costs through flexibility in how and when room attendants are used. Costs can be saved by paying cleaners to work only when rooms need to be cleaned; by removing the hotel's obligation to pay nonwage benefits or social contributions; and by externalizing to temp agencies and outside cleaning companies the costs of recruiting and training room attendants. "Exit options" enlarge employers' room for maneuver with respect to labor-use strategies, as discussed by Gerhard Bosch, Ken Mayhew, and Jérôme Gautié (this volume). As a result, nonstandard work arrangements are on the rise.

Although managers in all countries were pursuing flexibility, exactly how they secured a more flexible workforce differed. The United States offers a clear model of internal flexibility. Room attendants were simply not called in to work if the hotel was not full. In union hotels, schedules were assigned on the basis of seniority, and in non-union hotels by management decisions alone; in both cases, however, workers faced a continuing fluctuation in hours that corresponded directly to hotel occupancy rates. As a result, part-time hours were a common feature for U.S. room attendants, with more than 43 percent working less than full-time (forty hours per week).

Part-time hours were also common in the five European countries, though these were often achieved through nonstandard work contracts. Just short of 40 percent of all U.K. hotel employees work part-time (People 1st 2006). Some of our U.K. hotels offered only part-time contracts, while others offered full-time contracts for a core group of workers, supplemented by either casual workers or temp workers. In German hotels, there has been a strong increase in the use of short-term, part-time "mini-jobs," created by national policy reforms intended to boost employment. Although part-time work has not increased in France, French hotels make significant use of so-called extras—room attendants who work just a few hours a day, for a maximum of sixty days during a given quarter.[3] Both Dutch and Danish hotels are increasingly using part-time workers; Dutch hotels also use "minimum-term" workers, who work only when needed and are paid only for actual hours worked (Bispo 2007, 189; EMIRE 2007). None of these practices are unusual. Analysis of the European Establishment Survey on Working Time reveals that the hospitality industry (primarily hotels and restaurants) is characterized by more nonstandardized work arrangements than is the norm for Europe (Anxo et al. 2007; Kümmerling and Lehndorff 2007).

In addition to internal flexibility strategies, hotels in a number of European countries have begun to externalize the room-cleaning function, either through outsourcing to cleaning companies or through the use of temp workers. This possibility is made easier by the fact that room cleaning is a highly routinized, standardized task for which employees do not need extensive training (Espino-Rodríguez, Lai, and Baum 2008). The outsourcing of room cleaning offers hotels the opportunity to better match staffing with fluctuations in demand (Osborne 2005; Rodríguez-Díaz and Espino-Rodríguez 2006). It also offers the opportunity to cut wages.

In our case study hotels, outsourcing often allowed managers to pursue formal or actual piece-rate pay strategies. Management recognized that piece rates created wage instability for room attendants, but they legitimized the strategy by referring to the fluctuating demand for cleaning: "We can't afford not to [pay by the room], it's as simple as that, because it doesn't take a rocket scientist to work out, if the hotel's full, we're going to make money, if the hotel is empty, we're going to struggle," said the operations director of a U.K. cleaning company. In Germany, firms with outsourced cleaning contracts are legally required to pay the rate set by collective bargaining at the industry level. In practice, however, these firms often pay by the number of rooms cleaned, and the result can be a lower pay rate: "If the cleaner who is paid per room does not reach four rooms in an hour, he will not get the collectively agreed wage," explained the owner of a German cleaning firm.

During the years of our research, there was already a high level of outsourcing of room attendant jobs in Germany and the Netherlands, and the trend was growing in the French and Danish hotels. But the picture is not so simple. In the United Kingdom, several of our case study hotels had once contracted out cleaning services, but had recently stopped doing so out of worry about the low quality of cleaning by external staff. (Nonetheless, several hotels continued to use temp agencies to supplement their core staff.) And some of our Dutch and German case study hotels deliberately avoided outsourcing in the belief that direct employees were more reliable, motivated, and willing to work long hours when needed.

That said, it seems clear that in Europe, as Dawne Lamminmaki (2005, 517) states, "outsourcing has become a significant facet of modern hotel management." At the same time, the available evidence suggests that the extent of subcontracting in hotels is uneven across countries. A comparative study by David Finegold, Karin Wagner, and Geoff Mason (2000, 509) showed that the incidence of outsourcing was highest in Germany (66 percent), much lower in the United Kingdom (7 percent), and not apparent in U.S. hotels (which may well reflect the already high level of internal flexibility afforded to hotel managers in the United States). In the Netherlands, an internal study of the Dutch Executive Housekeepers Association in 2004 showed that 48 percent of hotels had outsourced room cleaning (Hermanussen 2008, 178). Data on outsourcing are unavailable for Denmark, though interviews with trade unionists confirmed its spread.

How can cross-country differences in the use of subcontracting for room cleaning be explained? There are indications that institutional factors play an important role here. One reason is that the gains that employers accrue from outsourcing vary among these countries. In Denmark, wage differentials between internal and external cleaning staff are small, and so managers do not perceive cost reductions to be decisive (Eriksson and Li 2008). By contrast, wage differentials between in-house and external room attendants are greater in Germany, France, and the Netherlands. In the Netherlands, for example, the value of cleaning contracts has decreased by 10 to 20 percent over the last five years. "The large hotel chains in particular had succeeded in putting tariffs under pressure, and fierce competition had forced cleaning companies to accept lower prices," according to Ria Hermanussen (2008, 190). The Dutch case studies also reveal that hotel managers used nonstandard work arrangements to try to avoid having to participate in their employees' sick leave and occupational disability costs (Hermanussen 2008, 189).

The case of Germany illustrates the additional role of product market deregulation. After the government reduced market entry barriers to the cleaning sector in 2004, the number of cleaning firms increased sharply. And because traditional markets for contract cleaning (for example, offices) have become saturated, cleaning providers are now looking for other clients, such as hotels (Vanselow 2008). The result is increased competition among contract cleaning companies, which translates into significantly lower wages for room attendants, as well as work intensification.

There are also indications of the use of illegal practices among contract cleaning companies. Although collective agreements exist for the cleaning sector, many firms pay wages under the level of these agreements in order to win contracts, and they are able to do so because of weak enforcement and, relatedly, the lack of union presence in workplaces. Government agencies have documented cases of drastic underpayment by cleaning firms, especially in the case of "posted" workers from eastern Europe (see Bosch, Mayhew, and Gautié, this volume).[4] In one case, cleaners of a hotel service firm in Munich received an hourly rate of only €2.50 rather than the regular wage of €8.15 ($11.15, 2007 dollars). These workers were cleaning rooms in luxury hotels such as the Ritz Carlton, Sheraton, and Hilton Hotels (Gewerkschaft Nahrung-Genuss-Gaststätten 2008).

In sum, outsourcing was being used as a strategy to cut costs and further intensify work. Even when contract cleaners earned the same wages as in-house cleaners, contract cleaners were preferred because they would work more quickly or because they did not have to be paid for downtime. Our findings in this respect are not exceptional. The research of Yara Evans and her colleagues (2007) among migrant workers and trade unionists in London similarly found that external staff have inferior pay and working conditions, compared to those directly employed by hotels. Externalization therefore suggests a race to the bottom, which has a negative impact on the job quality of room attendants, particularly with regard to wages—the issue to which we next turn.

Wages

Up to this point, we have found similarities in the content and work organization of room attendant jobs across all six countries under study, with some differences in strategies around flexibility. We turn now to an analysis of wage outcomes, and here the picture is more mixed. In all countries, room attendants receive relatively low pay. But what differs is how low their wages are, especially relative to the labor market overall, and the implication of those low wages for economic well-being.

Broadly speaking, low wages are clearly a defining feature of the hotel industry. Table 7.2 shows the percentage of hotel workers who fall below each country's low-wage threshold.[5] The first point to note is that in all countries the prevalence of low-wage work in hotels is at least double and even triple the national rate, putting the industry squarely at the floor of the national labor market. That said, the six countries do differ in the severity of the low-wage problem. Industry pay is consistently low in Germany, the United Kingdom, and the United States, with between 45 and 71 percent of the hotel workforce falling below the respective low-wage thresholds.[6] By contrast, in the French, Danish, and Dutch hotel industries, only 20 to 26 percent of hotel workers fall below the low-wage threshold.

This variation is largely driven by differences in where the countries set their wage floors. As shown in the second row of table 7.2, room attendant wages are effectively pegged to the national minimum wage (France, the Netherlands, the United Kingdom), a "minimum tariff" (Denmark), or the prevailing wage floor (Germany, the United States). But as we will see in the next section, there are marked differences in exactly where these floors are set relative to the overall economy. In Denmark and France in particular, that floor rests significantly closer to the national median wage than it does in the other four countries—resulting in the lower prevalence of low-wage work both overall and in the hotel industry.

In the European Union, workers receive mandatory nonwage benefits and entitlements from their employers, such as paid holidays and sick leave. They and their families are also entitled to a range of services and work supports, including state-provided rental accommodation, subsidized child care, and health care free at the point of need; all of services are funded by a combination of taxation and employer and employee contributions (see Mason and Salverda, this volume). The outcome can be dramatic, as research on the lives of low-wage workers in the United Kingdom (Toynbee 2003) and in the United States (Ehrenreich 2001) reveals. In the United Kingdom, for example, low-wage workers had access to low-cost government housing and free health care, while their counterparts in the United States worked while suffering from untreated illnesses and had to resort to extreme measures such as sleeping in their vehicles in car parks.

A number of other findings about wages in the hotel industry warrant comment. First, we found striking consistency in room attendant wages across all hotels, regardless of market segment, challenging the common assumption of causal linkages between product market strategies and workers' skills and pay. The wages of room attendants in upmarket hotels were barely, if at all, higher than those of room attendants working in midmarket hotels (see also Dutton et al. 2008). "We're finding that whether it's top end or the bottom end of the hotel value chain, they're paying at or slightly above the minimum wage," said a U.K.-based living wage campaigner. "They're getting a lot from customers for this quality product and paying the

Table 7.2 Room Attendant Wages

	Denmark	France	Germany	Netherlands	United Kingdom	United States
Low-wage workers nationally	9%	11%	23%	18%	22%	25%
Low-wage workers in the hotel industry[a]	25% in hotels with restaurants, 19% in hotels without restaurants	20%	71%	26%	59%	45%
Wages for room attendants	Set at €15.08 ($18.92, 2006 dollars) per hour by CLA in 2006; wages for non-union workers pegged to the national "minimum tariff" of €13.26 ($16.64, 2006 dollars) per hour.	Largely pegged to the national minimum wage (€8.27 per hour in 2005) ($10.29, 2005 dollars).	CLA wages differ by region; €7.38 ($9.26, 2006 dollars) per hour in the North Rhine–Westphalia CLA in 2005–2006).[b] Most (86 percent) earn below low-wage threshold.	Set at national minimum wage (€7.73 per hour in 2006) ($9.70, 2006 dollars) by hotel CLA.	Largely pegged to the national minimum wage (£5.05 per hour in 2005) ($9.18, 2005 dollars). Most (89 percent) earn below low-wage threshold.	$8.21 per hour in 2005 (national minimum wage was $5.15 per hour in 2005). Most (72 percent) earn below low-wage threshold.

Evidence of employers paying below minimum wage or CLA wage	Yes	Yes, especially for mini-jobbers and for cleaning contractors	Yes, for cleaning companies in Amsterdam	Yes	Yes, in lower-end, non-union hotels

Sources: Authors' compilation based on Bernhardt, Dresser, and Hatton (2003); Dutton et al. (2008); Eriksson and Li (2008); Guégnard and Mériot (2008b); Hermanussen (2008); Vanselow (2008); and unpublished material, especially industry reports, from the international low-wage work project by the Russell Sage Foundation.

a. Percentage figures for Denmark in the first and second rows are drawn from 2005; from 2005 for France in the first row and 2002 for the second row; from 2005 for Germany in the first row and 2003 in the second row; from 2002 for the Netherlands in the first row and 2005 in the second row; from 2005 for the United Kingdom, and from 2003 for the United States in the first row and 2005 in the second row.

b. A Land (or regional state) of Germany.

same to staff as their low-cost, cheaper competitors," the campaigner added.

That said, some hotels, especially upmarket ones, tried to find ways to offer stronger remuneration packages to their workers as a way of tackling recruitment and retention problems (for example, loyalty bonuses, free meals or uniforms, and performance awards such a free dinner for two in the hotel restaurant).[7] In one upmarket U.K. hotel, all staff were entitled to discounted stays in the hotel chain world-wide or use of the employing hotel's leisure facilities. However, the feasibility of taking up such offers was questionable for such low-wage workers; some were even oblivious to their existence. Performance-related pay or bonuses, which was offered in some of the bigger chain hotels, was generally limited for room attendants, though some hotels might pay annual bonuses. And a financial bonus might be offered to a room attendant for remaining employed with the hotel for a lengthy period of time.

Second, having permanent, full-time contracts at least provided some measure of *wage stability*, if not higher income. Moves by some hotels to externalize room cleaning through subcontracting and the use of temporary work agencies removed that stability, as cleaners on the subsequent nonstandard work arrangements were then paid piece rates, either effectively or in actuality. In French budget hotels, the per-room pay rate could be as little as €1.90, or the equivalent of the price of a cup of coffee. In the Netherlands, workers often cited unstable pay as the reason for quitting cleaning companies that paid by the room.

Third, we did find some evidence of a union effect on wages for several countries. In the U.S. hotel industry, union wages were on average 17 percent higher than non-union wages in 2000; in cities with high union density, the union effect was even stronger, raising wages by as much as $3.00 an hour (Bernhard, Dresser, and Hatton 2003). In Denmark (the one European country where hotel union membership is sizable), union wages were set at €15.08 per hour in 2006 ($18.92, 2006 dollars), while wages for non-union workers were set at €13.26 per hour ($16.64, 2006 dollars), representing a 14 percent union premium. On balance, however, the main conclusion from the European case studies is the striking failure of collective bargaining institutions to deliver significant wage increases in the hotel industry—an issue on which we focus later.

Finally, and perhaps of most concern, we found evidence of substandard wages for room attendants across the six countries—wages that violated either minimum-wage laws or CLAs. For example, some cleaning contractors in Germany and the Netherlands operated without regard for their CLA. There is also evidence from the French and U.K. case studies of minimum-wage violations: piece-rate workers found that their daily targets were too tight (Guégnard and Mériot 2008a) and that rooms required much longer to clean (Warhurst, Lloyd, and Dutton 2008). In one five-star U.K. hotel, a room attendant explained, by way of example, that a romantic weekend couple had left a bathtub rim encircled with hardened candle wax that took an hour to scrape and clean—time that was supposed to be spent cleaning other rooms. A French room attendant explained: "Personally I find that the thirty minutes we are allowed per room, for a four-star hotel, isn't fair, as it takes forty minutes to get a room spick-and-span." As a result, actual pay can fall below the rate of the national minimum wage—a practice that is illegal but not uncommon.

THE ROLE OF INDUSTRY DRIVERS, INDUSTRIAL RELATIONS, AND THE MINIMUM WAGE

A useful way to summarize these findings is to imagine holding up pictures of room attendants at work in each of our six countries: on many dimensions, it would be very hard to guess where the pictures were taken. There is little cross-country variation in work organization and content. Opportunities for upward mobility are limited or nonexistent. Workloads have intensified with the growth in room quotas and in the number of amenities to be cleaned and stocked. Hotels in all countries are increasingly searching for flexibility in when and how room attendants are deployed (though strategies for achieving flexibility differ by country). Once we attach wages to each of these pictures, however, the countries begin to differentiate themselves. Although room attendants generally work at (and sometimes below) the wage floor in all of the countries, the level of that floor is different, as is the impact of low wages on economic well-being. The upshot is that we are left with the following puzzle: Why do job quality outcomes for room attendants look so similar across a half-dozen different countries? And what explains the few (but important) differences that we do observe?

To begin, it is worth making the baseline point that the similarities in job quality outcomes across countries reflect the strong imprint of the hotel industry itself. Across countries, management techniques put pressure on the terms of employment by increasing workloads and using temp agencies and contract cleaning companies to cut labor costs and adapt to fluctuations in demand. Thus, while low skill and low wages are long-standing features of the hotel sector, industry consolidation and corporatization are leading to ever more competitive product markets (both local and global), resulting in management strategies that further degrade the working conditions of many hotel room attendants (Scully-Russ 2005; Appelbaum, Bernhardt, and Murnane 2003).

Such strategies, however, do not operate in a vacuum but are initiated and implemented within institutional contexts that allow choices about (and also impose constraints upon) how to organize work and production. The implication therefore is that labor market institutions might make a difference to the outcome of the job quality of room attendants. To wit, from the U.S. perspective, it would have been expected that the European institutional setting would deliver significantly better outcomes for workers. Instead, excepting differences in the social wage (see Mason and Salverda, this volume; Bosch, Mayhew, and Gautié, this volume), we find what are most accurately described as weak differences between countries. In what follows, we analyze why the apparently stronger collective bargaining systems in Europe have partly or wholly failed the hotel industry, and how state regulation of the wage floor has stepped in to fill the void.

INDUSTRIAL RELATIONS IN A DIFFICULT CONTEXT

In Europe, strong industrial relations—expressed as high rates of union density and collective bargaining coverage—are still associated with higher average wages, better fringe benefits, and greater training opportunities. That said, it is also the case that trade unions are coming under growing pressure and losing members and influence (Philips and Eamets 2007; see also Bosch, Mayhew, and Gautié, this volume). In the hotel industry, however, trade unions historically have always been weak (Dutton et al. 2008; Klein Hesselink et al. 2004; Jossart and Walthery 2001; Wood 1992). No wonder that in the recent industrial relations report of the European Commission, hospitality serves as an example for low unionization: "When you ask a young, female, part-time, contingent worker employed in a small hotel or restaurant if she is a union member, the answer will almost always be 'no'" (EC 2006b, 28).

Indeed, table 7.3 shows that, in all six countries, hotel industrial relations differ from the norm.[8] Union density (as measured by membership) in the hotel industry is noticeably lower than average in all of our countries. Union density in the industry is highest in Denmark (30 percent) and lowest in France (2 percent), although density is also low in the Netherlands (16 percent) and the United States (12 percent), and it is very low in Germany (5 percent) and the United Kingdom (4 percent). There is some evidence that the management paternalism of small, independent hotels substitutes for interest representation through trade unions (Dutton et al. 2008; Mériot 2000) and that an anti-union management culture exists in some multinational companies (see, for example, ILO 2001, 123). Moreover, employers' associations in the hotel industry are very well organized. The density of the big hospitality employers' associations in European countries ranges from 40 percent in the United Kingdom to 66 percent in Denmark (Jossart and Walthery 2001). In France, the lobbying strength of employers has resulted in the hospitality industry having a number of legal dispensations from the National Labor Code with respect to the minimum wage, working time regulation, and work contracts. Although aggressive anti-unionism is not unknown in European hotels, particularly in the United Kingdom (Dutton et al. 2008), labor-management relations between employers and unions tend to be more cooperative in Europe, especially in Denmark, than in the United States.

There are, however, important differences across the countries in the form and coverage of collective bargaining, as chapter 3 in this volume highlights. In particular, union *coverage* is significantly higher than union *membership* in all of the countries except the United Kingdom and the United States. In these two countries, bargaining is fragmented and decentralized, with only firm-specific agreements between employers and unions. The other four countries have sector-wide agreements between employers and unions that extend beyond union members to cover some or even all workers in non-unionized hotels and companies. These CLAs cover pay and working conditions negotiated between unions and employers. In Denmark, France, and the Netherlands, these agreements are made at the national level, and in Germany at the regional level. At least on paper, these "exten-

Table 7.3 Industrial Relations in the Hotel Industry

	Denmark	France	Germany	Netherlands	United Kingdom	United States
Union density nationally	71%	6%	23%	26%	29%	12%
Union density in the hotel industry	30	2	5	16	4	12
CLA coverage in the hotel industry	72	100	55	93	7	NA
Bargaining trends in the industry	Employer-driven attempt to decentralize to firm level.	No trend, but a "historical" CLA was reached in 2005, introducing the 39-hour workweek and other changes.	Some decentralization to firm. Employers can be members of employers' association without being part of CLA.	New hospitality CLA was reached in 2005, with worsening of wage and job security	No change—already decentralized and fragmented.	No change—already decentralized and fragmented.

Sources: Authors' compilation based on EC (2004b); Tijdens and van Klaveren (2007); London Economics (2003). Data for union density relate to 2003 and for CLA coverage to September 2006. The trends are those identified from our own research.

sion agreements" result in a higher coverage of firms despite low union density. In the Netherlands, for example, 16 percent of hotel workers are union members, but 93 percent are covered by collective labor agreements.

The problem is that without strong representation on the shop floor, institutional arrangements such as sectorwide collectively agreed wages and working conditions lack bite. Unfortunately, such a situation exists in the European hotel industry: although union coverage is wide, union presence is often absent in the workplace, and so monitoring and enforcement of CLAs is weak, particularly in relation to room attendants. Although it is difficult to measure enforcement of CLAs, there are indications from both our primary research and secondary data that enforcement is problematic. In Germany, for example, the employers' association stated that collectively agreed holiday pay is not enforced in almost half of hotels (Vanselow 2008). In the Netherlands, a new law had to be introduced in 2007 to give the Dutch Labor Inspectorate the power to fine employers who pay less than the statutory minimum wage (van het Kaar 2007). Even in Denmark, where enforcement is strong for in-house room attendants, it is weaker for cleaners employed by subcontractors.

In Germany, the Netherlands, and France, works councils—sometimes with and sometimes without trade unions—have the capacity to restrain management (see Bosch, Mayhew, and Gautié, this volume), but in the hotel industry their effectiveness is often limited.[9] A key reason is that many hotels are too small to have systems of collective employee representation. In France, for example, unions can designate a staff representative only in hotels with more than twenty employees and a works council in hotels with more than fifty employees. Moreover, the hotel unions that usually underpin works councils are often weak or simply absent within the workplace. As a consequence, French hotel managers are strong, and labor laws can be violated, with evidence of unpaid work and undeclared or illegal work.

In some of our larger case study hotels in Germany, works councils did have some impact: they negotiated with management on behalf of in-house room attendants on issues such as working time and outsourcing, and they also enforced labor agreements. This restraining capacity ended, however, when housekeeping was outsourced, since cleaners working for subcontractors cannot be represented by a hotel's works council (and subcontractor cleaners are rarely unionized; see Gather, Gerhard, and Schroth 2005). The Dutch hotel industry has a collective bargaining system similar to Germany's, with the key added advantage that unions can still negotiate for room attendants even if they are outsourced. The hotel employers' association is strong, however, and has refused recently to extend the new CLA across the industry. It now works with a relatively small union that is prepared to support a collective agreement that is more amenable to employers' use of flexible employment contracts and working hours (Hermanussen 2008). In Denmark, hotel unions are more successful, featuring strong, consensus-based collective bargaining that is underpinned by the national importance of wage compression as a feature of social solidarity (McLaughlin 2007). Even here, however, Danish employers are increasingly pressing to shift from industry-wide agreements to firm-level bargaining (Jørgensen 2007), which threatens to dilute union power.

In the United Kingdom and the United States, absent extension agreements, enforcement of union contracts largely becomes a question of the power of local unions within the particular hotels they represent. In the United States, enforcement is historically one of the key functions of unions across industries. Even when they are too weak to bargain for above-market wages and better working conditions, they generally are at least able to deliver enforcement of contract agreements as well as compliance with statutory employment and labor laws *within* the hotels that they represent. In the United Kingdom too, collective bargaining agreements are generally enforced, as are labor laws within unionized workplaces.

Across all six countries, then, the combination of low union density, poor workplace enforcement, and strong employers' associations means that hotel collective agreements are typically weak, setting wages near (or even below) the wage floor. For example, the current hotel CLA in the Netherlands explicitly sets baseline room attendant wages at the national minimum wage, and the implementation of the hospitality agreement in 2005 worsened wage and job security. In Germany, the 2004 collective wage agreement for the cleaning industry undercut previous wage rates, putting wages near the prevailing wage floor. In France, collectively negotiated hotel wage rates were so low that they were overtaken by the minimum wage rate. Hotel wage levels in the United Kingdom similarly have ended up near the minimum wage. In the United States, outside of a handful of cities where hotel unions have high density and therefore the power to set higher wages and working conditions, union contracts also generally set wages near the bottom of the market (though still above the national minimum wage, which has dropped so low as to be largely irrelevant to wage setting).

Although our overall assessment of the role of unions in the hotel industry is bleak, we did find some evidence of positive impact. In the United States, in those cities where unions have high density, they are able to set significantly higher wages for room attendants and to bargain for better working conditions (such as reduced room quotas). And in recent years, the main hotel union has succeeded in effectively bypassing local management to deal instead with corporate executives, a strategy that, it is hoped, will lead hotel chains to negotiate nationwide neutrality agreements (Sherwyn, Eigen, and Wagner 2006). Dani Zuberi (2007) documents greater job security, better working conditions, more in-kind benefits such as free meals and bus passes, and slightly higher wages for unionized hotel workers in the United States.

Germany also provides an example of significant intracountry variation in union impact, but for a different reason: its regional sectoral bargaining system, which created eighteen tariff regions. CLAs in around half of these regions have remained unchanged for many years—a massive failure of the collective bargaining system. By contrast, in the North Rhine–Westphalia region, the union and employers' association signed a collective agreement in 2008 to improve employment for low-wage workers in the hotel and restaurant industry. The lowest wage groups were abolished, entry-level hourly wages were increased to €7.64 ($10.45, 2007 dollars), and it was agreed to apply to the federal government for an extension of the agreement to cover all employees in the industry.

And in France, a collective agreement signed by employers and trade unions in July 2004 introduced a thirty-nine-hour week, a sixth week of annual holiday, and regulated night work and created a complimentary health insurance scheme for all workers. It was, stated one French hotel trade journal, "an historic agreement of the kind signed only once every thirty years in the field of hotels and restaurants" (quoted in Guégnard and Mériot 2008b, 177). In the United Kingdom, unions have joined forces with religious organizations and charities to instigate "name-and-shame" campaigns against particular employers in financial services and, more recently, the hotel industry—and with some success, as the action in London to force Hilton to reinternalize its cleaning services illustrates (Walton 2007).

In the end, however, what marks the hotel industry across all six countries is low union density, with the result that wages, working conditions, and enforcement of labor standards suffer. As a U.K. living wage campaigner stated, "Low-paid people have very little political voice, and they're not, for the main part, in trade unions." Looking back on his time in the German union NGG, a former senior union official concluded that, "due to the weakness of the trade union, some collective negotiations in the hotel and restaurant industry look like collective begging" (quoted in Pohl 2007, 64).[10]

Minimum-Wage Regulation

In the absence of union capacity to raise industry standards, it is minimum-wage regulation that has played a crucial role in establishing a wage floor for the hotel industry, and in particular the wages of room attendants.

Four of our countries—France, the Netherlands, the United Kingdom, and the United States—have a statutory national minimum wage for the whole economy (see Bosch, Mayhew, and Gautié, this volume). Denmark has no statutory minimum wage, but it does have a national "minimum tariff" that is negotiated and agreed upon by the social partners. (For the sake of simplicity, we include this tariff when referring to the minimum wage.) In the absence of high union density and strong collective agreements, room attendants' wages in European hotels are now driven by these minimum-wage rates. As such, these intended *minimum* rates have increasingly become the *going* rate or benchmark. In the United Kingdom, for example, employers initially opposed the introduction of the national minimum wage, but since its introduction, the number of hotels aligning their wages to the national minimum wage has risen from two-thirds to almost nine-tenths, according to an Income Data Services (2007) survey. A similar situation exists in France, where employers likewise avoid discussion of wages higher than the minimum rate. Room attendants in France reflect ruefully on this situation: "It's a hard job," said one. "They could pay us more, but we only get the SMIC."[11] In the United States, room attendant wages are actually higher than the low national minimum wage, but sit at what is effectively the wage floor for the labor market. Germany has no national minimum wage, meaning that the weak and incomplete CLAs define working conditions in the industry (as discussed earlier).

In all five countries, the level of the minimum wage is low—below

Figure 7.1 Ratio of Median to Minimum Wage in Five
Countries, 1970 to 2003

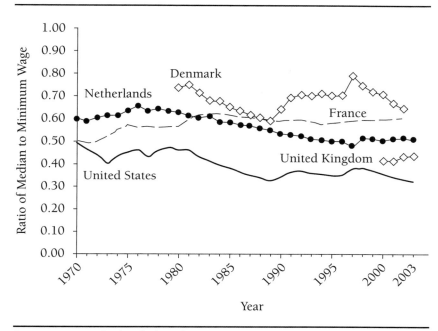

Source: Mason and Salverda (2007).
Note: "Minimum tariff" shown for Denmark.

the commonly accepted low-wage threshold of earning less than two-
thirds of the gross hourly median wage (see Bosch, Mayhew, and
Gautié, this volume). Nonetheless, there are significant differences in
just how low the minimum wage floors are. Figure 7.1 shows the
value of the minimum wage relative to the national median wage over
time. Denmark's minimum wage was almost two-thirds of the national median wage in 2003, with France running a close second at
61 percent. The Netherlands and the United Kingdom lagged further
behind on this measure (52 percent and 44 percent, respectively),
and the United States, not surprisingly, was dead last (33 percent).
The current strength of each country's minimum wage is largely a
function of how well it has kept its value over time. In all of these
countries except the United States, the minimum wage is frequently
readjusted, typically yearly (see Mason and Salverda, this volume).
Denmark and France have done a better job of keeping a strong wage

floor over time than the Netherlands. The national minimum wage in the United States has been raised only once in the last ten years and has declined steeply since its historic height in 1968.[12] The United Kingdom only recently instituted a national minimum wage, making it difficult to judge the trend relative to the country's median wage.

It should also be emphasized that the wage floor is not always solid. First, in the four countries with a national minimum wage, there are lower rates for young people. Until recently, these dispensations included employers being legally entitled to deduct in-kind benefits, such as meals, resulting in a lower minimum wage (Guégnard and Mériot 2008a). Second, as we documented earlier, outright violations of minimum-wage standards were reported in all of our countries. Third, some workers—illegal workers in France and Germany, migrant workers in the United Kingdom, and immigrant workers in Denmark and the United States—are sometimes paid below the minimum rate, either because they lack employment rights or because they are ignorant of those rights (Guégnard and Mériot 2008b; Vanselow 2008; Pai 2006; Bernhardt, McGrath, and DeFilippis 2007).

The national contexts in which minimum wages are introduced help explain their strength or weakness. In Denmark, the minimum tariff relates to the social partners' desire to promote social solidarity through wage compression (McLaughlin 2007). As a consequence, compared to similar wage regulation in other countries in our study, the Danish minimum wage rate has been high and stable. Elsewhere, employer opposition to raising wages through regulation, as in the United Kingdom (see Warhurst, Lloyd, and Dutton 2008), helps to explain why the minimum-wage floor is low—and also why it is so permeable and weak. Commenting on previous state attempts in the United Kingdom to regulate wages in the hotel industry, Wood (1995, 80) urged caution about the introduction of the national minimum wage, suggesting that "the history of the industry tells us . . . that even with (albeit limited) wages regulation and monitoring, hospitality sector employers are skilled at either ignoring the law or finding ways around it."

SUMMARY AND DISCUSSION

Our comparative study has focused on the job quality of hotel room attendants in the United States and five countries in Europe. The poor job quality that is so evident for U.S. hotel room attendants motivated this transatlantic investigation. Throughout this chapter, we have sought to identify how the stronger labor market regulations and institutions in Europe might better support room attendants. To our surprise, we found less effect on job quality in Europe than we expected. In this section, we begin by summarizing the major conclusions of our comparison.

As we noted at the outset, hotel jobs cannot be exported—a business traveler to New York cannot be supplied with a hotel room from Mumbai in India. Even so, the industry is not immune to the effects of globalization. The hotel industry is consolidating and is increasingly dominated by large international corporations. Although small independent family businesses are still numerous, large international chains account for a disproportionate share of hotel beds and industry jobs and are driving industry trends, especially those that affect job quality. At the same time, the hotel industry has suffered an oversupply of hotel accommodation in many markets, leading to increased competition and, in some cases, price wars between hotels. Hotels have responded with a dual strategy of improving service quality while cutting costs wherever possible. These industry trends are evident across the countries of our study. Instead of improving the job quality in low-paid jobs, the hotel industry, both in Europe and the United States, has relied on women, immigrants, and workers of color to fill these jobs. Globalization is not happening in the location of hotels but in their workforce.

Table 7.4 summarizes key trends for room attendant jobs in the six countries. First, in terms of work content, room attendants' work looks remarkably similar. Regardless of country, room cleaning is a physically hard, psychologically taxing, and increasingly demanding job. The work of cleaning, tidying, and re-presenting rooms does not vary across countries or across market segments. Because it is regarded as women's work and many room attendants lack formal education and training, the job is perceived as low- or no-skill.

Across all countries, room attendants have few avenues for advancement. Because of the flat organizational structure of housekeeping and the subsequent lack of training and career development opportunities, there is a very small internal labor market through which room attendants might progress upward in the industry. Subcontracting of housekeeping makes advancement there even less likely. Moreover, because many of these workers lack transferable, certified skills, opportunities in the external labor market are also re-

Table 7.4 Trends in Room Attendant Jobs in the Six Countries, Early 2000s

	Denmark	France	Germany	Netherlands	United Kingdom	United States
Work content	Low-skill, routinized, demanding jobs with minimal access to training or career ladders. Growing standardization and especially intensification of work.					
Employment trends	Some use of outsourcing, strong use of part-time workers	Some use of outsourcing, strong use of part-time and other contingent workers	Strong use of outsourcing, strong use of part-time and other contingent workers	Strong use of outsourcing, strong use of part-time and other contingent workers	Strong use of part-time work, some use of temp workers, limited use of outsourcing	Strong use of part-time work, no use of outsourcing
Room attendant wages	Largely pegged to the national minimum tariff	Largely pegged to the national minimum wage	Largely set at the national wage floor through regional CLAs	Largely pegged to the national minimum wage	Largely pegged to the national minimum wage	Largely set at the wage floor
Hotel industry collective bargaining	Strong collective bargaining, but under pressure recently	Strong CLA coverage, but weak in practice	Weak regional collective bargaining	Strong CLA coverage, but weak in practice	Collective bargaining fragmented and weak	Collective bargaining fragmented and weak, except in large metropolitan areas with high density
Minimum-wage regulation	High minimum tariff, set by the social partners, has kept value over time	High minimum wage has kept value over time	No minimum wage regulation	Moderately strong national minimum wage, but has lost value over time	National minimum wage only recently introduced, no trend yet discernible	Weak national minimum wage has lost value over time

Sources: Authors' compilation based on Bernhardt, Dresser, and Hatton (2003); Dutton et al. (2008); Eriksson and Li (2008); Guégnard and Mériot (2008b); Hermanussen (2008); and Vanselow (2008).

stricted. Where student labor is more prevalent—for example, in Danish hotels—these workers at least are less likely to be trapped in the job over the long term. For most other workers, however, advancement is a very remote possibility.

Meanwhile, job quality is diminishing in all the countries we studied. First, work intensification is salient across all six countries. Room attendants have to do more work in each room as they clean, and they must clean more rooms during their shift. There is, as Annette Bernhardt, Laura Dresser, and Erin Hatton (2003, 59) note, "a bewildering increase in amenities in recent years." At the same time, the time calculated by management to clean rooms is being shortened—though this development is contested where unions are present. Second, employers are pursuing flexibility to better match fluctuating occupancy rates with staffing levels. These strategies are shaped by national regulation and institutions, but their aim of flexibility is consistent. Some hotels are increasingly splitting the job between full-time permanent staff and part-time staff with variable-hours contracts. In some cases, hotels are outsourcing room cleaning or employing temporary work agency staff. As management seeks to reduce the hotel's risk, the outcome is employment insecurity and wage instability for many room attendants.

In all six countries, room attendants work right at their national wage floor. Both workers and managers recognized and lamented this low pay, although managers legitimized it by referring to their tight budgetary constraints. It is interesting that there was no major difference between the pay of room attendants in upmarket and midmarket hotels, despite the former having a high-value-added product strategy and the latter typically a low-value-added strategy.

Importantly, given the low wages for room attendants, the European workers in our study benefit from the provision of an expansive and more inclusive social wage. In the United States, room attendants rarely have health insurance or private pension plans, nor can they count on substantial sick leave and vacation benefits. In this way, U.S. hotel room attendants clearly fall behind their counterparts in Europe.

Well-known differences exist across the six countries in their industrial relations systems. But even where these systems are nationally robust, they have only weak purchase in the hotel industry. In all of our countries, hotel union density is significantly lower than the national average (though Denmark's density is significantly higher than in the other countries). With the exception of the United Kingdom and the United States, the other countries in our study have collective bargaining agreements whose coverage stretches far beyond just those hotels with union members. Unfortunately, such agreements tend to be weakly enforced for room attendants because these workers lack effective workplace interest representation. Further, some collective agreements are being dissolved or entirely bypassed—evidence of growing stress within these collective bargaining systems.

In the absence of effective union intervention, the existence of minimum wages plays a crucial part in establishing and maintaining the wage floor for room attendants. Four countries operate a statutory minimum wage (France, the Netherlands, the United Kingdom, and the United States) and one country—Denmark—has a minimum tariff based on collective agreement between the social partners. Relative to its median wage, Denmark has the highest effective wage floor, with France a close second. The weak floor in the United States leaves hotel workers much further below the median. Germany has no wage floor, and the negative effects for room attendants are clear in the diminution of the CLA for contract cleaning companies and, perhaps more important, the increasing number of contract cleaners that simply operate outside the agreement. With the exception of the United States (where the minimum wage is too low to be economically relevant), these minimum rates have become the going rate for room attendant pay rather than a minimum from which better, higher rates might have been expected.

In sum, across the six countries that we studied, hotel room cleaning is a job with poor pay and prospects. The work is hard and is becoming more so with intensification. Nonstandard work arrangements are further limiting career development and destabilizing hours, and weak collective labor agreements give little relief. As a consequence, room attendant pay is at the wage floor in each of our countries, though the level of that floor varies comparatively across the countries.

Although the job quality of room attendants is poor, there is the possibility that it might become even worse as new industry and labor market developments take hold. First, as discussed in this chapter, the hotel industry has become increasingly dominated by large, publicly traded corporations. This trend of private-to-public ownership is being reversed in some cases, however, as companies are "re-privatized" through new private equity–leveraged buyouts that see these companies' shares bought up by a small group of investors. Indeed, private equity is establishing "a significant presence" in the industry, according to the trade journal *Caterer and Hotelkeeper* (2006, 2). In 2006 the U.S.-owned Hilton Hotels Corporation took over the U.K.-based Hilton Group Plc, which, since 1964, had run all non-U.S. Hilton hotels (Gunn 2005). In 2007 this company was itself the subject of a £10 billion ($500 million, 2007 dollars) private equity takeover (Thomas 2007). In the United States, Equity Inns and Highland Hospitality have also fallen prey to private equity purchases, with analysts predicting more such transactions over the coming years (Marino 2007).

These buyouts affect the operation of these hotel chains. Taking them off the stock market, "expert investors" take direct control of these companies with the express purpose of profit maximization and an expectation of selling or refloating the company on the stock market within three to five years. During this time, the investors claim to make these companies more efficient and so improve their competitiveness (Cohen 2007). But significant transparency is lost because private equity firms do not have to comply with a range of regulations, such as producing regular reports for shareholders. It is difficult to assess the impact of private equity on workers' job quality (*Labor Research* 2007), but where private equity is already well established in other industries—for example, retail—there is evidence of job losses in just under half of such deals. With accusations of asset stripping and shedding jobs, private equity managers have been called "locusts" by the former vice chancellor of Germany, Franz Müntefering. Already concerned about the job cuts that sometimes occur after private equity buyouts, trade unionists are worried about the future of the hotel industry.

Second, there is little existing pressure from the labor market on hotels to improve job quality, and all of our countries have the potential to tap new sources of labor. Although the hotel industry cannot export its room-cleaning jobs to countries with lower wage rates, governments can "import" cheaper workers from those countries on behalf of the industry, and it is an issue being actively discussed by employers' associations—in Germany, for example (DEHOGA 2004). The United Kingdom and the United States already have a well-developed migrant labor market, and the other four European countries of our study are scheduled in 2009 to also open their borders to workers from the EU accession countries. Compared to the "old EU," wage levels are significantly lower in these accession countries. The low monthly gross wages of our room attendants are high by comparison to average tourist industry monthly wages paid in these accession countries: Latvia €157 ($177.20, 2003 dollars), Hungary €340 ($383.75, 2003 dollars), Czech Republic €471 ($443.09, 2002 dollars), and Poland €280 to €980 ($316.03 to $1106.09, 2003 dollars) (Deutscher Bundestag 2003, 41). It is likely, therefore, that after 2009 there will be economic migration from these countries to the old EU. The precedent exists: the United Kingdom has already opened its borders to the accession countries and attracted a significant number of workers to its hotel industry (Murphy 2006; Salt and Millar 2006).[13] The U.K. hotel industry has even become dependent upon these migrant workers (McEwen 2005). Denmark has so far avoided significant use of migrant workers, but hotels in that country instead employ significant numbers of students, particularly in major cities (see Gautié et al., this volume). Given the expansion of higher education across the EU as a matter of policy (EC 2004a), the supply of students who are likely to work in order to support their studies is likely to increase, and many of these students will seek to enter low-entry-barrier industries such as hospitality, as evidence from the United Kingdom (Canny 2002) and the Netherlands (Hofman and Steijn 2003) is beginning to reveal. In both cases, given the potential supply of labor from students and, particularly, migrants, as well as the increasing physical workload, it is possible that more male room attendants will be employed in this hitherto female-dominated occupation in the future (see BHA 2005; Hermanussen 2008).

It is more probable, however, that the occupation will remain "women's work." With little population growth and concern about shrinking labor markets, there is concern within the EU about levering parents—in reality, mothers—into the workforce. The push by the EU for greater work-life balance is evidence of this initiative, as employers and national governments are exhorted to provide family-friendly employment polices (Eikhof, Warhurst, and Haunschild 2007; MacInnes 2008). In addition, some "workfare"-style initiatives by governments in the countries of our study are also intended to lever into jobs more women with domestic responsibilities. For example, in 2007 the U.K. government announced a shake-up of the welfare system that will require single parents (the vast majority of whom are women) to look for a job (Dutton et al. 2005; Mulholland

2007). Women are more likely than men to take temporary or non-permanent jobs (Osborne 2005). As Harald Bielenski, Gerhard Bosch, and Alexandra Wagner (2002) note, part-time work constitutes a form of labor market entry for women, and the main reason women work part-time is because of domestic responsibilities, usually child care, for which they still have the most responsibility. Thus, part-time work, such as that offered increasingly by hotels, provides a way of reconciling paid work and domestic responsibilities. Consequently, there are likely to be fewer supply pressures on employers that might, in other circumstances, force them to improve job quality in order to recruit and retain cleaning staff. As Christine Guégnard and Sylvie-Anne Mériot (2008a, 17) conclude in their analysis of room attendants in France: "Hotel directors are ready to admit that the job is tedious and badly paid, but few are prepared to adopt strategies that would benefit their staff." The possibility is that, in the absence of such strategies, the job quality of room attendants in Europe will edge closer to what is found in the United States.

Although the "low road" looms, our research reveals a potential for some "high-road" diversions. The U.S. hotel study shows that a combination of market segment, union representation, and union density within a region can offer real improvement to the wages and working conditions for room attendants. Workers are "better paid and better informed," note Bernhardt, Dresser, and Hatton (2003, 64), and this aids increased worker awareness and resistance to the negative effects of restructuring. High-road elements could also be found in the European study. Hotels that were keen to retain housekeeping employees offered permanent contracts and opportunities for job advancement and accepted interest representation through CLAs and on the shop floor. This "human-resource oriented approach" (Hermanussen 2008), however, again seems to be limited in the European industry. Furthermore, better wage and working conditions that depend on the goodwill of the employer are less sustainable than when introduced and enforced through employee rights set out in CLAs and labor laws. It is here that the EU has some advantage over the United States for room attendants.

The active attention of unions to room attendants at specific properties is likely to become increasingly relevant in both the United States and Europe. Having an actual work-site presence is one way to ensure and enforce wage standards. Further, especially as the workforce diversifies through migration and immigration, hotel and other service industries will be the places where many such workers first encounter worker representation (both unions and works councils in the EU). That these structures represent and enforce the interests of room attendants and other service workers is one way to build stronger and broader public support for the institutional infrastructure that has protected and promoted the interests of so many other workers. The hotel union experience in the United States of reaching out to and embracing immigrant workers may be an important model as more EU countries grapple with migration.

The trend toward industry concentration and consolidation may actually have a positive side as well. The negatives of consolidation are obvious: the work intensification and other speedups documented in this chapter. But consolidation also creates an opportunity for unions to leverage connections in one location to change conditions at another. In the United States, the largest union representing hotel workers (UNITE HERE) has consistently leveraged relationships with firms to help extend its reach into new properties. Also important, with consolidation, victories or embarrassments in a single location can affect the practice of entire chains. The decision in 2007 by Hilton hotels in London to bring cleaning back in-house—after it was revealed that cleaners hired through agencies were being paid less than the national minimum wage and receiving no overtime pay—occurred as a result of a "name-and-shame" campaign by community and trade union activists (Walton 2007). This retreat from outsourcing follows that of Accor in France in 2002: cleaners with the subcontracting company went on strike for better pay and conditions, and as in the London case, it was a public relations disaster. Accor has since also brought cleaning back in-house (Puech 2004, cited in Guégnard and Mériot 2008b). In these ways, while the costs of consolidation can be high, there is also potential for leveraging change at more hotel establishments through organizing, public relations, and other campaigns. Indeed, this is one area that is ripe for transnational and transatlantic learning and strategy, and given U.S. success in leveraging corporate, political, and media connections to win wage increases, this area is one in which American practice may be instructive in Europe. Already the living wage campaign of London, which was behind the Hilton about-face, has drawn on the example and financial support of UNITE HERE (Dutton et al. 2008).

Despite the rhetoric of shifts toward becoming high-skill, high-wage, knowledge-intensive, and ideas-driven economies (Reich

1991; Florida 2002), these optimistic accounts of the future of work recognize that routine service work will be the largest type of job in the United States and elsewhere. Indeed, it is more likely that a polarization is occurring in the labor market. The "low-end . . . menial jobs" of serving the more fortunate knowledge and creative workers, as Richard Florida (2002, 74, 71) laments, offer little more than a minimum-wage life that is "a gruelling struggle for existence amid the wealth of others." He has subsequently acknowledged that ways need to be found to make these jobs "less deadening" (Florida 2005, 5). Given that many of these jobs, such as our room attendants, are fixed in terms of location, there is scope for localized intervention in global economies. However, governments need to act, because employers will not and trade unions, currently, cannot. In particular, governments need to better ensure the wage floor, most obviously through enhanced minimum wages and better workplace monitoring and enforcement of minimum-wage regulations. Government inspectors can provide this enforcement, but their numbers are limited. It is a role more appropriate for trade unions, and a role that unions would willingly undertake (Kloosterboer 2007). The challenge for trade unions, however, is to develop strategies for organizing and representing a diversified workforce in a fragmented service industry.

The authors would like to thank all of the national teams' researchers who provided the data from which much of this comparative chapter is derived: Tor Eriksson, Eli Dutton, Christine Guégnard, Erin Hatton, Ria Hermanussen, Susan James, Jinkun Li, Caroline Lloyd, Sylvie-Anne Mériot, and Dennis Nickson. We are also grateful to Dani Zuberi for his comments on an earlier version of this chapter. Chris Warhurst also gratefully acknowledges the support of the Royal Society of Edinburgh and the Caledonian Research Foundation in enabling him to work directly with Achim Vanselow on this chapter. Last but not least, we thank all of the staff and associates of the Russell Sage Foundation for their support throughout this project.

NOTES

1. Precise figures are difficult because statistics are collated for "hospitality," which also includes cafés and restaurants, or enveloped within "tourism," which includes airlines.

2. As Roy Wood (1992) noted long ago, there is little conceptual clarity in the hotel industry about the use of the terms "migrant" and "immigrant" labor. We use "migrant" to refer to transitory workers and "immigrant" to refer to workers who intend to take up permanent residency in the host country.

3. An "extra" who works continuously for more than sixty days has a legal right to claim a permanent contract, but enforcement is difficult.

4. Posted workers are dispatched, or "posted," from their home country to work in a foreign host country, but under current EU law, they remain employed by their home-country employer while on the posted temporary assignment (see Fellini, Ferro, and Fullin 2007).

5. The definition of low wage is earning less than two-thirds of the gross hourly median wage; see Mason and Salverda (this volume).

6. The statistics are even worse when we focus only on room attendants: 86 percent earn below the low-pay threshold in Germany, 89 percent in the United Kingdom, and 72 percent in the United States.

7. Tipping was not common among the room attendants in our case studies, in line with other research findings (IDS 2005). Long-serving housekeepers in our hotels noted that only regular guests might leave tips and that tipping seemed to be disappearing as chain hotels became more prominent. At best, therefore, the occasional few cents left on a pillow was about as much as many room attendants could expect.

8. We refer here to "hospitality" because for some of the countries there is a lack of hotel-specific data, and in any case, union organization stretches beyond hotels to include restaurants and cafés. In Denmark in particular, unions are typically organized by occupation rather than industry.

9. While the general purpose of works councils is very similar in all countries—to represent employee interests—their legal framework and form of operation are different between countries. In Germany and the Netherlands, interest representation in the workplace is mainly through works councils; the law makes no provision for unions in this respect. In France, both unions and works councils tend to be present at the workplace level (Philips and Eamets 2007, 24–28).

10. The sectoral union NGG (Nahrung, Genuss, Gaststätten) organizes the food and luxury food industry and the hotel and restaurant industry.

11. SMIC is the French national minimum wage (see Bosch, Mayhew, and Goutié, this volume).

12. Although forty-four states have their own supplementary minimum wage, of which about one-third are higher than the national rate (Carley 2006).

13. Only the United Kingdom, Ireland, and Sweden allowed unrestricted

labor market access to workers from the A8 central and eastern European new EU member countries in 2004.

REFERENCES

Anxo, Dominique, Colette Fagan, Mark Smith, Marie-Thérèse Letablier, and Corinne Perraudin. 2007. *Part-Time Work in European Companies: Establishment Survey on Working Time 2004–2005*. Dublin: European Foundation for the Improvement of Living and Working Conditions.

Appelbaum, Eileen, Annette Bernhardt, and Richard J. Murnane. 2003. *Low-Wage America*. New York: Russell Sage Foundation.

Bernhardt, Annette, Laura Dresser, and Erin Hatton. 2003. "The Coffee Pot Wars: Unions and Firm Restructuring in the Hotel Industry." In *Low-Wage America*, edited by Eileen Appelbaum, Annette Bernhardt, and Richard J. Murnane. New York: Russell Sage Foundation.

Bernhardt, Annette, Siobhan McGrath, and James DeFilippis. 2007. "Unregulated Work in the Global City: Employment and Labor Law Violations in New York City." New York: New York University School of Law, Brennan Center for Justice.

Bielenski, Harald, Gerhard Bosch, and Alexandra Wagner. 2002. *Working Time Preferences in Sixteen European Countries*. Dublin: European Foundation for the Improvement of Living and Working Conditions.

Bispo, Arménio. 2007. *Labor Market Segmentation: An Investigation into the Dutch Hospitality Industry*. ERIM PhD Series Research in Management 108. Rotterdam: Erasmus Research Institute of Management (ERIM).

British Hospitality Association (BHA). 2005. *Trends and Statistics*. London: BHA.

Burgess, Cathy. 2007. "Is There a Future for Hotel Financial Controllers?" *Hospitality Management* 26(1): 161–74.

Business Travel Europe (BTE). 2005. *European Hotels on Way to Recovery—Deloitte*. Newsletter 47. Available at Air and Business Travel News, http://www.businesstraveleurope.com/newsletter.php?typ=n&id=281&iss=47 (accessed November 29, 2007).

Canny, Angela. 2002. "Flexible Labor? The Growth of Student Employment in the U.K." *Journal of Education and Work* 15(3): 277–301.

Carley, Mark. 2006. "Key Themes in Global Industrial Relations: Minimum Wages and Relocation of Production." Internet report. Dublin: European Foundation for the Improvement of Living and Working Conditions. Available at: http://www.eurofound.europa.eu/publications/htmlfiles/ef05138.htm (accessed June 11, 2009)

Caterer and Hotelkeeper. 2002. "The Future Lies in Outsourcing, Says GM." *Caterer and Hotelkeeper* (December 5). Available at Caterersearch.com, http://www.caterersearch.com/Articles/2002/12/06/46014/the-future-lies-in-outsourcing-says-gm.html (accessed May 23, 2006).

———. 2003. "Worldwide Briefing." *Caterer and Hotelkeeper* (March 11). Available at Caterersearch.com, http://www.caterersearch.com/Articles/2003/03/11/47424/worldwide-briefing.html (accessed May 23, 2006).

———. 2005. "European Hotel Market Recovers." *Caterer and Hotelkeeper* (July 19). Available at Caterersearch.com, http://www.caterersearch.com/Articles/2005/07/19/301578/european-hotel-market-recovers.html (accessed May 23, 2006).

———. 2006. "Market Snapshot: Hotels." *Caterer and Hotelkeeper* (April 24). Available at: http://www.caterersearch.com/Articles/2006/04/24/57630/market-snapshot-hotels.html (accessed May 23, 2006).

Cohen, Ronald. 2007. "How I Rode the Rising Wave of Private Equity." *Sunday Times*, November 4, 2007, 13.

DEHOGA (Deutscher Hotel- und Gaststättenverband—German Hotel and Restaurant Association). 2004. *Wir machen Branchenpolitik: Jahrbuch 2003–2004*. Berlin: DEHOGA.

Deloitte. 2007. *HotelBenchmark™ Survey: Monthly Bulletin—Global January*, was available at: http://www.hotelbenchmark.com/Services/Publications/Forms/GlobalBulletin.pdf (accessed November 5, 2007).

Deutscher Bundestag. 2003. "Antwort der Bundesregierung auf eine Grosse Anfrage der Abgeordneten Jürgen Klimke, Klaus Brämig und weiterer Abgeordneter der Fraktion der CDU/CSU: Auswirkungen der EU-Osterweiterung auf den Tourismus und die deutsche Tourismuswirtschaft (Answer of the German Government to a great inquiry of the members of the Bundestag Jürgen Klimke, Klaus Brämig and other members of the faction of CDU/CSU: Impact of the Eastern European expansion of the EU on tourism and the German tourism industry." Deutscher Bundestag, 15. Wahlperiode, Drucksache (German Bundestag, 15. Legislation period. Official Records of Parliament) 15/1267. December 15.

Dutton, Eli, Chris Warhurst, Caroline Lloyd, Susan James, Johanna Commander, and Dennis Nickson. 2008. "Just Like the Elves in Harry Potter." In *Low-Wage Work in the United Kingdom*, edited by Caroline Lloyd, Geoff Mason, and Ken Mayhew. New York: Russell Sage Foundation.

Dutton, Eli, Chris Warhurst, Dennis Nickson, and Cliff Lockyer. 2005. "Lone Parents, the New Deal, and the Opportunities and Barriers to Retail Employment." *Policy Studies* 26(1): 85–101.

Ehrenreich, Barbara. 2001. *Nickel and Dimed*. New York: Metropolitan.

Eikhof, Doris Ruth, Chris Warhurst, and Axel Haunschild. 2007. "What Work? What Life? What Balance? Critical Reflections on the Work-Life Balance Debate." *Employee Relations* 29(4): 325–33.

EMIRE. 2007. "Minimum-Terms Workers." European industrial relations glossaries provided by the European Foundation for the Improvement

of Living and Working Conditions, Dublin. Available at: http://www
.eurofound.europa.eu/emire/NETHERLANDS/MINIMUMTERMS
WORKER-NL.htm (accessed January 10, 2008).

Eriksson, Tor, and Jinkun Li. 2008. "Restructuring Meets Flexicurity:
Housekeeping Work in Danish Hotels." In *Low-Wage Work in Denmark*,
edited by Niels Westergaard-Nielsen. New York: Russell Sage Foundation.

Espino-Rodríguez, Tomás F., and Antonia Ma Gil-Padilla. 2005. "Determinants of Information Systems Outsourcing in Hotels from the Resource-
Based View: An Empirical Study." *International Journal of Tourism Research*
7(1): 35–47.

Espino-Rodríguez, Tomás F., Pei-Chun Lai, and Tom Baum. 2008. "Asset
Specificity in Make or Buy Decisions for Service Operations." *International Journal of Service Industry Management* 19(1): 111–33.

European Commission (EC). 2003. *E-Commerce and the Internet in European
Businesses: Data 2001–2002*. Luxembourg: Office for Official Publications
of the European Communities.

———. 2004a. *Facing the Challenges*. Luxembourg: Office for Official Publications of the European Communities.

———. 2004b. *Industrial Relations*. Luxembourg: Office for Official Publications of the European Communities.

———. 2006a. *Panorama on Tourism*. Luxembourg: Office for Official Publications of the European Communities.

———. 2006b. *Industrial Relations in Europe 2006*. Luxembourg: Office for
Official Publications of the European Communities.

Evans, Yara, Jane Wills, Kavita Datta, Joanna Herbert, Jon May, and Cathy
McIlwaine. 2007. "Subcontracting by Stealth in London's Hotels: Impacts
and Implications for Labor Organizing." *Just Labor: A Canadian Journal of
Work and Society* 10: 85–97.

Fellini, Ivana, Anna Ferro, and Giovanna Fullin. 2007. "Recruitment
Processes and Labor Mobility: The Construction Industry in Europe."
Work, Employment, and Society 21(2): 277–98.

Finegold, David, Karin Wagner, and Geoff Mason. 2000. "National Skill-
Creation Systems and Career Paths for Service Workers: Hotels in the
United States, Germany, and the United Kingdom." *International Journal
of Human Resource Management* 11(3): 497–516.

Florida, Richard L. 2002. *The Rise of the Creative Class*. New York: Basic
Books.

———. 2005. *Cities and the Creative Class*. London: Routledge.

Gather, Claudia, Ute Gerhard, and Heidi Schroth. 2005. *Vergeben und
vergessen? Gebäudereinigung im Spannungsfeld zwischen kommunalen Dien-
sten und Privatisierung (Forgive and Forgotten? Janitorial Services as Field
of Tension Between Municipal Services and Privatization)*. Hamburg: VSA.

Gewerkschaft Nahrung-Genuss-Gaststätten (NGG, Food and Allied Workers' Union). 2008. "Hotelreinigung: Rosenberger: Fremdfirmen müssen Mindestlohn zahlen!" ("Hotel Cleaning: Rosenberger: Service Firms Have to Pay the Minimum Wage!"). Press release (January 30).

Grugulis, Irena, Chris Warhurst, and Ewart Keep. 2004. "What's Happening to Skill?" In *The Skills That Matter*, edited by Chris Warhurst, Ewart Keep, and Irena Grugulis. London: Palgrave Macmillan.

Guégnard, Christine, and Sylvie-Anne Mériot. 2008a. "Employable Workers and Attractive Employers?" Paper presented to the twenty-sixth annual International Labor Process Conference. University College Dublin (March 18–20).

———. 2008b. "Housekeepers in French Hotels: Cinderella in the Shadows." In *Low-Wage Work in France*, edited by Ève Caroli and Jérôme Gautié. New York: Russell Sage Foundation.

Gunn, Jessica. 2005. "HHC to Finalize Hilton Group Deal This Year." *Caterer and Hotelkeeper* (December 22). Available at: http://www.cater ersearch.com/Articles/2005/12/22/304176/hhc-to-finalise-hilton-group-deal-this-year.html (accessed December 6, 2007).

Hemmington, Nigel, and Christopher King. 2000. "Key Dimensions of Outsourcing Hotel Food and Beverage Services." *International Journal of Contemporary Hospitality Management* 12(4): 256–65.

Hermanussen, Ria. 2008. "Hotels: Industry Restructuring and Room Attendants' Jobs." In *Low-Wage Work in the Netherlands*, edited by Wiemer Salverda, Maarten van Klaveren, and Marc van der Meer. New York: Russell Sage Foundation.

Hofman, Wiecher, and Abraham Steijn. 2003. "Students or Lower-Skilled Workers? 'Displacement' at the Bottom of the Labor Market." *Higher Education* 45: 127–46.

Income Data Services (IDS). 2005. "Pay in Hotels." *IDS Pay Report* 943(January): 11–15.

———. 2007. "Pay in Hotels." *IDS Pay Report* 968(January): 13–17.

International Labor Organization (ILO). 2001. *Human Resources Development, Employment, and Globalization in the Hotel, Catering, and Tourism Sector*. Geneva: ILO.

Jørgensen, Carsten. 2007. "New Employer Organization Favors More Company-Level Agreements." Available at EIROnline (European Industrial Relations Observatory), http://www.eurofound.europa.eu/eiro/2006/11/articles/DK0611029I.htm (accessed November 16, 2007). Dublin: European Foundation for the Improvement of Living and Working Conditions.

Jossart, Alexandre, and Pierre Walthery. 2001. *Sectoral Unions and Employers' Organizations in the EU Hotel, Restaurant, and Cafés Sector (NACE 55)*. Annual report on social concertation and collective bargaining. Project V/001/97. Louvain-la-Neuve, Belgium: Université Catholique de Louvain [online only, no longer available].

Klein Hesselink, John, Irene Houtman, Ruurt van den Berg, Seth van den Bossche, and Floor van den Heuvel. 2004. *EU Hotel and Restaurant Sector: Work and Employment Conditions.* Dublin: European Foundation for the Improvement of Living and Working Conditions.

Kloosterboer, Dirk. 2007. *Innovative Trade Union Strategies.* Utrecht: Stichting FNV Pers.

Kümmerling, Angelika, and Steffen Lehndorff. 2007. *Extended and Unusual Working Hours in European Companies: Establishment Survey on Working Time 2004–2005.* Dublin: European Foundation for the Improvement of Living and Working Conditions.

Labor Research. 2007. "The True Cost of Private Equity." *Labor Research* (May): 23–25.

Lai, Pei-Chun, and Tom Baum. 2005. "Just-in-Time Labor Supply in the Hotel Sector: The Role of Agencies." *Employee Relations* 27(1): 86–102.

Lamminmaki, Dawne. 2005. "Why Do Hotels Outsource? An Investigation Using Asset Specificity." *International Journal of Contemporary Hospitality Management* 17(6): 516–28.

Leidner, Rudiger. 2004. *The European Tourism Industry: A Multi-Sector with Dynamic Markets.* Luxembourg: Office for Official Publications of the European Communities.

London Economics. 2003. *Working Conditions in—Hotels and Restaurants: National Report for France.* Dublin: European Foundation for the Improvement of Living and Working Conditions.

MacInnes, John. 2008. "Work-Life Balance: Three Terms in Search of a Definition." In *Work Less, Live More?* edited by Chris Warhurst, Doris Ruth Eikhof, and Axel Haunschild. London: Palgrave Macmillan.

Malik, Zaiba. 2006. "A Dirty Business." *Guardian*, December 9, 47–57.

Mandelbaum, Robert. 2007. "Once Again Revenue Gains Overcome Expense Growth." Hotel News Resource, available at: http://www.hotelnews resource.com/pdf/dyn/28873.pdf (accessed November 5, 2007).

Marino, Vivian. 2007. "In Hotel Companies, Amenities for Investors." *New York Times*, July 22, 28.

Mason, Geoff, and Wiemar Salverda. 2007. "Russell Sage Foundation Benchmarking Study for Phase 2: Low-Wage Employment in Western Europe and the United States." Report to Russell Sage Foundation, p. 82.

McEwen, Alan. 2005. "Eastern Europeans Save Capital Hotels from Staff Crisis." *Edinburgh Evening News*, May 4, 3.

McLaughlin, Colm. 2007. "Challenging the Neo-Liberal Prescription: The Industrial Relations Lessons from Denmark, Ireland, and New Zealand." Paper presented to the Fifth International Conference in Commemoration of Marco Biagi. University of Modena (March 17–21).

Mériot, Sylvie-Anne. 2000. "Employment Prospects in the Hotel and Catering Trade: A Franco-American Comparison." *Training and Employment* 40: 1–4.

Mintel. 2004. *Hotels—United Kingdom.* London: Mintel.

Mitchell, Jackie. 2007. "Suite Inspiration." *Caterer and Hotelkeeper*, May 10, 44–48.

Mulholland, Hélène. 2007. "More Parents to Work in Welfare Shake-up." *Guardian*, December 13, 6.

Murphy, Noelle. 2006. "Employing Migrant Workers." *IRS Employment Review* 844: 42–45.

Nickson, Dennis. 2007. *Human Resource Management for the Hospitality and Tourism Industries.* Oxford: Butterworth Heinemann.

O'Connor, Peter, and Jamie Murphy. 2004. "Research on Information Technology in the Hospitality Industry." *International Journal of Hospitality Management* 23(5): 473–84.

Osborne, Matthew. 2005. "Industry Report: Temporary Work Agencies in the United Kingdom." Unpublished paper. National Institute of Economic and Social Research, London.

Pai, Hsiao-Hung. 2006. "Our Eyes Have Been Opened by the Abuse." *Guardian*, April 29, 10–11.

Parent-Thirion, Agnès, Enrique Fernández Macías, John Hurley, and Greet Vermeylen. 2007. *Fourth European Working Conditions Survey.* Dublin: European Foundation for the Improvement of Living and Working Conditions.

People 1st. 2006. *Hotels: Industry Report.* London: People 1st.

Philips, Kaia, and Raul Eamets. 2007. *Impact of Globalization on Industrial Relations in the EU and Other Major Economies.* Dublin: European Foundation for the Improvement of Living and Working Conditions.

Pohl, Gerd. 2007. "Tariflose Zustände und Tariferosion. Erfahrungen aus dem Gastgewerbe (Non-Coverage by Collective Agreements and the Erosion of Collective Bargaining. Experiences from the Hotel and Restaurant Trade)." In *Wohin treibt das Tarifsystem? (Where is the Collective Bargaining System Heading?)*, edited by R. Bispinck. Hamburg: VSA.

Puech, I. 2004. "Le Temps du remue-ménage: Conditions d'emploi et de travail des femmes de chamber (Times of Confusion: Employment and Working Conditions of Chambermaids)." *Sociologie du Travail* 46(2): 150–67.

Reich, Robert. 1991. *The Work of Nations.* New York: Alfred Knopf.

Ritzer, George, and Craig D. Lair. 2009. "The Globalization of Nothing and the Outsourcing of Service Work." In *Service Work: Critical Perspectives*, edited by Cameron Macdonald and Marek Korczynski. London: Routledge.

Rodríguez-Díaz, Manuel, and Tomás F. Espino-Rodríguez. 2006. "Developing Relational Capabilities in Hotels." *International Journal of Contemporary Hospitality Management* 18(1): 25–40.

Salt, John, and Jane Millar. 2006. "Foreign Labor in the United Kingdom:

Current Patterns and Trends." *Labor Market Trends* (October): 335–55.

Sandoff, Mette. 2005. "Customization and Standardization in Hotels: A Paradox or Not?" *International Journal of Contemporary Hospitality* 17(6): 529–35.

Scottish Centre for Employment Research (SCER). 2006. *Valuable Assets: A General Formal Investigation into the Role and Status of Classroom Assistants in Scotland's Primary Schools.* SCER report 11, University of Strathclyde. Available at Equality and Human Rights Commission, http://83.137.212.42/sitearchive/eoc/Docs/VAssets_Overtime_%20research_report.doc?page=20368 (accessed June 8, 2009).

Scully-Russ, Ellen. 2005. "Agency Versus Structure: Path Dependency and Choice in Low-Wage Labor Markets." *Human Resource Development Review* 4(3): 254–78.

Sherwyn, David, Zev Eigen, and Paul Wagner. 2006. "The Hotel Industry's Summer of 2006: A Watershed Moment for America's Labor Unions?" *Cornell Hotel and Restaurant Administration Quarterly* 47(4): 337–49.

Thomas, Daniel. 2007. "£10b Hilton Deal Will Not Be the Last." *Caterer and Hotelkeeper*, July 12. Available at: http://www.caterersearch.com/Articles/2007/07/12/314834/10b-hilton-deal-will-not-be-the-last.html (accessed December 6, 2007).

Tijdens, Kea, and Maarten van Klaveren. 2007. *WIBAR Report No. 5: Collective Bargaining Coverage.* Amsterdam: University of Amsterdam, Amsterdam Institute for Advanced Studies.

Toynbee, Polly. 2003. *Hard Work.* London: Bloomsbury.

UniteHere. 2006. *Creating Luxury, Enduring Pain: How Hotel Work Is Hurting Housekeepers.* Available at: http://www.hotelworkersrising.org/pdf/Injury_Paper.pdf (accessed January 25, 2002).

U.S. Bureau of Labor Statistics (BLS). 2008. *Career Guide to Industries, Hotels, and Other Accomodations.* Available at: http://www.bls.gov/oco/cg/cgs036.htm#emply (accessed August 28, 2008).

U.S. Department of Labor. 2001. "Table 1: Incidence Rates of Nonfatal Occupational Injuries and Illnesses by Industry and Selected Case Types, 2000." Available at: http://www.bls.gov/iif/oshwc/osh/os/ostb1001.pdf (accessed January 25, 2002).

Van het Kaar, Robbert. 2007. "Crackdown on Breaches of Minimum Wage Law." Dublin: European Foundation for the Improvement of Living and Working Conditions. Available at EIROnline (European Industrial Relations Observatory), http://www.eurofound.europa.eu/eiro/2007/07/articles/nl0707049i.htm (accessed November 16, 2007).

Vanselow, Achim. 2008. "Still Lost and Forgotten? The Work of Hotel Room Attendants in Germany." In *Low-Wage Work in Germany*, edited by Gerhard Bosch and Claudia Weinkopf. New York: Russell Sage Foundation.

Walton, Christopher. 2007. "Hilton Agency Staff Were Paid Less Than the Minimum Wage." (November 1). Available at: Caterersearch.com, http://www.caterersearch.com/Articles/2007/11/01/317037/hilton-agency-staff-were-paid-less-than-the-minimum.html (accessed November 5, 2007).

Warhurst, Chris, Caroline Lloyd, and Eli Dutton. 2008. "The National Minimum Wage, Low Pay, and the U.K. Hotel Industry: The Case of Room Attendants." *Sociology* 42(6): 1228–36.

Watkins, Ed. 2000. "The Consolidation Conundrum." *Lodging Hospitality* 56(15): 2.

Wood, Roy C. 1992. *Working in Hotels and Catering.* London: Routledge.

———. 1995. "Wages Council Abolition: Doing Labor a Favor?" *Renewal* 3(1): 72–81.

Zuberi, Dani. 2007. "Organizing for Better Working Conditions and Wages: The UNITE Here! Hotel Workers Rising Campaign." *Just Labor: A Canadian Journal of Work and Society* 10: 60–73.

CHAPTER 8

Cleaning and Nursing in Hospitals: Institutional Variety and the Reshaping of Low-Wage Jobs

Philippe Méhaut, Peter Berg, Damian Grimshaw, and Karen Jaehrling, with Marc van der Meer and Jacob Eskildsen

In their research on low-wage and low-skill work in U.S. hospitals, Eileen Appelbaum and her colleagues (2003) found a high incidence of low-wage work among cleaners and nursing assistants. At the time of their study, U.S. hospitals were struggling with high turnover and difficulties in recruiting low-skilled workers. Rather than raise wages, hospitals, responding in some cases to trade union pressure, experimented with increased training and alternative forms of work organization that broadened job tasks. One of the key assumptions behind these experiments was that creating more interesting jobs and improving job satisfaction would increase the ability of hospitals to recruit and retain labor and that cost savings could be achieved by switching job tasks among nursing assistants and nurses. Nevertheless, such changes have not had a significant effect on the incidence of low-wage work; nor is there any evidence of significant diffusion of so-called high-road human resource (HR) practices in U.S. hospitals.

In Europe, the picture varies considerably from country to country. In three countries (Denmark, France, and the Netherlands), there is in fact very little evidence of low-wage work among cleaners and nursing assistants in hospitals. Only the United Kingdom registers a high incidence of low-wage work, at a level close to that of the United States. In Germany, the incidence is increasing among cleaners.

Despite these differences, U.S. and European hospitals have faced similar pressures in recent years, including an aging population, budget constraints, concerns over the quality of care, and new demands from patients. In many respects, hospitals have responded in fairly similar ways—with efforts to increase patient throughput, reform funding schemes, and shift the care and rehabilitation of patients outside hospitals. Attempts to reorganize work, however, have varied significantly, in large part because of the reality that human resource strategies are embedded within national employment systems and the diverse roles and influences of the social partners.

The first three sections of this chapter set out the background to conditions in the hospital sector. The first describes the commonalities and differences in the hospital sector (ownership, cost pressures, industry organization, and so on) across the six countries. The next section presents the main characteristics of the division of labor and work organization, as well as the labor supply. Unlike the other industries analyzed in this book, the hospital industry presents huge intercountry differences, despite the fact that our analysis focuses on a common set of tasks (cleaning patients' rooms and basic nursing) and similar job titles (cleaner and nursing assistant). We emphasize job categories, qualifications, and training in our analysis because these factors play an important role in our understanding of the incidence of low pay in this sector. The third section compares the incidence of low-wage work in hospital occupations and considers the role of wage regulation and wage structure in explaining country differences.

The next three sections of the chapter then focus on three main trends affecting the quality of low-wage, low-skill work. When they are not putting direct pressure on wages, hospitals can develop alternative HR strategies. They can save costs and gain in flexibility by outsourcing their cleaning activities or using alternative "exit options." Depending on the country in question, these possibilities are facilitated or impeded by the main domestic labor market institutions. The European hospitals in our sample have reshaped work organization as part of a more systematic and more positive up-skilling process than that observed in the U.S. hospitals. Another option available to hospitals is to increase workloads; however, the extent to which this has occurred, as perceived by workers, varies across countries.

These three trends are an important part of the dynamic of low-wage, low-skill work and are reflected in, among other things, persistently high wage differences in the United States, stability of and/or improvement in the wage and skill positions in Denmark and the Netherlands, and an increase in low-wage work among cleaners in Germany.

We conclude by emphasizing the importance of the interplay between a broad set of labor market institutions (collective agreements, the minimum wage, training facilities) and health institutions (funding rules, monitoring of care quality) in explaining the development of virtuous or vicious circles in the six countries investigated here.

As in the other chapters of this book, our data are derived from the common methodology designed for the entire research project on low-wage work: a mix of industry-level analysis of the hospital sector and in-depth case studies in a sample of hospitals (fifteen for the United States, eight per country for Europe) that involved interviews with managers, union representatives, and workers. To enhance comparability, most of the interviews in the European countries were undertaken in medical wards in general (non-university or teaching) hospitals. Some of our conclusions are more specific to this aspect of hospital care. The U.S. case data were gathered in fifteen community hospitals between 2000 and 2002 (five years before the European research). In addition to over one hundred interviews with managers, supervisors, and union officials, the original U.S. research team conducted a telephone survey of 589 low-wage workers across the fifteen hospitals.[1]

THE HOSPITAL SERVICES SECTOR: DISTINCTIVE STRUCTURES BUT RELATIVELY COMMON PRESSURES FOR CHANGE

Hospital structure and financing vary considerably across the six countries. Nevertheless, the hospital services sector faces relatively common challenges, including those related to an aging population, the need for stricter funding principles, changing patient expectations, and the demand for improved medical technologies.

PRIVATE OR PUBLIC FUNDING? PRIVATE OR PUBLIC HOSPITALS?

The most striking difference is that while U.S. hospitals are financed by a mix of public and private funds (taxation, plus private insurance and out-of-pocket payments), hospitals in Europe, both public and private, rely almost entirely on public spending raised through either taxation (Denmark and the United Kingdom) or social insurance (France, Germany, and the Netherlands). According to Organization for Economic Cooperation and Development (OECD) health data for 2005, public funding accounts for 94 to 96 percent of hospital income in Denmark, the United Kingdom, and France, 88 percent in Germany, and 77 percent in the Netherlands, but just 57 percent in the United States. Moreover, only the United States among our six selected countries has significantly reduced the share of public funding since the mid-1990s, from 61 percent in 1995 to 57 percent in the mid-2000s (see table 8.1).

Furthermore, there are stark intercountry differences in the mix of public and private ownership of hospitals and in the shares of for-profit and not-for-profit operation. In Denmark, the Netherlands, and the United Kingdom, hospitals are located almost entirely in the public sector. In the other three countries, the private sector accounts for one in three (France), two in three (Germany), and three in four (the United States) hospitals (table 8.1). In France, private for-profit hospitals handle a larger share of acute hospital activity than private nonprofit hospitals, the ratio being around five to two. The opposite is true in Germany and the United States, where nonprofit hospitals play a larger role than for-profit hospitals, especially in the United States. The situation in Germany is changing, however, since there has been a rapid rise in the share of for-profit hospitals (up from 15 percent in 1990 to 25 percent in 2004) as a result of policies to privatize public hospitals. Nevertheless, the share of nonprofit hospitals has remained stable at around 38 percent.

Trends in expenditures per head of population on hospital treatment diverged markedly between 1998 and 2005. There appears to be no simple relationship between such expenditures and the particular system of financing and hospital ownership. Of the three countries where hospitals are largely financed through social insurance, one saw a relatively large increase in funding (Netherlands) and two relatively small rises (France and Germany). There were moderate increases in both the United States, with its private insurance system, and Denmark, where hospitals are funded largely by taxation (see table 8.1). Harmonized OECD data are unfortunately not available for the United Kingdom, but national data show a substantial increase in hospital spending (and in public funding) of around 54 percent over the period 1998 to 2005.

Common Pressures for Change

Despite country differences in the form of hospital finance, ownership structure, and the trend in expenditures, hospitals in all six

	Denmark	France	Germany	Netherlands	United Kingdom	United States
Main system of financing	General taxation	Social insurance	Social insurance	Social insurance and private insurance	General taxation	Private insurance and social insurance
Public- or private-sector funding	Public-sector (96 percent)	Public-sector (94 percent)	Public-sector (88 percent)	Public-sector (77 percent)	Public-sector (96 percent)[a]	Public-private mix (57 percent and 43 percent)
Increase in hospital expenditures per head of population, 1998 to 2005[b]	6.9%	6.0%	6.7%	29.5%	NA	29.4%
Ownership of hospitals:[c]						
Public	100	65	37	100	NA	23
Private non-profit		9	38			51
Private for-profit		26	25			26
Number of beds per 1,000 people and trend 1995 to 2005	3.8 beds,[d] decline from 4.9	7.5 beds, decline from 8.9	8.5 beds, decline from 9.7	5.1 beds,[e] decline from 5.3	3.9 beds, decline from 4.8	3.2 beds,[c] decline from 4.1

Sources: OECD Health Data (various years; www.sourceoecd.org) and World Health Organization (various years; http://data.euro.who.int). U.S. ownership data: American Hospital Association (2006).

a. 1999 data (latest available data from OECD for the United Kingdom).
b. Authors' calculations using expenditures per head of population on hospital services in national currency units at 2000 GDP price level.
c. National sources of data for France (2004 data from Méhaut et al. 2008), Germany (Jaehrling 2008), and the United States (Cutler 2000).
d. 2004 data.
e. 2003 data.

countries face relatively common pressures for change. Pressures on unit costs have intensified and play a strong role in the reshaping (by government, hospitals, and other bodies) of finance and governance rules in the sector. In the United States, hospitals face enormous problems in aligning cost structures with an imperfect insurance system for managing and funding health care. On the one hand, the high proportion of uninsured patients is a factor in the large volume of medical bills that remain unpaid; in 2000 alone, U.S. hospitals wrote off an estimated $20 billion in bad debt related to treatment of the uninsured. On the other hand, insured patients also pose cost problems for hospitals owing to the difficulties of claiming reimbursements from insurance companies that match the cost of service provision. Insurance companies are constantly evaluating what they are willing to pay for health care services. In some cases, hospitals find that they cannot offer services at the prescribed level of reimbursement and have to take losses on those services. The effect of providing care to one party and receiving payment from another party that determines what it is willing to pay has been to keep U.S. hospitals under continuous cost pressure. This effect is similar for public insurance schemes, such as Medicare and Medicaid, in that pressures on the federal government budget (reflecting political goals as well as pressures from a cost-conscious taxpaying public) force hospitals to search for ways to meet lower reimbursement rates (see also Appelbaum and Skromme 1986).

Cost pressures in Europe are similarly strong, albeit different in nature. Although there are important differences in the growth trend in health care expenditures (table 8.1), budget pressures in funding public health care systems are forcing hospitals in all countries to reduce the cost of delivering care. In all five European countries, new funding principles inspired by the U.S. diagnosis-related groups have been implemented, though only recently and under different rules in some countries. The common principle involves fixing an average price for each hospital activity and funding hospitals "ex post" on that basis, regardless of the real costs. This new principle of financing health care is part of a wider package of reforms in each country instituted in the early 1990s that represents a shift toward a quasi-market regulation of hospital service provision (Kirkpatrick and Martinez Lucio 1996; Le Grand and Bartlett 1993), which in turn has made the rules governing the costing of hospital activities more stringent. The overall result is to establish a form of market pressure on hospital managers to make year-on-year cost savings and to identify those activities operating at above-average cost.

Aging populations are a further important source of cost pressures for hospitals. The increasing number of older people has raised demand for health care and the need for acute and chronic treatment, thereby raising the cost of providing health care services. When combined with public budget pressures—or with servicing an uninsured population, as in the United States—the increase in acute treatment squeezes hospitals even more tightly.

New pressures on the organization of hospital services also arise from reduced hospital stays among patients. On the one hand, patients are increasingly likely to opt for shorter stays in the hospital— a decision facilitated by new medical techniques. On the other hand, hospitals have developed outpatient facilities and accelerated the transfer of patients to other types of health care providers for rehabilitation. Over the last decade, there has been a growth in the use of home care and long-term care facilities. Patients who in the past would have required hospitalization are now seen in outpatient clinics for day surgery or treatment. In all six countries, these developments are reflected in downward trends in the number of hospital beds per capita (table 8.1). The decline in the number of beds per one thousand people between 1995 and 2005 was greatest in the United States (where the number of beds was already the lowest in 1995) and smallest in the Netherlands. The other four countries saw reductions of between 12 and 19 percent. One consequence of increased patient turnover is an increase in the workloads associated with the servicing of hospital wards, especially for cleaning and auxiliary nursing staff.

Despite these common trends, we will see in the remainder of the chapter that:

1. Our comparative investigation of the cleaning of patients' rooms and basic nursing reveals significant country differences in work organization and job definition, unlike in the other sectors investigated in this book.

2. The incidence of low-wage work is very different across our six countries, largely as a result of variations in work organization and the degree of inclusiveness in the wage-setting arrangements.

WHO WASHES THE PATIENTS? WHO MOPS THE FLOOR?

To improve the comparative analysis, data collection in each case study focused on common job tasks—namely, cleaning patients' rooms and basic nursing tasks. The two most common job titles are those of nursing assistant and cleaner. However, the same tasks can be part of a broad range of jobs with very different task profiles, skill requirements, and occupational labels. In the countries in our sample, both the vertical and the horizontal integration of tasks vary considerably, particularly when it comes to basic nursing tasks. This needs to be taken into account when comparing wage structures across countries.

The Nursing Assistant: An Unskilled or Skilled Job?

As Brian Abel-Smith (1960) argues in the U.K. context, much of the history of the division of labor in nursing has been a struggle over the "second portal"—that is, the nature of a skilled grade of nurse deployed to assist a nurse with a higher level of skills and qualifications. Although there was a period of time when such a second portal existed in all six countries, country trends have diverged since.[2] These divergent trends were already at work when the hospital sector began to face the changes and challenges outlined earlier, and they shaped the very different national responses to these "external" pressures. Today, as a result, three different models of work organization can be identified in nursing (see table 8.2 for detailed figures):

- Primarily *one portal*: Qualified nurses constitute the overwhelming majority of nursing personnel, and the number of nursing assistants is very limited (the Netherlands and Germany).

- Strong *second portal*: High use is made of nursing assistants, the bulk of whom have received regulated, formal vocational training (France and, to a lesser extent, Denmark).

- Strong *third portal*: High use is made of nursing assistants, the bulk of whom have little or no compulsory vocational training (the United Kingdom and the United States).

Table 8.2 Occupational Groups Among Nursing Staff in Hospitals, Mid-2000s

	Netherlands[a] (2007)	Germany (2005)	Denmark (2004)	France[b] (2002)	United States (2006)	United Kingdom (England, 2006)[c]
Qualified nurses	76,000	355,000	27,000	228,000	1,374,000	299,000
Nurse assistants	4,300	38,000	8,000	210,000	554,000	129,000
Second portal	4,300	18,000	5,000	200,000[b]	171,000	9,000
Third portal	Not relevant	20,000	3,000	10,000	383,000	120,000
Ratio of nurses to nursing assistants	17:7	9:4	3:3	1:1	2:5	2:3

Sources: Authors' compilation based on: Netherlands—Netherlands Centre of Excellence in Nursing, available at: www.lev.nl; United Kingdom—Department of Health, NHS hospital and community health services nonmedical staff in England, 1996 to 2006 (table 1a, 2), full-time-equivalents (FTEs); Germany—Statistisches Bundesamt (2008), Grunddaten der Krankenhäuser, vol. 2006, headcounts; France—Drees, statistique annuelle des établissements de santé, headcounts; United States—U.S. Bureau of Labor Statistics (2006), headcounts; Denmark—Eskildsen and Løkke-Nielsen (2008), FTEs.

a. General hospitals only.
b. Estimation by the authors.
c. Figures include staff working for the National Health Service (NHS) in ambulatory health services outside hospitals.

Hence, in four out of six countries, basic nursing tasks, such as washing patients, are either integrated into the nurses' job profile (Germany, the Netherlands) or assigned to nursing assistants who have completed at least twelve months of formal vocational training (France, Denmark). Moreover, in some countries where we found skilled nursing assistants, such as France and Denmark, the job territory of nursing assistants overlaps with that of nurses. In France, the nursing assistant sometimes has complete access to patients' records and can provide information in response to certain requests. Under the guidance of a nurse or supervisor, a nursing assistant can help in tasks such as providing medicines, recording patients' temperature, tending patients immediately after surgery (including checking blood pressure), and changing dressings. The more technical the health care and the busier the nurses, the more tasks overlap. In Denmark, the trend is similar. We found a high share of nursing assistants in the United Kingdom, where they are concentrated in the "third portal": nursing assistant jobs are less skilled than in France and Denmark (training is provided in U.K. hospitals, but no qualifications are as yet required), and the job scope is narrower, with less physical care of patients and less involvement in administrative duties. In the United States, nursing assistants have traditionally been responsible for bathing and feeding the patient as well as assisting registered nurses as needed. However, U.S. hospitals have been shifting more nursing functions to nursing assistants as a cost-saving measure. These tasks include taking and recording vital signs, drawing blood, and conducting basic sterile procedures, although the nursing assistants do not necessarily receive any significant additional training (Berg and Frost 2005).

Mopping the Floor or Doing More?

Different models of labor division can also be found in housekeeping. Cleaning and other housekeeping tasks can be divided, in a "Taylorist" manner, into a multitude of jobs with narrowly confined duties, or they can be combined to form a broader job profile. Although hospitals in all countries have begun experimenting with redesigning these roles, the broader job profile remains the exception. This phenomenon is most evident in Denmark and, to a lesser extent, in France. In the other countries, cleaning patients' rooms is the primary occupation of a group of cleaners who are employed either by the hospital itself or by an external service provider.

Linking Work Organization and Labor Supply: Women and Migrants

A notable difference between the United States and Europe is the composition of the workforce. In both the United States and the European countries, the two target occupations are strongly female-dominated (more than 80 percent). Differences appear, however, when ethnicity is taken into account. Although we did not collect detailed comparable data on the number of employees from ethnic minority backgrounds, the case studies and a few national statistical sources clearly indicate that their share is relatively low in most of the European countries—not only compared to the United States but also compared to other low-wage occupations studied in this volume (on hotels, for example, see Vanselow et al., this volume). Is there a causal relation between the two phenomena—that is, between the low share of both low-wage work and immigrants in the workforce? An answer to this question needs to take into account not only the wider economic and sociopolitical context that shapes the labor supply for these occupations but also the choices in work organization. For cleaning staff, a Taylorist mode of organization with a low level of patient contact could allow hospitals to hire workers who are non-native speakers. In contrast, if cleaners perform other tasks that bring them in close contact with patients and their families (for example, helping with feeding, providing vases for flowers), then language skills become a key issue. Work organization could explain why in some countries, such as France and Denmark, we found hardly any migrant workers in our case studies. The higher the number and qualifications of the native workers competing for these jobs, the more real or attributed deficits in the (accredited) formal qualifications and language skills among immigrants will make a difference—particularly if employers also display a preference for skilled over unskilled employees, even for jobs at the lower end of the skill hierarchy. Thus, much depends on the extent to which employers can recruit among natives with the same or higher qualifications; this in turn is dependent on the alternatives available to potential job applicants, that is, on the availability and attractiveness of other jobs or other income sources provided by the tax and benefit system.

With regard to tax and benefit systems, Gautié and his colleagues (this volume) show that social assistance in most European countries is more generous than in the United States, and this generosity reduces the pressure on individuals to take up low-paid jobs. Generous social assistance has a particular impact on the labor supply of immigrants, given that this population tends to be overrepresented among recipients of social assistance (for lack of other resources, such as unemployment benefits). However, this factor is far from determining the share of immigrants within an occupational group, as the example of Germany shows: within the same tax and benefit system, the share of immigrants among cleaners differs strongly between East and West Germany. In East Germany, where the overall unemployment rate is very high, hospitals have no problems recruiting German nationals; in West Germany, on the other hand, women from ethnic minority backgrounds make up a large share—sometimes even the majority—of cleaning staff in hospitals. This difference is due not only to different regional unemployment rates but also to differences in the prevailing norms with regard to female labor market participation. In East Germany, the historically strong "dual-earner" norm is one of the factors that help to maintain the female labor supply at a generally higher level. Thus, high unemployment rates and culturally embedded norms help to mitigate the impact of the tax-benefit system on workforce composition.

Apart from the factors "pushing" female nationals to compete for these jobs, there are also a number of "pulling" factors linked to the jobs' relative attractiveness. In the European countries, as opposed to the United States, pay and working conditions for the two target occupations tend to be better in hospitals than in other parts of the health sector or in other low-skilled jobs. This might partly explain why even in a country like Denmark, with its low overall unemployment rate and high unemployment rate among immigrants, the latter are rather underrepresented in our two target occupations. On the other hand, the case of the United Kingdom illustrates that a job's relative attractiveness is not necessarily linked to particularly favorable working conditions but might also be due to a lack of other jobs that facilitate the reconciliation of work and family life. Evidence from U.K. case studies suggests that many women working in the target occupations are considerably overeducated or have higher than expected skill levels acquired in previous employment. One of the major reasons for occupational downgrading is that individuals in better-paid but highly constraining jobs decide to seek jobs that offer flexible (typically part-time) working hours that are more compatible with family commitments.

In sum, in our female-dominated occupations, the share of workers from ethnic minority backgrounds seems to be closely linked to gender issues and, more specifically, to the size and structure of the female labor supply for jobs at the lower end of the pay/skill hierarchy. A number of factors can help to increase the competition for these jobs from female nationals, including high unemployment rates, culturally embedded norms favoring female labor market participation, favorable working conditions (for example, relatively good pay), or the lack of other available jobs that enable workers to reconcile work and family life; however, these factors all have the same impact on immigrant workers.

These differences in work organization and labor force structure interact with the wage structure and the incidence of low-wage work.

THE INCIDENCE OF LOW-WAGE WORK, THE ROLE OF WAGE REGULATION, AND THE WAGE/BENEFIT STRUCTURE

As emphasized by Mason and Salverda (this volume), the incidence of low pay differs considerably across countries. This is also true of the hospital sector. Some peculiarities must be emphasized, however, namely, those concerning the binding power of collective agreements and civil servant status, which help to explain why, in some countries, the incidence of low wages in the hospital sector does not conform fully to the national pattern.

COMPARING THE INCIDENCE OF LOW-WAGE WORK

Using the common statistical definition, the incidence of low-wage work varies widely among cleaners and nursing assistants (table 8.3). In the United States and the United Kingdom, the incidence is very high among cleaners (more than 50 percent), but also high among nursing assistants (more than 20 percent). Germany occupies an intermediate position, with figures of 9 percent for nursing assistants and 20 percent for cleaners. France would appear to have a significantly lower incidence (less than 5 percent in both categories). Finally, in Denmark and the Netherlands, the incidence seems to be virtually zero except for cleaners in Denmark.

The data thus suggest an extraordinarily wide intercountry range in the prevalence of low-wage work in hospitals, ranging from high prevalence in the United States to negligible in Denmark. Such differences demonstrate the need for further empirical inquiry that includes an examination of country institutions, employer human resource practices, and patterns of work organization. Before proceeding, however, a number of reservations concerning the low-wage data in table 8.3 need to be examined.

First, the wage data for hospital employees exclude many low-wage workers defined as employed within a different industry sector, largely because of outsourcing. In Germany, for example, the number of hospital cleaners and other ancillary services personnel declined

Table 8.3 The Incidence of Low-Wage Work in the Hospital Sector
         Mid-2000s

	United States	United Kingdom	Germany	Netherlands[a]	France	Denma
Cleaners	50.4%	55%	19.6%	10%	3.2% (public) 4.4 (private)	11.7ᶜ
Nurse assistants	38.2	21	8.8	None	0.9 (public) 4.6 (private)	2.2
Labor market conditions	Tight	Tight	Soft	Tight	Soft	Tight

Source: Authors' calculations using national data (see note 1 at end of this chapter).
a. In general hospitals.

by more than 40 percent between 1991 and 2004, largely because of outsourcing. A similar trend can be observed in the United Kingdom. For neither country is it possible to estimate the volume of employment excluded from the statistics for the hospital sector, nor is it possible to estimate the aggregate earnings of hospital and outsourced employees combined. The result is that the data in table 8.3 are somewhat problematic.

A second caveat concerns country differences in providing public wage subsidies. In France, some jobs are subsidized in the form of public schemes for the unemployed and paid at the minimum wage. These jobs are only partially accounted for in the national data. If it is assumed that about 5 percent of cleaners' jobs are subsidized, this would double the incidence of low-wage work in France, taking it to 10 percent—which is still well below the figures for the United Kingdom, the United States, and Germany, but close to Denmark.

Taking these caveats into account, we may not be able to specify with precision the share of low-wage workers in hospitals in each country. Nevertheless, we can still usefully arrange the countries along a continuum from high to low incidence. This continuum is not far removed from the national picture as seen in chapter 2. It clearly opposes, on the one hand, the United States and the United

Kingdom and, on the other hand, the continental European countries, with Germany in an intermediate position.

THE ROLE OF INCLUSIVE AND EXCLUSIVE WAGE-SETTING SYSTEMS

To understand why the question of low wages is not necessarily a key issue in some European countries, we must enlarge the analysis to consider the wider dimensions of the wage-setting system. The major argument of this book is that the degree of "inclusiveness" of a country's system of wage-setting (and industrial relations, more broadly defined) has an important influence on the incidence of low-wage work. Bosch, Mayhew, and Gautié (this volume) describe the labor markets of Denmark, the Netherlands, and France as strongly inclusive in this respect, since they have a high level of collective bargaining coverage combined with the use of formal mechanisms to extend the terms of pay, benefits, and working conditions negotiated by unions and employers to firms or sectors where workers do not enjoy strong bargaining power. The United Kingdom and the United States, in contrast, are strongly exclusive, with only a minority of workers covered by collective bargaining and limited examples of governments using extension mechanisms to make the prevailing joint regulation of pay and other employment conditions more inclusive. Germany, which lies somewhere in between the two poles, has witnessed a dramatic shift toward a less inclusive system since the 1990s as many employers have withdrawn from sector wage agreements, mini-jobs and posted workers have increased in number, and employer outsourcing practices have become more widespread.

The argument put forward by Bosch, Mayhew, and Gautié (this volume) is that such institutions play a major role in explaining cross-national differences in low-wage work. This general argument is certainly supported by the data in this chapter. Indeed, the country ranking by incidence of low-wage work in hospitals correlates very well with the exclusive/inclusive nature of the corresponding wage-setting systems. However, inclusiveness at the national level is not necessarily matched in all six countries by inclusiveness at the level of the hospital sector.[3] Figure 8.1 shows that the three countries broadly defined as having inclusive country-level systems—France, Denmark, and the Netherlands—also have inclusive systems within

Figure 8.1 Inclusive and Exclusive Systems of Wage-Setting at the Country and Hospital Sector Levels

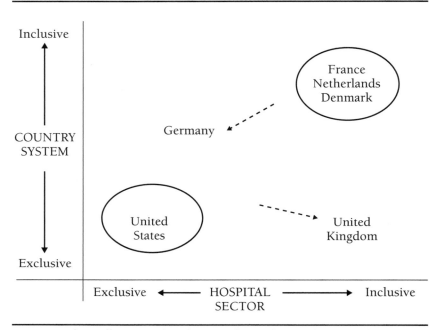

Sources: Authors' illustration based on Bosch, Mayhew, and Gautié (this volume) and Grimshaw et al. (2007).

the hospital sector, although they differ in nature. For example, since 1986, public-sector hospital employees in France have enjoyed full national civil servant status, which strengthens inclusiveness (albeit with the risk that the government can impose pay settlements below inflation, as it has in recent years). France also enjoys informal coordination between private- and public-sector hospitals. Unions organize across sectors, and in 2002 an agreement was signed on wage rate convergence. In the Netherlands, by contrast, while the degree of inclusiveness is similarly strong in terms of collective bargaining coverage, the hospital wage-setting arrangement is not integrated with other parts of the public sector. Since 1998, indeed, the agreement for health and social care has been further separated from the public sector as a whole, with separate agreements being concluded for each particular type of care.

The degree of inclusiveness in the U.S. hospital sector reflects that of the country as a whole. However, the picture for the United Kingdom, the other exclusive-type country, is rather different. Here we find that the hospital sector is atypical, with a relatively high level of collective bargaining coverage, centralized wage determination for all public-sector hospitals, a national integrated pay scale for all hospital employees (except doctors, dentists, and senior managers), and the quasi-extension of the national wage agreement to employees of companies that provide outsourced hospital services, such as cleaning (known as the "two-tier code"). Key dimensions of this strongly inclusive sectoral model have only recently been implemented and consequently cannot be expected to have shaped the earnings data reported here, although it is likely that future years will see a reduction in the incidence of low-wage work.

Finally, a note of explanation is needed for Germany, since, as figure 8.1 suggests, the hospital sector, like the country more generally, has experienced a steady fragmentation of the system of wage determination. Key elements of change include: the withdrawal of the Bundesländer (federal states) from negotiations on a new public-sector agreement, which introduced a common pay spine for manual and nonmanual hospital workers in both the federal and municipal sectors; the decision by the doctors' union, the Marburger Bund, to cease collaboration with the public-sector union Ver.di in negotiations with hospital employers; the breakaway of private-sector agreements (nonprofit and for-profit) from the settlements agreed to for public hospitals; and the separate regulation, through the collective agreement for the private cleaning industry, of terms and conditions for cleaners working in private subcontractor firms. The combined effect of these changes is likely to be an increase in the incidence of low-wage work in the sector.

THE WAGE HIERARCHY IN THE COLLECTIVE AGREEMENTS: THE LOW-WAGE THRESHOLD, THE SENIORITY PREMIUM, AND WAGE COMPRESSION BETWEEN CLEANERS, NURSING ASSISTANTS, AND NURSES

In the collective agreements of three countries—Denmark, the Netherlands, and France—the entry wage rate for a cleaner is at or slightly below the low-wage threshold, whereas in the United Kingdom and Germany the entry wage is pitched significantly below the threshold. This difference is compounded by the fact that, in Denmark, the Netherlands, and France, the collectively agreed wage scale (along with the minimum wage) in practice operates as a safety net. The pay scale for cleaners (and other groups) incorporates a seniority premium: with low staff turnover, cleaners can move quickly above the low-wage threshold. In these three countries, therefore, the strong inclusiveness of the national collective agreements clearly protects cleaners from low wages. In France, the situation is somewhat complicated by the fact that the pay scale collectively agreed to for the private for-profit hospitals includes lower rates than that for civil servants. Nevertheless, there is increasing evidence of coordination between the two agreements, and it is still possible to speak of inclusiveness.

Germany and the United Kingdom provide a contrasting scenario. In Germany, the collective agreement for public-sector hospitals in West Germany has the highest wage rates in the hospital sector. In East Germany, the public-sector agreement and, especially, the collective agreement covering private hospitals include lower wage rates. Nevertheless, even taking into account the most generous collective agreement, the entry wage for cleaners falls below the low-wage threshold. Fragmentation, exclusiveness, and the absence of a national minimum wage are the factors that explain the high incidence of low wages. In the United Kingdom, the entry rate also falls well below the low-wage threshold, and unlike the pay scale in the French collective agreement, the U.K. pay scale offers limited opportunity to escape low pay through seniority pay progression.

A second important observation from this intercountry comparison is that the wage differential between cleaners and nursing assistants differs considerably. In the United Kingdom, France, and Germany (where they exist), nursing assistants have a better wage career than cleaners, even if at the entry point the wage gap is not large. Hospitals in Denmark follow the national pattern, with greater wage compression than in the other countries.

For the United States, the only data available are median hourly wages. The cleaners' median wage is 91 percent of the nursing assistants' and 81 percent of the low-wage threshold. Seniority pay increments improve the position of low-paid cleaners and nursing assistants in the United States, although in non-union hospitals seniority pay is less generous than in European hospitals. Nursing assistants in the United States, as in Europe, have more extensive promotion opportunities than cleaners, who typically can advance only from cleaner 1 to cleaner 2, with a small increase in pay.

Nurses' wages must be analyzed also, since they are relevant to the division of labor between nurses and nursing assistants. As we have seen before (table 8.2), nursing assistants scarcely exist in the Netherlands and Germany. In both countries, the wage differential between nursing assistants and nurses (who are not graduates) is low. Hospitals prefer to hire nurses to cover the full range of tasks, including many of those undertaken by nursing assistants in the other countries. The wage differential is widest in France and the United Kingdom. Both countries train nurses up to the university degree level. This partly explains why the ratio of nurses to nursing assistants is lowest in these countries. Denmark occupies an intermediate position; there, as we discuss later, the nursing assistant job has been evolving. In the United States, median wages for nursing assistants are 44 percent of the median nurse's wage and 120 percent of the low-wage threshold. Whereas registered nurses require two years of community college or four years of university training, nursing assistants can become certified with as little as six weeks of training.

Thus, while entry wage rates fall below the low-wage threshold in some countries, the possibility of seniority-related pay increases for nursing assistants and, to a lesser extent, cleaners partly explains the low incidence of low-wage work compared to the other sectors considered in this book. A few bonus payments and one or two years of seniority are sufficient to cross the threshold. Indeed, as we show later, hospital work is attractive in part because seniority is generally high and turnover fairly low, so that many workers do climb up the pay scale; the familiar exceptions, once again, are the United States and workers in outsourced jobs in the European countries.

BASIC PAY AND THE SOCIAL WAGE

In addition to basic pay, a key issue for understanding low-wage work is the social wage, as emphasized in chapters 2 and 3, including pension conditions and entitlement to sickness pay and other benefits. The elements of the social wage vary across countries. In the United States, cleaners and nursing assistants typically have paid vacation, sick days, overtime pay, and some form of pension plan for full-time workers. The higher unionization rate among hospital workers (20 percent) compared with other sectors is one of the reasons why they enjoy better benefits. In the five European countries, bonuses for shift work or unsocial working hours can be as high as 20 to 50 percent of basic pay; the other benefits associated with a hospital job tend to follow the national framework. In some cases, however, hospitals provide more generous entitlements, often in accordance with the national collective agreements. In France, for example, civil servants in public hospitals enjoy better pensions than their counterparts in the private sector, and women working in care departments have the option of retiring at a relatively early age. Moreover, in both public- and private-sector hospitals in France, sickness leave duration (at full pay) is relatively generous compared to other sectors. Some French hospitals also provide nurseries for young children. In all six countries, pension rates are typically relatively generous, either because they fall under the public service scheme, as in France and Germany, or because of the supplementary pension schemes set up by hospitals (as in Denmark and the United Kingdom).

These social benefits, combined in some countries with wages significantly above the low-wage threshold, partly explain the attractiveness of hospital jobs. Even in countries with fairly tight labor markets, such as Denmark and the Netherlands, hospitals have little difficulty in recruiting staff, and turnover is low. This contrasts sharply with the American situation.

THE EXIT OPTIONS: SHIFTING THE BOUNDARIES OF THE CORE WORKFORCE

As stated in the previous section, the statistical incidence of low-wage work is highly dependent on the boundaries of the sector. Outsourcing and the use of temp agencies or atypical contracts are all practices used by hospitals to build a "second-tier" workforce. For hospitals, the objective is to manage the increased flexibility constraints produced by high patient turnover and the drive to maximize bed occupancy rates. They are also seeking to bear down on their wage bills, notably through outsourcing. In some cases, finally, hospitals are attempting, like enterprises in many other sectors, to refocus on their core business—the provision of medical care—and to delegate their other functions, particularly "hotel" services. Nevertheless, as the following section also shows, the separation between care functions and hotel functions is less simple than it seems and is frequently a source of tensions. The consequences have implications for workers' pay as well as their opportunities for mobility.

OUTSOURCING

The employer response of outsourcing a low-wage activity, such as hospital cleaning, is generally viewed as a "low-road" strategy associated with deteriorations in pay, career opportunities, and job security. Under pressure to reduce costs, hospitals may be willing to outsource workers to a specialist subcontractor firm that offers less generous rates of pay and may operate outside the protection of collective bargaining. Career prospects are contingent upon the employer's commitment to multi-skilling and the transparency of promotion ladders, but there is a risk that working in, say, a specialist cleaning firm reduces opportunities to progress to other hospital jobs that require different skills, such as nursing assistant or administrator. Moreover, outsourcing constitutes an obvious threat to job security—both at the outset, when the activity is subcontracted for the first time and the bond of job security with the hospital employer is broken, and subsequently with each round of recurrent subcontracting.

Our data show that outsourcing is not a universal practice in hospitals in the six countries. Differences in the degree of inclusiveness or exclusiveness in collective bargaining systems help explain the prevalence of outsourcing, but our data also reveal unanticipated "hybrid" examples of outsourcing. The six countries split between those where hospitals retain a relatively integrated model of service provision (delivering integrated hotel services alongside medical care), those that outsource hotel services, and a third group that outsource management roles only (table 8.4).

In the former group, without outsourcing, only two hospitals out of twenty-three investigated in Denmark, France, and the Netherlands outsourced some or all of their ancillary services. Limited use of outsourcing fits with the strongly inclusive systems of collective bargaining in these three countries, which reduce opportunities for hospitals to reduce costs through outsourcing. This institutional constraint on hospital managers can also be interpreted as a catalyst that encourages them to improve the efficiencies associated with in-house cleaning services. For example, managers in the Danish hospitals emphasized the inherent benefits of internalized provision, in-

Table 8.4 Case Study Evidence of Outsourcing Practices in the Six Countries

	Number of Hospitals Outsourcing Cleaning	Factors Constraining or Encouraging Outsourcing	Implications of Outsourcing for Employment Conditions
Denmark	0 of 9 hospitals	Expanded role of cleaner (hospital service assistant) limits possibilities for outsourcing jobs. Solidaristic and inclusive collective bargaining between sectors.	NA
France	1 of 8 hospitals	Examples of agreements with unions to exchange job cuts for services in-house. Example of outsourcing rationalized as measure to simplify hospital management structure.	Pay protected for transferred staff but loss of benefits. Possible emergence of two-tier conditions in subcontracting firm with lower pay for new recruits.
Germany	7 of 8 hospitals	Outsourcing to exploit lower costs of private cleaning sector collective agreement. Hospitals in less prosperous regions more likely to outsource. Division of job into narrow tasks facilitates outsourcing.	Not clear that pay is protected for transferring staff under TUPE. Pay in private cleaning up to 40 percent less than in public sector and problems of compliance. Outsourcing hinders career paths to better-paid jobs (for example, nurse assistants) in the hospital.

Country			
Netherlands	1 of 6 hospitals	Management desire for external flexibility.	Other collective agreements, lower wages, but fewer differences regarding the professional attitude, productivity, and working conditions than in the other countries.
United Kingdom	5 of 7 hospitals	Legal requirement to consider relative costs of external bids for ancillary services. Legal requirement to outsource to acquire new buildings financed by private capital. Public pressure to improve quality standards an obstacle to outsourcing.	Pay protected for transferring staff, but loss of generous public-sector pensions. Until 2005, two-tier conditions in subcontracting firm due to lower pay for new recruits. Outsourcing hinders career paths to better-paid jobs (for example, nurse assistants) in the hospital.
United States	1 of 16 hospitals[a] 0 of 6 hospitals[b] Most hospitals (for example, 5 of 6)[b] outsource the management of food services and housekeeping	Hospital objective to retain control over quality of employees and very limited potential for cost savings. Aim to utilize higher-caliber, specialist management from external firm.	Fewer days of annual leave, higher health insurance copayments. Better career prospects for managers across different hospitals, but no differences for hospital employees.

Source: Authors' calculations using national data (see note 1 at end of this chapter).
a. Appelbaum et al. (2003).
b. Erickcek, Houseman, and Kalleberg (2003). Other countries, see note 1.

cluding direct control over task flexibility, worker stability, and service quality. Moreover, managers had broadened cleaners' job descriptions—redefining them as "hospital service assistants"—thereby making it more difficult for external specialist firms to bid for the work. Interestingly, a Danish firm that was well known in the United Kingdom as one of the main hospital subcontractors was operating in some of our U.K. case study hospitals but not in Denmark.

In the other three countries, there is extensive use of outsourcing, despite differences in the inclusiveness or exclusiveness of collective bargaining (table 8.4). However, the data do point to considerable variation in the factors influencing outsourcing, the operational model of outsourcing, and the implications for employment conditions. In Germany, hospital managers outsourced cleaners either to a subsidiary company (a "Service-GmbH") or to a different company; in both cases, the cleaning firm was covered by a less generous collective bargaining agreement. The one German case study hospital that did not outsource cleaning was located in a relatively prosperous region and benefited from a greater proportion of privately insured patients, whose higher payments reduced cost pressures. In the United Kingdom, outsourcing of cleaning was either the result of 1980s legislation obliging hospitals to put certain ancillary services out to competitive tender or associated with new building projects financed by private capital that required (until 2006) the outsourcing of all ancillary services. It is worth noting that two of the seven U.K. hospitals investigated had retained cleaning in-house and that this strategy was strongly supported by the HR management team. For example, one HR director stated that, while he had a legal duty to consider outsourcing, "there's a real issue that you should never compromise quality for what would be relatively marginal financial gain. . . . There have been so many [outsourcing] horror stories from different organizations."

In both Germany and the United Kingdom, the case study evidence suggests that outsourcing of the cleaning function worsens employment conditions, although there has been a reversal of fortunes in the United Kingdom. In Germany, outsourced cleaners are covered by a generally binding collective agreement that applies to the cleaning sector. Consequently, cleaning workers still enjoy the protection of what is a relatively inclusive system of employment regulation. The evidence reveals problems of compliance, however, among some private-sector cleaning firms that fail to provide pension schemes. Even without that, the total pay package is reduced by up to 30 percent compared with cleaners employed by public hospitals. The hourly rate for West German regions in the 2005 private cleaning industry agreement was 7.87 compared to 8.28 to 11.73 in the new public hospitals agreement (TvÖd, or Tarifvertrag für den öffentlichen Dienst [Collective Agreement for Public Sector Employees]). In the United Kingdom, although pay for transferred staff is protected under TUPE legislation (the European Acquired Rights Directive), pensions are not included and TUPE does not apply to new recruits. Until 2005, new recruits hired by subcontracting firms tended to be offered less favorable terms and conditions; that practice created what the public-sector unions have dubbed a "two-tier workforce." Following pressure from public-sector trade unions, however, the government introduced a new code of practice (dubbed the "two-tier code"). It applied first to local government and then was extended to other areas of the public sector, including health. It requires private-sector service providers to offer terms and conditions to new recruits that are "not less favorable" than those of transferred employees covered by TUPE legislation. In practice, it amounts to an extension of the public-sector hospitals' national pay structure to all workers employed by subcontractor firms, and it has significantly boosted the terms and conditions for many thousands of outsourced cleaners (and other ancillary services workers). Besides pay, outsourcing also shapes career paths, and the evidence from Germany and the United Kingdom suggests that outsourced cleaners find it more difficult to gain access to better-paid jobs in the hospital, such as nursing assistant or low-level administrative posts.

U.S. hospitals have adopted a hybrid outsourcing model. The data suggest that it is relatively rare for a hospital to outsource its entire housekeeping, but fairly typical to outsource the management of housekeeping services. This practice ostensibly allows hospitals to bring in higher-caliber managers than would be available through direct employment, partly because of the difficulties that hospitals experience in recruiting managers to posts where career ladders are limited. The practice also allows hospitals to retain control over the quality of their cleaning staff, directly managing their recruitment, retention, and skill development. There were no differences observed in work organization for employees when management was outsourced, but there was evidence of job reductions (usually through natural attrition) and an emphasis on performance discipline and the promise of improved productivity. Interestingly, a similar practice has been introduced in some U.K. hospitals, with supervisory and management posts being outsourced and nonsupervisory staff retained in-house. This "retention of employment" model was practiced in one of the seven U.K. case study hospitals and was said by managers to be more advantageous than total outsourcing, since it protected the generous public-sector pensions of lower-paid nonsupervisory staff, provided them with direct career paths within the hospital (for example, to nursing assistant posts), and also opened up the managerial career path for mid- and high-level managers of ancillary services. Cleaners also preferred this new arrangement. As one of them put it, "I'd rather stay with the [public sector] because at least you've got something substantial there. Because these contract people, they're not very good. Some of our women have worked for ISS Mediclean before, like in Asda [Wal-Mart], and they're a terrible firm."

In sum, the data suggest that hospitals in countries with relatively stable forms of inclusive collective bargaining make limited use of outsourcing as a flexibility strategy. Minimum wages set at a relatively high level are one barrier to outsourcing (as in France, for example), and high collective bargaining coverage is another. The evidence from France, Denmark, and the Netherlands (as well as the United Kingdom) also demonstrates the ability of trade unions to fight against outsourcing policies.

We would expect countries with either exclusive systems or inclusive systems that have fragmented bargaining structures to make greater use of outsourcing. We find, however, that the extent of outsourcing in these systems is variable. German hospitals make the greatest use of total outsourcing of cleaning services, which can be explained by the opportunities they have to outsource workers into weaker and less generous collective agreements. Hybrid outsourcing practices focusing on the outsourcing of the management of cleaning services are found in the United Kingdom and the United States. In the exclusive U.S. system, wages for hospital cleaners are relatively low and comparable to those of other cleaning service workers. Contrary to expectations, the cost benefits of outsourcing are not as great as in the high-paying, public-sector hospitals in other countries. There is more incentive in the United States to outsource the management function as a spur to improving the productivity of in-house cleaning services. Although the United Kingdom has an exclusive system at the national level, wage setting within the hospital sector is more inclusive. Outsourcing of cleaning workers continues to be a relatively common practice, encouraged by the government's use of private capital to fund hospital building and maintenance programs. In contrast to Germany, however, there have been innovative efforts recently to strengthen the inclusiveness of existing collective bargaining agreements, as in the two-tier code and the retention-of-employment approach, which encourages the outsourcing of supervisory and management staff only.

TEMPORARY AGENCY WORKERS

A second possible source of external flexibility is the use of temporary agency workers in hospitals. Each of the six countries has its own regulatory system governing agency work, and it is these national systems that shaped the frequency of use of agency work in the hospitals in our study (see Bosch, Mayhew, and Gautié, this volume; and Arrowsmith 2006). One important finding from our research is that the use of external agency work is far less common than the use of internally managed pools of temporary, on-call workers (table 8.5). In fact, it is only in the United States that hospitals make significant use of external temporary work agencies to fill vacancies for cleaners and nursing assistants. There is evidence of limited use in France for cleaners in private-sector hospitals (where external agencies seem to provide the main port of entry) and as a backup strategy for filling nursing assistant vacancies in U.K. hospitals. The reluctance to hire from external agencies is illustrated by the comments of a deputy chief nurse at one of the U.K. hospitals: "Some of the quality of the people you get through the agencies is very poor, and I don't know what a lot of those agencies do in terms of their selection procedures, but I don't think they're at a level we would like them to be." In general, the use of external agencies by hospitals in Europe is confined to sourcing specialist technical and professional medical staff.

In the United States, interviews with hospital managers suggest numerous reasons for using external agencies, but it is unclear why internally managed pools are not more developed. The reasons for using external agencies include recruitment difficulties, the slow and bureaucratic hospital hiring process, and the value of screening agency workers for prospective job posts because they are so much easier to dismiss. In several U.S. hospitals, agency workers earned

Table 8.5 Use of Internal and External Temporary Workers in the Six Countries

| | Internal or External Source of Temporary Workers | | |
	Cleaners	Nurse Assistants	Issues
Denmark	Internal agency	Internal agency	External agencies used only irregularly. Cover also provided by extending hours of incumbent staff.
France	Internal pool (public hospitals) External agency (private hospitals)	Internal pool	Private hospitals use external agencies primarily for qualified nurses and technicians and only rarely for nursing assistants.
Germany	None	Internal pool and external agency in one case	
Netherlands	Limited use	Internal pool	Regular contracts with external temporary staff are not permitted in hospitals (mainly used for specialist health professionals).
United Kingdom	None	Internal agency	Internal agency takes two forms: local pool managed by the hospital and a national agency managed by the NHS.
United States	External agency	External agency	Agencies used to circumvent the slow hiring processes in hospitals, to facilitate screening and quick dismissals, and to respond to recruitment difficulties. Morale problems are caused by pay differentials.

Source: Please refer to note 1 at the end of this chapter.

more than regular workers, and such pay differentials caused resentment. Also, perceptions of unreliability caused one hospital to reduce its use of agency workers by offering regular workers overtime, bringing their total working time to sixty hours per week.

Evidence from the hospitals in Europe suggests that there is value in establishing an internal pool of reserve workers, in terms of both cost-effectiveness and employment conditions. The examples of the Netherlands and the United Kingdom are illustrative. All six hospitals in the Dutch research used an internal "flexpool" to fill nurse vacancies, supplemented by offers of overtime to regular staff.[4] According to hospital managers, the advantages included relative cost and an ability to control service quality by controlling the selection of staff for the pool. Four of the U.K. hospitals investigated used an internal pool, and three contracted with a national, public-sector agency governed within the National Health Service (NHS). The NHS not-for-profit agency was established in 2004 in response to concern about the escalating costs of for-profit agencies, inefficient management of some hospitals' internal pools, and inconsistent pay policies. It charges half the fee of a for-profit agency and works closely with hospital management to reduce spending on temporary cover. Agency workers also receive terms and conditions equivalent to those for other NHS workers (including the pension scheme and access to training).

Nonstandard Labor Contracts

France provides an example of a third way between outsourcing and the use of temp agencies. Here the main tool of flexibility is extensive use of nonstandard labor contracts. The French case studies reveal that, despite protections afforded by civil servant status, public hospitals use fixed-term contracts of varying length, primarily for cleaners. In some case study hospitals, approximately half the total cleaner workforce was employed on fixed-term contracts. Private hospitals also use fixed-term contracts, albeit less extensively in those visited by our research team. In both sectors, employees with nonstandard contracts do not enjoy the same rights and entitlements as regular employees, such as access to seniority pay increments and wage premiums. This is a good example of an "exit option" that bypasses collective agreements. These contracts are also a screening device for the hospitals, which can use them to select those who will be included in the core workforce at a later stage. Although many fixed-term workers lose their jobs, for others, a temporary contract is a bridge to a permanent position. These contracts act as a waiting list; some workers may stay on it for five years, or even longer, in the hope of being recruited as a permanent worker with civil servant status.

This bypassing process is also sometimes reinforced by government employment policy. In France, subsidized jobs for the long-term unemployed (fixed-term, part-time contracts paid at the minimum wage) are used by public-sector hospitals. In local areas with high unemployment, hospital managers are obliged to fill a quota of such jobs, and sometimes they may make more extensive use of these contracts in order to recruit higher numbers at lower cost. A comparable example of the impact of public policy on the labor market is the "mini-job" widely used by German hospitals (and subcontractor companies) to recruit cleaners.

ENHANCING WORK ORGANIZATION AND CAREER OPPORTUNITIES

Reorganizing work is another way in which hospitals in all of our countries have responded to increasing competitive pressures. In some cases, it is a reaction to difficulties in recruiting cleaners and nursing assistants (as well as doctors and nurses) that have caused certain tasks to be transferred to other levels. It is also a response to technological developments (for example, some modern equipment can easily be operated by a nursing assistant). Finally, work reorganization is a way for hospitals to support their attempts to refocus on their core business— delivering the most advanced health care to patients, who will then leave the hospital to be cared for elsewhere. Hospitals' choices of work organization strategies reflect national education and training systems and labor market conditions, as well as the nature of national collective bargaining models and, of course, national health policies.

Cleaners: Between the "Hostel" and the "Care" Models

As a general rule, work organization in this occupational area is characterized by dynamics of change that are even stronger than those for nursing assistants. The outcomes are not always stable, however, because hospitals tend to adapt their work organization models by trial and error: they might redesign occupational roles and after a while return to the model previously in place.

In the United States, one strategy adopted by hospitals in response to the tighter labor market for low-skilled employees in the second half of the 1990s was to create multi-skilled positions for housekeepers by combining tasks from several functional areas (for example, patient transport, cleaning, food service) into one profile. The aim of this reorganization was to improve job satisfaction for these workers, thereby reducing absenteeism and high turnover among housekeeping staff and the related direct costs of recruiting and training (see Appelbaum et al. 2003). It is unclear how many U.S. hospitals made use of these "patient care associates" or "service support associates" (two frequently used titles), but several national consulting firms recommended this approach. However, at the time of the research done by Appelbaum and her colleagues (2003), some hospitals had already reverted to more Taylorist forms of work organization because of the costs associated with implementing the restructured jobs and management issues around patient care. Patient care associates were often employed with minimal training, tended to do only certain tasks well, and lacked the social skills necessary to interact with patients. In addition, patients were uncomfortable with having their food delivered by the same person who cleaned their room. Also, nurse managers lacked knowledge of the housekeeping function and did not use patient care associates efficiently (see Berg and Frost 2005, 667).

Contrary to what might be expected, however, differences in the tightness of labor markets and in labor turnover cannot fully explain the differences between countries in the reorganization of housekeeping, as the example of the United Kingdom shows.

Denmark is yet another example, although in the opposite direction. Despite a lack of recruitment problems, Denmark is the country where the enhancement of job organization has been pursued most systematically. Many hospitals have implemented a redesigned profile for the position of "hospital service assistant," a move that was encouraged by the introduction of a new national vocational training program some fifteen years ago. A hospital service assistant's job consists of cleaning, bed-making, linen service, replenishing supplies, cooking and serving meals, moving patients, and maintaining patients' personal hygiene. Although the traditional model of work organization persists in some hospitals, many seem to have implemented the new concept and have retrained their employees (usually with one or two years of supplementary training at a vocational school, depending on previous work experience). In this case, one aim might have been to improve job and service quality for the employee groups involved, but the reorganization was also a way of dealing with the general transfer of tasks from higher to lower positions in the skill hierarchy that was necessary because of shortages of doctors and qualified nurses. Apart from the transfer of tasks from nurses to nursing assistants, there has been a similar transfer in some hospitals from nursing assistants to hospital service assistants. In these cases, hospital service assistants have taken over some of the nursing assistants' routine tasks, such as replenishing supplies and handing out food. As a result of this reorganization, the number of porters and specialized cleaners in hospitals has decreased significantly, and they have been replaced, at least partially, by hospital service assistants, with a better pay scale. The implementation of this new model was fully supported by the unions. It was a way, on the one hand, of countering the risk of outsourcing and, on the other, of improving skills and wages.

The same developments were observed in some case studies in the Netherlands and the United Kingdom. In the Netherlands, one hospital was implementing a new "joint assist occupation" in an attempt to integrate the assisting, cleaning, and nutrition functions. The three aims of the enhanced work organization project were to raise employee and patient satisfaction, to gain greater insight into costs, and, if possible, to obtain a financial benefit. After nine months, the majority of employees were satisfied, and nurses saw working with an assistant as innovative and an improvement over their previous situation. Nurses were performing considerably fewer assist tasks and, consequently, had more time for patients. Nutritionist assistants, however, proved to be unhappy about exchanging the care and nutritional aspects of their jobs for general hospitality and cleaning tasks. Patients appeared to be rather pleased with the innovation. It was difficult to measure the overall costs of introducing the assistant position. However, the move seems to have been a positive one.

In the United Kingdom, three of the seven hospitals had introduced the new post of "ward housekeeper," and the private firms in three hospitals had introduced a similar new role, the "patient services assistant" or "ward steward." These new roles were introduced nationally with the aim of improving the patient environment and lowering rates of hospital-acquired infections. Their duties involve serving drinks, arranging flowers, and generally keeping the patient area tidy. They are defined as higher posts on the wage grid and thus potentially provide a new career path for cleaners, However, while cleaners welcomed the potential to earn higher pay, they did not believe that the housekeeper role was of a higher value in terms of the duties required. Here a higher incidence of recruitment problems did not lead hospitals to adopt an effective enhanced model of work organization; instead, improvements in job quality focused mainly on better remuneration.

These new models highlight the difference between a "hotel and office" model, in which cleaners only clean and have little if any patient contact, and a more integrated model in which they also provide certain services for patients. The second model involves more vocational training (except in the United States) and helps to up-skill jobs; these enhanced jobs are sometimes also better-paid. The choice between these two models is often linked to considerations about the quality of cleaning. In the United Kingdom, there has been a lot of debate about the decline in hospital cleaning standards and the increase in hospital-acquired infections. This decline has sometimes been attributed to the poor quality of outsourced work and the lack of cooperation between care staff (nurses and nursing assistants) and cleaning staff.

Nevertheless, there seem to be big differences in terms of the job quality and job satisfaction associated with these forms of work organization. One of the rather surprising results of a survey of employees in the U.S. case study hospitals is that work organization and job redesign had little impact on employee job satisfaction. Rather, employees complained about increased workloads; consequently, inadequate staffing levels proved to be a more important factor in determining job satisfaction. This can be explained by the wider context and the goals underlying the work redesign efforts, since they were specifically intended to reduce staffing levels by increasing individual workloads. As Peter Berg and Ann Frost (2005, 676) argue, "The jobs held by these workers are so poorly paid, so physically demanding, and so unrewarding that adjusting their contours does little to ameliorate the situation." This contrasts with the situation in Denmark, where hospital service workers report high job satisfaction, even though they experience their jobs as highly stressful. Moreover, as emphasized in some of the interviews with assist staff and housekeepers in Denmark, the Netherlands, and France, they differentiated themselves from hotel housekeepers, emphasizing their pride in providing patient services. This also explains the greater attractiveness of these jobs in hospitals, even in tight labor markets.

Another consequence of the choice of work organization is the opportunity it provides for mobility among cleaners. In Denmark, for example, the new ward assistant positions are better-paid and require more training. Nevertheless, few of them are able to move to nursing assistant positions, access to which is difficult because of the high levels of qualification required. In France, the traditional organization of the broad cleaning function, which required a high level of co-operation with nursing assistants, provided a possible route into nursing assistant training school (with wage and training costs paid by the hospital) and thence into nursing assistant jobs. In some of the case study hospitals, it had been quite common for five to ten cleaners to take this path each year. It was also a way for hospitals to meet their needs for qualified nursing assistants. At the time the studies were carried out, this path was disappearing because hospitals were concentrating their training funds on nurses. Since then, however, it has been opened up again as a result of national negotiations with the unions. Moreover, a new way of acquiring the nursing assistant's qualification through the accreditation of work experience combined with shorter training courses has been introduced, with some success. This also provides cleaners (and the unions) with a strong incentive to defend the integrated, in-ward model of the cleaning function as the best way to acquire work experience.

Nursing Assistants: Reinforcing the Second Portal?

In some of the countries investigated, the job of nursing assistant and the associated skills are also changing. The best example is Denmark. Although the share of nursing assistants has fallen, the nursing assistant position was included in a comprehensive transfer of tasks from higher to lower levels in the skill hierarchy that—in contrast to the U.S. case—was accompanied by an up-skilling process for all employee groups involved. To offset the lack of doctors and nurses, nursing assistants at some of the Danish case study hospitals received additional training to enable them to distribute drugs, catheterize patients, and carry out other nursing tasks, such as accompanying doctors on their rounds. Prior to this, a new certification for nursing assistants was introduced in 1992, and a lot of nursing assistants undertook vocational training programs in order to qualify for the new certificate. It is now no longer possible to obtain a nursing assistant job without the new certificate, which requires a training program of thirty-four months, of which a minimum of fifty-six weeks is theoretical.

In France, changes in the skill mix are less evident, since the nurse to nursing assistant ratio has remained more or less stable. Nevertheless, the process of eliminating nursing assistants without qualifications has been ongoing since the beginning of the 1980s. First, job vacancies caused by retirements are filled by qualified nursing assistants. Second, as in Denmark, a strong vocational policy has been developed in order to train unqualified nursing assistants. Furthermore, most of the case studies show that nursing assistants' tasks are increasingly overlapping those of nurses.

In the United Kingdom, where the "third portal" (unqualified nursing assistants) is dominant, the nursing assistants in all of the case study hospitals were being encouraged to take the National Vocational Qualification Level 2 (NVQ2) in care.[5] There were also several examples of new higher-band posts that required NVQ3 skills, and these were being offered as possible paths of progression for band 2 assistant nurses. For example, two hospitals had introduced the new role of "junior doctor's assistant." These were assistant nurses who were on-call and trained to assist junior doctors by carrying out routine procedures such as cannulation and phlebotomy. Also, four hospitals had introduced the new post of "assistant practitioner" for assistant nurses who wished to further their career but without taking the academic route into nursing. This post, which attracted higher rates of pay, involved completing an NVQ3 plus a two-year foundation degree and qualified the person to carry out procedures such as venepuncture and ECG (electrocardiogram) recording. Despite these opportunities, there were also obstacles to progression. First, several interviewees had completed the NVQ3 qualification but had not been promoted to a band 3 post because promotion occurred only when a post became available. Unsurprisingly, therefore, we found evidence of dissatisfaction among those assistant nurses who had been funded, and encouraged, to complete a level 3 qualification but were still being paid at the same rate as those with a level 2 or those with no qualification at all. A second obstacle to progression was in part a response to this issue, combined with cost pressures on the funding for training provision and on the pay bill. In some hospitals, we discovered, managers had changed their strategy toward skill development and during 2005 restricted opportunities to complete a level 3 qualification to those who either were occupying a role defined as requiring level 3 skills or had been earmarked for a forthcoming band 3 post vacancy.

Some similar trends were found in the U.S. hospitals. To improve outcomes and reduce costs, hospitals frequently redefined nursing assistant (and registered nurse) job responsibilities and sought to integrate nursing assistants more fully into the patient care team. Because of the wage and education differences between nursing assistants and registered nurses—registered nurses typically earned over $20 per hour—many hospitals had shifted routine tasks from registered nurses to nursing assistants. These tasks included taking vital signs, drawing blood, and conducting basic sterile procedures. The next change in nursing assistant work was to integrate nursing assistants more fully into a specific team of care providers. As such, in contrast to the previous work organization model, nursing assistants could now work with a single registered nurse (or two) and conduct a broader set of tasks for these nurses' patients. Nevertheless, two key differences with the European countries must be emphasized. First, the use of nursing assistants in this capacity was the result of individual hospital strategic decisions, not of a national coordinated public policy. Second, although enhancing, the job tasks of nursing assistants generally demand no more than additional on-the-job training—they do not necessarily require additional formal certification.

A GENERALIZED INCREASE IN WORKLOAD

Low-wage work is often considered low-productivity work. Low-wage workers are typically thought to be low-skilled workers who make a small contribution to output. The information gathered for this study challenges that notion. It is virtually impossible to conduct a detailed comparison of work intensity and labor productivity given the diversity of forms of work organization in our sample—for example, nurses with or without responsibility for cleaning and household tasks and cleaners with varying degrees of specialization. Depending on the hospital in question, the specification for a cleaner's job might be to clean thirty to forty rooms in half a working day or 150 square meters per hour; alternatively, one cleaner might be allocated for every ten rooms and expected to combine cleaning duties with other tasks.

Despite the absence of detailed data, a whole set of indicators, including employee interviews, strongly suggest that work in hospitals has intensified. This intensification is a response to the pressures being exerted on hospitals, notably those of a budgetary nature. However, it is also a consequence of the reduction in patient stays.

In virtually all the countries, the number of cleaners has declined more quickly than the number of beds, and to a greater extent than can be explained by outsourcing alone. This is the case in Denmark, where outsourcing is not used, in the Netherlands, and in France. The same is true of nursing auxiliaries, whose numbers have either fallen (Denmark, Germany) or stagnated (the United Kingdom). The number of fully qualified nurses has increased as a result of job substitution and skill upgrading; however, this has not been sufficient to cover the increasing workload. In all the countries, the length of hospital stays has fallen, and the bed occupancy rate has remained very high. This increase in the patient turnover rate has several consequences for our two occupational categories. In the early part of their stay, patients are more dependent on the nursing care provided. Nurses and nursing assistants must check patients frequently, and help with mobility is more frequently required in the early days of treatment. Moreover, employees frequently report that patients have become more demanding, in terms of both service quality and information about their disease and the treatment. "The desire for information has increased, which is good, in some ways, but also takes up more time," said a head nurse in a German hospital. The higher patient turnover increases the administrative burden, particularly for nurses and nursing assistants, as in Denmark, for example. Rooms have to be cleaned and beds made up more frequently. And the cleaning process must follow stricter rules, as part of the fight against hospital-acquired diseases. Despite technological improvements, such as floor-cleaning machines and electric beds, cleaners' workloads are also increasing. This is even more apparent in the case of outsourcing. Thus, in Germany, the increase in the performance standard (150 to 260 square meters per hour, sometimes far in excess of the recommendations of the specialist institutions) is particularly noticeable in outsourced services.

Several surveys confirm this phenomenon. In a survey of working conditions carried out in the Netherlands, 63 percent of hospital workers said their work was physically hard, and 44 percent said it was emotionally hard, both figures being above the national average (Bekker et al. 2004). In France, national surveys show a sharp deterioration in the perception of working conditions in hospitals between 1998 and 2003 (Le Lan and Baubeau 2004). This phenomenon was aggravated by the introduction of the thirty-five-hour week: insufficient new jobs were created to make up for the hours lost.

Some German employers have even adopted a voluntary strategy of reducing weekly working hours in order to make sure that their employees are able to withstand the stresses and strains of their jobs. A manager of a public hospital's subsidiary service company, for instance, explained why the company recruits new staff only on part-time contracts: "Simply because we assume that someone who works 50, 65, or 75 percent of the day can manage the workload far better than someone who has to work 100 percent."

Nevertheless, the perception of the workload, and of its consequences, differed from country to country. In the employee interviews and the case studies, two benchmarks were used to assess hospital work. The first was linked to the previous career trajectories of cleaners and nursing assistants. Some had experience of factory work, work in private households, or office cleaning jobs. Some chose hospital work because it enabled them to strike a better balance between family life and paid work (United Kingdom, France, the Netherlands). As a general rule, they tended to judge working conditions in hospitals more favorably than their previous experiences. For the other benchmark, hospital work was contrasted with other areas of care work and home help services or with other unskilled female jobs. Here too, most of the indicators were positive. In general, hospital work offered better pay levels, except in the United States and, to a lesser degree, the United Kingdom. Working conditions, particularly working hours, were often regarded as more favorable or more predictable, with the exception of outsourced services. In addition, work involving patient contact was valued more highly by hospital workers. Those integrated into nursing teams valued cooperation with other staff members and the team atmosphere highly. This was particularly true for nursing assistants, for ward assistants in Denmark, the Netherlands, and France, and for most of the cleaners in France and, to a lesser degree, in the United Kingdom and Germany. In these countries, hospital work remained attractive and turnover was rather low. In the U.K. case studies, however, arduous working conditions were one explanation offered for the high turnover rate among cleaners ill prepared for the hospital environment. The U.S. case studies and survey of 589 employees also showed that the work was perceived to be physically demanding and that workers felt that they did not have sufficient resources to do it properly (Berg and Frost 2005). The demanding work of nursing assistants and the low value placed on cleaning in hospitals relative to other environments, such as hotels, contributes to a high turnover rate of cleaners and nursing assistants in U.S. hospitals. Annual turnover rates of 50 percent are not uncommon. At one U.S. hospital, the turnover rate for cleaners approached 100 percent for the month of June.

TRENDS: WAGES MORE OR LESS SHELTERED FROM COMPETITIVE PRESSURES

If we return now to the question of pay and adopt a dynamic perspective, several different groups of countries can be identified by combining wage trends with the other structural changes in work organization, training, and workload.

Two countries (the Netherlands and Denmark) are clearly pursuing the high-road model. In Denmark, a restructuring of the pay scales has led to an average pay increase of between 3 and 4 percent. In the Netherlands, a reform of the job classification system introduced in the year 2000 led to pay increases for nurses and other categories. These pay policies go hand in hand, as we have seen, with low use of outsourcing and up-skilling policies for cleaners and, in Denmark, nursing assistants.

France seems to be following a slight downward trend. On the one hand, the number of workers who do not belong to the core hospital workforce (non–civil servants employed in public hospitals on fixed-term contracts) is fairly high, and these workers enjoy fewer benefits. On the other hand, the general civil service pay policy has resulted in below-inflation pay rises and a relative decline in pay compared with the private, profit-making hospital sector, particularly for the lower job categories, which were relatively advantaged. The gap between the public and private hospital sectors, however, is still on the order of 10 percent in favor of the former. Nevertheless, to avoid an entry pay level below the minimum wage, the civil service pay scale was revised for the lowest categories between 2005 and 2007, with a slight increase in the basic wage at the entry level and a longer wage trajectory. And as the nurse qualification and position in the collective agreements is to be upgraded, it is highly probable that the position of the nursing assistant will also be upgraded in the future. In that sense, France will remain close to the Netherlands and Denmark.

Germany and the United Kingdom are two radically different cases. In Germany, pay levels have been cut very significantly as a result of outsourcing and changes to the collective agreements. This is the case in church-run hospitals, where collectively agreed pay rates for cleaners have fallen by up to 25 percent. Moreover, public hospitals now offer a starting wage for cleaners that is only very slightly higher than the wages paid by outside companies providing outsourced cleaning services. Combined with outsourcing, the changes constitute a low-road approach similar to that adopted by the so-called liberal market model countries. However, nursing assistants are not affected by this development. The steady decrease in their numbers and their replacement by nurses reflects hospitals' search for internal flexibility based on an increase in skill levels.

The trend in the United Kingdom is in the opposite direction. After years of efforts to decentralize wage setting and cuts in the NHS budget, recent years have seen the renaissance of a national wage-setting system and substantial increases in the hospital budget. The changes to the pay determination system (Department of Health 2004) introduced new rules and scales that granted a one-off pay rise of up to 20 percent for an experienced cleaner, or 7 percent for a newly recruited nursing assistant. The workers interviewed were of the view that they were paid relatively well, particularly compared with other sectors. Nevertheless, the reforms initially posed a threat to generous shift bonuses and wage premiums for working unsocial hours, although strong trade union resistance may prove successful in reaching a compromise that retains generous bonuses and premiums for low-wage workers. Consequently, it is likely that the incidence of low-wage work will diminish, particularly once this reform combines with others that seek to improve access to training courses. In this case, the U.K. hospital sector would paradoxically be drawing closer to the continental model just as Germany has begun to depart from it.

The wage trends for hospital nursing assistants and cleaners in the

United States have followed the overall downward pressure on real wages for low-wage workers. From 2000 to 2006, median real wages for cleaners declined by 14.5 percent, from $11.70 to $10.00 per hour. This drop can be explained in part by the decline in unionized workers. Although the union wages are still higher than the non-union wages, the median wage for cleaners in 2006 mirrored the median non-union wage of $10 rather than the union wage of $12.06 per hour. With regard to nursing assistants, the median wage for this group has remained virtually unchanged since 2000, at $11 per hour, and declined by less than 1 percent from 2000 to 2006. Unionized nursing assistants, however, have seen a drop in their wages. The median union wage declined 9.4 percent, from $14.04 to $12.72 per hour, between 2000 and 2006 (Current Population Survey calculations). And despite a number of attempts to improve work organization that we came across in our case studies, there is nothing to suggest that high-road strategies are gaining any ground.

CONCLUSION

The starting point for this chapter was an observation that, on the face of it, might have seemed somewhat surprising. Hospitals that are fairly similar in size and range of services and subject to similar economic and technological pressures have developed very different strategies for carrying out two basic tasks—cleaning and nursing—that are, in theory at least, the same in all hospitals.

It turns out that hospitals are fully integrated into national employment models; in some cases, they exacerbate or exaggerate the characteristics and dynamics of those models, while in others they attenuate them somewhat. In countries where the incidence of low-wage work is high (the United States and the United Kingdom) or increasing (Germany), this is also the case in hospitals. In countries where it is moderate or low (France, Denmark, and the Netherlands), it is also low in hospitals and often lower than in other similar sectors or jobs. Over and above these marked differences in the incidence of low-wage work, however, the other aspects of employment and working conditions—employment status, work organization, the use of skilled or unskilled labor—also vary considerably from one country to another. The only point the countries have in common is the intensification of cleaners' and nursing assistants' work, although even this intensification takes different forms: some hospitals adopt more Taylorist strategies, and others emphasize enriching and extending the scope of work. The empirical evidence presented in this chapter underlines the close interrelationship of wages and the other aspects of working conditions. Wages tend to be low *because* of specific forms of work organization, training, and so on, while work organization tends to be enhanced *because* the opportunity costs of lowering wages are too high. The empirical evidence reveals the difficulties associated with strategies that target just one side of this equation, while at the same time it shows that institutions and strategies that have an impact on both sides of the equation can lead to the establishment of virtuous or vicious circles.

As in other industries studied in this book, Denmark offers an example of a virtuous circle: a low incidence of poorly paid work owing to strong collective regulation of all wages, few if any exit options, a reorganization of work supported by the trade unions, which has driven up workforce skills, and extensive use of training. The Netherlands is close to this model, albeit with a few small differences. Here too, the incidence of low-wage work is low, with collective regulation playing its role. Task enrichment has been implemented for cleaners, although in a less rigorous way and on more of a case-by-case basis. On the other hand, the absence of nursing assistants reflects a preference for a decidedly high-skill approach to nursing tasks. Although the case studies did not reveal any exit options, the extensive use of part-time jobs with very short hours and on-call jobs could be regarded as a functional equivalent. However, this is consistent with the dominant national model of women's employment. Although it does not consistently display all these characteristics, France is similar in many respects to these two countries: it has a low incidence of low-wage work, uses strategies for driving up skill levels in both categories, and enjoys high levels of job stability. Nevertheless, there is greater indecision in hospitals as to whether to adopt a traditional integrated model or a Taylorist model for cleaners' tasks, as well as more opportunities to bypass collective agreements through the use of fixed-term employment contracts.

In the United Kingdom, the dominant trend is toward adoption of the "continental" model. Although the incidence of low-wage work is high, the changes currently being introduced suggest that the relative position of our two job categories will improve. The creation of the new position of housekeeper, improved training for nursing assistants, a restructuring of pay scales, and a leveling-up of wages in hospitals and subcontractor firms were all emerging trends when our interviews were being conducted, and they should lead to a reduction in the incidence of low-wage work.

In Germany, the situation varies depending on the job category in question. In the case of cleaners, hospitals have followed the national trend toward the fragmentation of labor market institutions and a deterioration in pay and employment conditions. Thus, as far as this highly vulnerable category is concerned, hospitals are tending to converge with the American model. The case of nursing assistants, on the other hand, is less clear, since these jobs are declining or even disappearing, as they are in the Netherlands, in favor of more-skilled nurses.

In contrast to most of the European countries, and despite attempts to improve work organization, both cleaners and, to a lesser extent, nursing assistants in the United States suffer from cumulative disadvantages, including low pay, poor working conditions, and low mobility prospects. True, the case studies did reveal some attempts to escape from this vicious circle, particularly where trade unions wield influence and in areas where labor market tensions are greater. There is no evidence, however, that a stable high-road approach has been adopted to any significant extent at the national level. Moreover, these case studies demonstrate the ambiguity of partial solutions: task enrichment unsupported by training and without any uprating of pay does not improve job satisfaction and does not necessarily have any significant effect on turnover or commitment to work.

Thus, our comparative analysis of the six countries enables us to draw several conclusions about the interplay of institutions. First, it needs to be emphasized that, although many hospitals are part of the public or not-for-profit sector, they are fully embedded in their respective national models, the effects and dynamics of which they reproduce and sometimes exaggerate. Sectoral specificities, though certainly real enough, are not sufficient to explain all the differences, which also arise in part out of these national models.

Second, in this area, after all, national health care systems and policies have a greater impact than in other sectors that supply private goods and services. American hospitals' greater dependence on fragmented and competing sources of finance and the absence of funding for populations not covered by health insurance explain why their responses are so diverse and why it is difficult to put high-road strategies in place. This is less the case in Europe, where patients' social coverage is based more on a unitary and integrative public system. Despite increasing competition between hospitals, this coverage is more regulated centrally by the health care institutions. Moreover, as the British example underlines, NHS policies cannot be understood without taking account of the crisis of confidence in the hospital system that originated in the Thatcher era, when waiting lists grew long and there were recurrent problems with the quality of care and the cleanliness of hospitals. Thus, the policies adopted by U.K. hospitals, all of them operating within the NHS, must be sensitive to national health policy options and the health service budget in terms of their consequences for pay policy, outsourcing, and even concerns about the quality of care and the fight against hospital-acquired infections.

The third and final conclusion to be drawn from this chapter concerns the interrelationship between the various aspects of low-wage and low-skilled work and the various labor market institutions. As we have seen, the use of outsourcing, which tends to have a negative impact on cleaners' wage levels and mobility prospects, cannot be understood without taking into account the extent to which collective agreements are inclusive or exclusive, as well as the role and level of the minimum wage, the size of the available labor supply, the degree to which available labor is willing to submit to this constraint, and the nature of the relevant training policies. In this respect, Denmark is an emblematic case: a strong trade union presence, unity on the employers' side, and a national collective agreement all help to create the conditions for integration. This effect is reinforced by policies that promote intersectoral solidarity, which protects against outsourcing, and is further supported by the importance attached to training and the policies on improving work organization associated with it.

Germany and France are particularly interesting cases. In both countries, the hospital system is a mixture of public and private establishments. In both countries, the female unemployment rate is high, and public policies exert considerable pressures on the unemployed. In both countries, the coverage rate of collective agreements is high. And yet, as we have seen with regard to outsourcing, the trends in the two countries are divergent. The gradual fragmentation of collective agreements in Germany, the increasing opportunities for hospitals to exploit opt-out clauses, and the absence of a national minimum wage prevent collective agreements from fulfilling their integrative function, from the industry level down to the establishment level. This trend is reinforced by the fact that the female labor supply is still strongly influenced, in western Germany, by the male bread-winner model, which weakens women's position in the labor market. And paradoxically, for a country with a strong tradition of vocational training, the weakness of the training provided for low-skilled jobs tends to polarize the skill mix, to the detriment of the least-skilled. It would appear that everything is pushing France in the same direction. Nevertheless, three factors work in the opposite direction, toward a virtuous circle: a different provider mix with a much lower share of private hospitals, greater unity on the employers' side, and forms of state-controlled coordination between the public and private sectors, which is also found on the trade union side; the existence of a national minimum wage, which plays a strongly integrative role by limiting the attractiveness of outsourcing; and a supply of intermediate-level training that tends to encourage hospitals to opt for skilled or semi-skilled jobs, even for cleaners.

Compared with the European countries (including the United Kingdom, the country that most resembles it), the United States offers the most fragmented picture with regard to both health care and labor market institutions. High-road initiatives face many more obstacles because of the absence of national institutions and forms of coordination.

NOTES

1. Except where indicated, the national results are taken from the following chapters published in a series of national books about low-wage work by the Russell Sage foundation: Appelbaum et al. (2003); Eskildsen and Løkke Nielsen (2008); Grimshaw and Carroll (2008); Jaehrling (2008); Méhaut et al. (2008); van der Meer (2008).
2. Under different occupational labels—for example, "licensed practical nurse" (the United States), "state enrolled nurse" (the United Kingdom), or "Krankenpflegehelfer/in" (Denmark).
3. The following brief summary draws on the more detailed discussion of collective bargaining patterns and trends in the public hospitals sector in Grimshaw et al. (2007).
4. Bearing in mind that in the Netherlands there were no nursing assistants in our sample of hospitals.
5. NVQs are work-related, competence-based qualifications, based on national occupational standards of performance. They can be completed

by full-time or part-time employees or by students at schools and colleges and thus have no age limits or entry requirements. Within public-sector hospitals, NVQ training for nursing assistants has been supported by government investment in so-called NHS Learning Accounts, amounting to more than £150 million during the period 2003 to 2005.

REFERENCES

Abel-Smith, Brian. 1960. *A History of the Nursing Profession.* London: Heinemann.

American Hospital Association. 2006. *Fast Facts on U.S. Hospitals.* Chicago: AHA. Available at: http://www.aha.org/aha/resource-center/Statistics-and-Studies/fast-facts.html.

Appelbaum, Eileen, Peter Berg, Ann Frost, and Gil Preuss. 2003. "The Effects of Work Restructuring on Low-Wage, Low-Skilled Workers in U.S. Hospitals." In *Low-Wage America: How Employers Are Reshaping Opportunity in the Workplace*, edited by Eileen Appelbaum, Annette Bernhardt, and Richard J. Murnane. New York: Russell Sage Foundation.

Appelbaum, Eileen G., and Cherlyn Skromme. 1986. "Hospital Employment Under Revised Medicare Payment Schedule." *Monthly Labor Review* (August): 37–45.

Arrowsmith, James. 2006. *Temporary Agency Work in an Enlarged EU.* Dublin: European Foundation for the Improvement of Living and Working Conditions.

Bekker, Sonja, Gerard van Essen, Edith Josten, and Hanne Meihizen. 2004. "Trendrappport aanbod van arbeid in zorg en welzijn 2003 (Trend report on labour supply in care and welfare in 2003)." *OSA publicatie* (ZW47, April).

Berg, Peter, and Ann C. Frost. 2005. "Dignity of Work for Low-Wage, Low-Skill Service Workers." In *Relations Industrielles (Industrial Relations)* 60(4): 657–82.

Cutler, David M., ed. 2000. *The Changing Hospital Industry: Comparing Not-for-Profit and For-Profit Institutions.* National Bureau of Economic Research report. Chicago: University of Chicago Press.

Department of Health. 2004. *Agenda for Change: Final Agreement.* London: Department of Health. Available at: www.dh.gov.uk (accessed March 2006).

Direction de la Récherche, des Études, des Evaluations et de la Statistique (DREES). 2008. *Les établissements de santé: un panorama pour 2006.* Paris: Ministère de la santé (Ministry of Health). Available at: http://www.sante.gouv.fr/drees/donnees/es2006/es2006.htm.

Erickcek, George A., Susan N. Houseman, and Arne L. Kalleberg. 2003. "The Effects of Temporary Services and Contracting Out on Low-Skilled Workers: Evidence from Auto Suppliers, Hospitals, and Public Schools." In *Low-Wage America: How Employers are Reshaping Opportunity in the*

Work Place, edited by Eileen Appelbaum, Annette Bernhardt, Richard J. Murnane. New York: Russell Sage Foundation.

Eskildsen, Jacob K., and Ann-Kristina Løkke-Nielsen. 2008. "The Upgrading of Skills in the Danish Public-Sector Hospitals." In *Low-Wage Work in Denmark*, edited by Niels Westergaard-Nielsen. New York: Russell Sage Foundation.

Grimshaw, Damian, and Marylin Carroll. 2008. "Improving the Position of Low-Wage Workers Through New Coordinating Institutions: The Case of Public Hospitals." In *Low-Wage Work in the United Kingdom*, edited by Caroline Lloyd, Geoff Mason, and Ken Mayhew. New York: Russell Sage Foundation.

Grimshaw, Damian, Karen Jaehrling, Marc van der Meer, Philippe Méhaut, and Nirit Shimron. 2007. "Convergent and Divergent Country Trends in Coordinated Wage Setting and Collective Bargaining in the Public Hospitals Sector." *Industrial Relations Journal* 38(6): 591–613.

Jaehrling, Karen. 2008. "Polarization of Working Conditions: Cleaners and Nursing Assistants in Hospitals." In *Low-Wage Work in Germany*, edited by Gerhard Bosch and Claudia Weinkopf. New York: Russell Sage Foundation.

Kirkpatrick, Ian, and Miguel Martinez Lucio. 1996. "The Contract State and the Future of Public Management." *Public Administration* 74(1): 1–8.

Le Grand, Julian, and Will Bartlett. 1993. *Quasi-Markets and Social Policy*. London: Palgrave Macmillan.

Le Lan, Romuald, and Dominique Baubeau. 2004. "Les Conditions de travail perçues par les professionnels des établissements de santé." *Études et Résultats* 335: 11.

Méhaut, Philippe, Anne Marie Arborio, Jacques Bouteiller, Lise Causse, and Philippe Mossé. 2008. "Good Jobs, Hard Work? The Employment Model of Cleaners and Nurse Assistants in the French Hospitals." In *Low-Wage Work in France*, edited by Ève Caroli and Jérôme Gautié. New York: Russell Sage Foundation.

Organisation for Economic Co-operation and Development (OECD). Various years. OECD Health Data. Available at: http://titania.sourceoecd.org/vl=7446525/cl=58/nw=1/rpsv/ij/oecdstats/99991012/v1n1/s1/p1 (accessed December 2007).

Statistisches Bundesamt. 2008. Grunddaten der Krankenhäuser 2006, Fachserie 12, Reihe 6.1.1, Wiesbaden.

U.K. Department of Health. 1996–2006. NHS Staff 1996–2006 (Non-Medical). Available at: http://www.ic.nhs.uk/statistics-and-data-collections/workforce/nhs-staff-numbers/nhs-staff-1996—2006-non-medical.

U.S. Bureau of Labor Statistics (BLS). 2006. Occupational Employment and Wages Estimates, May. Washington: BLS. Available at: http://www.bls.gov/oes/current/oes_alph.htm.

Van der Meer, Marc. 2008. "Health Care: Integrated Quality Care Sheltered from Cost Control?" In *Low-Wage Work in the Netherlands*, edited by Wiemer Salverda, Maarten van Klaveren, and Marc van der Meer. New York: Russell Sage Foundation.

World Health Organization (WHO). Various years. European Health for All Database (HFA-DB). Available at http://data.euro.who.int/hfadb (accessed December 2007).

CHAPTER 9

Tough Meat, Hard Candy: Implications for Low-Wage Work in the Food-Processing Industry

Klaus G. Grunert, Susan James, and Philip Moss

Food processing is traditionally a low-wage area. It is also usually one of the biggest manufacturing sectors of a national economy, it is heavily tied to national culture, and it is at the same time strongly affected by reduced trade barriers and increased globalization. The food manufacturing industry is highly competitive (Wilson and Hogarth 2003), and companies have been faced with many challenges arising from changing economic conditions. In each of the countries in this study, the food-processing sector plays a prominent role and is often regarded as one of the more successful manufacturing areas. Furthermore, the food-processing industries in many parts of the world face similar challenges these days and deal with them within the constraints of different national institutional systems and cultural differences that affect not only the demand for food and drink but also a range of other issues, such as the prevalent business strategy in food processing, management practices, and issues of human resource development.

The purpose of this chapter is to analyze how the employment and working conditions in the food-processing sector have been affected by the challenges the sector is facing, with a focus on national differences in how these challenges are dealt with and the role of national institutions in explaining these differences. The chapter is based on research completed in the food-processing sectors of five European countries—Denmark, France, Germany, the Netherlands, and the United Kingdom (see Caroli, Gautié, and Lamanthe 2008; Czommer 2008; Esbjerg and Grunert 2008; James and Lloyd 2008; van Halem 2008)—and draws on case studies in the meat-processing and confectionery subsectors. Where relevant information was available, we have included comparisons with the situation in the United States.

Our study focuses on the working conditions of process operatives, who account for the largest group of workers in the food manufacturing industry, although previous studies conducted on the
food-processing sector often neglect this role. The various tasks in
food processing follow rather common patterns across the various
subsectors: incoming raw materials are washed, cut, and mixed, then
subjected to various mechanical, chemical, and thermal treatments,
and the resulting products are cooled down and packed. On-line operative jobs involve routine, often tedious, manual operations and are
highly repetitive, with short, intense cycle times. One operative at a
U.K. confectionery company explained:

> At the moment I am doing the new product, and it's actually counting
> ten sweets, they are twist-wrapped and five in each hand in each box,
> and we are doing an average speed of seventeen boxes a minute. So
> that's one hundred seventy sweets a minute we can put into a box.

Off-line operative positions include palletizing or mixing ingredients; some positions have more responsibility, such as quality control. Many operatives work in a team where the work revolves around
a specific line; however, this does not indicate that a variety of roles
are necessarily undertaken within the line. Some operatives advance
to team leader and are responsible for the workers of a specific line.
With the increase in automation, the job has changed from being
classified as reasonably skilled manual labor to more monitoring of
production processes and machinery. The responsibility of machine
process operatives for the daily running of the equipment mainly involves monitoring duties; however, because engineers are on hand
for breakdowns, machine operative roles remain relatively unskilled.
Consequently, many common problems in the work of operatives
pertain to poor work positions, repetitive and monotonous movements, lifting heavy objects, stench, noise, dust, high or low temperatures, and drafts as well as poor ventilation in the factories.

We begin the chapter by describing the challenges that a globalized food sector poses for the various national food-processing sectors. We discuss the generic ways in which food companies can deal
with these challenges, distinguishing low- and high-road strategies,
and we briefly characterize the different settings within which companies in the selected countries have to deal with these challenges.
We then describe the ensuing differences these strategies make for

working conditions, discussing the effects on compensation pressure, the use of temporary and immigrant labor, numerical and functional flexibility, de- and up-skilling, and health and safety issues. We close by speculating about the future development of the food-processing sector, especially the likely prevalence of high- and low-road strategies in dealing with competitive pressures and the effects this will have on workers.

SCOPE AND METHODOLOGY

The two subsectors that were the focus of the research—meat processing and confectionery—differ in a number of important ways. Confectionery ranges from small, craftsman-type operations to large mass operation plants, and the sector includes some major multinational players. The subsector is still dominated by manufacturer brands, some of which have considerable international brand equity, and a correspondingly low share of private labels. Automation started early in the confectionery sector, which has a high share of female operators. Meat processing, on the other hand, while also including a number of large players, is not dominated by multinationals, has a weak degree of branding, started automation later than confectionery, and, because of considerable physical demands, is male-dominated.

The characteristics of the firms and the methodology were coordinated across the five European countries.[1] Overall, thirty-five companies across the five European countries were involved (detailed in table 9A.1). A semi-structured interview schedule was approved between the five countries. Face-to-face interviews were conducted in each of the companies with a range of managers, team leaders, production operatives, trade union and employee representatives, a multi-employer group manager (in France), managers of temporary work agencies, professional and employers' organizations, actors in the field of training and working conditions improvement, and labor inspectors.

Comparisons, where possible, are made to the food-processing industry in the United States. These comparisons are based on a study in the United States that focuses on the labor market in the food service industry, with some attention to food manufacturing (Lane et al. 2003). In addition, case studies done as part of the general study on which that paper was based, including one in meat processing and one in confectionery manufacturing, were used, as well as published data and other research on the U.S. food-processing industry. We realize that there are limitations of generalizability in following this format; however, the data gathered in the U.S. study do provide the opportunity for comparison and contextualization between Europe and the United States, highlighting points of similarity and departure.

Securing access was homogeneously problematic across the six countries. The intense competitive pressure that companies are under could be an explanation. Furthermore, it could be assumed that the companies that did agree to give us access were examples of the better-than-average employer in the food-processing sector. Management predominantly put forward individuals for interviews, raising the issue of selection bias, but the interviews yielded a range of opinions and substantial data that provided useful insights into employee perspectives and were balanced with the information and opinions provided by managers. Some quantitative data were provided by some of the companies on aspects such as pay rates, employee numbers, breakdowns on age and gender, and performance figures and were used with the qualitative data.

FOOD PROCESSING: GLOBAL COMPETITION AND NATIONAL INDUSTRIES

CHALLENGES IN FOOD PROCESSING

The challenges affecting food-processing companies in the countries studied have been remarkably similar. The highly competitive environment has made it difficult for companies, multinational corporations (MNCs), and small to medium-sized enterprises (SMEs) alike to operate profitably (one case company operates with a profit margin as low as 1 percent). Retail pressure, increasing international competition, and changing consumer demands are three of the key challenges having an impact on firms' ability to maintain good performance.

The power of the retailers, with their centralized buying policies and distribution channels, are such that a supply chain pressure (see, for example, Grimshaw et al. 2005) is placed on the manufacturers to provide goods at the lowest possible prices and is amplified by consumers' demands (Codron et al. 2005). The competition between supermarkets is intense, and with the increasing use of supermarket "own labels," these companies compete on price as well as quality. The rise of supermarket own-label products can be seen in all six countries. To compete on price, the retailers expect manufacturers to be able to respond to orders and deliver according to their "just-in-time" requirements. This is less of a problem in confectionery, with its longer product shelf life; however, meat is a highly perishable product, and availability is dependent on an animal's growth cycle.

Retailers exert power not only in relation to cost but also through their audits. In conducting audits, retailers are imposing their particular requirements or criteria for the way the production process happens above and beyond health and safety legislation requirements (for further discussion, see Lloyd and James 2008). For instance, in France and the United Kingdom, where the share of supermarket own-label products is highest, retailers are adamant in their demands for differentiated production: in many cases, they demand that a production line be used only for their own products. This requirement places a huge capital investment burden on companies and increases the power relation of supermarkets, since the manufacturer relies on their custom. One way in which manufacturers have been trying to counteract this pressure is by strengthening their own brands, so that consumers will demand those products on the shelves, thus strengthening manufacturers in the power relationship with retailers. This practice is especially prevalent in confectionery, where a number of multinational companies have established well-known brands instantly recognizable by consumers.

The retailers' revenue depends on consumer demands being met (Grunert 2002), such as demands for recognizable brands, expectations of variation and discounts, and ways of addressing consumers' (and governments') health concerns—for instance, obesity in relation to sugar and confectionery products and junk food. Furthermore, consumers' lifestyle demands have resulted in the expansion of the convenience food market, which can be seen across all six countries in this study. However, consumers' increasing concern about health and safety issues—notably expressed in the BSE (bovine spongiform encephalopathy, commonly known as mad-cow disease) crisis in the United Kingdom in 2005 and the spread of the avian bird flu in chicken processing—has provided some companies in the food manufacturing industry with the opportunity to expand and concentrate in certain areas and thus retain some power and control over their profits (for example, French beef, British poultry, Danish pork). The opportunities provided by consumer demand thus allow manufacturing companies to differentiate their products.

Mergers and acquisitions and increased consolidation across Europe and the United States have increased international competition among fewer players (Lane et al. 2003). A consequence is the downsizing of many multinational corporations' production facilities and the transfer of some production facilities to eastern Europe.

Overall, supply chain pressures and changing consumer demands influence at many levels the constraints weighing on companies: cost reductions, increased quality and specialization, and greater responsiveness and adaptability to demand in terms of quality and quantity. This in turn has an effect on the job of the process operative.

How Food-Processing Companies React

There are two basic ways in which food-processing companies have been trying to address the challenges described in the previous section: by reducing costs and by finding new ways to create value for their customers. These two ways do not rule each other out, but the weight with which they have been pursued differs widely.

Trying to bring down the per-unit cost of production is an obvious reaction to retailer price pressure and increasing competition from producers in low-cost countries. It usually involves attempts to bring down labor costs by putting pressure on hourly wages, reducing piece rates, reducing overtime payment and bonus schemes, and implementing other measures that have an impact on the cost of labor. In addition, food processing has a long history of cost reduction by automation. Degrees of automation vary enormously, both between various subsectors of food processing and between companies. The process usually starts with certain tasks being automated, like the cutting or mixing of ingredients; when more and more tasks are subsequently automated, the result is production lines in which machines of different vintages are interlinked by the remaining manual tasks. Eventually production is moved to integrated, computer-controlled production lines.

Attempts to increase efficiency relate not only to lowering per-unit costs but also to increasing numerical flexibility in production, so that short-term fluctuations in retailer demand, often coupled with requirements for speedy just-in-time delivery, can be met alongside the more predictable seasonal variations that characterize many branches of food processing. Such increased flexibility can be achieved by greater use of temporary and seasonal workers (external flexibility) or by introducing flexible working hour arrangements like annualized working times.

Finally, attempts to increase efficiency can involve moving whole sections of production. Parts of production may be offshored to other countries with lower labor costs, or parts of production may be outsourced to suppliers that are more efficient with regard to the specific type of manufacturing task.

Although the food-processing industry has responded to the competitive challenges in all these ways, there is a widespread belief in the European food industry that such measures will not be enough to ensure long-term survival in the face of low-cost competition and retailer pressure and that they will have to be supplemented by new ways of creating more value for the customer. There are three reasons for this widespread belief. First, the challenge of more fragmented, heterogeneous, and dynamic consumer demand provides opportunity to obtain competitive advantage by achieving a better understanding of consumer wants and developing products accordingly, creating more value in the eyes of the end user. Second, when attempts to increase efficiency are not enough to match the lower cost level of new competitors, competitive position can be ensured only by offering products for which customers are willing to pay a premium (Day and Wensley 1988). Third, high-value products that are adapted to specific consumer needs give some protection against retailer threats to switch suppliers unless there are further price cuts (Grunert 2006).

Adding additional value in food processing can be done by differentiation and by additional processing. Additional processing can match new consumer demands for convenience, for healthy products, and for new and unusual sensory experiences. Differentiation can match consumer demands for variation and some consumers' specific requirements for certain characteristics of the production process, like organic production, fair trade, or animal welfare.

The urge to find new ways of adding value to agricultural raw material has led to much emphasis on innovation and new product development in the food-processing industry. At the same time, the failure rates of new food products introduced on the market are notoriously high, indicating that the road to high-value products is not an easy one to take and not necessarily everyone has the necessary competencies (Kristensen, Østergaard, and Juhl 1998). In the search for new high-value products, there has been a renewed interest in regional products, among which are a number of successful premium products; smaller food-processing companies in particular may see this as a way of fighting the pressure.

Furthermore, branding has become a focal topic in food processing. Well-established brands add value to products, command price premiums, and give protection against excessive pressure from retailers. In food, there are some international icon brands (Heinz ketchup, Mars chocolate bars), and in every country there are national icon brands (Cadbury chocolate in the United Kingdom, Stryhn's liver paté in Denmark), but the degree of branding varies widely between different food categories, and many food brands are weak. Brands provide a means of differentiation, however, and are a necessary tool in communicating some of the more intangible ways of creating added value in food processing, such as the origin of the product, the type of production, and certain pleasure characteristics (Marsden 1987).

The mix of means by which food-processing companies address the competitive challenges is affected by their position in the value chain and by the predominant form of governance of that chain. A smaller food producer that supplies retailers who are exerting price pressure, and that is forced to source deliveries from world markets where prices are rising, will find it difficult to react in any other way than trying to cut costs. A smaller food producer with access to local deliveries with contractually guaranteed special quality characteristics (like meat from special breeds or from organic production) may succeed in developing high-quality niche products that can be distributed through specialty outlets in addition to supermarkets, thus diminishing pressures from both sides. A multinational producer of branded products can stand up to the power exerted by retailers and put pressure on its own suppliers. A large company selling semi-processed products of differentiated quality to next-level processing companies worldwide will be less affected by retailer pressure and can find new ways of creating value for its main customers.

The distinction of low-cost and high-value strategies is well established in the business strategy literature (dating back to Porter 1980). When discussing reactions to competitive pressure and their implications for working conditions, sometimes the notion of high- versus low-road strategies is used. We should note here that a low-cost strategy is not necessarily low-road in terms of working conditions, and a high-value strategy is not necessarily high-road. Low costs can, in principle, be achieved by high degrees of automation, leaving only a few jobs with relatively good working conditions. High value can, in principle, be produced by lots of manual labor, repetitive tasks, and poor working conditions. In this chapter, we talk about low- and high-road strategies only when we believe there are indicators that the strategies pursued indeed have less or more positive consequences for the conditions of food-processing operatives.

Although the arsenal of possible reactions to the competitive challenges that the food-processing industry is facing is generic, and elements of each of these possible reactions can be found across countries and specific subsectors, different points of departure can make different types of reactions more obvious and more prevalent. These different points of departure relate both to differences in the business environment in various countries and to differences at the company level.

DIFFERENT FRAMES OF REFERENCE

Although the competitive challenges and possible ways of handling them are quite similar in the six countries in our comparison, the state of the food-processing industry in general and the two subsectors addressed in our study in particular—confectionery and meat processing—differ considerably between the six countries.

In the United States, food manufacturing employed 1,469,730 workers in 2005—11 percent of all manufacturing workers. Within food manufacturing, the two subsectors, meat processing, including poultry (506,947), and sugar confectionery processing (60,107), employed 567,054 workers, or 37 percent of all food-processing workers. Food manufacturing was about 12 percent of value-added in manufacturing in 2005. Meat processing constituted 27 percent of food-processing value-added, and confectionery added another 6 percent.[2] Foreign trade plays only a modest role in food manufacturing, with the exception of imports of confectionery products. Exports and imports of manufactured food products stand at approximately 17 percent of total value-added. Within the meat-processing subsector, 19 percent of value-added is exported, while 13 percent of value-added is imported. The percentages for confectionery are 11 percent of value-added exported and 30 percent imported.[3]

Food processing pays relatively low wages in the United States. Average hourly wages among food-processing workers was $13.13 in 2006, in comparison to $16.76, the average for all private industry workers. Within food processing, sugar- and confectionery-processing workers did a bit better than the average food-processing worker at $15.19, while meat-processing workers were particularly low-paid at $11.49.[4] In addition, injury rates were relatively high: 7.4 cases of work-related injury or illness per 100 full-time food manufacturing workers compared to 4.4 for the entire private sector. Nineteen percent of food manufacturing workers are union members or are covered by a collective bargaining agreement.[5] The rate is a bit lower in meat and confectionery processing, at about 16 percent.[6] Finally, 18 percent of the workers in food processing were on some type of contingent work arrangement as independent contractors or on-call workers, or they were paid by temp agencies. The comparable figure for all sectors is 13.7 percent.[7]

All segments of the U.S. food industry have experienced significant consolidation. The top four firms account for 52 percent of sales among food service contractors; 28 percent among general line grocery wholesalers; 20 percent among grocery stores; 17 percent among food manufacturers; 42 percent in meat products; and 38 percent in sugar and confectionery processing.[8] The consolidation among the top two distributors—Sysco and U.S. Food—was over 43 percent in 2001 (Lane et al. 2003).

Within meat processing, concentration is particularly striking in beef, pork, and poultry. The top four beef packers—Tyson Foods, Cargill, Swift & Company, and National Beef Packing Company—control fully 83.5 percent of the market. In pork packing, 66 percent of the market is controlled by the top four: Smithfield Foods, Tyson Foods, Swift & Company, and Cargill. Finally, within poultry, 58.5 percent of the market for the largest-selling product, broilers, is controlled by the top four: Pilgrim's Pride, Tyson Foods, Purdue, and Sanderson Farms (Hendrickson and Heffernan 2007). Within sugar and confectionery processing, the concentration ratio in confectionery processing of chocolate from cacao beans is very high, at 69 percent.[9]

The U.K. food-processing sector is one of the largest manufacturing sectors of the country, employing more than 400,000 workers, who represent about 13 percent of manufacturing employment. The sector serves mostly the domestic market, with exports accounting for only 15 percent of sales. Imports, though not dominant at 26 percent of overall food sales, are rising. The sector has been in slow decline, having lost its position as Europe's biggest food manufacturing sector to France and Germany. Ninety percent of the companies are small (fewer than 20 people), although companies with more than 250 employees account for three-quarters of industry output. About one-third of the jobs in food processing are below the low-pay threshold, and more than half of the workers have qualifications below basic school-leaving expectations.

Industry structure and product market strategies differ between our two focal subsectors. In confectionery, three multinationals—Cadbury Schweppes, Masterfoods, and Nestle Rowntree—have together two-thirds of the U.K. market, and the sector is characterized by a high number of branded products, diversity in distribution channels, and a comparatively higher profit margin. Meat processing, by contrast, is not dominated by a small number of players, and by far the most products are sold through retailers under retailers' private labels, with considerably lower profit margins.

Both sectors employ large numbers of low-skilled and low-wage workers. In spite of a generally tight labor market in the United Kingdom, companies in food processing have had no problems in recruiting low-cost labor for unskilled work, owing to regulations that have opened job markets to workers from the new EU member countries and also measures to attract workers specifically to meat and fish processing from outside the EU. Many of these workers work on temporary contracts through agencies, and their pay is close to the national minimum wage (NMW). Median hourly pay for operatives in the case companies varied between £5.64 ($11.15) and £7.61 ($15.04), with agency workers generally paid just a little above £5.00 ($9.88).[10] Workers received some additional benefits, such as paid breaks, additional holidays, and sick pay, but these varied a good deal between companies.

The role of unions in food processing is generally weak. One major role that they seem to have retained is monitoring the work health and safety standards for these workplaces characterized by repetitive manual tasks, nuisances due to noise, wet, cold, and heat, and the widespread use of moving and cutting machinery, combined with widely varying levels of management attention to such matters.

The German food-processing sector has a number of similarities with the U.K. one. Its relative importance as a manufacturing sector is about the same, as is the level of imports and exports. Also, in Germany the sector is very fragmented. The large majority of businesses are small or medium-sized, including many that are still family-run. The ten largest producers have only a 15 percent share of the industry. There is an ongoing structural change, however, and multinationals have been acquiring smaller businesses, often subsequently changing their product market strategy and business operations; for example, the Dutch Vion Food Group has taken over major players in meat processing. The sector has a sizable proportion of unskilled and low-wage work, just as in the United Kingdom. In 2003, 23 percent of the workforce in the food industry had not completed any vocational training, compared to 16 percent in the total economy.

Although the role of unions in the food industry is generally weak (degrees of unionization are 10 to 20 percent in SMEs and higher in larger companies), and collective bargaining is more fragmented than in any other German industry, there are some significant differences between our two focal subsectors. The production of confectionery in Germany went through an early period of industrialization, with high degrees of automation and the development of a low-skill industrial workforce. This again led to strong union activity and the establishment of a tradition of collective bargaining that persists today: a nationwide collective agreement continues to regulate working conditions and various regional collective pay agreements. The industrialization of meat processing took place much later, and in terms of collective agreements and trade union influence, meat processing is quite the opposite case from confectionery. There are no industrywide collective agreements; those that exist are at the regional or (mostly) company level, and many companies have none at all.

As in the United Kingdom, the confectionery subsector in Germany includes some producers of branded premium products with good growth and profitability, whereas producers of products for the budget segment seem to be struggling more. Also here, distribution channels are more diversified for confectionery. Meat products are largely distributed through supermarkets, and the conditions of meat-processing companies are affected by the very high market shares of discounters in the German retailing scene, resulting in 40 percent of prepacked sausage and meat products being sold through discounters, with corresponding price pressure on manufacturers.

Both subsectors employ large numbers of low-skilled and low-wage workers. Fifty percent of operators in meat processing and 60 percent in confectionery have no vocational training, and 49 percent in meat processing and 29 percent in confectionery received wages below the low-wage threshold. The lowest pay grades for production and packing workers in confectionery are, according to the national collective agreement, between €8.40 and €8.90 ($13.08 and $13.86) per hour. The situation in meat processing, where no such agreement exists, is different. The collectively agreed lowest pay in the case studies varied from €6.98 to €9.83 ($10.87 to $15.31) per hour and is assumed to be between €6.00 and €8.00 ($9.34 and $12.46) in companies without a collective agreement. Parts of meat processing, however, make widespread use of cheap labor from eastern Europe, especially Poland, where labor is subcontracted to gang-masters at wages as low as €3.00 ($4.67) per hour.

France has one of the strongest food cultures in the world, and the food-processing sector is of corresponding national importance. It is the leading manufacturing sector in France in terms of sales and the third most important in terms of employment; France is also the biggest European food producer. As in the United Kingdom and Germany, the French food-processing sector is quite fragmented, with a large majority of small and medium-sized firms: only one-third of the companies employ more than five hundred workers. There is also some structural change, and in confectionery three big groups—Cadbury, Haribo, and Wrigley—have two-thirds of the market. Meat processing is much more fragmented, with the ten largest firms accounting for only 25 percent of the sales. The level of imports and exports is comparable (in relative terms) to that of Germany and the United Kingdom.

Four types of companies can be distinguished in the French food-processing sector. The first is the big firm, sometimes a multinational, that produces its own brands. The second is the firm that specializes in high-volume, low-quality mass production, acting as a subcontractor for other producers or as a supplier to retailers' private labels. The third type is the medium-sized company that pursues a mixed strategy based on a diversification of products (some with its own brand) and distribution channels and tries to combine the economies of scale achieved by supplying large retail chains with the advantages of selling high-value-added products produced in small batches. Finally, there is the small business that produces niche products, sometimes with protected geographical origin.

Also, in France, food processing employs a high proportion of un-

skilled labor. Forty-four percent of all blue-collar jobs in food processing are officially classified as unskilled, compared to 32 percent
in other manufacturing sectors. Still, most of this work is not paid below the low-wage threshold: only 7.2 percent of the workforce in
meat processing and 6.2 percent in confectionery receive wages that
low. Gross salaries consist of a base wage determined by the level in a
national job classification scheme plus a large range of bonuses and
extra pay, such as a thirteenth month salary and compensation for
night shifts, dressing and undressing, and so on. Although the hourly
wage at the lowest level of the job classification is close to the national minimum wage and would be low-wage, the various extra payments lift it above the threshold; in addition, most workers are paid
at higher levels in the job classification scheme so that most labor in
food processing is above the low-wage threshold. In meat processing,
minimum hourly wages for the various levels of the job classification
scheme vary from €8.12 to €9.48 ($12.65 to $14.76, slightly lower
for confectionery), but with all bonuses taken into account, a worker
in meat processing at a medium level of the job classification would
earn at least €9.50 ($14.80).

Various forms of temporary labor play a big role in French food
processing. Workers from temporary agencies are widely used; their
pay is often a little higher than that of permanent employees with low
tenure (not taking into account profit-sharing—that is, those arrangements whereby workers are paid bonuses based on company profits),
since they are paid an obligatory job insecurity premium. French
meat processing also has a system of gang-masters and their workers,
but in contrast to the German version, these are well-paid specialists.
Seasonal workers are the lowest-paid in the sector, since most seasonal workers have the lowest job classification and most bonuses
and extra payments do not apply to them. In contrast to the German
and U.K. situation, immigrant labor does not play a major role in
French food processing.

Industrial relations in food processing are quite similar to those in
France in general, meaning that unions are weak at the firm level but
active at the sector or industry level. Legal collective bargaining
agreements apply to all companies and settle not only minimum
wages for the various job classifications but also the numerous
bonuses. In addition to unions, a number of other institutions play a
role in providing continuous training for the sector and advice on issues of health and working conditions.

Food processing in France, like other sectors of the French economy, has been affected by the implementation of the laws on the thirty-five-hour week. In food processing, this has often taken the form of annualized working times, which match the sector's need for flexibility in production, and cuts in overtime hours. As a result of these changes, the monthly income of many food-processing workers has declined.

In the Netherlands, food processing is an export-oriented industry: 55 percent of food sales are exported. Multinational companies like Unilever, Heineken, Sara Lee, Nestle, and Masterfoods play a big role, as do some large farmers' cooperatives like FCDF and Vion Food. With regard to our two subsectors, the export orientation is strongest in confectionery, where several multinationals have strong export-oriented brands. Just as in some of the other countries, confectionery is somewhat less dependent on the retail trade and has better profit margins than meat processing. In meat processing, both branding and the export orientation are weaker, and 90 percent of sales go through supermarkets.

Both confectionery and meat processing employ high numbers of unskilled workers who have either no secondary vocational education or no vocational education at all.

Labor relations in both subsectors are governed by collective labor agreements that are signed by the employers' associations and by the unions and then are legally extended to cover the whole sector. Thus, the collective agreements have 100 percent coverage, even though degrees of unionization are on average no higher than 20 percent, with higher union density in the bigger firms. The collective agreements cover not only wages but also pension schemes, vocational training, and issues of work health and safety.

Wages are based on a job evaluation scheme that is part of the collective agreement. The scheme specifies both different job categories and a range of payment levels for each category, to be reached in nine or ten yearly steps. The lowest negotiated entry-wage level in confectionery corresponds to an hourly wage of €10.30 ($16.04), with the highest maximum wage corresponding to €15.89 ($24.75). The figures for meat processing are €8.71 and €12.48 ($13.56 and $19.44). Entry wages are below the low-wage threshold, but maximum wages are above it. Most companies pay 5 to 10 percent above those rates, however, because of tight labor markets. In addition, a number of other benefits are collectively regulated, like a holiday allowance, health insurance payments, a pension premium, an annual bonus, and some firm-specific bonuses. (Figures for the proportion of workers under the low-wage threshold were not available for the subsectors.)

A labor shortage some years ago resulted in widespread recruitment across Europe by temporary work agencies, a form of work now also collectively regulated by a "covenant" on keeping a flexible workforce. These temporary workers constitute the biggest part of the workforce that is in the low-wage category. Temporary workers are used not only during shortages and to manage seasonal variation, but increasingly as a source of recruitment for new workers.

The Danish food-processing sector is one of the strongholds of the Danish economy, accounting for 22 percent of total production in industry, 18 percent of industrial employment, and 16 percent of all exported goods. The Danish food sector is highly concentrated; the top ten companies in the sector account for 49.9 percent of total industry turnover. The large companies are among the largest in their respective subsectors in the world: Danish Crown in meat processing, Arla Foods in dairy, Carlsberg in brewing, and Danisco Cultor in food ingredients. The Danish food sector is export-oriented, with more than two-thirds of total production exported.

Our two focal subsectors differ considerably in Denmark. Meat processing is the most export-oriented subsector, the major item being pork-based products, 85 percent of which are exported, making Denmark the biggest exporter of pork in the world. Most of the exported products are chilled or frozen cuts to be processed further in the importing country, although the share of more highly processed products has been rising. The subsector has gone through a period of mergers and acquisitions that has resulted in the domination of one large company, Danish Crown, a farmers' cooperative that also owns operating plants outside Denmark. The Danish Meat and Bacon Council, the sector's trade association, had fifty-four members in 1970, operating sixty plants. Today it has two members operating sixteen plants, reflecting the concentration process and structural change that has been going on in the industry. Also, more than half of Danish poultry production is exported.

Confectionery, on the other hand, is comparatively small. It consists of a number of smaller producers that mainly serve the domestic market; many products are branded, and some of them are household icons. One bigger player, Dandy, has been very export-oriented but sold its main brands (including the Stimorol chewing gum brand) to Cadbury Schweppes a few years ago. As in the other countries, confectionery has a more varied distribution channel than meat.

Skill requirements for workers in food processing are limited in Denmark, with most employees having either a vocational education (most likely in meat processing) or no education beyond primary school. Ten percent of the workforce are immigrants, which is double the rate of the Danish economy as a whole. There are no recruitment problems at present, though this may change as the Danish labor market in general tightens.

Food processing is not a low-wage sector in Denmark: the proportions of low-wage earners in both subsectors are way below 5 percent. The negotiated minimum hourly wage for adult slaughterhouse workers is DKR152 ($31.76), though in reality they earn much more owing to piece-rate agreements, bringing their average salary up to DKR224 ($46.73). In confectionery, the negotiated minimum wage is DKR93 ($19.42).[11] The Danish food-processing sector has been characterized by formal or de facto closed-shop agreements, though this may change now that such agreements have been declared illegal by the European Court of Human Rights.

A notable aspect of the Danish food-processing sector is its emphasis on research and innovation. There is a long tradition in the sector of subsidizing research and development, with the Innovation Act of 2001 being the latest in a series of measures that provide support for the development of new products and production processes. The meat-processing sector has its own research institute, the Danish Meat Research Institute, which conducts research on product quality, food safety, and automation of production processes.

IMPLICATIONS FOR LOW-WAGE LABOR

The challenges that companies are facing have numerous implications for low-wage work and workers. In this second part of the chapter, we analyze how companies in the selected countries have reacted to the competitive challenges within their national contexts. We show that, while the impact on low-wage work can be analyzed using common dimensions, the ways in which companies have reacted differ widely and have differing effects on workers. We describe these differences and try to explain some of them against the background of national differences in institutional factors and market factors.

COMPENSATION PRESSURE

The pressure on companies to reduce costs to remain competitive is enormous. The simplest way to begin is by reducing labor costs, which historically have been the highest cost involved in production (although this situation is changing with increased automation). In all countries, there were indications of pressure on wages and wage-related benefits and of work intensification. The extent of this pressure varied, however, both between and within countries.

In all countries, there was pressure to lower wages. This was not primarily aimed at lowering the base wage but involved a variety of other measures such as reducing piece rates, converting overtime to regular working hours, and changing wage progressions. Often such measures were applied only to new employees, who would start at lower wages and/or with reduced benefits compared to incumbents; a decline in labor costs over the long term was thus achieved, while the wage status of current workers was preserved. Although observed in all countries, such wage pressures were most pronounced in the German and U.K. cases. These cases also demonstrated the strongest examples of reduction of wage-related benefits, though some of this was also visible in the French and Dutch cases. Among the benefits reduced were sick pay, payment of bonuses, and pension schemes.

To explain the differences found in the extent of compensation pressure, both within and between countries, we can distinguish between institutional factors, the prevalence of or access to other ways to counteract competitive pressures, and market factors.

It seems plausible that the existence of strong unions slows down the pressure on wages and benefits. In the two areas where compensation pressure was felt most—both the confectionery and meat subsectors in the United Kingdom and the meat-processing subsector in Germany—unions are weak, the degree of unionization is low, and collective agreements, if present at all, are fragmented and exist only at the local or company level. Compensation pressure was clearly less intense in Denmark, where the degree of unionization is high, up to the level of closed-shop agreements (until recently), and also in France and the Netherlands, where the degree of unionization is lower than in Denmark but the legal extension of collective agreements to the whole sector strengthens the role of unions at the sector level (on differences in the use of collective agreements between the countries, see Bosch, Mayhew, and Gautié, this volume).

Other elements of the national labor market "model" affect compensation pressure as well. Working time regulations were found to have effects on compensation pressure, though they may have been unintended by regulators. In France, the implementation of the thirty-five-hour week has led to a number of measures that, while aimed at maintaining income levels in the short run in spite of reductions in working time, will probably lead to reduced wages in the long run as companies that promised to leave monthly incomes unchanged are allowed to suppress seniority premiums for new entrants and limit wage increases. Also, the annualization of working time, which many companies have adopted in response to the implementation of the thirty-five-hour week, has led to the substitution of regular working hours for higher-paid overtime. A similar effect was found in the United Kingdom, where efforts to reduce overtime work—largely for reasons of health and safety and through legislation in the form of the EU Working Time Directive (WTD)—have had the result that some of the work previously done by permanent employees working overtime is now done by cheaper temporary workers: "From a financial level," said a confectionery company section leader, "let's be brutal about it, we have no commitment to them [temp workers] other than during the time they are here . . . from a cost point of view, although we are paying for their hourly rate, the pensions, holiday, sickness, etc., again that's gone."

The minimum wage, where it exists (France, Netherlands, the United Kingdom), acts as a floor with regard to wage pressure. There are signs that it leads to wage compression in the lower wage areas, as we could expect when the overall wage level in the sector does not keep up with general developments in wages. The statutory minimum wage does.

Finally, legislation affecting the availability of cheap immigrant labor has had an effect on compensation pressures in what might otherwise have been tight local labor markets. This effect has been most noticeable in the United Kingdom, which not only has opened its labor market to workers from the new EU member countries but has also adopted measures to attract unskilled labor from outside the EU to jobs in food processing. An ample supply of cheap immigrant labor also played a role in the Netherlands and in Germany. Usually these workers are employed through temporary work agencies or, in the extreme low-wage cases, through subcontracts to gang-masters (especially in German meat processing). Immigrant labor played a much lesser role in Denmark and France. In both countries, immigration policies are more restrictive, and regulations in France make it more difficult to recruit immigrants as posted or temporary workers.

As noted earlier in this chapter, putting pressure on wages and wage-related benefits is only one among several ways in which companies in this sector deal with increased competitive pressure. The degree of compensation pressure can therefore be related to their use of other strategies and to how difficult it is for them to use these other ways. We are dealing with a case of interdependence rather than causality—for example, better possibilities for automation may lead to less pressure on wages, but then more difficulties in pressuring wages may lead to more emphasis on automation.

In the United States, the decline of union density and power and the increasing use of immigrant labor have kept pressure to increase wages at bay. Labor relations with the major union that represents food-processing workers, the United Food and Commercial Workers (UFCW), have been very contentious at Smithfield Food, the largest pork producer in the United States. UFCW tried to organize a major Smithfield plant in North Carolina before finally succeeding, and only after Smithfield had been cited with numerous unfair labor practices.[12] Immigrants have become a major source of labor for food processors, and this has helped neutralize wage pressure that might have arisen on the labor supply side. This was clear in the meat-processing and confectionery manufacturing case study firms that were analyzed in an earlier U.S. study (Lane et al. 2003). Starting hourly pay was in the range of $7.00 to $7.50 at both firms during 2002 and 2003, when the interviews were conducted, and there was no talk of raising wages. Our meatpacking case study firm, Quality Meats, is a unionized plant organized by the UFCW, and Family Pastries is non-union. The UFCW has not had a great deal of influence on the general rate of pay or the use of immigrant labor at Quality Meats.

We observed widespread use of increased automation as a way of dealing with competitive pressures. Access to and use of this avenue differed widely, however, and we got the impression that compensation pressure was highest on those companies that found access to automation more difficult. A major factor seems to be related to company size. Automation requires investment, and the higher levels of investment that involve integrated computerized production lines may not be accessible to independent small and medium-sized companies; their efforts may be limited to the upgrading of single machines. Local competence clusters may also play a role in implementing advanced levels of automation. The fact that Danish meat processing is a world leader in automation of this particular part of food processing is related to several factors: strong mother companies providing access to financial resources, a scale of operations that makes automation pay off more easily, and a long history of automation in the sector and a well-established network of food-processing companies, suppliers of machinery, and research institutions.

In response to pressure on wages, manufacturing can be offshored to a low-wage area. Two forms of this strategy have been observed for food processing: a multinational restructuring its portfolio of production sites, as has been the case in the confectionery sector, which has seen the closing of production in some high-wage countries like Denmark and the concentration of production in existing production sites in other EU countries; and a national player moving some of its production to a new site in a low-wage country. In both meat processing and confectionery, we found that German companies had moved some of their production to Poland, and in meat processing the major Danish player had moved some of its production to Germany. However, we also observed cases of companies shunning offshoring or trying it and then bringing production back in-house. Not every manufacturing task can be simply moved somewhere else without consequences for the work carried out. We may venture the simple but plausible hypothesis that the more simple the manufacturing task, the more simple it is to offshore it. It is less clear, however, what "simple" means. We saw a case of a German confectionery producer who had to bring production back from Poland because retailers complained about the deteriorating quality of the packaging. There was no clear pattern relating the amount or the possibility of offshoring to compensation pressure on those workers who remained.

Trying to counter competitive pressure by developing new products with added value was mentioned in almost all the cases we investigated. We also found a range of successes. There is no clear pattern in these successes, but we may note that new product development in the food sector is inherently risky—the large majority of new product introductions fail on the market—and that just for reasons of professionalism and access to resources, large multinationals may be better equipped for successful innovation than SMEs, which thus far have produced only a few pretty basic products. On the other hand, SMEs that have a history in niche production or that can draw on regional traditions in food craftsmanship may be well equipped for this avenue. Success with new value-added products may not only reduce compensation pressure but actually modify work tasks in such a way that both the number of workers and wages increase, as was seen in one French case.

We should also mention that we found some cases of the introduction of new, more performance-based wage systems. This took a variety of forms, from the introduction of personal bonuses based on assessment interviews (as found in a French case) to a new, performance-based interpretation of existing wage categories that has become part of a collective agreement (as in the Netherlands). Although such systems are meant to decrease labor costs for the manufacturer, the effects on workers depend on a host of factors. Monthly income may go up or down, and although work intensity may increase, job satisfaction may increase or decrease, depending on the type of work reorganization involved and whether the particular employee values stability or autonomy the most.

The factors discussed already indicate that a number of characteristics of the industry play a role. Maybe most importantly, compensation pressure seems to be highest where sectors are fragmented and dominated by SMEs, particularly SMEs that produce standard products; they find it difficult to get access to capital for large-scale automation, and they have no tradition for producing high-value niche products. We found examples of this especially among the German and U.K. cases. The situation may be different for French SMEs because their embeddedness in a strong local food culture makes it easier for them to focus on, for example, regional labeled products that have a specific value proposition.

The overall impression is that while the food-processing sector as a whole is in a period of pressure on wages and related compensation, both national institutions and industry-related factors play a major role in how strongly that pressure is felt. Compensation pressure was clearly less in countries where unions had a strong role in food processing or where collective agreements were legally extended to the whole sector. In addition, large companies seemed better able to react to competitive pressures with a mix of measures: where compensation pressure is combined with increased automation, new forms of work organization and new product development may occur, whereas the only way, or at least the most important way, of dealing with competitive pressures for SMEs that produce basic products is to put pressure on wages and benefits.

VARYING USE OF TEMPORARY AND IMMIGRANT WORKERS

The use of temporary workers is one way for a company to enhance its numerical flexibility to deal with fluctuating demand, as discussed in the next section. Food processors in all of the countries studied used temporary workers for this purpose to some extent, and the use of these workers was increasing in all countries except Denmark. The increase in the use of temporary workers has reduced costs for food processors because temporary workers carry a relatively low wage, except in France, and are not entitled to many of the benefits that permanent workers enjoy, such as holiday payments, pensions, and sick pay (there are exceptions in France and the Netherlands). However, it is necessary to differentiate between the different forms of temporary workers across the countries. These are summarized in table 9.1.

Considering the degree to which temporary work is used and is increasing, the different countries might be grouped as follows. Denmark and France are at the lower end, in both the amount of temporary work and the degree to which temporary workers are "lower-level" workers in pay, status, or protection. At the upper end are the United Kingdom and Germany, where the gap between the pay, status, and protection of temporary workers and that of the permanent workforce seems to be widest. In the middle is the Netherlands. Despite the fact that temporary work has increased a great deal in the Netherlands and the wage rates for temporary workers are lower than for permanent workers, the terms under which temporary workers may be hired, and from what agencies, are regulated to some extent by national laws, and they are included in the formal central labor agreements that govern employment practices in the food-processing sector. In Germany and the United Kingdom, the use of temporary workers seems much more at the will of employers, and there is less social or institutional restraint than in the other three countries (for a general discussion of the

Table 9.1 Types of Temporary Workers

Country	Type of Temporary Worker in Each Country			
	Type 1	Type 2	Type 3	Type 4
United Kingdom	Temporary work agency (TWA)—predominantly immigrants	Company's temporary workers		
France	TWA—predominantly French	Fixed-term contract	Seasonal workers	Tâcherons (piece workers)—meat processing only; officially posted workers
Germany	TWA—predominantly immigrants	Temporary seasonal workers (mini-jobs)	Foreign posted workers (country-of-origin principle applies)	
Netherlands	TWA—predominantly immigrants	Fixed-term contract		
Denmark	TWA	Temporary contract	Seasonal workers (short-term contracts)	
United States	Immigrant workers employed directly by companies under contracts with no job security protection	Undocumented immigrant workers employed directly by companies under contracts with no job security protection		

Source: Authors' compilation.

conditions of temporary workers in the six countries, see Bosch, Mayhew, and Gautié, this volume).

This grouping of the countries also accords with the degree to which the use of temporary work has eroded not only the overall incomes of food-processing workers but also the obligations that employers have traditionally maintained toward their employees. The same constellation of factors that have conditioned the reduction of wages and benefits across the six countries—competitive strategies (the high-road versus low-road relative mix of cost reduction, product and process innovation, and higher-than-average quality), union strength, social norms, food culture, and national regulatory standards—is at work in constraining the replacement of more permanent conditions of employment with more contingent ones.

In Denmark, there is relatively less use of temporary workers than in the other countries, owing to a combination of factors: the food-processing industry's history of research and development and greater use of technology, which results in and facilitates a higher-road competitive strategy; the concentration of the industry in both subsectors in a few very large firms; the development of a sizable export market based on very high-quality products; and the strength of the social resistance of employee groups (through unions and in other ways) to the substitution of temporary workers for permanent workers. Most notably, however, Danish labor market regulations make it possible for anyone to be laid off, and agreements are reached at the workplace level that working hours can vary over time. This flexibility with current workers reduces companies' need for temporary workers.

Temporary workers are used in France for all the same reasons they are used in other countries: to manage seasonal demand fluctuations, to recruit for the permanent workforce, to replace permanent workers on vacation (this need having increased with the implementation of the thirty-five-hour week), and to handle some particularly difficult-to-fill job assignments.[13] What is interesting in France is that there are two classes of temporary workers: the relatively higher class of workers who come through temporary agencies (the TWAs), and the lower class of workers who are on seasonal contracts. Seasonal workers receive the lowest wage coefficients on the wage evaluation scales. Workers from the TWAs, on the other hand, are paid at a somewhat higher rate and receive a "precariousness" bonus to compensate for the temporary conditions of their contract. (Workers on seasonal contracts do not receive this bonus.) In this way, TWA workers do not occupy as low a rung on the wage ladder as temporary workers in the other European countries. TWAs are still less expensive than permanent workers for the firms because TWAs do not qualify for other benefits that must be paid to permanent workers, such as seniority premiums and gain sharing. In meat processing, there is also a third class, the so-called tâcherons. Tâcherons are contract workers (or "posted workers"—that is, they are officially paid by another firm) who perform specialized tasks that involve particularly difficult work with greater-than-average health risks, such as deboning. Even if they officially receive a fixed monthly wage (with some additional premiums to cover, for instance, transportation costs), they are in fact paid on a piece-rate basis.

Since the conditions and pay of seasonal workers are relatively low, where does the supply of workers come from? First, rural versus urban location appears to be the major factor affecting the local availability of workers who are willing to accept the poorer conditions of the seasonal work contracts. Many of the food processors in France are in rural areas where there are few alternative employment opportunities. Second, firms recruit their permanent workers from the seasonal workers. This prospect makes putting up with the lower wages and nonpermanent status more attractive. Finally, although there are no statistical data available, evidence from the case studies suggests that there is a greater representation of women and younger workers among the seasonal workers than among the permanent workers. Women and young workers sometimes prefer nonpermanent work situations, but gender discrimination may be at work as well.

Firms in urban areas where there are more employment alternatives to working in food processing have more difficulty attracting employees under the low-paid seasonal labor contracts. By turning to the TWAs and paying a more attractive wage plus the precariousness and holiday bonuses, these firms are better able to enlist workers who are willing to accept nonpermanent labor contracts. The firms in the urban areas also use the TWAs as a pool from which to recruit permanent workers. This further increases the attractiveness of the TWA arrangement for potential employees. The number of TWAs is increasing significantly among French food processors. So far the French have not turned to immigrant workers and are managing their increased need for flexibility with native French workers who are willing to accept relatively lower-paid work arrangements—

which are nevertheless not as low-paid as the contingent arrangements found in the other countries studied.

The use of temporary workers is greater in the Netherlands than it is in either Denmark or France, as mentioned in the previous section. In addition, unlike Danish or French firms, but similar to German and U.K. ones, Dutch firms are recruiting temporary workers from outside the Netherlands, in eastern Europe by and large. Unlike the case in Germany and the United Kingdom, the process and terms for hiring temporary workers have become part of the centralized negotiated labor agreements and are regulated to an extent by national regulations. Food-processing firms in the Netherlands employ temporary workers through TWAs, which, being covered by the central labor agreements, hold the line to a degree on the wages and conditions of temporary work.

In both meat and confectionery, the recruitment of new workers has been pretty much turned over to the TWAs. A fraction of TWA workers become permanent workers. Wages for TWA workers are lower than for non-TWA workers and are just above the national minimum wage. After six months, TWA workers' wages are raised to the CLA wage for the industry, although remaining in the lower grades of the pay scale, and the TWA workers receive neither a pension nor some other benefits. Unions appear to have recognized the need for employers to reduce costs and increase flexibility in order to stave off more extreme adaptations, such as plant closings and restructuring or relocating production outside the country. They have responded in a way that protects permanent native workers by sanctioning, but regulating, the greater hiring of temporary workers from outside the country, primarily Poland. Such non-native workers do not raise the same level of concern about job protection. Presumably, the conditions of the temporary workers have been allowed to deteriorate to the degree that the firms cannot resist the temptation to substitute temporary for permanent workers on a much wider scale than at present.

In both Germany and the United Kingdom, in comparison to the other countries in this study, there has been more extensive use of temporary workers, less protection and regulation of temporary work from the institutional structure, and more overt or tacit discretion accorded to firms as to who they may hire and under what terms. The United Kingdom seems to have gone further in this direction than Germany. Temporary workers are a greater fraction of the workforce in food processing in the United Kingdom than in Germany. There appear to be more brakes on expanding the use of temporary workers in Germany. In particular, there appears to be more concern that even greater use of temporary workers would undermine firms' capacity to compete on high-quality products. Conditions appear to be worse for temporary workers in the United Kingdom than they are in Germany.

The two countries are similar, however, along a number of dimensions. Unions in both countries have had little power to influence the use or pay of temporary workers. Compared to the other countries, the use of temporary workers in these two countries has gone far beyond the need primarily for temporary workers to staff peaks in demand and toward using them as a regular and easily accessible workforce for the lower-end jobs. This arrangement serves to hold down the cost of staffing lower-paid jobs because the easily recruited labor supply blunts wage pressure for otherwise undesirable jobs. In both Germany and the United Kingdom, there has been publicity about the abusive health and safety conditions under which some temporary workers must labor. Both countries have adopted the practice of contracting with gang-masters to bring in teams of temporary workers for particularly low-level jobs.[14]

The much greater use of immigrant workers for temporary work in the United Kingdom and Germany is likely both cause and effect of the greater, less officially regulated, and more abusive use of temporary workers in these two countries. In Germany, the "country-of-origin" principle allows German firms to employ labor under the legislated regulations of the workers' home countries, which exacerbates unequal treatment (for a discussion of the use of posted workers in Germany, see Bosch, Mayhew, and Gautié, this volume). Reports have been heard in the United Kingdom of employers using the essentially inexhaustible supply of temporary workers to discipline permanent workers if they request better pay or conditions. One confectionery manager observed: "If they don't like it here, they can leave. There are ten more where they came from."

The pattern of employing immigrant workers across the countries studied is much the same as the pattern of use of temporary workers. Denmark and France do not make much use of immigrant labor, the United Kingdom and Germany employ large numbers, and the Netherlands falls between these two groups. Although not exactly the same, the factors that influence whether employers make more or less use of immigrant workers are very similar to those that influence the use of temporary workers. In many cases, immigrant workers are the temporary workers. Even if they are not hired on purely temporary contracts, immigrant workers are generally paid less than permanent native workers, and they are more flexibly deployed. So hiring immigrant workers allows firms to reduce labor costs, increase flexibility, and maintain some degree of security and income for the permanent native workforce.

The availability of immigrant workers also allows for more use of nonpermanent contracts. Causation is likely to go both ways. Lower-wage and temporary employment contracts are more difficult to fill with native workers, who would compare them with the norms of the permanent contracts that other native workers have. Immigrant workers are less likely to object to these arrangements, because they are not substandard in comparison with their home country, and indeed, many immigrant workers do not see themselves as staying in the employing country, but as earning a nest egg for their family to whom they plan to return. As foreigners in lower-paid jobs, immigrant workers are also less likely to trigger the same level of social concern expressed when native workers are "stuck" in less desirable temporary working circumstances. The caliber of immigrant workers is seen as an additional advantage, as noted by a U.K. meat-processing company section leader:

> [I] would say each year . . . it's got better and better, so that the caliber of people that come to us [is] extremely good. . . . Of course, if they are coming from, say, eastern Europe, wages are so poor there that the attraction of what is a considerable wage, not for living standards here but what can be taken home, means that they want to work, and that's incredible, people who are coming here who are intelligent, who really want to work even though the job may be repetitive and boring.

With that kind of bargain for firms, one has to ask what constrains even more widespread use of immigrant workers in all the countries studied. Certainly with the entry of the accession countries in 2004, the availability of immigrant workers has greatly increased. The list of factors limiting greater use appears to include the strength of institutional restraints, such as national labor standards, regulations, and unions; social restraints on mixing and managing foreign workers' interactions with native workers and native communities; the degree to which more advanced technology is used; the degree to which competition is based on quality; the nature of the country's food culture; and the availability and ease of recruiting foreign workers. Danish firms are somewhat hesitant to hire non-Danish-speaking workers because of the increasing use of sophisticated technology that requires monitoring and controlling machinery. In addition, the strength of unions, while falling in Denmark, is still greater than in most other countries, and employers have worked to maintain good industrial relations as they rationalize and restructure to compete. Also, the flexible labor market in Denmark reduces the need for temporary workers, as permanent workers can be used in a flexible way.

As in most manufacturing as well as lower-paid service industries, the United States makes extensive use of immigrant labor in food processing. The stories from a meatpacking plant in New England and a pastry manufacturer in the mid-Atlantic area are similar and seem to be common. Family Pastries, a seventy-employee fresh and frozen pastry manufacturer, switched from African American employees to Latin American ones over the last couple of decades. Like other lower-wage employers throughout the United States, Family Pastries trumpets the superior work ethic of immigrant over non-immigrant U.S. employees (see, for example, Moss and Tilly 2001; Waldinger and Lichter 2003). Deluxe Meats has adopted the same human resource strategy. It is a medium-sized beef-packing plant whose primary product is frozen hamburger patties for fast-food and chain restaurants and frozen meatballs for grocery stores. Deluxe Meats was purchased by Tyson Foods, the largest food-processing corporation in the United States, in 2002. Its workforce is primarily Mexican immigrants but also includes recent Bosnian and Sudanese immigrants. Deluxe Meats indicated that it could not survive without the immigrant labor supply.

In the United States, the use of immigrant labor is confounded with the concern over illegal ("undocumented") immigration into the country, which has been an extremely controversial and polarizing issue in U.S. politics. The situation of illegal immigrants working in meat processing was put into high relief by the much-publicized raids by federal agents at Swift and Company meatpacking plants in December 2006. U.S. Immigration and Customs Enforcement (ICE) arrested over thirteen hundred employees at plants in six states. Without new legislation or major increases in enforcement budgets, neither of which appears likely, it is likely that such raids will have only a very temporary effect on the use of illegal immigrants in food processing.

NUMERICAL AND FUNCTIONAL FLEXIBILITY

Food producers are introducing and increasing a variety of forms of labor flexibility, primarily to reduce costs. Flexibility in staffing and hour levels beyond those dictated by the relevant standard full-time, full-year contract is numerical flexibility. Flexibility in the level and mix of tasks that individual workers perform is functional flexibility. Both types of flexibility help reduce costs. Numerical flexibility affects the cost of adapting output to changes in demand; for example, flexibility achieved by paying overtime may lead to higher labor costs than flexibility achieved by the use of temporary workers. Functional flexibility, facilitated by job rotation or cross-training, can increase labor productivity by developing more broadly skilled workers, by allowing workers to fill in at jobs that are in temporary demand because they are seasonal or because other workers are absent, or simply by making employees take on more tasks. This type of functional flexibility is more simply known as "stretch-out." In addition, functional flexibility through job rotation may help reduce exposure to health risks from repetitive jobs.

Both confectionery and meat-processing firms in all the five countries as well as in the United States are pursuing greater numerical and functional flexibility. The degree and the mix are different in the different countries. The various forms and levels of change are interesting in their own right and for their different implications for lower-wage workers. Of particular interest are differences in the mix of flexibility enhancements that, on average, lower the incomes or quality of work life of the workers producing food versus those that boost productivity without such effects. Because many of the forms of increased flexibility act to lower overall payments to labor, the differences in the degree of flexibility introduced across countries and sectors also provide a window into what restrains firms from competing by squeezing labor and retreating from the past norms of "fair" labor contracts.

The primary means by which food-processing firms in the United Kingdom have introduced flexibility into operations has been numerical flexibility through increased use of temporary workers, a strategy that has been used to a greater extent in the United Kingdom relative to some of the other countries. All save one of the sample firms had a rotating, two-shift pattern in place, but there were no reports of increases in the use of shift arrangements. Only one firm reported the use of annualized hours to avoid overtime payments. Overtime work has otherwise been a major instrument used by U.K. manufacturers to achieve numerical flexibility, and the extra income generated by it is viewed by many workers as indispensable for making ends meet. U.K. food processors have recruited large numbers of workers from the accession countries that joined the EU in 2004 as a source of their growing numbers of temporary workers. In this respect, the United Kingdom appears to be ahead of the other countries in the study.

Job rotation, often used to achieve greater functional flexibility or skill development, was instead used by firms in the United Kingdom as a means to deal with health and safety risks. Since much of the work in food processing is physically demanding and repetitive, job rotation is seen as a means to lessen repetitive motion disorders and reduce accidents that might be caused by boredom. There were no reports of changes in job design to address health and safety dangers, which presumably would be a much more expensive strategy than having workers take turns across jobs. The workers interviewed in these firms reported that job rotation was not much of a benefit, since they were simply moving from one boring, repetitive job to another. The firm with the worst health and safety record had no job rotation scheme, although there were probably many other factors that differentiated that firm from the others.

In France, food-processing firms in meat and confectionery have made extensive use of numerical flexibility through nonpermanent employment contracts, the use of TWAs, shift work, and annualized hours arrangements that reduce the need for overtime. Firms are increasingly adopting job rotation to boost functional flexibility so as to reduce slack time and allow more senior workers to train recently hired ones.

Although the actions taken to add flexibility in the workplace to remain competitive have definitely intensified work in the eyes of the workers we interviewed, the changes in France, in comparison to those in most of the other countries we studied, appear to have had somewhat less of an impact on worker incomes. Two- and three-shift arrangements have been part of work organization in France for over a decade. A bonus is paid, however, for night work. Incomes have been reduced by firms' adoption of annualization of work hours to reduce the need for overtime, but annualization of work hours typically followed the passage of the Robien and Aubry laws (1998), which reduced the workweek without lowering pay.

Some permanent workers in France find job rotation to be a burden because of the stress of shifting between different jobs. Plus, job rotation was adopted to reduce slack time across different job tasks, and therefore, with rotation, workers are more likely to have to work at full pace, all the time. Moreover, skilled workers may occasionally be asked to take on unskilled jobs during slack times. But there is some compensation for the burden of shouldering the various tasks: workers maintain the rate of pay of their highest job classification throughout their job rotation.

There have also been examples of French firms trying to substitute internal (functional) for external flexibility by cutting down on temporary workers and increasing automation, job rotation, and multiskilling training. Another interesting approach to internalizing flexibility in France is the multi-employer contract: workers are hired by an association of employers that rotates the workers among member firms.

German food-processing firms have implemented a number of initiatives to reduce the costs associated with keeping up the numerical flexibility required by seasonal variations, mainly by making employees bank leave time and work intensively during peak periods. The arrangements varied across the firms in the sample, but most firms had adopted one or another way of reducing the cumulative amount paid to their employees over the year. Because they face such heavy peak production before the holiday period, confectionery firms operate three shifts and in some cases Saturday and Sunday shifts. The bonus for shift work, other than Saturday and Sunday shifts, appears to be quite low, so firms gain a great deal by running these shifts.

One of the confectionery firms in the sample of Danish firms we studied had introduced an annualized hours scheme to handle the distribution of work hours in its permanent workforce over peak and slack times. Other firms were interested in following the lead of this firm, but had not yet done so. Some firms used shifts to handle peak work times, but the practice was not widespread because of the bonus that must be added to wages for evening and night work. The Danish Working Environment Authority has mandated that firms institute job rotation when there is repetitive work. The goal is to reduce worker health hazards. Workers complain about the burdens of job rotation, but some firms report benefits: the broader range of skills in which workers are being trained makes flexible deployment of workers easier to accomplish.

Danish firms make use of temporary workers during periods of high demand, both by offering workers temporary contracts and by contracting with temporary agencies. Although not that pervasive, the use of temporary workers and temporary work agencies is increasing. Permanent employees and worker representatives have voiced opposition, however, to firms' greater reliance on temporary workers.

Flexibility in the Dutch food-processing industry is controlled more by the institutional regulatory structure than it is in the other countries studied. The collective labor agreements (CLAs) that have been agreed to jointly by the major unions and employers' associations have constrained the kind of steps toward greater numerical and functional flexibility that firms in other countries have taken. For example, annualizing hours, which has been adopted in some of the other countries, is limited by the CLAs in food processing. Individual plants may work out a plan with their unions, but it does not appear to happen very often. Shift work and overtime are more important tools than annualized hours for staffing varying levels of demand.

Job rotation is used to some extent, but less as a tool to achieve broader skill capacity in workers, and hence functional flexibility, than as a means to avoid repetitive stress disorders and other task exposure risks. There is a wage cost to firms if they develop multiple skills in their employees, because CLAs require wage bonuses for increased task competencies. This reduces the incentive for developing functional flexibility through job rotation.

The primary way in which flexibility has been introduced into food processing in the Netherlands is through increased deployment of temporary workers. Temporary worker agencies have become important players. Temporary workers are increasingly being used not only for the traditional role of staffing during peak demand times, but also for jobs with higher health risks that require little skill. TWAs are also serving more and more often as the general recruiters for employees, some of whom may become permanent workers for food processors, and the TWAs are stepping up their recruitment in eastern Europe for workers. The operation of TWAs is now regulated to a degree by CLAs and by national legislation, although compliance with the CLA is less than perfect.

DE- AND UP-SKILLING

Jobs in food manufacturing companies have changed vastly with the increased use of automation. A company's level of automation depends on its product market strategy. With increased consolidation among companies both within and across countries, strategies tend to fall into one of two camps: high-quality, value-added, often branded products or supermarket own label; and more basic products. The strategy adopted influences the level of automation. By definition, high-quality, value-added products require a higher degree of attention and processing; this leaves more room for automation, but also may increase reliance on more skilled labor that is more difficult to automate. With more basic products it is easier to automate the task, but the level of labor may be such that retaining low-skill workers is cheaper than introducing more complex automation. All companies across the five countries had introduced technology, to varying degrees, over the last twenty years to remain competitive. The exceptions were two companies, one in Denmark and one in the United Kingdom, that produced handmade products. The strategies adopted and levels of automation varied between the companies across the five countries, as shown in table 9.2.

The increasing use of automation in the meat-processing and confectionery sectors is the result of a number of factors: the downward pressure on prices from the food retail sector, increased competition, increasing productivity demands, a desire to improve working conditions (predominantly in France and Denmark), and cost—particularly labor costs. The emphasis on each of these factors varied, however, across the countries. In Denmark and France, it was less about reducing labor costs and more about improving product efficiency and suppressing the most physically demanding jobs, whereas in Germany, the Netherlands, and the United Kingdom reducing labor costs was a major factor because the food retail sector in those countries places more and more pressure on manufacturers.

Each of these strategies makes perfect economic sense for companies trying to stay afloat and make a profit in such a competitive environment. Small to medium-sized enterprises are the least likely to invest in automation, owing to the capital-intense investment re-

Table 9.2 Product Strategy and Automation

Country	Confectionery Companies		
Denmark	Brand Confectionery	Family Chocolate	PL Confectionery
Product strategy 1		Handmade chocolates	No
Product strategy 2		No	Yes
Automation	Highly automated	Automated	Highly automated
Germany	Confect_A	Confect_B	Confect_C
Product strategy 1	Yes	Yes	Yes
Product strategy 2	Yes	Yes	Yes
Automation	Highly automated	Highly automated	Highly automated
France	Chocchris	Chocind	Regsweet
Product strategy 1	Yes	No	Yes
Product strategy 2	Yes	Yes	No
Automation	Highly automated	Automated	Highly automated
Netherlands	CON A	CON B	CON C
Product strategy 1	No	Yes	No
Product strategy 2	Yes	No	Yes
Automation	Automated	Highly automated	Automated
United Kingdom	Chocs	Sweetco	Novelty
Product strategy 1	Yes, some handmade	Yes	No
Product strategy 2		No	Yes
Automation	Automated	Highly automated	Automated

Source: Authors' compilation based on previous volumes in series.
Notes:
Product strategy 1: high-quality, value-added, often branded.
Product strategy 2: supermarket own label, private label, and more basic products.

quired; a number of manual positions can still be found in these firms. SMEs are prominent in Germany, France, and the United Kingdom, although a number of them have been bought by multinational corporations in these countries.

The increased use of automation has been a double-edged sword for many low-wage workers. The introduction of automated machinery can replace the more-skilled craft and artisan jobs, resulting in a

	Chicken	Danish Liver	Multi-food	JV-Food
		Meat Companies		
	Yes	Yes	Yes	Yes
	Yes	No	No	Yes
	Highly automated	Highly automated	Highly automated	Highly automated
	Meat_A	Meat_B	Meat_C	Meat_D
	Yes	Yes	Yes	Yes
	No	No	No	No
	Automated	Automated	Highly automated	Highly automated
	Canpat	Hambac	Multiprod	Regsaus
	Yes	No	Yes	Yes
	Yes	Yes	Yes	Yes
	Highly automated	Highly automated	Automated	Highly automated
CON D	MEA A	MEA B	MEA C	MEA D
Yes	Yes	No	Yes	Yes
No	Yes	Yes	No	Yes
Highly automated	Automated	Automated	Increasing automation	Highly automated
	Clucks	Poultryco	Baconco	
	Yes	Yes		
	No	Yes	Yes	
	Highly automated	Automated	Automated	

Highly automated: automated integrated product lines.
Automated: some tasks automated, but manual labor involved to produce parts of the product line and, in some places, to connect the automated aspects of the production lines.

de-skilling of the majority of factory process operatives. What are left are the mundane jobs along the process line, particularly in those companies where the introduction of technology is in its early stages and has been piecemeal, as was the case in the German and U.K. companies. As a result, the machines often have to be "patched together" by the intervention of simple manual operations. Clucks, a U.K. case company, had invested in a continuous cooker and automated packing machine, but the meat still had to be individually placed by hand onto the conveyor belt to enter the cooker (James and Lloyd 2008). On the other hand, in Denmark, France, and the Netherlands, where automation has been widely adopted across the board, sorting and packing positions are no longer available. For many workers, the content of jobs is changing from manual labor to being more skilled. As the labor-intensive positions are automated, the machines and the production processes need to be monitored, and workers are trained and up-skilled to machine operator positions and technicians. Workers in all countries were given some training when they began at any of the companies participating in this study; however, this training was predominantly oriented toward health and safety. Further, role-specific training occurred on the job and often involved training from the company that produced the machinery involved.

Consequently, an up-skilling of segments of the workforce is occurring at the same time that workers are being de-skilled. As smaller companies are bought by MNCs, capital intensity will increase, new technological innovation will be introduced, and the divide between skilled and unskilled workers will increase. Ultimately, low-skill occupations will be a thing of the past. Robots are already being tried out in Denmark, Germany, and the United Kingdom.

Health and Safety

Not only is the food-processing sector renowned for low wages, but it also has a reputation for having one of the worst health and safety records in the manufacturing industry. Specifically, in each of the five countries, the working conditions of process operatives were reported as being rife with stench, noise, dust, high or low temperatures, and drafts as well as poor ventilation; process operatives were also required to work in poor positions, engage in repetitive and monotonous movements, and lift heavy objects. In comparing the Danish and U.S. meat-processing subsector, Lars Esbjerg and Klaus Grunert (2008, 111–12) note from Human Rights Watch that "in many ways, at the turn of the 21st century meatpacking in the U.S. resembled the situation 100 years earlier":

> Meatpacking plants at the turn of the twentieth century were more than sweatshops. They were bloodshops, and not only for animal

slaughter. The industry operated with low wages, long hours, brutal treatment and sometimes deadly exploitation of mostly immigrant workers. (Human Rights Watch 2005, 11)

The case study work on which this chapter is based includes ample evidence of problems in European production sites as well. An operative with the U.K. company Clucks reported:

We shift and sort ten tons plus a day, the five of us on that line, so, lifting and throwing it on the line and moving it about. You do a lot of lifting, and it is now starting to play my back up.

Another U.K. operative, a shop steward at Baconco, described the brutal consequences of improper training:

He [a Polish trainee] said, "I go on holiday tomorrow, what's the point of me going in there for one or two hours" [he was not trained in that area], and the supervisor say, "Get your backside in there, you do it," pressure and pressure and he took his finger straight off within five minutes of doing the job. . . . So that's what we call training.

Evidence from the Netherlands (van Halem 2008, 283) indicates that the use of migrant workers is strategic in order to deal with health and safety issues: "Deboning has been outsourced to two teams of ten to twelve employees each, the majority of them Polish, by a secondment contract at piece rates. Management decided to outsource this work because of the high health and safety risks." In France, the same high-risk task is carried out by specialists contracted for this task only, the tâcherons mentioned earlier, who are paid on a piece-rate basis but face health problems and possibly health-related unemployment later in life. Automation can be used as a strategy to reduce not only labor costs but also the risks of suffering disabling sickness or injury from performing dangerous tasks.

Legislation and union impact have somewhat improved working conditions for food process operatives across the five countries, although it does seem that meat processing is worse than confectionery. For example, in the United Kingdom, the official injury rate for food and drink manufacturing has decreased by 37 percent over the last fifteen years, but the official injury rate is still 1,775 per 100,000 workers, which is nearly double the manufacturing average of 989 per 100,000 workers (Health and Safety Executive 2005). In France, although no data were available on whether conditions were improving or worsening, empirical evidence from the interviews suggested that physical hardship was diminishing with automation; nevertheless, workers complained about increasing stress and work intensification. In Denmark, as mentioned earlier, the Working Environment Authority addresses repetitive work by demanding job rotation to reduce health hazards. Similarly, in the Netherlands, a collective agreement was signed for both confectionery and meat processing in 2003 that imposed job rotation in order to limit repetitive strain injuries.

In the United States, injury rates in the meat and poultry processing industries have historically been among the highest compared to all other manufacturing industries. For example, in the early 1990s, the injury rate in meatpacking was four times the rate for all private industries, and three times the rate for all manufacturing industries. The rate for meat processing and poultry processing was approximately three times the overall private industry rate and twice the manufacturing rate, with poultry processing slightly higher than meat processing. Official government statistics have shown a remarkable improvement, however, in the last decade and a half. There have been declines in the rates in the confectionery industry as well, although not as large as the drop in meat and poultry processing. For example, in meat processing, the illness and injury rate for 1994 was 20.4 per 100 workers. In 2006 it had fallen to 9.8. The confectionery sector saw rates decline from 13.4 in 1994 to 9.6 in 2000, to 7.8 in 2006.[15] Both the industry associations and the Occupational Safety and Health Administration (OSHA) ascribe the fall in injury rates to increased priority, scrutiny, and workplace safety programs implemented by companies, the promulgation of voluntary ergonomic guidelines issued by OSHA (there are no mandatory standards), partnerships with OSHA in voluntary protection programs, and grants that OSHA has issued to universities, such as the Georgia Institute of Technology, to provide assistance to meat and poultry producers.[16] Others have argued, however, that these improved rates are to a large degree due to changes in reporting methodology (Leigh, Marcin, and Miller 2004; Rosenman et al. 2006).

In the case of meat processing, Human Rights Watch (2005) cites several studies and its own interviews with workers, labor officials, and industry representatives to illustrate how the numbers are under-reported or manipulated by companies and various reasons for why this happens. The safety record in the United States, therefore, is difficult to assess in its own right, let alone compare to the five European countries. The health and safety experience in meat and poultry processing in the United States appears to reflect two changes: a substantial reduction of regulatory oversight, through reduced standards and reduced implementation of standards as well as through reduced budgets for regulatory agencies; and an increase in the use of immigrant labor, especially undocumented immigrant labor. The alleged result is a continued high level of worker exposure to harm. In this way, the U.S. situation poses an important comparison case for any analysis of the increased use of vulnerable labor and the effects of standards and their enforcement in the European countries, where these two developments have occurred to a much lesser degree, and in the United Kingdom, which is intermediate between the United States and the other countries. Another implication of the U.S. experience for other countries is that the attempt to raise standards and enforcement could increase the incentives for companies to underreport and to increase their use of legal and especially illegal immigrants. We can also speculate that higher standards will increase the likelihood that companies will move operations out of their home country.

Automation and new forms of work organization, especially multitasking and job rotation, have been a result of the tightening of health and safety legislation and have been adopted, to greater or lesser extents, in each country. It should be noted, however, that job rotation and multi-skilling were not always introduced primarily in order to improve health and safety. In the Netherlands, improvements in health and safety have been a positive by-product of companies introducing job rotation to improve efficiency; in Germany, "the aim [of multi-skilling] was to meet the unrelenting competitive pressure by increasing quality and safety standards, whilst at the same time increasing productivity on the lines" (Czommer 2008, 163). And automation also has negative effects on health and safety. An operator with the French company Regsweet reported to Caroli, Gautié, and Lamanthe (2008, 112):

> As they've automated practically everything, there are machines everywhere now, work space is small, there's no room, it's not adapted. . . . There was a time after everything was automated when there were a lot of accidents, cuts, fingers cut . . . just to make us work faster.

While job rotation and multi-skilling seemed a positive step toward improving work conditions and tackling health and safety problems, and there was evidence that many employees in each country saw these strategies as positive—employees in France, the United Kingdom, and Denmark reported being less tired and bored—there were also limits to how much could be achieved by work reorganization based on job rotation. The use of job rotation may be limited by hygiene norms—in the production and packaging of fresh products, the various stages of the production process have to be clearly separated (Hambac in France and Clucks in the United Kingdom were examples of this). In Denmark, France, and the United Kingdom, both managers and employees at some companies noted the difficulty of implementing job rotation schemes when employees were resistant. It seems that once some employees found a niche with a task, they were reluctant, even unwilling in some cases, to perform a different task. Esbjerg and Grunert (2008, 116) state that "workers tend to find frequent rotation mandated by the Danish Working Environment Authority (WEA) in order to reduce the amount of repetitive work, to be a nuisance." Job rotation can make work less physically demanding, but the need to pay more attention to work can lead to increased mental strain. Finally, the use of job rotation and multi-skilling depends, of course, on management's choice and will. Evidence across the countries showed that a positive management and paternalistic company philosophy more often resulted in a positive trickle-down effect to the workers with more frequent training for multi-skilling and job rotation.

Gender Differences

Surprisingly, gender did not seem to feature strongly in confectionery in most of the countries. With the increasing use of temporary labor, it was found that both men and women were doing the same low-skilled tasks. In the United Kingdom, there was mention that females found it easier to pack the high-end chocolates into the boxes in a specific way because they had smaller hands, but this certainly did not prohibit companies from having males in these positions. In France, women were also overrepresented in the packaging activities, where wages tend to be lower than in the production activities. Seasonal workers—the least favorable employment status—were also more often women.

Some firms declared an explicit policy to tackle the gender difference in pay (implementing for instance the "Equal" program funded by the European Social Fund). There was no explicit mention of gen-

der differentiation in the production process in the other countries—
the dualism being more between permanent and temporary workers,
who were often foreign-born males. In meat, however, there was gender differentiation, as expected, between slaughterhouses and meat
processing. In the slaughterhouses, which were not directly studied
in our research but were nevertheless discussed as part of the process,
the work was predominantly done by males. In the meat-processing
factories, there did not seem to be any great differentiation on the
lines between males and females undertaking various jobs, but there
was no evidence from which to draw firmer conclusions. That gender
differentiation was not a distinguishing feature, particularly in terms
of health and safety, across the countries could be considered a finding in and of itself.

THE FUTURE OF LOW- AND HIGH-ROAD STRATEGIES FOR WORKING CONDITIONS IN FOOD PROCESSING

In this chapter, we have reviewed how the food-processing sector,
specifically the meat processing and confectionery sectors, cope with
increasing competitive pressures in five European countries, with
some comparison to the U.S. situation. We have shown how the pressures on food producers are quite similar across these countries and
are caused by the same global forces—namely, increased retail pressure, new low-cost competitors, and changing consumer demands.

In dealing with these pressures, we have found a mixture of low-
and high-road strategies to handle working conditions for food
process operatives. There were plenty of examples of pressure on
wages, cuts in benefits, increased pace of work, and use of more temporary forms of employment. But there were also plenty of examples
of food processing workers still being paid way above the low-wage
threshold (sometimes far above), of job up-skilling due to a need for
functional flexibility and/or automation, and of improvements in
health and safety conditions in an industry that historically has had
somewhat worse than average problems with health and safety.

In trying to explain which factors may further high- versus low-
road strategies, we can distinguish three groups of (interrelated) factors: the different points of departure in the various countries, the
different sets of institutional and cultural arrangements, and the different competitive positions and strategies of the companies.

It was clear that the point of departure in the five European countries differed enormously. This was most pronounced with regard to wages, but also with regard to nonwage benefits, the use of immigrant and temporary labor, working time regulations, and focus on work health and safety. The existence of these differences does not imply, however, that they will last. If food producers across countries experience similar competitive pressures, their reactions may lead to working conditions in the food-processing sector that converge at the low level. This is the bitter forecast for the future of food processing: as competitive pressures increase, producers in countries with better working conditions will either be forced down the low road or, if institutional or cultural constraints prevent this, be forced to offshore or outsource production, so that local labor markets for food operatives in these countries will collapse and the food-processing sector will eventually disappear, except for some local niche production.

There are limits to how far this development could go. Food is a product category that is strongly embedded in national and local culture, resulting in specific local preferences for certain kinds of foods. Closeness to the end user is therefore important for food producers and becomes more important moving from universal, staple products to differentiated, value-added products. Also, transportation costs provide a limit to outsourcing, and current debates on the environmental impact of food production, especially on food miles, provides additional barriers to any attempt by the food sector to rely mostly on production outsourced to areas where labor costs are low.

But more importantly, we have seen examples of the high-road approach as well—companies reacting to competitive challenges with innovation, added value, and automation in ways that allow the payment of higher wages, maintain high standards of health and safety, and lead to jobs that are more attractive in terms of diversity of tasks and skills required. Automation can have a positive effect on working conditions, especially when food-processing companies make the qualitative leap from piecemeal automation to integrated automated process lines. High-value-added products based on craftsman-type niche production result in more specialized jobs. Although it is difficult to predict what mass-produced, high-value-added products will do to the jobs of food processing operatives in the longer run, we should at least suspect that an economically viable production of high-value-added products also makes it easier to take the high road with regard to work conditions.

Choosing the high road will work only if companies have, or can acquire, the necessary competencies; can gain access to the necessary capital; and can gain access to markets that demand high value and differentiated products. It seems plausible that domestic markets with a strong food culture, like France, may fulfill that condition more than weaker food cultures, as in the remaining five countries. Also, the increasing income inequality in many countries may lead to a higher demand for higher-end products. Otherwise, the feasibility of the high road may be linked to access to export markets. Thus, following the high road may also be linked to having competencies in exporting.

The research presented in this chapter suggests that there are country differences in the extent to which the low versus the high road is pursued. Food producers in Germany and the United Kingdom seem to have advanced more along the low road than food producers in the other three countries. This raises the question of whether countries are only at different stages of a common pattern of development, and whether the other countries eventually will follow Germany and the United Kingdom on that route. It is clear that national policies in Denmark, France, and the Netherlands have implemented measures (in the form of minimum wages, other forms of regulation of compensation and work conditions, strong unions, and compulsory collective agreements) that make it more difficult for food companies to react to competitive challenges by following the low road. We may venture the hypothesis that the existence of such measures—which have been part of the national institutional setup in these countries for a long time—has motivated food producers in these countries to develop competencies and business strategies that combine production efficiency with the creation of added customer value, thus making it possible to pursue a high-road approach.

This does not mean that copying such measures in settings where they are not so much a part of the traditional institutional setup will by itself encourage companies to seek the high road. As noted earlier, countering competitive challenges by innovation, automation, and added value requires different competencies in the food-processing sector, and public policy can have a role in helping the sector acquire these competencies. Innovation policy is especially important here: supporting the research and development relevant for the cost-effective production of high-value food products; encouraging knowledge transfer between research institutions and food companies; sharing knowledge through clustering and networking; and taking measures to build up market-related competencies that enable food-producing companies to translate changing consumer demands into successful high-value food products.

Table 9A.1 Case Information

Country	Confectionery Companies		
Denmark	Brand Confec-tionery	Family Chocolate	PL Confectionery
Firm size	1,200 to 1,500 employees	Fewer than 50 employees	400 to 500 employees
Annual sales	DKR1.7 billion	DKR186 million	DKR805 million
Business strategy	Manufacturer brands; some private label	High-quality, fresh, handmade	Private label and OEM
Union	Yes—very high	Unknown	Yes—very high
Temps/Agency	Limited	Yes—50 percent during peak season	Yes—recent
Pay (hourly)[a]	DKR98	Basic rate: un-skilled, DKR108; skilled, DKR120	DKR98
Germany	Confect_A	Confect_B	Confect_C
Firm size	More than 700 employees	About 400 employees	400 employees
Annual sales	€225 million	€397 million	More than €4 billion
Business strategy	Seasonal product suppliers; en-larging product range	Consolidation, mass orientation, efficiency with-out seasonal fluctuations	Low and high market seg-ments with high degree of tech-nical and prod-uct innovation
Union	Yes—20 to 40 percent	Yes—approxi-mately 34 percent	Yes—60 percent
Temps	Yes	Yes—minimal	Yes—maximum 80
Pay (hourly)[a]	€8.60	€8.60	€8.60

Meat Companies			
Chicken	Danish Liver	Multi-food	JV-Food
More than 1,000 employees	200 to 250 employees	More than 3,000 employees	More than 1,800 employees
DKR1.4 billion	DKR28 million	DKR4.8 billion	DKR2.6 billion
Trend toward value-added products	Quality and strong brands	Tasty, high-quality products; intense cost focus; on-going rationalization	Trend toward value-added products
Yes—99.9 percent	Yes—100 percent	Yes—100 percent	Yes—very high
Use students on holidays	No	No	No
Approximately DKR112	DKR112, increasing to DKR142 after two years	Approximately DKR224	Approximately DKR224
Meat_A	Meat_B	Meat_C	Meat_D
200 to 300 employees	Fewer than 100 employees	800 to 900 employees	700 to 800 employees
€39 million	€1 million	€250 million	Approximately €150 million
Premium products; avoid dependence from market discounters	Organic premium products; strong social policy orientation	High-quality, large branded-product range	Production of premium products
Yes—10 to 15 percent	No	Yes—50 percent	Yes—45 percent
No; high number of migrant workers	No; low number of migrant workers	Seasonal; migrant workers 20 percent	No; 16 migrant workers
€6.98	€8.60	€9.30	€9.83

(*Table continues on p. 414.*)

Table 9A.1 (*Continued*)

Country	Confectionery Companies			
France	Chochris	Chocind	Regsweet	
Firm size	200 to 300 employees	100 to 150 employees	Fewer than 100 employees	
Annual sales	NA	NA	NA	
Business strategy	Medium- and high-quality own-label brand and retail brand products	Mass production of industrial chocolate	High-quality regional, own-label brand and retail brand products	
Union	Yes (recent)—low	Yes—low	No	
Temp agency/ other temporary workers	Almost no temps; many seasonal workers; very few foreign workers	High rate of temps (20 to 25 percent); very few seasonal workers; high share of workers from ethnic minorities	Intensive use of fixed-term contracts and temps during the high season	
Pay[b]	Basic salary + premiums	Basic salary + premiums	Basic salary + premiums	
Netherlands	CON A	CON B	CON C	CON D
Firm size	150 to 200 employees	Fewer than 150 employees	Fewer than 100 employees	100 employe
Annual sales	NA	NA	NA	NA
Business strategy	Specialist private-label family sweet producers	Branded MNC producing one particular line of sweets	Private-label, family-owned chocolate producer	Niche and branded fam owned com
Union	Yes—65 percent (manufacturing 100 percent)	Yes—30 percent	Yes—95 percent (manufacturing 100 percent)	Yes—60 perc
Temps/agency	Yes—average 10 percent; 40 percent immigrants	Yes—10 to 30 percent; immigrants 30 percent	Yes—average 35 percent; 45 percent immigrants	Yes—average percent; 10 cent immigr
Pay (hourly)	Grade B: €11.34 Grade C: €11.62	Grade B: €11.38 Grade C: €11.63	Grade 1: €11.10 Grade 2: €11.27 Grade 3: €11.58 Grade 4: €12.00	Mostly grade €11.58

Meat Companies			
Canpat	Hambac	Multiprod	Regsaus
150 to 200 employees	500 to 600 employees	About 1,000 employees	Fewer than 100 employees
NA	NA	NA	NA
Medium- and high-quality own-label brand and retail brand products	Mass production of retail brand and no-brand products	Medium- and high-quality own-label brand and retail brand products	High-quality own-label brand and retail brand products
Yes—low	Yes—high	Yes—low	No
Almost none	Intensive use of tâcherons, temps, fixed-term contracts	Use of temps and seasonal work	Intensive use of fixed-term contracts and temps during the high season
Basic + premiums	Basic + premiums	Basic + premiums	Basic + premiums
MEA A	MEA B	MEA C	MEA D
Fewer than 100 employees	Fewer than 100 employees	100 to 150 employees	Fewer than 100 employees
€32 million	€24 million	€55 million	NA
Singular meat products for brand and private label	Private-label sausage producers	Private-label, family-owned, bacon products and sausages	MNC branded and private-label sausage products
Yes—20 percent	Yes—75 percent	Yes—20 percent	Yes—15 percent
Yes—average 14 percent; 12.5 percent immigrants	Yes—average 5 percent NA	Yes—45 percent; 30 to 40 percent immigrants	Yes—up to 20 percent; 20 percent immigrants
€8.95	Grade 2: €8.42 Grade 3: €8.98	Grade A: €8.85	€8.95

(*Table continues on p. 416.*)

Table 9A.1 (*Continued*)

Country	Confectionery Companies		
United Kingdom	Chocs	Sweetco	Novelty
Firm size	150 to 200 employees	More than 500 employees in two plants	100 to 150 employees
Annual sales	£30 million	£48 million	£15 million
Business strategy	New investment, new products in new market, new management	Niche markets, short runs, constant R&D, recent technological investment	Emphasis on cost-cutting, efficiency, and product variations, increasing automation
Union	Yes—very low	No	Yes
Temps/agency	Yes; over 100	Yes; over 300	Yes; increases in high season
Pay (hourly)[a]	2 shifts: €8.23	2 shifts: training starts at €8.03	2 shifts: packers €12.64; operatives €13.29

Source: Authors' compilation based on Carolis, Gautié, and Lamanthe (2008); Czommer (2008); Esbjerg and Grunert (2008); James and Lloyd (2008); and van Halem (2008).
a. Lowest amount paid for an operative (not training rate) in that company.
b. Actual figures for pay rates were not available for French cases.

NOTES

1. For further information on the methodology used and on the food-processing industry in the individual countries, see Caroli, Gautié, and Lamanthe (2008), Czommer (2008), Esbjerg and Grunert (2008), James and Lloyd (2008), and van Halem (2008).

2. U.S. Census Department, Bureau of Economic Analysis. County Business Patterns, 2005, available at: http://censtats.census.gov/cgi-bin/cbpnaic/cbpdetl.pl; and Economic Census of Manufactures, 2002, available at: http://www.census.gov/econ/census02/guide/INDRPT31.HTM

3. U.S. Census Bureau, "Foreign Trade Statistics," available at: http://www.census.gov/foreign-trade/statistics/country/index.html.

4. U.S. Bureau of Labor Statistics (BLS), "Career Guide to Industries: Food Manufacturing," available at: http://www.bls.gov/oco/cg/cgs011.htm.

Meat Companies		
Clucks	Poultryco	Baconco
Plant: more than 600 employees	Plant: 500 to 600 employees	Plant: more than 150 employees
£40 million	£210 million in U.K.	£1,952 million (whole company)
Increasing technology to replace manual labor; produce large volumes and cut costs	Expanding into value-added meals and developing new products, recent de-layering	Work intensification, new products from another factory
Yes—low	Yes—low	Yes—50 percent
Yes—increasing	Yes	Yes—increasing
2 shifts: €8.80	2 shifts: €9.08	2 shifts: €11.11

5. Ibid.
6. U.S. Census Bureau, Current Population Survey. Author's tabulation from Current Population Survey micro data for 2000, available at: http://www.census.gov/cps.
7. U.S. BLS, "Contingent and Alternative Employment Arrangements," supplement to the Current Population Survey, 2005. February 2005. Authors' tabulation from microdata. Available at: http://www.census .gov/cps.
8. Lane et al. (2003), based on U.S. Census Bureau, "Concentration Ratios: 2002 Economic Census, Manufacturing," available at: http://www .census.gov/prod/ec02/ec0231sr1.pdf.
9. U.S. Census Bureau, "Concentration Ratios: 2002," May 2006. Available at: http://www.census.gov/prod/ec02/ec0231sr1.pdf.
10. At the time of the field research, the NMW was £5.05 ($9.98) and scheduled to rise to £5.35 ($10.58) in October 2006.
11. It should be noted that Denmark has a rather high income tax, with

tax rates of about 44 percent (before tax deductions for rent payments and payments to unions and unemployment schemes) even for low wages.
12. UFCW won a union representation election on December 17, 2008.
13. Many firms have implemented the reduction of working time to thirty-five hours per week by increasing the number of days off.
14. The death of twenty-one Chinese cockle pickers working illegally for a gang-master in Morecombe Bay in 2004 brought this issue to the fore in the United Kingdom and provided the impetus for regulation. Since August 2006, all agencies and employers providing labor to the food-processing industry must have a license.
15. U.S. BLS, "Injuries, Illnesses, and Fatalities," available at: http://www .bls.gov/iif/oshsum.htm#06Summary%20Tables.
16. See, for example, U.S. Department of Labor, Occupational Safety and Health Administration (OSHA), "OSHA Recognizes Five Nebraska Meat Processing Facilities for Safety" (news release), November 16, 2005, available at: http://www.osha.gov/pls/oshaweb/owadisp.show _document?p_table=NEWS_RELEASES&p_id=11694; and U.S. BLS, "Career Guide to Industries: Food Manufacturing" (see note 4).

REFERENCES

Caroli, Ève, Jérôme Gautié, and Annie Lamanthe. 2008. "Operators in Food-Processing Industries: Coping with Increasing Competitive Pressure." In *Low-Wage Work in France*, edited by Ève Caroli and Jérôme Gautié. New York: Russell Sage Foundation.

Codron, Jean-Marie, Klaus Grunert, Eric Giraud-Heraud, Louis-Georges Soler, and Anita Regmi. 2005. "Retail Sector Responses to Changing Consumer Preferences: The European Experience." In *New Directions in Global Food Markets*, edited by Anita Regmi and Mark Gehlhar. Washington: U.S. Department of Agriculture, Economic Research Service.

Czommer, Lars. 2008. "Wild West Conditions in Germany?! Low-Skill Jobs in Food Processing." In *Low-Wage Work in Germany*, edited by Gerhard Bosch and Claudia Weinkopf. New York: Russell Sage Foundation.

Day, George S., and Robin Wensley. 1988. "Assessing Advantage: A Framework for Diagnosing Competitive Superiority." *Journal of Marketing* 52(1): 1–20.

Esbjerg, Lars, and Klaus Grunert. 2008. "Feeling the Gale or Enjoying a Breeze in the Eye of the Storm? The Consequences of Globalization for Work and Workers in the Danish Food-Processing Industry." In *Low-Wage Work in Denmark*, edited by Niels Westergaard-Nielsen. New York: Russell Sage Foundation.

Grimshaw, Damian, Mick Marchington, Jill Rubery, and Hugh Willmott.

2005. "Conclusion: Redrawing Boundaries, Reflecting on Practice and Policy." In *Fragmenting Work: Blurring Organizational Boundaries and Disordering Hierarchies*, edited by Mick Marchington, Damian Grimshaw, Jill Rubbery, and Hugh Willmott. Oxford: Oxford University Press.

Grunert, Klaus G. 2002. "Current Issues in the Understanding of Consumer Food Choice." *Trends in Food Science and Technology* 13(8): 275–85.

———. 2006. "How Changes in Consumer Behavior and Retailing Affect Competence Requirements for Food Producers and Processors." *Economía y Recursos Naturales* 6(11): 3–22.

Health and Safety Executive. 2005. *A Recipe for Safety: Occupational Health and Safety in Food and Drink Manufacture*. Sudbury, U.K.: HSE Books.

Hendrickson, Mary, and William D. Heffernan. 2007. "Concentration of Agricultural Markets." Food Circle Networking Project. Columbia: University of Missouri (April). Available at: http://www.nfu.org/wp-content/2007-heffernanreport.pdf.

Human Rights Watch. 2005. *Blood, Sweat, and Fear: Workers' Rights in U.S. Meat and Poultry Plants*. Human Rights Watch report (January). Available at: http://www.hrw.org/reports/2005/usa0105/index.htm.

James, Susan, and Caroline Lloyd. 2008. "Supply Chain Pressures and Migrant Workers: Deteriorating Job Quality in the United Kingdom Food-Processing Industry." In *Low-Wage Work in the United Kingdom*, edited by Caroline Lloyd, Geoff Mason, and Ken Mayhew. New York: Russell Sage Foundation.

Kristensen, Kai, Peder Østergaard, and Hans Jørn Juhl. 1998. "Success and Failure of Product Development in the Danish Food Sector." *Food Quality and Preference* 9(5): 333–42.

Lane, Julia, Phillip Moss, Harold Salzman, and Christopher Tilly. 2003. "Too Many Cooks? Tracking Internal Labor Market Dynamics in Food Service with Case Studies and Quantitative Data." In *Low-Wage America*, edited by Eileen Appelbaum, Annette Bernhardt, and Richard J. Murnane. New York: Russell Sage Foundation.

Leigh, J. Paul, James P. Marcin, and Ted R. Miller. 2004. "An Estimate of the U.S. Government's Undercount of Nonfatal Occupational Injuries." *Journal of Occupational and Environmental Medicine* 46(1): 10–18.

Lloyd, Caroline, and Susan James. 2008. "Too Much Pressure? Retailer Power and Occupational Health and Safety in the Food Processing Industry." *Work, Employment & Society* 22(4): 713–30.

Marsden, Andrew. 1987. "The Brand Management of Food Products." *Food Marketing* 2(3): 101–9.

Moss, Phillip, and Christopher Tilly. 2001. *Stories Employers Tell: Race, Skill, and Hiring in America*. New York: Russell Sage Foundation.

Porter, Michael E. 1980. *Competitive Strategy*. San Francisco: Freeman.

Rosenman, Kenneth D., Alice Kalush, Mary Jo Reilly, Joseph C. Gardiner,

Mathew Reeves, and Zhewui Luo. 2006. "How Much Work-Related Injury and Illness Is Missed by the Current National Surveillance System?"
Journal of Occupational and Environmental Medicine 48(4): 357–65.

Van Halem, Arjen. 2008. "The Food Industry: Meat Processing and Confectionery." In *Low-Wage Work in the Netherlands*, edited by Wiemer
Salverda, Maarten van Klaveren, and Marc van der Meer. New York: Russell Sage Foundation.

Waldinger, Roger, and Michael Lichter. 2003. *How the Other Half Works: Immigration and the Social Organization of Labor*. Berkeley: University of California Press.

Wilson, Rob, and Terence Hogarth. 2003. *Tackling the Low Skills Equilibrium*. London: DTI.

CHAPTER 10

Restructuring Customer Service: Labor Market Institutions and Call Center Workers in Europe and the United States

Caroline Lloyd, Claudia Weinkopf, and Rosemary Batt

Call centers emerged as an important source of employment in advanced economies in the 1990s. Made possible by advances in digital technologies and the declining costs of transmission, these technology-mediated centers were viewed by firms as a cost-effective service and sales channel for their customers, and a number of governments viewed them as a solution to unemployment. At the same time, these developments made it possible to relocate, outsource, or offshore call center work to low-wage regions and countries. Thus, there were substantial incentives for employers to treat call center work as an opportunity to reduce costs and realize economies of scale. As a result, call centers quickly developed a reputation for offering poor customer service and routinized work at low pay.

As the number of call centers rapidly expanded, academic studies began to paint a more complex picture of these newly created jobs. Call center work was found to vary considerably in terms of the level of service quality, job complexity, skill requirements, and pay across different employers and industries (Frenkel et al. 1999; Batt 2001). Nevertheless, call centers present employers with several dilemmas. On the one hand, advanced information technologies allow them to implement highly automated work processes. Employers can set algorithms, for example, that limit the discretion and independent decisionmaking of workers when they interact with customers. These technologies facilitate business strategies that target high-volume, low-cost solutions to customer interactions and allow firms to compete by minimizing costs. These strategies and technologies are attractive to firms that concentrate on maximizing short-run profits. They also put downward pressure on overall wages and working conditions.

On the other hand, beyond simple transactions, the demands of customization and the negotiation of products and services may be sufficiently complex to require a higher level of competency on the part of workers in terms of product knowledge, literacy, numeracy, and communication skills. These demands put a certain upward pressure on the skill levels required by workers—and potentially on their rates of pay—and are likely to provide incentives for a longer-term approach to business strategy based on quality, customer loyalty, and long-term revenue horizons. The variation in employer strategies and workers' jobs and pay reflect these tensions (Taylor and Bain 1999, 2001; Hutchinson, Purcell, and Kinnie 2000; Deery and Kinnie 2004; Korczynski 2002).

The purpose of this chapter is to explore the factors that shape the level of pay and organization of work in call centers in Europe and the United States. It goes beyond prior research, which has focused primarily on the intrinsic quality of jobs and has tended to draw on studies within countries, particularly the United States and the United Kingdom. Here we examine variation across countries, specifically focusing on how differences in labor market institutions shape employer strategies, working conditions, and pay across national borders as well as within them. We are interested in whether pay and job quality are higher or lower in countries with historically high levels of labor market protections and collective representation compared to those with lower levels of labor market regulation. We also explore whether institutional variation leads to differences in employer strategies in setting pay and organizing work. The call center example is a particularly useful one to examine because, as an emerging phenomenon, it has afforded opportunities for employers to set up workplaces outside of traditional industrial relations systems.

To compare the role of different national institutions, we draw on parallel case study research from five European countries—Denmark, France, Germany, the Netherlands, and the United Kingdom—and we compare our findings to prior research on call centers in the United States. In comparison to the European examples, the United States has the most lightly regulated labor market environment. Prior research on call centers in the United States has shown that within this context employers are permitted greater leeway in making employment decisions; as a result, the variation in pay and working conditions is substantial. Business strategies and unionization play central roles in shaping pay levels and working conditions (Batt 2001; Batt, Hunter, and Wilk 2003).

To make comparisons across countries, each country team focused on three types of centers: those in financial services, those in utilities, and those operated by subcontractors. Within these three contexts, we focused on the jobs that the overwhelming majority of call center workers hold; answering in-bound calls that involve service or sales interactions with customers in the mass market. These are the jobs that are likely to be lower-paying and to offer less discretion and task complexity than those in business-to-business centers or technical services. Each country team conducted between six and eight case studies at in-house finance and utility call centers and at subcontractors serving one of these sectors. The typical case study included interviews with the call center manager, the human resource manager, team leaders, call center agents, and union representatives. The country teams conducted more than 350 interviews between January 2005 and June 2006 at the workplace level, while a range of other interviews took place with sectoral bodies, such as employers' associations and trade unions (for details, see Beraud et al. 2008; Lloyd et al. 2008; Sørenson 2008; van Klaveren and Sprenger 2008; Weinkopf 2008).[1]

We offer several central findings. The first concerns variation in employment systems across countries. With respect to pay levels, we find that the extent of low-wage work in call centers varies substantially across countries: the proportion of workers who are low-paid is relatively low in Denmark and France, fairly high in the United Kingdom and the United States, and highest in Germany and the Netherlands. Cross-national variation in work organization also emerges as an important theme. We identify two clusters of countries, based on case studies and survey evidence. In Denmark, France, and Germany, call center employers are more likely to create operations in which each call center agent is expected to be able to deal with a broad range of products and services. As a result, workers need to be more functionally flexible, and they utilize more discretion and judgment in meeting customer needs. In the Netherlands, the United Kingdom, and the United States, by contrast, we found that employers are more likely to divide up the operations of the customer service or sales function into separate departments, with work organized on the basis of standardized, Taylorist methods. In these workplaces there is a greater emphasis on the use of scripts, electronic monitoring, and adherence to performance metrics.

However, while variation across countries is notable, we do not want to overstate this argument. The call center "sector" is a complex phenomenon that emerged within each country from a series of different industries with distinct historical legacies. These legacies create remarkable variation within each country, whereby call center pay and work organization tend to reflect the industry in which the center is embedded. In addition, there are major differences in pay and work organization between in-house centers tied to particular industry standards and centers operated by subcontractors, which are relatively free from institutional norms.

In the following section, we describe call center work and the influence of changes in the financial services and utility industries on patterns of development in call centers. We then move on to examine, first, variation in pay and, second, differences in work organization both within and across countries. We conclude by highlighting the key factors that help explain patterns of low pay and work organization, focusing on the contribution of different institutional and regulatory frameworks.

THE EMERGENCE OF CALL CENTER OPERATIONS

Call centers are a prominent and growing feature in each of the six national economies in this study, although they employ a significantly higher percentage of the workforce (between 2.5 percent and 3 percent) in the Netherlands, the United Kingdom, and the United States than they do in Denmark, France and Germany (see table 10.1). Unfortunately, official government data are generally not collected on call centers in these countries, and accurate estimates of employment trends, pay, and working conditions are therefore difficult to obtain. Call centers do not form an "industry" but rather are service and sales centers embedded within different industries or operated by subcontractors. In addition, many studies have been written by technology consultants or others who have a self-interested stake in the growth of the sector. In this study, we triangulated between available secondary data and the Global Call Center Survey (GCC), an identical establishment-level survey conducted in each of the six countries in 2004 and 2005.[2]

Table 10.1 Estimated Call Center Employment, 2004
              to 2005

	Employment	Percentage of National Workforce	Percentage Employed by Subcontractors
Denmark	23,000	1.0%	33%
France	210,000	0.75	38
Germany	330,000	1.0	50
Netherlands	180,000	2.4	15 to 20
United Kingdom	742,000	3.0	10
United States	3,900,000	3.0	23

Sources: Estimates based on Batt, Doellgast, and Kwon (2005); Beraud et al. (2008); Lloyd et al. (2008); Sørenson (2008); van Klaveren and Sprenger (2008); and Weinkopf (2008).

Call centers grew dramatically in the mid and late 1990s in all of the six countries under study as advanced call center technologies diffused rapidly and the costs of transmission plummeted. Growth rates appear to have slowed in the 2000s, based on consultants' estimates of the sale of call center technology, the slowdown in the establishment of new call centers, and the limited growth in employment levels (Beraud et al. 2008; Lloyd et al. 2008; Sørenson 2008; van Klaveren and Sprenger 2008; Weinkopf 2008). The overwhelming majority of workers in these centers are operators who handle inbound inquiries from customers or make outbound calls and simultaneously use computers to process customer orders and complete transactions. Most of these workplaces are inbound rather than outbound centers, serve the mass customer market as opposed to business customers, rely on telephones rather than other communications technologies (such as email or the Internet), and provide services to their own domestic market rather than an international market (Holman, Batt, and Holtgrewe 2007).

In addition to new technology, the deregulation of national product markets, particularly in finance, utilities, and telecommunications, during the 1980s and 1990s provided a major impetus for the growth of call centers. Firms faced heightened cost competition, and call centers were viewed as a cost-effective solution to customer service. Many firms sought cost advantages by consolidating and centralizing customer services into large call centers and closing branch offices. Alongside cost imperatives, deregulation also allowed firms to sell a broader range of services, and the call center offered a direct vehicle for the cross-selling of products. The financial services and utility industries, which we focus on in this study, are prime examples of this process. The financial services industry (along with telecommunications companies) was a driving force in the development of call center operations and continues to be the largest user of call centers in Europe (Beraud et al. 2008; Lloyd et al. 2008; Sørenson 2008; van Klaveren and Sprenger 2008; Weinkopf 2008).

Across Europe, the financial services industry was one of the early examples of deregulation. Beginning in the 1980s, national governments relaxed regulatory controls on financial markets, allowing more open systems both domestically and internationally. In particular, they removed controls on credits and restrictions on interest rates, lessened barriers to entry, and reduced or lifted demarcations between different types of firms—for example, between insurance providers and banks (Bongini 2003). Intensified competition between the established companies was exacerbated by the emergence of new entrants that provided a much lower-cost, telephone-only (and later Internet) insurance and banking service. Although Internet banking has grown, there is little evidence as yet that it has reduced employment in call centers.

The utility industry provides a useful comparison, since it has undergone rapid and more recent privatization and deregulation and thus offers the opportunity to examine differences in work practices between centers and countries at different points in the deregulation process. Since the late 1990s, European Union liberalization has opened up domestic markets to competition. The effect has been wide-ranging privatization and deregulation, although some countries have retained a greater level of protection (France and, to a lesser extent, the Netherlands and Germany) (DG Tren 2004), and some sectors remain either highly regulated or monopolies—for example, water. In the United States, a similar pattern of liberalization took place in financial services, but the deregulation of utilities has largely stalled; most energy providers continue to be regionally owned and operated, as well as regulated, by state and federal authorities.

An ongoing threat to the employment and wages of call center workers has been the growth of outsourcing and offshoring. While the 1990s saw the growth of subcontractors within national borders, after 2000 the strategy of offshoring became more prominent, primarily for English-speaking countries (the United Kingdom and the United States). The potential for offshoring is an important differentiator across countries based primarily on language; the opportunities are very low for Denmark and the Netherlands and moderately low for Germany (with East Germany serving as a low-cost location). French firms have experimented with offshoring to Morocco and other parts of North Africa, but the numbers remain relatively small. The United Kingdom and the United States offer the greatest opportunities for offshoring: large multinationals have opened subsidiaries or hired subcontractors in Ireland, Canada, India, South Africa, and the Philippines. Nevertheless, estimates for the United Kingdom, where relocation has predominantly been to India, indicate that the levels remain relatively low, at around forty thousand jobs in India (Bain and Taylor 2008). Similarly, Indian call centers provide a relatively small fraction of all services to customers in the United States.

Outsourcing within a country features prominently in Germany, and across all countries this practice has emerged primarily as a cheap alternative to in-house service provision (see table 10.1). A high proportion of subcontractors continue to be cost-driven, bottom-end providers of simplified tasks (Holman, Batt, and Holtgrewe 2007). However, intensifying competition, concerns about quality, and the spread of call centers to a broader range of services and industries have led to a more diversified range of subcontractors, with some targeting high-value-added markets that offer specialist services. Among the subcontractors in our case studies, we found workers in France engaged in giving legal advice and agents in the United Kingdom providing a disability rights advice line under a government contract.

WORKING IN A CALL CENTER

The call center workforce in the six countries in this study share a number of common characteristics (table 10.2). The majority of call center workers—between 60 and 75 percent—are female, and the workforce is disproportionately young. For most workers, call centers provide full-time jobs, although the proportion of workers who are part-time is higher than the national average in Denmark, Germany, and the Netherlands. Dutch employers also appear to be particularly reliant on contingent workers, with an estimated 40 percent

Table 10.2 Call Center Workers' Characteristics, 2004 to 2005

	Women	Under Age Thirty	Part-Time	Contingent[a]	Educational Level: Two Most Common[b]	
Denmark	64%	57%	23%	7%	Vocational (one to three years)	46%
					High school	33
France	66	66	9	25	At least some college	72
					High school	25
Germany	74	50	40 to 50	20	Vocational (three to four years)	75
					At least some college	10
Netherlands	75	46	50	40	High school	52
					Secondary school	30
United Kingdom	61	56	26	9	Secondary school	38
					High school	31
United States	66	68	11	7	At least some college	60
					High school	40

Sources: These figures represent best estimates based on the following sources: Global Call Center Survey (GCC); de Grip, Sieben, and van Jaarsveld (2005); Beraud et al. (2008); Lloyd et al. (2008); Sorenson (2008); van Klaveren and Sprenger (2008); and Weinkopf (2008).
a. Includes temporary, agency, and freelancers.
b. "Secondary school" refers to successful completion, typically by age sixteen, of compulsory education, which may include passing examinations at specified levels. "High school" refers to attainment of academic qualifications normally taken at age eighteen—for example, the Baccalauréat in France, the HAVO/VWO diploma in the Netherlands, a high school diploma in the United States, and A levels in the United Kingdom. "College" refers to higher education such as universities.

of the workforce on some form of temporary contract, working for an agency, or freelancing. There is some evidence that ethnic minorities are overrepresented in French call centers, possibly reflecting a pattern of discrimination they experience in gaining access to face-to-face jobs (Beraud et al. 2008). The use of migrant workers, in contrast, is rare, due to the requirement for high levels of fluency in the native language.

Education levels vary both within and across countries, but some general patterns are discernable (GCC survey; Beraud et al. 2008; Lloyd et al. 2008; Sørenson 2008; van Klaveren and Sprenger 2008; Weinkopf 2008). French and German call center agents are the most highly qualified; the typical French worker has completed two years of university, and the majority of German workers have completed a three- or four-year apprenticeship. In the United States, almost all workers have a high school diploma, and a majority have at least some college education. Danish workers are more likely to have undertaken vocational education of between one and three years after leaving compulsory secondary school (at age sixteen). In the Netherlands and the United Kingdom, the majority of workers have qualifications somewhat lower—equivalent to secondary school and high school diplomas. Despite these differences, call centers in all countries employed a substantial number of university graduates, and some also provided opportunities for those with very limited, if any, qualifications.

Although workers' educational levels are often quite high, call center jobs tend to be seen as relatively low-paid, highly monotonous, subject to performance monitoring and control, and stressful because of the incessant interaction with callers. Most of the managers in our case study organizations identified labor turnover as a serious problem, particularly for those jobs that were lower-paid or highly repetitive. The exception was in Germany, where labor turnover rates were generally low, reflecting a combination of lower levels of job dissatisfaction, higher levels of unemployment, and a lack of alternative job opportunities.

In the five European countries, the two chosen sectors—financial services and utilities—are generally better-paying than the average call center and offer relatively good benefit packages (for example, sick pay, pensions, extra holidays, and maternity leave where state provision is relatively low). These workers tend to be covered by the existing institutional frameworks—banking or utility sectoral collective agreements and/or individual company collective bargaining—or by the norms and traditions of the specific industry or company. Similarly, in the United States, call center agents in financial services and utilities tend to be better-paid and also receive a range of holiday, sickness, health, and pension benefits, although on average they are provided at somewhat higher levels in the unionized utility call centers.

Outsourcing provides companies with "exit options" that allow them to escape from the higher costs associated with these types of arrangements that are typical of in-house centers in financial services and utilities. Although some new institutional structures are emerging in France and the Netherlands for call center workers employed by subcontractors, the minimum rates of pay and benefits remain substantially below what is set in existing sectoral agreements. In stark contrast to the United States, however, even workers at subcontractor centers and temporary agency staff across Europe are entitled to at least twenty days of paid holiday a year and have access to a range of nonwage benefits, including health provision, sick pay, parental leave plans, and pensions. These benefits vary considerably in terms of the level of minimum entitlements and are funded by country-specific combinations of taxes and contributions of employees and employers (see Mason and Salverda, this volume). In the U.S. subcontracting sector, where almost one-quarter of call center workers are found, paid holidays are likely to be limited to one or two weeks, and there is little if any access to health insurance or pension plans.

In the following sections, we first turn to a more detailed consideration of pay patterns within and across countries and then examine trends in work organization.

PAY LEVELS

In our research, we found substantial variation in call center wage levels both within and across countries. Our findings draw on the case studies carried out by the national teams, reviews of prior research and secondary sources, and findings of the Global Call Center survey. The GCC survey helps to assess the incidence of low pay among call center agents that, in contrast to the other industries, cannot be derived from national statistics.[3]

Three major findings are salient. First, across the six countries in the study, the proportion of call center workers below the low-pay threshold varies considerably: levels are low in Denmark and France, fairly high in the United Kingdom and the United States, and highest in the Netherlands and Germany. Second, both survey data and case study findings suggest that for most workers call center jobs are neither minimum-wage jobs nor at the bottom of the occupational hierarchy. Third, within countries there are considerable variations in the level of call center wages. Our case studies of call centers in finance and utilities and among subcontractors found that hourly wage levels ranged between 64 and 112 percent of the national median wage in Denmark, between 63 and 122 percent in France, between 57 and 130 percent in the United Kingdom, and between 40 and 151 percent in Germany.[4] In the Netherlands, the collective bargaining agreements covering adult call center agents set hourly rates that ranged from 53 to 95 percent of the national median. Evidence from the GCC survey indicates that wage dispersion is even higher in the United States than in the European countries.

Several factors contribute to the high levels of within-country variation in pay. Call centers, in fact, do not constitute an "industry" but rather a new form of work organization that has emerged in various industries. As such, in-house call centers tend to be governed by collective bargaining agreements and other institutional norms of their respective industries. At the same time, subcontractors have emerged outside of industry boundaries, and these employers operate with fewer institutional constraints and potentially more latitude in setting pay rates. Task characteristics and the complexity of jobs can also be quite different from one call center to another. Even in the same call center, jobs may vary from simple, routine transactions to complex ones involving negotiations with business customers over product features, prices, and customized bundling of services. How employers choose to design jobs and allocate tasks is explored later in the chapter.

Our case studies document these patterns of wage variation. In the financial services and utility sectors, employers generally conformed to the industrial relations systems (although those systems varied across countries), and overall we found little evidence of low-paid work in the case study call centers. Pay levels tended to reflect the historical legacy of industry characteristics and union coverage and were similar to findings in the United States. Where low-paid work did exist, it was predominantly among agency workers, new entrants or trainees, and those holding low-skilled temporary positions, including students. By contrast, our case studies of subcontractors serving those sectors showed that they often paid wages below those of in-house centers and provided more examples of wage rates below the low-pay threshold. The GCC survey also found systematic differences in pay levels between in-house centers and subcontractors (Holman, Batt, and Holtgrewe 2007, 28), although the extent varied across countries. Some differences in pay are due to variations in the sectors served by the call centers or in the complexity of tasks undertaken by call center agents. However, in regression analyses that controlled for industry sector, union coverage, and organizational, task, and human capital characteristics, there were statistically significant differences in pay between in-house centers and subcontractors in all of the countries in this study, with the exception of the United Kingdom. Subcontractors paid 8 percent lower than in-house centers in Denmark, 7 percent lower in France, 26 percent lower in Germany, 23 percent lower in the Netherlands, and 8 percent lower in the United States (see Batt and Nohara 2008).

Explaining Variation: Labor Market Institutions and Employment Regulations

How do we explain the diverging national patterns of pay found in the GCC surveys? Two of the most important factors that explain cross-national variation in call center pay are differences in collective bargaining systems and in the existence and level of legally mandated minimum wages, both of which influence the inclusiveness of labor market protections. Collective bargaining systems vary in the extent of centralization (whether contracts are negotiated at the level of the firm, the industry, or some combination of both) and the extent to which the agreement is automatically extended to all employers in the industry (regardless of whether they are members of the employers' association). More centralized systems, mandatory extensions, and high relative minimum-wage standards increase the proportion of workers who are included in labor market protections (see Bosch, Mayhew, and Gautié, this volume).

Our analysis demonstrates that these institutions matter: inclusive (though different) formal institutions in France and Denmark are associated with relatively few low-wage workers. However, be-cause call centers are a relatively new development, employers are presented with more exit options and opportunities to reconfigure prior institutional arrangements to their advantage. This potential is particularly apparent in Germany, where employers make substan-tial use of subcontractors, and in the Netherlands, where there is a heavy reliance on contingent workers. The United Kingdom and the United States, by contrast, are well known for their traditionally weaker institutional frameworks. Table 10.3 provides estimates for the levels of low pay and the extent of collective bargaining coverage for call centers in each of the six countries. Table 10.4 presents the key patterns of collective bargaining coverage in the finance, utility, and subcontracting sectors and specific arrangements for temporary work agencies.

The lowest shares of low pay in call centers are found in France and Denmark, where rates are below that of the national average in each economy (see Mason and Salverda, this volume). Although there are wage differentials between in-house centers and subcon-tractors in both countries, the extent of low pay is relatively lim-ited, even for subcontractors. These findings suggest that call cen-ters are generally included within the standard regulatory framework of the two countries. As a result, employers appear to have very few exit options to escape from the usual standards. However, the patterns of regulation in the two countries are very distinctive, each having its own particular impact on pay levels in call centers. In France, the combination of high coverage by in-dustry collective agreements and their quasi-automatic extension and the relatively high level of the national minimum wage creates a very inclusive regulatory framework for call centers. In Den-mark, by contrast, the institutional framework for call centers could be regarded as fairly weak: only the financial call centers have high levels of union density and collective agreements. De-spite a relatively weak *formal* set of industrial relations institu-tions, employers appear to be limited in their ability to exploit the situation because of the relative power of unions in Denmark as a whole (Sørenson 2008).

The collective bargaining coverage of French call centers is high, according to the GCC survey, covering 81 percent of all call centers, including over two-thirds of subcontractors, and there are no signifi-cant differences in pay between centers with and without union cov-

Table 10.3 Incidence of Low Pay, by Country and Industry, 2004 to 2005

	Workers Covered by Collective Bargaining			Pay Difference by Collective Bargaining Coverage[a]	Low-Wage Incidence		
	All Call Centers	In-House	Subcontractor		All Call Centers	In-House	Subcontractor
Denmark	65%	76%	22%	8%	5%	3%	13%
France	81	89	68	0	4	1	20
Germany[b]	30	46	15	29	36	10 (West)	43 (West)
Netherlands	65	73	59	16	41	38	45
United Kingdom	46	58	27	0	28	17	51
United States	5	10	1	22	19	17	23

Sources: Authors' compilation based on Holman, Batt, and Holtgrewe (2007); Batt and Nohara (2008); additional calculations of GCC data.

a. The union pay differential is based on regression analyses that control for industry sector and the organizational, task, and human capital characteristics of the center (based on Batt and Nohara 2008).

b. Figures for Germany are complicated by the large difference in pay levels between East and West Germany. The low-wage incidence figures presented for in-house workers and subcontractors refer to West Germany only. The German GCC sample includes a very high proportion of subcontractors (two-thirds), whereas other surveys suggest that the number of in-house workers and subcontractors may be more balanced. Taking this into account, estimates for Germany have been readjusted.

Table 10.4 Patterns of Collective Bargaining Coverage, by Industry, 2005 to 2006

	Utilities	Finance	Subcontractors	Temporary Agency Workers
Denmark	Company level Low coverage	Sectoral level High coverage	Company level Low coverage	Company level Medium coverage
France	Sectoral level High coverage	Sectoral level High coverage	Sectoral level High coverage	Equal pay plus 10 percent
Germany	Company level High coverage	Company level High coverage	Company level Low coverage	Sectoral level High coverage
Netherlands	Sectoral level High coverage	Company level Medium coverage	Sectoral level Medium coverage	Sectoral level High coverage
United Kingdom	Company level Medium coverage	Company level Medium coverage	Company level Low coverage	Company level Low coverage
United States	Company level High coverage	Company level Very low coverage	No coverage	No coverage

Sources: Authors' compilation based on Beraud et al. (2008); Lloyd et al. (2008); Sørenson (2008); van Klaveren and Sprenger (2008); and Weinkopf (2008).
Notes: "Level" refers to the predominant level at which collective bargaining occurs; "coverage" refers to the extent to which workers are covered by collective agreement. "High" refers to 80 percent coverage or more; "medium" 30 to 80 percent; "low" 10 to 30 percent; "very low" below 10 percent.

erage. Collective agreements are negotiated at the relevant industry level, and national law mandates their extension to virtually all employers in the industry. This bargaining system, together with a relatively high national minimum wage and pay protection for agency workers, has more or less obstructed a passage to low-pay strategies. Nevertheless, the sectoral collective bargaining agreements covering financial services and utility companies do not set specific rates for call center workers, although they do provide minimum pay levels and the total wage range for the industry. As a result, the relative position of call center pay within the sectoral wage scale has to be set at the company or establishment level, with or without negotiations with trade unions. Actual wage levels therefore depend partly on the power and organizational strength of the relevant unions at the local level. In the utility sector, unions have traditionally been relatively strong. In addition, subcontractors are covered by one of two sectoral collective bargaining agreements (telecommunications and service providers), and these agreements, depending on the specific area of activity, are binding on all the relevant subcontractors. These collective agreements offer very different levels of protection, however, with the service provider agreement setting only basic minimum standards.

The evidence from our case studies confirms that this institutional framework limits low-wage work. The French team found low-wage workers only among newly hired trainees in one financial services company and among workers in the lowest job grades within two subcontractors. Notably, because temporary and agency workers are entitled to equal pay rates as well as a 10 percent insecurity premium, these workers are typically not low-paid. Not only does the institutional effect ensure that there are few low-wage workers, but relatively high labor costs also appear to provide an impetus to organizations to focus on business strategies that add value rather than cut costs and to invest in the skills of the workforce (for more detail, see Beraud et al. 2008).

In contrast to France, the Danes have managed to sustain relatively high levels of call center pay without a formal inclusive institutional framework. The collective bargaining coverage of call centers, according to the GCC survey, is at 65 percent, with only 22 percent coverage for subcontractors, a far lower rate than in France. Compared to France, where there is no union wage differential, the differential in Denmark is about 8 percent. This is similar to the level reported for other Danish industries (see, for instance, the discussion of the hotel industry in Vanselow et al., this volume). Sectoral bargaining in Danish call centers occurs in the financial services industry, but not in utilities or among subcontractors, and Denmark has no statutory national minimum wage. For call centers, both collective bargaining and union membership are uneven—extensive in the well-organized financial services sector, low among utility companies, and extremely low among subcontractors. However, despite the low level of collective agreements, utility firms and subcontractors tend to pay very similar wages to those specified in the agreements that do exist. In a country where the reservation wage is high and a large part of the economy is covered by union agreements, companies that diverge from the collectively agreed pay rates are likely to suffer not just from recruitment and retention problems but also from intensive public campaigns from trade unions. As a result, Danish managers appear to follow collective agreements voluntarily, yet their actions are backed up by the threat of a strong union response if they fail to comply.

The Danish case studies revealed that the call center workers who received the lowest pay were those on temporary contracts and freelancers working on the most routine tasks, many of whom were students. Wage differentials between permanent and temporary workers were generally substantial, although these tended to reflect the different skill levels of the jobs that were held. At one financial services call center, average pay for permanent workers in 2005 was DKR161.70 ($27.00) per hour, nearly 50 percent higher than the DKR110.00 ($18.30) per hour paid to temporary workers. Although some workers were paid below the low-pay threshold, the Danish research found only one case—a subcontractor—where the introductory wage for new permanent employees was (slightly) below the low-pay threshold. This center provided relatively low-complexity tasks to the utility sector.

Surprisingly, the Netherlands and Germany, both traditionally known as countries with a relatively inclusive framework, are the countries with the highest incidence of low-wage work among call centers from our sample. Although the available data on pay in both countries are somewhat mixed, even the lowest estimates indicate that low pay is much more widespread than in the other four countries—at above 40 percent in the Netherlands and around 36 percent in Germany. In both countries, wage differentials between call centers that are covered or not covered by collective agreements are pronounced, even when controlling for several factors; these are estimated at 16 percent and 29 percent, respectively (see table 10.3). As noted earlier, the pay differences between in-house centers and subcontractors are also substantial, at 26 percent in the Netherlands and 23 percent in Germany.

The Dutch formal institutional arrangements are, to a certain extent, quite similar to those in France, yet the coverage of call centers by collective agreements is somewhat lower. In part, lower coverage reflects a collective labor agreement for subcontractors that has been more recently established and is applicable only to those (the majority) that are members of the employers' organization. Although coverage in the Netherlands is at a level similar to Denmark's, the incidence of low pay among call center workers is much higher. These findings suggest that the Dutch labor market regulatory framework is not as inclusive as it first appears. Despite having minimum-wage laws and collective agreements that cover a high proportion of workers, low pay in call centers is widespread—a major contrast to some of the other Dutch jobs explored in this volume that are less frequently low-paying. One explanation is that the minimum wage has been set at a very low rate and youth rates (applied to those age twenty-three or younger) are even lower. Yet this low standard does not explain the low wages in call centers, as it is common across all industries.

More central to the call center story is that employers have successfully negotiated collective wage agreements that maintain low levels of minimum pay in entry-level positions. This outcome is the case not only for subcontractors but also for temporary agency workers and youth rates in the finance sector, which may explain why in-house centers show a relatively high low-pay incidence (at least against the background of national data). High levels of labor turnover lead to more workers being placed in (lower-paid) entry positions, while the high proportion of young and temporary agency workers allows employers to pay (negotiated) lower rates. Even in the higher grades in the agreements for subcontractors and temp agencies, all entry-level wages are below the low-wage threshold, with the lowest grade starting at €1,381 ($1,718) per month (about 53 percent of the national Dutch median wage). All of the maximum collectively agreed pay rates for subcontractors and the first two grades of one of the temporary work agency (TWA) agreements are also below the low-pay threshold (van Klaveren and Sprenger 2008, 262).[5] However, the collective bargaining agreement that covers subcontractors is a relatively recent development and does offer the potential for higher negotiated wages in the future.

The case study research revealed that within the Dutch financial and utility in-house centers, the low-paid were either young workers, who received legally sanctioned lower pay, part-time workers, or temporary agency workers who had limited tenure and therefore were subject to relatively low entry wages under the collective agreements. The research also found that women and students disproportionately received lower pay, while men were more likely to be employed in permanent jobs and to be undertaking more complex tasks.

In Germany, by contrast, the high incidence of low pay is mainly due to the very high rates of low pay at subcontractors, whereas pay rates at in-house centers are typically above the low-pay threshold, at least in West Germany. In recent years, East Germany has provided a route for a kind of internal offshoring from higher-paid areas in the West. German trade unions have not been successful in negotiating sectoral collective agreements for subcontractors, nor have they achieved many contracts at the company level. Unions have made little effort to secure agreements, owing in part to the lack of employers' associations with which to negotiate collectively. Moreover, there is no statutory minimum wage that would define a generally binding minimum-wage floor. In the context of high levels of unemployment, wage levels at subcontractors are sometimes extremely low. At one of the case study centers, the entry level of wages was around €6.00 ($7.50) per hour, corresponding to only 40 percent of the West German median wage, a relative level that would be illegal in most of the other countries.

In the financial services and utility sectors, the level of collectively agreed wages has traditionally been quite high owing to strong unions and works councils. Utility companies were part of the public sector, with its history of relatively high pay levels even for low-skill functions. In-house call centers became subject to the same collective wage agreements as their parent companies. Moreover, collective agreements or negotiations at the company level and dismissal protections in both sectors have ensured that workers whose former positions were eliminated and who were transferred to call centers retained their existing salary and all of their rights and union protections. As a result, many call center agents in the in-house case study organizations received wages above the national median (and in some cases considerably more).

However, the German institutional framework has come under pressure since the mid-1990s. While industry-level collective bargaining traditionally protected workers, bargaining has increasingly devolved to the firm level, with more employers refusing to follow industry norms. Outside of the utility and finance sectors, and particularly among subcontractors, institutional protections and collectively agreed wage standards are much weaker or even nonexistent. Here we see particularly high proportions of workers below the low-pay threshold. The difference between in-house centers and subcontractors creates significant incentives for German employers to escape from union and in-house employment contracts.

The wide differential in pay between in-house centers covered by collective agreements and subcontractors that are not is probably also key to understanding the high proportion of subcontractors in Germany (estimated at 40 percent or even higher). Not only do subcontractors tend to pay low wages, but their widespread low-cost strategies place considerable pressure on the wages and conditions of in-house employees. In all but one of the in-house case study call centers, unions had agreed, or were in discussions over, a reduced pay rate for the lowest grades. Representatives emphasized in several interviews that "otherwise we can't keep the jobs." Lower pay rates mainly affected new entrants, leading to wide variations in wages within each call center. In the utility company with the overall highest pay rates for call center employees (108 to 134 percent of the West German median wage), the negotiated pay rate for new entrants was below the low-pay threshold (61 percent of the median wage).

The United Kingdom and the United States, as liberal market economies, are well known for a traditionally much weaker institutional framework compared to the continental European countries. Nevertheless, the low-pay incidence among call centers, although substantial, is surprisingly lower than in the Netherlands and Germany—about 30 percent for the United Kingdom and 19 percent for the United States.[6] As for the other two pairs of countries, there are different kinds of institutional configurations that create these outcomes. Similar to the Netherlands and Germany, the United States has a substantial union wage premium for call center workers, but the United Kingdom presents a different picture. Analysis of the GCC survey data suggests that in the United Kingdom there are no significant pay differentials between union and non-union call centers, or between in-house centers and subcontractors, once sectoral and other organizational characteristics are taken into account (Batt and Nohara 2008). This result reflects wider evidence that the union wage premium in the United Kingdom has virtually disappeared as union bargaining power has declined over recent decades (Blanchflower and Bryson 2002). Compared to Germany, however, the national minimum wage ensures that pay at the bottom has at least some floor, even if it is relatively low. In addition, minimum-wage rates for young people (between eighteen and twenty-one) are a higher percentage of the adult rate (around 83 percent) than in the Netherlands, where eighteen-year-olds are entitled to only 50 percent of the adult rate.

As a historically regulated industry, the finance sector has a tradition of union organization, with 31 percent of workers still covered by collective bargaining, compared to 20 percent for the whole of the private sector (Grainger and Crowther 2007). Many of the non-union companies in financial services succeeded in retaining their non-union status by matching the pay and benefits of their unionized counterparts. The utility sector was part of the public sector and had an associated set of collective bargaining systems. With privatization, unions managed to retain a substantial foothold, with 63 percent collective bargaining coverage in 2006. The result of these historical legacies is that in both industries pay tends to be higher, and this picture is reflected in the call center case studies. Only one of the in-house call centers paid wages below the low-pay threshold (for agency workers in the first three months of employment).

Although union coverage of call center workers in both sectors is quite widespread (and even the coverage of subcontractors may be higher than in Denmark), pay differentials appear to be a combination of sector- and company-specific factors and local labor market conditions. Employers in the United Kingdom often take advantage of regional variations by locating call centers in low-wage areas and by differentiating pay rates according to local labor market conditions. An in-house utility company had starting pay rates that varied by 20 percent according to the location of the call center, an outsourcer had midgrade rates that varied by 30 percent, and one temporary agency's lowest grades differed by 40 percent. Pay tends to be higher in those areas with significant competition for call center agents and lower where there is either high unemployment or few similar types of jobs. For the case study in-house centers, the minimum wage appeared to be largely irrelevant. In low-paying sectors, however, such as retail and teleworking, it is likely to be of more importance. At one of the subcontractors, starting pay was just above the national minimum wage, and average pay was £5.80 ($10.50) per hour in 2005 (61 percent of the national median wage).

One reason for the limited size of the subcontracting sector in the United Kingdom (around 10 percent) may relate to the limited legal regulation governing temporary agency work compared to the other European economies. Agency workers are not normally covered by collective agreements; they can be used in any situation, except for replacing workers during a strike; and they can be paid at different rates from direct employees. They are also not entitled to the additional company benefits that many of the case study employers provided for directly employed staff. At one of the utility case studies, agency workers received on average only 57 percent of the wage of permanent employees. However, even when wage differentials were much less—typically between 10 and 20 percent—managers were able to make substantial cost savings by matching workers more directly to the peaks and flows in call volumes. At one call center, 86 percent of the agents were temporary agency workers.

The United States presents a different picture again. Unlike the United Kingdom, the legal minimum wage is set at such a low rate that it has virtually no effect on wage levels in call centers. Although the United States also has a very decentralized system of collective bargaining, the union wage premium for call center workers is substantial, at about 20 percent (Batt 2001; Batt and Nohara 2008). This figure is consistent with national estimates of the union/non-union wage gap in the United States. However, unionization in call centers is concentrated in the telecommunications and utilities industries. In the utility sector, union-negotiated pay and benefits remain relatively high, in large part because deregulation has proceeded only in fits and starts, limiting national consolidation, and retaining regional ownership patterns. As a result, consolidation of work into large remote centers, as well as outsourcing and offshoring, has been limited. Case study comparisons of union and non-union call centers are instructive. In a typical union contract in 2005, hourly wages began at around $14.00 for new hires (just below the national median wage of $14.30) and rose to about $18.00 for experienced workers (considerably above the median). By contrast, in a comparable non-union center, entry-level pay began at about $10.00 per hour (just above the low-pay threshold), while an experienced worker earned a maximum of $13.00 per hour. Workers in many non-union workplaces received no sick leave, minimal vacation time, and had to pay substantial monthly premiums for health insurance.

As in the European countries, deregulation in the financial industry in the United States has proceeded rapidly, leading to ongoing mergers, heightened price competition, and a blurring of boundaries between banks, insurance companies, and other financial services providers (Hunter et al. 2001). Unlike in Europe, the financial services sector is almost completely non-union. However, even though large call centers were established in remote areas, pay still tends to be above the low pay threshold (Batt, Hunter, and Wilk 2003). Case study and survey research undertaken by Rosemary Batt and Virginia

Doellgast found that pay levels in the utilities and financial services sector were generally somewhat higher than the low-pay threshold ($9.53 in 2005). In contrast, subcontractors were typically bottom-end employers, with rates of pay in some companies of between $7.50 and $8.50 per hour in 2005.

One reason why these levels of low pay are not higher in both the United States and the United Kingdom may be that many lower-skilled jobs have been sent offshore to other English-speaking countries. This practice is easier and more widespread than in the other European countries, and more prevalent particularly in the United States, where call center jobs are relocated to Canada as well as to India and the Philippines. The evidence presented in the next section suggests, however, that both the United Kingdom and the United States continue to host a disproportionate number of low-discretion call center jobs. A possible reason as to why jobs tend to be paid somewhat above the minimum wage is that employers require (native) fluency in English, as well as numeracy and communication skills, which place some limits on the available labor supply; for example, most migrant workers are excluded. In the context of relatively low levels of unemployment in both of these countries, employers may find that they have to pay above the minimum wage to attract and retain workers who will deliver the required levels of service quality.

In summary, across all of the country cases, we found few low-wage call center workers in the utility and financial service sectors, a reflection of the characteristics of these particular industries. These sectors are relatively higher-paying in comparison to sectors such as retail and outbound call centers. In each of the countries, subcontractors were more likely to pay lower wages. Variations in the nature and extent of collective bargaining between in-house centers and subcontractors in each country help to explain these differences in pay. In addition, subcontractors have a lower level of interest representation at the firm level and, as will be shown in the next section, disproportionately handle tasks of lower complexity. Cross-national differences in labor market institutions also translate into differences in the size of the pay gap between in-house centers and subcontractors.

WORK ORGANIZATION

Working in a mass-market call center and answering predominantly inbound calls from customers involves a number of common features across all of the countries in this study. Agents spend most of their time in front of a computer, receiving telephone calls from an automatic call distribution system. Call center technology provides the employee with detailed information on customer characteristics and the employer with detailed metrics on employee performance. This technology is widely available and has diffused within and across countries. What matters, however, is how and if employers use the information. As one Danish manager explained: "Don't ask me whether we have the figures. We measure everything. The question is how we use it." Employers are able to measure employees by the number of calls answered, the amount of time callers have to wait, the number of callers waiting in line, the length of each call, the time in between calls, the time spent away from the workstation, and the volume and value of sales, among other things.

Despite the technology-driven nature of this work, our case study research confirms the evidence from existing studies that the organization of work varies considerably within countries in relation to the scope of tasks and the level of employee discretion (Beraud et al. 2008; Lloyd et al. 2008; Sørenson 2008; van Klaveren and Sprenger 2008; Weinkopf 2008). A customer phoning a bank to pay a bill and to request a loan may be dealt with by one agent trained to undertake a broad range of tasks. Alternatively, the caller may end up dealing with several agents because each one is only able to respond to a specific part of the query. Workers undertaking a more limited range of tasks require fewer skills and less training and are therefore more easily replaceable. Our case studies indicate that more routine tasks allow managers to make greater use of contingent workers, such as agency staff (the Netherlands, the United Kingdom), temporary workers (the Netherlands, France) and students (Denmark). In Germany, outsourcing of this work is more common, often to East Germany, while in the United States and the United Kingdom employers are also sending some of the more routine work offshore. Data from the GCC survey confirm that employers report a significantly higher proportion of low-discretion jobs at subcontractors compared to in-house call centers (table 10.5).

Our case study research provides evidence that different trends have emerged in how work tends to be organized across the countries (table 10.6). Workplaces in the Netherlands, the United Kingdom, and the United States can be seen to reflect more closely the predominant image of the mass-market call center. Employers relied heavily

Table 10.5 Workers by Level of Discretion, 2004 to 2005

	Low Discretion			Moderate Discretion			High Discretion		
	All	In-House	Subcontractor	All	In-House	Subcontractor	All	In-House	Subcontractor
Denmark	30%	25%	46%	43%	42%	48%	27%	32%	6%
France	49	44	57	35	35	36	16	21	7
Germany	26	3	31	45	77	37	29	20	32
Netherlands	57	NA	NA	40	NA	NA	2	NA	NA
United Kingdom	64	57	75	32	41	16	4	2	8
United States	63	61	70	26	31	10	10	8	20

Source: Rosemary Batt's calculations of GCC data.

Notes: Discretion was measured on a scale of 1 to 5, by a series of questions regarding discretion over pace of work, daily tasks, work methods, lunch breaks, revising work methods, what to say to customers, handling additional customers, and settling customer complaints. Low discretion = 1.00 to 2.59; moderate discretion = 2.60 to 3.39; high discretion = 3.40 to 5.00.

NA: Not available owing to limited observations.

Table 10.6 Dominant Pattern of Work Organization in the In-House Case Study Call Centers, 2005 to 2006

	Relative Range of Tasks	Individual Performance Monitoring	Use of Scripts	Union/Works Council Involvement in Job Design	Progression Opportunities
Denmark	Moderate range, including nontelephone activities	Common: some link to pay/promotion but not to disciplinary process	Rare	Common	Some to wider organization
France	Broad range, including nontelephone activities	Common: but mostly no link to pay/promotion	Rare	Limited	Common to wider organization
Germany	Broad range	Limited	Rare	Some	Exist, but blocked due to low turnover
Netherlands	Narrow range	Extensive: link to performance management but generally not to pay	Common	Limited	Limited to call center
United Kingdom	Narrow range	Extensive: link to pay/promotion/disciplinary process	Common	Limited	Mainly limited to call center
United States	Narrow range	Extensive: link to pay/promotion/disciplinary process	Common	Limited	Limited to call center

Sources: Authors' compilation based on Beraud et al. (2008); Lloyd et al. (2008); Sørenson (2008); van Klaveren and Sprenger (2008); and Weinkopf (2008).

on customer and product segmentation strategies, took a more Taylorized approach to organizing work, and made extensive use of electronic performance monitoring. In contrast, there were many cases, particularly of in-house call centers, in Denmark, France, and Germany where employers organized work to cover a broad range of customer groups or a wide range of services and created jobs that required more functionally flexible staff with higher levels of discretion. These findings from the case studies are consistent with the survey results of the GCC data, which found a significantly smaller proportion of low-discretion jobs in Denmark, France, and Germany (table 10.5).

TRENDS TO ROUTINIZE JOBS

Work organization in call centers in the Netherlands, the United Kingdom, and the United States has a number of common features that were more prevalent than in the other three countries. Employers were more likely to design jobs that were narrow in terms of the tasks undertaken, with agents spending virtually all of their working time on the telephone and undertaking only simple after-call operations. Agents normally passed additional work to other departments and sent more complex issues to separate specialist groups. In all three countries, there were many examples from the case studies of managers relying heavily on scripted texts, while electronic performance monitoring linked to individual targets was endemic. In the United Kingdom and the United States, managers emphasized individual performance monitoring and metrics, with targets including call quality and accuracy, call length, after-call time, sales and retention, timekeeping, and attendance. They also tied meeting targets to disciplinary action, including dismissal, as well as performance-based pay and bonuses.

One factor that partly explains the structure of low-discretion, fragmented jobs is the strategy of customer segmentation. If companies segment their customers according to their demand characteristics or value-added, they can design work to match the specific characteristics and inquiries of the targeted customer group. This strategy creates a more specialized division of labor for each call center within a given company; it is a well-developed strategy in the United States. Companies can stratify centers by the level of complexity of tasks, with more transactional centers offering lower discretion and pay and higher-value-added centers offering the opposite. Companies benefit because they can adjust labor costs to the value of the customer segment, and they claim that customers can also benefit from more customized service (Batt 2001, 2002).

Our research also found that, in the United Kingdom, segmentation strategies were common within the same call center, with one department dealing with higher-value-added customers and others with mass-market customers. In addition, companies further segmented services among groups of mass-market customers. In one utility company, for example, each of its five call centers specialized in a different activity: one dealt just with new customers and retaining old customers, while another handled only calls about payments. Similarly, a water company allocated workers to specialized teams that dealt with particular areas. One team handled calls relating to blocked drains, sewerage, and flooding issues; a second team dealt with calls relating to water supply and leaks; and a third team handled only billing issues. Similarly in a finance company, one set of employees dealt with savings, another group with loans, and a third group with mortgages.

Segmentation of services and the Taylorization of work that this allows can be seen as part of a fundamental strategy of cost reduction. Technological developments in relation to both telephone systems and information technology permit call centers to be located anywhere and enable managers to fragment tasks more easily and directly monitor workers. In the United States and the United Kingdom, employers taking this approach faced few constraints. Weak employment security regulations and the lack of sectoral collective bargaining coverage enabled companies to locate call centers in remote areas, often with relatively high levels of unemployment, while closing or downsizing preexisting customer-facing services. With a new workforce and few limitations on the way in which call centers could be organized, managers often chose to break up the work into very simple tasks and thus were able to hire workers for jobs that required few skills at significantly lower wages than the jobs they replaced. In a period of declining trade union power, union activity has focused on achieving company or workplace collective bargaining coverage rather than on the traditionally neglected issues of work organization.

Our research in the Netherlands and the United Kingdom found evidence that more recent pressures were leading managers to redesign jobs, although not necessarily in one direction. Regulatory changes in the banking and utility sectors across Europe have set new requirements and standards in relation to providing advice and selling. To ensure compliance, managers in a number of the case study firms in the Netherlands and the United Kingdom required agents to read out lengthy verbatim statements to callers. At an insurance center in the United Kingdom, for example, one agent described how the levels of discretion in selling had declined since the introduction of new Financial Services Authority (FSA) regulations: "There used to be quite a lot . . . in the good old days you could sort of get away with murder. But now the FSA, since January, it's a lot more strict. . . . So you can't say all kinds of things that you used to say, it is very scripted." Responding to regulations by using scripts may reflect a lack of management trust in workers and, particularly in the United Kingdom, the heavy costs associated with earlier periods of "mis-selling" products.

At the same time, deregulation has provided some incentives to expand call center jobs away from simple service operations as managers realize the potential for cross-selling when any contact is made with a call center. In some financial call centers, for example, workers who traditionally dealt only with the service aspects of customer accounts were now required to turn every call into a "selling opportunity." Some agents welcomed this change because it reduced monotony and, to some extent, broadened the knowledge requirements of the job. At a financial services center in the United Kingdom, management had recently merged the tasks of providing financial advice with the selling of targeted products. One agent explained that "there is a lot more variety now, it's bigger now, there are more things to do." Others found that taking on a more aggressive sales role could be a difficult transition. As one agent in the Netherlands explained following a similar process of change:

> Recently management changed the job content for all agents. . . . Personally, I felt very uncomfortable with the new targets. I have to try to sell as many products as possible during calls using "selling moments." We lost our thirteenth month of salary and have to "earn it back" by sales-related bonuses, with all the administrative fuzz connected. We never did those things before, and it makes you feel guilty towards the customer, who did not ask for any offer when phoning. (van Klaveren and Sprenger 2008, 256)

In the United Kingdom, where utility companies can offer a range of energy products and services, managers in three of the cases also defined every call as an opportunity to cross-sell. For example, in one electricity company, when customers called to pay their bills, the agent's job was to press them to switch their gas supply to the same company. In some instances, however, service segmentation had led to the possibility of losing business because cross-selling "leads" had to be forwarded to another agent or another call center specializing in that particular area.

A strategy of task fragmentation may allow employers to pay lower wages and, depending on the regulatory context, make more extensive use of agency and temporary workers. Whether firms are able to employ lower-waged, contingent workers partly depends on the existence and level of collective agreements, the extent to which the required service quality levels can be maintained, and the local labor market context. In the Netherlands, for example, collective agreements set minimum pay rates for jobs at different skill levels. A company agreement in 2006 set the maximum wage for a grade 5 (highest-skill) banking call center agent 40 percent higher than the maximum for a grade 1 (lowest-skill), thereby providing a cost incentive to create lower-skilled jobs. With relatively high levels of unemployment in recent years and a widespread demand for part-time work, employers appear to have had few problems in filling temporary and agency positions. Segmenting services and relying heavily on contingent workers, however, can lower the quality of service, particularly if turnover rates are excessively high. Public dissatisfaction with poor service levels at one of the Dutch utility firms led managers to shift to using more workers on permanent contracts and to provide extra training to agents. One agent commented: "We all went to extra training courses, to be able to answer more questions directly instead of connecting customers to the back offices. Since then, the number of complaints has gone down considerably."

In the United States and the United Kingdom, with pay levels set at the company or workplace level, the link between the pay and skill content of the jobs is often less direct. In the utility sector in the United States, where union contracts had established relatively high levels of pay and benefits, workers nonetheless tended to have narrow and low-discretion jobs. There was some evidence that managers were attempting to recoup higher labor costs by enhancing productivity through the use of more intensive electronic monitoring linked

to strict performance management systems and disciplinary procedures. Managers insisted on close adherence to scripts, scheduled
breaks, and performance objectives, such as sales quotas, call handling times, and politeness. Despite the higher pay, better benefits,
and greater job security offered by these unionized workplaces, labor
turnover was high because of the nature and intensity of the work.
Many unionized workers found that these jobs had become too
stressful and left to take lower-paid work elsewhere.

In the United Kingdom, task fragmentation has allowed the use of
lower-paid agency workers—in two of the case study firms, over 60
percent of the workforce were agency workers. Nonetheless, this approach was not sustainable in areas where local labor markets were
tight and where service quality levels had to be maintained. One
agent in a financial services center summed up his experience:

> It's hard to stay motivated and it's hard to sound motivated to a cus-
> tomer when you are just on the phone and do the same calls eight
> hours every day. And I found it was okay for six, eight months, but af-
> ter that it was just really boring. . . . But I think a lot of people feel the
> same thing, and I guess it's hardly motivating, someone who does the
> same job over and over, which is quite sad really. But I guess it's the
> call center environment in general (U.K. case studies).

The routine and repetitive nature of the jobs and, in a number of
cases, the high use of agency workers led to some very high levels of
labor turnover (over 50 percent). However, rather than exploring
ways of improving job design as a solution to recruitment and retention issues, management tended to focus on improving pay and other
working conditions.

One of the most routine jobs in our case studies was in a call center in the finance sector in the United Kingdom, where the majority
of agents dealt with only one main product. Management had designed work that was highly scripted and limited to routine transactions, with a range of individual performance targets linked to
bonuses. Calls typically lasted three or four minutes and involved
opening and closing accounts, making deposits and transfers, and
changing customer details. Any problems with on-line accounts or
customer service inquiries went to a different group of agents. As one
agent stated, "I would say it's very monotonous . . . it's boring, and it
needs to be over as soon as it starts". (U.K. case studies). The organ-

ization was still striving, however, for "high-quality customer service," and one of the most important targets related to "call quality." Managers attempted to deal with the negative consequences of poor job design by paying relatively well in the (tight) local labor market (a starting salary of £8.46 [$15.40] per hour), improving working hours, increasing initial training time, and encouraging a range of employee involvement initiatives. Managers in other call centers in the United Kingdom responded in similar ways when faced with major retention problems while also replacing temporary agency workers with permanent workers.

Although there was some variation in job redesign strategies in the Netherlands, the United Kingdom, and the United States, the predominant model of work organization in the case studies featured relatively narrowly defined jobs with low task discretion. High labor turnover stemmed from the pressures of constant interaction with customers on the telephone, intense performance monitoring, and routinized tasks. In addition, call center jobs offered few opportunities for progression beyond the position of team leader. As a result, workers in the case study organizations across the three countries often viewed their position as transitory; few were able or willing to stay in the job for more than a couple of years. Although pay rates in the finance and utility sectors are often well above the low-pay threshold and many workers receive additional company benefits, particularly in the United Kingdom and the United States, job quality still remains poor because of the predominant way in which work is organized.

The Prospects for More Broadly Defined Jobs

Managers of call centers in Denmark, Germany, and France had also pursued strategies of task fragmentation, but our case studies revealed many examples of jobs designed to meet a variety of caller needs. Agents often were expected to be able to handle a broad range of customer inquiries and, as a result, were required to be relatively functionally flexible and to exercise a certain level of discretion. Managers enabled employees to process a high percentage of calls to their conclusion, rather than passing them on to other agents or departments. By utilizing functionally flexible employees, as opposed to specialized agents, these managers were able to cope with variation in the volume of work and in the types of customer inquiries they received. As one German manager explained: "We need functionally flexible employees because too much specialization of the agents would restrict our capacities to cope with fluctuations in call volume." In these three countries, we found little or no use of individual monitoring for performance management or disciplinary purposes. In the German call centers, there was no individual monitoring. In the French centers, all workers were subject to monitoring, but the system was linked to pay, promotional prospects, and performance management in only a couple of cases. In Denmark, although monitoring covered all workers in the case studies, with some annual links to pay and promotion prospects, only a few centers used individual targets.

The case studies suggest that French and German in-house call centers were more likely to have been designed from the outset with relatively broad jobs and skill requirements. By contrast, some of the Danish centers began with fragmented jobs but were in the process of redesigning the work to broaden the range of tasks. In the French and German in-house utility and finance case study centers, agents had to be familiar with the range of available products and had to know the individual advisers who worked in the branches. At one of the German banks, agents dealt with a broad range of tasks, from routine changes in addresses and balance inquiries to investment fund management. Even at one of the subcontractors, each agent provided the full range of services to customers for at least two regional utility companies. At one of the French financial centers, a clear job ladder had been established. Newly hired workers started as receptionists, answering basic calls and providing appointments. Two years later, workers had typically progressed to "level 4," which enabled them to undertake all operations in relation to current account management, including buying and selling stock, administrative tasks, and direct marketing activities. A French utilities center directed callers, not to different departments, but to an agent who could handle calls that covered everything from moving house to making payments, canceling contracts, and making appointments with technicians.

In four out of eight French case study call centers, agents also undertook the administrative work associated with the call—for example, sending faxes or writing e-mails. In another three cases, management set aside distinct periods of time for agents to be relieved of telephone work and spend time on other related activities. In a number of Danish call centers, managers also provided specific periods of time for agents to be "off the phones." Some employers attempted to improve the organization of work by training employees to handle several types of products and different tasks, such as mail processing, quality control, emails, packing, and training colleagues. In all three countries, we found cases in which agents had some influence over their work schedules, including the timing of their daily breaks.

The ability to adopt a broader approach to job design partly depends on management rejecting the more extreme forms of customer and product segmentation that are so prevalent in the Netherlands, the United Kingdom, and the United States. In Denmark, with a population of only 5.5 million, the limited size of the domestic market tends to restrict the use of segmentation strategies. In Germany and France, however, where the size of the national market is generally not a limiting factor, we also found less reliance on product and service segmentation. In all three countries, call centers were more likely to be fully integrated into the core business rather than being considered as a mere cost center. Managers in the French banking sector tended to view the call center as simply "a new means . . . for executing a traditional banking function, namely 'advising clients'" (Beraud et al. 2008, 266). Danish and German companies in particular tended to locate their in-house centers close to corporate headquarters rather than in remote locations. These locational decisions signal that the call center is an important strategic asset for the company. Proximity enables call center managers to maintain close connections with corporate leaders and makes it more possible for call center employees to move to other positions in the company over time. In the United States, by contrast, firms typically establish call centers in remote locations far from corporate headquarters (Batt, Hunter, and Wilk 2003), a pattern that is also common in the United Kingdom.

Different approaches to jobs in call centers may partly reflect variations in consumer norms and expectations. In France, for example, customers still expect to have "direct" contact with the local branch of their bank. A French bank pursuing a centralized call center approach might therefore lose business. Beyond product market norms, however, we found that labor market institutions and regulations are a central influence on approaches to work organization.

In Denmark and Germany, strong collective agreements and legal regulations covering job security and dismissal substantially limit managerial prerogative. In many cases, managers could not simply set up a new work site with a new set of employees while existing staff were made redundant. In Germany, employers were frequently required to establish in-house call centers in banking and utilities using the company's existing employees. These workers tended to be well-paid and skilled, and had a three- or four-year apprenticeship certification in the relevant area plus considerable work experience. Managers in the case study call centers, seeking to utilize these skills, organized work in ways that tended to replicate the broad range of jobs that workers had previously held in individual branches and offices. Although the work was mediated by telephones rather than conducted in face-to-face encounters, agents undertook very similar activities. In a number of cases, however, some of the simpler operations and the handling of unsocial hours (evenings and weekends) were outsourced to lower-cost subcontractors.

In Denmark, banking employees effectively had "lifetime employment," and as managers closed down branches or offices, many were relocated to call centers. In this sector, with traditionally high levels of union density, unions continued to be actively involved in job design issues in a number of the call centers. At one Danish bank, for example, managers were engaged in a partnership with the union to redesign the work process, with a guiding principle that it would not resemble the "factories" they had visited in the United Kingdom. Another Danish bank had volunteered to participate in a work redesign project to improve job quality, funded by the European Union Social Fund. After a two-year effort that included social science researchers and extensive employee involvement, managers were engaged with unions in reorganizing the center along the lines of socio-technical systems principles, with self-directed, mixed-competency work teams.

In contrast, in the Danish utility sector, initially most call centers did not replace more traditional forms of work organization but were established to offer additional services to customers. As a result, they recruited a completely new set of workers. The historical weakness of the utility sector unions, stemming in part from earlier prohibitions on the use of strikes, combined with the inexperienced workforce to ensure that unions remained relatively marginal. Works councils were able to have an influence on management, however, as did broader negative publicity campaigns against specific high-profile employers. A campaign by the HK union depicted one utility company as the "worst call center in Denmark," while an active works councils attempted to influence job design. These efforts resulted in employees being given a range of different tasks, such as handling letters, emails, and coordination with other departments, in order to provide variation in the job and reduce the hours spent on the phone. Both the call center manager and the employees agreed that eight hours on the phone was too stressful and monotonous.

Trade unions and works councils also played a role in securing broader forms of job design in Germany. During the 1990s, German trade unions launched a number of initiatives, workshops, and projects that focused on improving working conditions in call centers—for example, reducing the time on the phones and enlarging the jobs to include administrative tasks. Although these activities slowed down in the 2000s, collective agreements and works councils still influence not only pay and working conditions but also the organization of work. Unions have been instrumental in enforcing legislation mandating five-minute hourly breaks from the computer screen. Works councils, backed by codetermination rights, have been able to block the use of individual performance monitoring. In call centers with active works councils, we found that individual workplace monitoring did not take place, thereby limiting the extent to which work could be intensively controlled. These outcomes are consistent with other findings on German call centers that works councils, particularly when backed by unions, have been able to limit individual monitoring and commission-based pay and have encouraged the establishment of group-based forms of work organization (Doellgast 2008).

As in Germany, many of the French banks and utility companies set up call centers to handle all of the activities that were previously undertaken by advisers in branch offices. Many French banking and insurance services operate at the regional level, and call center establishments reflect this pattern. Because they serve a smaller market, a high division of labor may offer few efficiency savings. The case studies also suggest that the relatively high cost of labor in France acts to prohibit a widespread strategy of providing only low-cost, simplified operations. In banking and utilities, sectoral collective agreements set some higher wage minimums, and social contributions add substantially to the cost of labor. Over recent years, French unions have also been actively involved in developing a number of company-based agreements that provide progression opportunities for call center agents. In some of the case study organizations, managers used the job of call center agent as an initial entry point into the company.

These jobs provided workers with broad-based training that allowed them to learn about the company's overall operations. After a couple of years in the call center, many employees were able to move into more traditional positions in the wider organization.

In addition to the regulatory framework and the role of collective organizations, labor market conditions may contribute to an understanding of developments in call center work organization. In the face of very high unemployment in recent years, German call centers have been successful at maintaining a well-qualified workforce by recruiting workers with three-year apprenticeships. Labor turnover rates among agents are low (particularly among in-house centers) because they have limited job opportunities both within and outside of the company. A continued supply of qualified workers, alongside low attrition rates, provides managers with little reason to fragment jobs, particularly when they are also able to extract collectively agreed wage concessions.

In France, high levels of unemployment have also enabled managers to recruit relatively highly qualified workers, reflected in the large proportion of call center agents with at least two years of higher education. In contrast to Germany, however, high labor turnover (on average about 22 percent) is an issue that could have two rather different consequences. On the one hand, at some subcontractors whose turnover is often much higher than average, managers have been able to avoid implementing the sort of work enhancement or career management policies that they might otherwise need if they had a stable, disgruntled workforce. On the other hand, in centers where the quality of service is important and training requirements are significant, turnover is much more costly in terms of training expenditure and the impact of poor service on customer relations. In these cases, managers have placed more emphasis on the development or maintenance of internal labor markets in the wider organization to ensure that their firms gain a "return on their investment."

Danish managers faced a similar choice: should they ensure sufficient training, establish career paths, and improve work organization to bring turnover down, or avoid investing too much in workers who were liable to leave? With unemployment relatively low, some of the case study call centers were experiencing major recruitment and retention issues (over 50 percent labor turnover rates in some cases). Managers tended to follow a job improvement route to deal with high labor turnover rather than pursue the pay and working conditions solution that was typical of employers in the United Kingdom. In addition to making efforts to redesign jobs, the Danish managers also took steps to reduce the pressure at work and to build career ladders to encourage workers to stay within the wider organization. The difference in managerial approach in Denmark may reflect a tighter labor market compared to the United Kingdom, as well as the more strategic and active role of trade unions in issues of job design. It may also be that with relatively flat payment systems and a universal right to substantial nonwage benefits, there is less opportunity to use the type of approach adopted in the United Kingdom.

Although call center jobs in Denmark and France incorporated more variety and discretion, many workers in the case study organizations still complained that the work quickly became routine and difficult to sustain. Several managers and employees in Denmark argued that workers could not, or would not, work in a call center for more than two to four years. A number of French workers complained about mental fatigue and exhaustion. At one center, some part-time call center agents claimed that the work intensity was such that they would have been incapable of working full-time. The result in both these countries was often high levels of labor turnover, suggesting that more broadly defined jobs have served only to alleviate rather than to resolve the central problems of poor work design in call centers.

In Germany, however, there was far less emphasis on problems of strain and stress in the job. These impressions were not only derived from interviews with workers in the case study organizations but are also supported by a survey of 650 call center employees carried out in 2001 (John and Schmitz 2002). Around 75 percent of respondents reported that they were "contented" with their work, compared to a small minority of 7 percent who were "discontented" or "very discontented." Fifty-eight percent confirmed that the statement "I do not feel overstrained even if the workload is high" was true or mainly true, while the rate of disagreement (mainly and completely) was only at about 16 percent. These findings may reflect the more broadly designed jobs found in many German call centers and the lack of individual monitoring. Nevertheless, young workers at one of the German finance case studies, who had just completed a three-year vocational training program for bank clerks, suffered from the frustration of being overqualified for their relatively low-paid jobs. They felt that there was also little prospect of progression because of lack of mobility further up the jobs ladder.

The case studies illustrate that a number of factors may be important in pushing firms to adopt forms of work organization that are less fragmented and provide more variety and discretion to workers. The existence of a well-trained, reasonably paid workforce that cannot be easily dismissed provides incentives to managers to utilize workers' skills more effectively. Trade unions and works councils can also play a role in campaigning and pressing managers to improve work organization. In France, the United Kingdom, and the United States, however, unions have had little involvement in job design issues, and they are unlikely to find employers willing to concede such an area of traditional managerial prerogative. Despite such positive incentives, the GCC evidence indicates that even at in-house call centers, there remain substantial numbers of low-discretion jobs in France (44 percent) and Denmark (25 percent) (table 10.5). The case study findings on work organization in these two countries may therefore reflect the specific institutional and product market features in the finance and utility sectors that tend to lead to both better-paid and better-designed jobs. German call centers show a different pattern: the GCC data indicate that only 3 percent of in-house call center workers are employed in low-discretion jobs. Even among subcontractors, only 31 percent are classified as low-discretion workers, with another one-third undertaking high-discretion jobs. This difference in the organization of work indicates that the picture found in the case studies for the finance and utility sectors is pervasive across other sectors of the German economy as well. The relatively high proportion of jobs with high discretion also suggests that German subcontractors do not necessarily provide only routine tasks with low complexity.

At a country level, there is no clear link between patterns of work organization and levels of low pay. While France and Denmark report few low-paid workers and evidence of broader forms of work organization, the German picture is more mixed. West German in-house centers provide broad and relatively well-paid jobs, yet a large proportion of subcontractors, often in East Germany, offer low-paid work that is not necessarily narrowly defined with limited discretion. It seems that it is relatively easy to outsource even the more complex jobs to low-paying employers, although in some cases there has been a reduction in service quality. With high levels of unemployment and limited worker mobility, subcontractors may be able to recruit and retain well-qualified workers despite paying low wages. In the other countries, the greater likelihood that low-paying employers will face recruitment difficulties and high labor turnover renders unsustainable any strategy based on low-paid, broadly designed jobs. In some instances, higher pay seems to have provided an incentive to develop broader forms of work organization (Germany, France, and Denmark), while in other cases (the United States) it has prompted further attempts at fragmentation and intensive monitoring. These findings suggest that rather than simple causal relationships, it is the interaction of a range of institutional, regulatory, and labor market factors that helps explain pressures to fragment or broaden the way call center jobs are organized.

SUMMARY AND CONCLUSIONS

Although the literature has emphasized the variation in the nature of call center work, our cross-country comparisons indicate that these jobs also have some distinctive characteristics within different countries. We found considerable variation in the extent of low-paid work, levels of wage dispersion, the share and usage of subcontractors, and patterns of work organization. Simple causal linkages, however, are not easily identified. Nevertheless, job quality appears to be mainly shaped by the institutional and regulatory framework, employer strategy, the relative power of trade unions, and the characteristics and size of the available workforce.

In Denmark, France, and Germany, jobs are organized in ways that tend to be broader and less fragmented than in the other three countries. In contrast, the patterns of pay are distinct, particularly in Germany, where there are substantially more low-paid workers, particularly at subcontractors. In France and Denmark, there are few low-wage workers, pay rates are close to the average wage, and there are relatively low levels of wage dispersion. In some cases, there are opportunities for career progression. In the other three countries, call center jobs tend be more fragmented, although with some variation in the patterns of pay. In the Netherlands and the United Kingdom, wage levels are relatively low compared to the average wage, and there are substantial numbers of low-wage workers. By comparison, in the United States, there are fewer low-wage workers, and the average call center wage is only just below the national average. In all three countries, monitoring is used extensively, although individualized forms of payment systems are far more widespread in the United

Kingdom and the United States. Work tends toward the low-discretion, low-complexity end of the continuum, and there are few opportunities for career progression.

What factors are critical in accounting for differences in the quality of jobs and pay in mass-market call centers? Despite the emergence of call centers largely as a response to employers' cost-cutting strategies, we found that institutions continue to play an important role in determining the quality of jobs in these new operations. In relation to pay, the in-house call centers have on the whole matched up to the existing country and sector institutional structures. We found that sectoral collective bargaining in finance and utilities is critical to ensuring that those "at the bottom" have a reasonable wage level and that it thereby minimizes the extent of low pay. In the absence of sectoral collective bargaining, within-industry variation in pay has the potential to be far greater because it depends more heavily on the presence and strength of trade unions, the strategic choices of management, and local labor market conditions. The relatively high cost of labor in certain in-house call centers may also be a factor in pushing firms to maximize employee input, through work intensification and/or a more extensive use of employee skill, and even to explore more quality-based product market strategies.

Employers can seek to escape traditional institutional structures or norms by outsourcing. The evidence indicates, however, that most organizations have retained call centers in-house, in part out of a desire to keep control over what is increasingly the predominant mechanism for interacting with customers. The relative cost savings that can be made by outsourcing does appear to vary substantially across countries and makes it a more or less attractive proposition. A crucial issue in some countries relates to the extent of inclusion of subcontractors in the regulatory framework. In Germany, employers are confronted with the relatively high pay of many in-house finance and utility call centers alongside the possibility of far lower wages and highly flexible employment contracts at subcontractors, particularly in the absence of any minimum wage and only a few collective agreements in this market segment. At some German subcontractors the entry-wage level was at or below 40 percent of the national median. Call centers thus provide a good example of the "German paradox": they employ relatively skilled workers in jobs that are functionally flexible and broadly defined, yet the industry has a higher share of low-wage workers than in the United Kingdom and the United

States, where work is far more Taylorized. In France, the financial incentives for subcontracting are much lower than in Germany because
the higher level of the national minimum wage and the extension
clauses for collective agreements clearly restrict wage differentiation
at the lower end. With little potential to utilize low-wage workers in
both Denmark and France, most subcontractors in these countries
have to adopt an alternative to a low-cost business strategy by, for example, offering flexibility or specific expertise.

Another crucial issue for pay levels is the extent of legal options
for a differentiation of pay by categories of workers. Whereas temporary and agency workers in France are entitled to receive equal pay
and an additional bonus of 10 percent, the limited regulation of
agency work in the United Kingdom allows call centers to utilize
highly flexible agency workers at lower pay rates. Even in Denmark,
there were examples of call centers paying substantially lower rates
for temporary and student workers.

Other regulations also have an impact on the ways in which employer strategy frames job quality and work organization. For instance, in the Netherlands and the United Kingdom, product market
regulations appeared to be of some importance. In finance, the requirement that staff comply with the relevant regulations and codes
of practice has led managers to introduce more scripts. In Germany
and Denmark, high levels of employment protection have affected
staff composition and union organization in some cases, since employers cannot easily dismiss long-term employees and hire new staff
at lower rates. These protections have had a positive effect not only
on pay but on the organization of work, because employers are faced
with a well-paid, skilled group of experienced workers capable of
handling a broad range of tasks. Trade unions and works councils
have also played a role in some countries in limiting the use of intensive forms of monitoring and individual performance metrics.

Finally, local labor market conditions influence employer approaches. Some of the cases in Denmark and the United Kingdom indicated that labor market shortages pushed them to increase pay levels, provide additional benefits, and pay attention to developing more
decent working conditions. In some companies in the United Kingdom, managers had rejected the use of agency workers, despite the
potential for lower wages and greater flexibility, because they were
unable to recruit suitable workers in the local area. Persistently high
unemployment rates in Germany, in contrast, had allowed several

call centers to continue to pay low wages or even reduce pay without the risk of losing their staff to other employers.

Compared to most of the other industries and jobs under study in this volume, the incidence of low pay in call centers is frequently lower, and working conditions and benefits are often significantly higher. Although the physical demands of the job may be less pronounced, a large proportion of these jobs are highly routine, mentally stressful, and tightly monitored and controlled. It appears that, outside of Germany, "burnout" is common after two or three years and often leads to high levels of labor turnover or low morale, particularly when workers have limited alternative employment options. Even in jobs that are better-paying and more broadly designed, the mental fatigue caused by the constant interaction on the phone can still be a problem. Our research shows, however, that there are ways to alleviate the worst aspects of call center jobs. These jobs do not have to be low-paid, and there are better ways to organize work by providing a broader range of tasks, including time off the phone, and eliminating overbearing targets and control mechanisms. The prospect for improving jobs depends primarily on strengthening institutional and regulatory frameworks, increasing the organizing capacity of trade unions, and creating an environment that seriously challenges many employers' current approaches to call center work.

This chapter draws on the work of the five country-based teams involved in the Russell Sage Foundation project on low-wage work. Part of this research has been published in the individual country studies (see note 1). The original research teams were Ole Henning Sørenson from Denmark; Mathieu Beraud, Thierry Colin, Emilie Fériel, and Benoit Grasser from France; Claudia Weinkopf and Bettina Hieming from Germany; Maarten van Klaveren and Wim Sprenger from the Netherlands; and Caroline Lloyd, Geoff Mason, Matt Osborne, and Jonathan Payne from the United Kingdom. Thanks in particular are due to Thierry Colin, Ole Henning Sørenson, Maarten van Klaveren, and Wim Sprenger for checking our interpretation of their research and for providing additional information, and to Virginia Doellgast, Jérôme Gautié, and John Schmitt for detailed comments on earlier drafts.

NOTES

1. The case study examples discussed in this chapter draw on the work of Mathieu Beraud, Thierry Colin, and Benoit Grasser (2008) for France, Caroline Lloyd and others (2008) for the United Kingdom, Ole Henning Sørenson (2008) for Denmark, Maarten van Klaveren and Wim Sprenger (2008) for the Netherlands, and Claudia Weinkopf (2008) for Germany. Additional material has also been provided by the country teams. Case examples for the United States draw on the fieldwork of Batt and Doellgast.
2. The Global Call Center Survey was funded by a number of organizations, including the Russell Sage Foundation, the Alfred P. Sloan Foundation, and the Hans Boeckler Foundation (see Holman, Batt, and Holtgrewe 2007; http://www.ilr.cornell.edu/globalcallcenter).
3. Apart from the United Kingdom, the governments of the countries in this study do not collect national data on call center pay. The GCC survey provides information on the hourly wages of "typical" agents in call centers (Holman, Batt, and Holtgrewe 2007; Batt and Nohara 2008). For this chapter, Batt calculated the share of agents below the national low-pay thresholds. Where these survey results differed from other sources, we used all the information available to make reasonable estimates.
4. Where employers pay regular bonuses or use commission-based pay, these are included in the figures.
5. There is another collective agreement for temporary work agencies that has lower rates of pay.
6. The U.K. figure is derived from the Annual Survey of Hours and Earnings for 2006 and is slightly above the GCC estimate.

REFERENCES

Bain, Peter, and Phil Taylor. 2008. "No Passage to India? Initial Responses of U.K. Trade Unions to Call Centre Offshoring." *Industrial Relations Journal* 39(1): 5–23.

Batt, Rosemary. 2001. "Explaining Intra-Occupational Wage Inequality in Telecommunications Services: Customer Segmentation, Human Resource Practices, and Union Decline." *Industrial and Labor Relations Review* 54(2A): 425–49.

———. 2002. "Managing Customer Services: Human Resource Practices, Quit Rates, and Sales Growth." *Academy of Management Journal* 45(3): 587–97.

Batt, Rosemary, Virginia Doellgast, and Hyunji Kwon. 2005. *The United States Call Center Industry: Strategy, HR Practices, and Performance*. Ithaca, N.Y.: Cornell University/ILR Press.

Batt, Rosemary, Larry Hunter, and Steffanie Wilk. 2003. "How and When Does Management Matter? Job Quality and Career Opportunities for Call Center Workers." In *Low-Wage America: How Employers Are Reshaping Opportunity in the Workplace*, edited by Eileen Appelbaum, Annette Bernhardt, and Richard J. Murnane. New York: Russell Sage Foundation.

Batt, Rosemary, and Hiro Nohara. 2008. "How Institutions and Business Strategies Affect Wages: A Cross-National Study of Call Centers." Unpublished paper. Cornell University, Ithaca, N.Y.

Beraud, Mathieu, Thierry Colin, and Benoit Grasser, with support by Emilie Fériel. 2008. "Job Quality and Career Opportunities for Call Center Workers: Contrasting Patterns in France." In *Low-Wage Work in France*, edited by Ève Caroli and Jérôme Gautié. New York: Russell Sage Foundation.

Blanchflower, David, and Alex Bryson. 2002. "Changes over Time in Union Relative Wage Effects in the United Kingdom and the United States Revisited." Working paper 9395. Cambridge, Mass.: National Bureau of Economic Research (December).

Bongini, Paola. 2003. *The EU Experience of Financial Services: Liberalization—A Model for GATS Negotiations*. Vienna: SUERF Studies.

Deery, Stephen, and Nick Kinnie. 2004. "Introduction: The Nature and Management of Call Centre Work." In *Call Centres and Human Resource Management: A Cross-National Perspective*, edited by Stephen Deery and Nick Kinnie. Basingstoke: Palgrave Macmillan.

De Grip, Andries, Inge Sieben, and Danielle van Jaarsveld. 2005. *Employment and Industrial Relations in the Dutch Call Centre Sector*. Maastricht: University of Maastricht.

Directorate-General for Transport and Energy (DG TREN). 2004. "Third Benchmarking Report on the Implementation of the Internal Electricity and Gas Market." Draft working paper. Brussels: Commission of the European Communities.

Doellgast, Virginia. 2008. "Collective Bargaining and High-Involvement Management in Comparative Perspective: Evidence from U.S. and German Call Centers." *Industrial Relations* 47(2): 284–319.

Frenkel, Stephen, Marek Korczynski, Karen Shire, and May Tam. 1999. *On the Front Line: Organization of Work in the Information Society*. Ithaca, N.Y.: Cornell University Press.

Grainger, Heidi, and Martin Crowther. 2007. *Trade Union Membership 2006*. London: Department of Trade and Industry.

Holman, David, Rosemary Batt, and Ursula Holtgrewe. 2007. *The Global Call Center Report: International Perspectives on Management and Employment*. Unpublished paper. Cornell University, Ithaca, N.Y. Available at: http://www.ilr.cornell.edu/globalcallcenter/upload/GCC-Intl-Rept-US-Version.pdf.

Hunter, Larry, Annette Bernhardt, Katherine Hughes, and Eva Skuratowicz. 2001. "It's Not Just the ATMs: Technology, Firm Strategies, Jobs, and Earnings in Retail Banking." *Industrial and Labor Relations Review* 54(2A): 402–24.

Hutchinson, Sue, John Purcell, and Nick Kinnie. 2000. "Evolving High Commitment Management and the Experience of the RAC Call Centre." *Human Resource Management Journal* 10(1): 63–78.

John, Hester, and Eva Schmitz. 2002. *Mitarbeitermotivation im Call Center: Ergebnisse der Mitarbeiterbefragung 2001 (Employees' Motivation in Call Centers. Results of an Employee Survey 2001).* Forschungsprojekt FREQUENZ. Personalmanagement Call Center und Handel, Band 2. Bonn: B+S.

Korczynski, Marek. 2002. *Human Resource Management in Service Work: The Fragile Social Order.* Basingstoke: Palgrave Macmillan.

Lloyd, Caroline, Geoff Mason, Matthew Osborne, and Jonathan Payne. 2008. "It's Just the Nature of the Job at the End of the Day": Pay and Job Quality in United Kingdom Mass-Market Call Centers." In *Low-Wage Work in the United Kingdom*, edited by Caroline Lloyd, Geoff Mason, and Ken Mayhew. New York: Russell Sage Foundation.

Sørenson, Ole Henning. 2008. "Pay and Job Quality in Danish Call Centers." In *Low-Wage Work in Denmark*, edited by Niels Westergaard-Nielsen. New York: Russell Sage Foundation.

Taylor, Phil, and Peter Bain. 1999. "An Assembly Line in the Head: Work and Employment Relations in the Call Centre." *Industrial Relations Journal* 30(2): 101–17.

———. 2001. "Trade Unions, Workers' Rights, and the Frontier of Control in U.K. Call Centres." *Economic and Industrial Democracy* 22: 39–66.

Van Klaveren, Maarten, and Wim Sprenger. 2008. "Call Center Employment: Diverging Jobs and Wages." In *Low-Wage Work in the Netherlands*, edited by Wiemer Salverda, Maarten van Klaveren, and Marc van der Meer. New York: Russell Sage Foundation.

Weinkopf, Claudia. 2008. "Pay in Customer Services Under Pressure: Call Center Agents." In *Low-Wage Work in Germany*, edited by Gerhard Bosch and Claudia Weinkopf. New York: Russell Sage Foundation.

Index

Boldface numbers refer to figures and tables